Bruce Lassen

# JUDICIAL DECEPTION

## REGINALD L. JENSEN

authorHOUSE®

*AuthorHouse*™
*1663 Liberty Drive*
*Bloomington, IN 47403*
*www.authorhouse.com*
*Phone: 1-800-839-8640*

*© 2010 Reginald L. Jensen. All rights reserved.*

*No part of this book may be reproduced, stored in a retrieval system, or transmitted by any means without the written permission of the author.*

*First published by AuthorHouse 1/25/2010*

*ISBN: 978-1-4490-2020-0 (e)*
*ISBN: 978-1-4490-2018-7 (sc)*
*ISBN: 978-1-4490-2019-4 (hc)*

*Library of Congress Control Number: 2009911374*

*Printed in the United States of America*
*Bloomington, Indiana*

*This book is printed on acid-free paper.*

If you purchase or read this book, you assume the obligation of convincing three others to do the same.

I want to express my thanks to my brother, Harold A. Jensen, Jr., for his help in modifying the FOREWARD to this book.

I want to thank Mr. David Kern of Dallastown, Pennsylvania and San Jose, California who conscientiously completed the editing of the book on my behalf.

Most of all I wish to express my thanks to my wife, Dorothy, for her endurance of the entire process we had to go through. Also, I give thanks for the continued love and concern of our three daughters, Wendy Sabin, Cynthia Campbell, and Leslie Morrison.

# FOREWARD

The legal system in the United States doesn't work the way most people assume. We've been taught to believe the blind lady holding the scales of justice protects those in the right. In reality, the scales of justice are a myth and the lady isn't blind. There are serious issues American citizens must tackle if they're to eliminate the myth and replace it with the desired reality. Remember the song "Do Re Mi?" In "Do Re Mi" we start at the very beginning and that's what needs to be done if you want to understand how the United States judicial system works. If the system works one way for me, a different way for you, and still a different way for many other people, we all need to know what's happening.

In his Sixth Annual message to Congress on December 2, 1806, President Thomas Jefferson said "[w]here under the characters of jurors, they exercise in person the greatest portion of the judiciary powers; where the laws are consequently so formed and administered as to bear with equal weight and favor on all, restraining no man in the pursuits of honest industry, and securing to every one the property which that acquires,…" reaffirming the judiciary is controlled by the people, not the judiciary. But as you shall see, control has been reversed.

One of the founding principles of our nation is that everyone is entitled to a trial by jury, whether the matter at hand is civil or criminal. The right to a jury trial in civil cases in federal court is governed by the Seventh Amendment:

> In Suits at Common Law, where the value in controversy shall exceed twenty dollars,[1] the right of trial by jury shall be preserved, and no fact tried to a jury, shall be otherwise reexamined in any Court of the United States, than according to the rules of the Common Law.

---

[1] The dollar amount has been increased.

Tocqueville reflects on his conversations in New England regarding the jury, and writes that the institution is the "most direct and most powerful application of the dogma of sovereignty."

But the requirement of receiving a jury trial has been lost. Statistics tell the story. The Bureau of Justice Statistics[2] tracks the percent of tort cases concluded by trial in U.S. District courts from 1970 to 2003. In 1970 there were 25,451 tort cases. Of those, 2,526 (9.9 percent) were decided by jury trial. In 2003 there were 49,166 tort cases. Of those 768 (1.56 percent) were decided by jury trial. In 1962, 11.5 percent of federal civil cases were disposed of by trial; by 2002, that figure had plummeted to 1.8 percent.[3] The records available in twenty-two states indicate only 0.6 percent of civil cases go to trial by jury. The Philadelphia Inquirer reported on September 26, 2004, that 1.7 percent of all criminal cases were tried before juries in 2002. The most commonly accepted margin of error in any statistical analysis is plus or minus 3 percent. Statistically, jury trials have been eliminated in the United States. If the members of the judiciary don't want you to have a trial, you won't have one. How does that stack up against Jefferson's vision of our judicial system? The judiciary has stolen control from the people and given it to itself.

Futhermore, the makeup of the judiciary itself tends to be unduly influenced by the legal profession at large. For example, judges in state courts rely on political contributions to finance their election and most of those contributions come from successful law firms. While judges in federal courts are appointed by the President with the approval of the Senate, the Senators from the states hosting the courts with vacancies are given the plum of selecting the candidates for appointment. Because the large law firms make substantial contributions to major politicians, the firms pass on their recommendations to the Senators regarding potential candidates for the bench. In most cases, several law firms will take credit for any appointment to the bench. As a result, those firms expect and receive preferential treatment in court.

---

[2] (http://www.ojp.usdoj.gov/bjs/glance/tables/torttrialtab.htm)

[3] A publication of the American Bar Association, *Litigation Online*, The Journal Of The Section Of Litigation, Volume 30 No. 2, Winter 2004, *Opening Statement The Vanishing Trial*, by Patricia Lee Refo, Chair, Section of Litigation, Page 2.

Attorneys represent themselves, not their clients. Their first question is always "What's in it for me?" If you go to court over any issue, always ask yourself what your attorney will want and what benefit your case will be to the attorney. Then you need to find out who controls the judge. Make no mistake, someone does in fact control the judge. To whom do the judges' loyalties lie? Theoretically, the judges should uphold and enforce the laws passed by Congress and signed by the president. The judges should perform on behalf of the law-abiding people. But they don't, they perform on behalf of the individuals and organizations that put them in office.

Anarchy is derived from the Greek word anarchos, which means "having no ruler." In English it means absence of governmental authority. A self-regulating organization is an anarchic organization when it has no superior authority to which it must answer. The United States Constitution is supposed to govern the judicial system, but, in fact, the judiciary has assumed the authority to govern itself by interpreting the Constitution as it applies to itself. The Constitution doesn't give that authority to the Supreme Court, it assumed that authority with its ruling in Marbury v. Madison.[4] (Chief Justice John Marshal was a compatriot of Aaron Burr.) The flaw becomes obvious because Congress is required to make changes in the judicial process. Congress is supposed to control the court's exceptions and regulations. The rule of law in the United States is supposed to be the Constitution, the statutes enacted by Congress, and case law (judicial decisions outlining precedent, or stare decisis), which supports and/or interprets either of the first two. The legal process allows a case to be decided in the trial court and the trial court's verdict, or decision, stands unless appealed. If the trial court results are not appealed, the case has no effect on any other case in the United States. But an appeal is supposed to change all that. The court of appeals either upholds

---

[4] Chief Justice Marshall said "The judicial power of the United States is extended to all cases arising under the constitution." But that isn't what the Constitution says. It says at Article. III. Section 2. "The judicial Power shall extend to all Cases, in Law and Equity, arising under this Constitution…" The Constitution then enumerates the powers of the judiciary. The Constitution then specifies in the second paragraph the cases where the Supreme Court has original jurisdiction. In cases where the Supreme Court does not have original jurisdiction it "shall have appellate Jurisdiction, both as to Law and Fact, with such Exceptions, and under such Regulations as the Congress shall make." The judiciary thus comes under control of Congress and Congress comes under control of the citizens.

or alters the trial court decision. When a trial court action is appealed, the court of appeals is required to verify the results are consistent with similar appellate court jurisdiction results or Supreme Court opinions bearing on the subject matter. The appellate court can reverse previous decisions, but the current rulings stand for all other cases in the circuit until reversed. If no other rulings have been made that bear on the subject matter, the issue may go to the Supreme Court and a new ruling (or opinion) created. If two different appellate courts rule inconsistently, the Supreme Court is supposed to review the lower-court rulings and reach a opinion that stands for all courts in the future. The Supreme Court takes very few petitions for appeal. The Supreme Court only reviews issues it thinks are important, which means the decision in the court of appeals is usually final. Whatever happens, the appealed decision is supposed to establish precedence unless precedence has already been established and the appellate decision merely supports previous decisions. The rule of law means the established law applies to you, me, and everyone else, under the same or similar circumstances.

The judges are doing what they are prohibited from doing according to the United States Constitution. If you ask members of the judiciary why they don't want jury trials the expected answer would be that it's inconvenient, it takes up too much of the courts valuable time. So, what is "valuable" about their time? They believe they're more competent to make decisions juries are required to make. But the primary purpose of the courts is to properly conduct jury trials. The only value of our judicial system is for it to supervise and monitor the presentation of evidence to juries of our peers.

Members of the judiciary have become self-guardians not guardians of the public trust. The President of the United States is independent from Congress and the judiciary, but not independent from the people. Congress is independent from the president and the judiciary, but not independent from the people. The judiciary is independent from the president and Congress and the people. The judiciary knows it isn't answerable to anyone and that's the primary reason it conducts its affairs the way it does. Since it can't be challenged, any absurdity is final, even condoning crimes, fraud and deception. The courts are supposed to apply the law to the facts, but most of the time they apply the facts (restated or recreated facts) to the law. On September 3, 2008, former

New York City Mayor and Republican presidential candidate Rudy Giuliani made this statement to the delegates at the Republican National Convention: "I learned as a trial lawyer a long time ago, if you don't have the facts, you've got to change them." Judges find the law they want to cite as the determination of an action and then turn the facts around to fit that law. This happens most often in summary judgments for the purpose of eliminating jury trials.

Turn to the United States Constitution for guidance as to how the judiciary can change its procedures. Article III, Section 2, second paragraph controls (see footnote #1). But as we shall see, the judges issue a new law for me, a different law for you, and something even more different for the next person, based upon the same or similar circumstances.

The federal and state courts have adopted a practice known as not for publication,[5] which effectively means the decision or ruling in the appealed case cannot be cited in any future lawsuit. This practice has never been approved by Congress, as the Constitution provides. *In fact, not for publication is a simple statement announcing the courts are applying a different rule of law, one they make up as they go along, to a particular litigant.* By adopting such a practice, the judiciary has removed a variety of lawsuits from recognition as a standard in guiding the future actions of the courts. The result of the "Not for Publication" appeal simply means the appeal has no standing, the appeal means nothing. Thus, the courts can reach any kind of decision—rational or irrational—and the court of appeals can uphold the action, claim its decision is not for publication, and then reverse its decision in any future action. This turns the judiciary into a faction that operates only in its own interest. The court becomes a kangaroo court.

The people employed in the justice system are victimized by two serious flaws in their thinking. The first is their belief that it's alright to "do a favor" for or "help out" another person in the same business when that person has "made a mistake" or committed a crime. They don't want to embarrass one of their own because they embarrass themselves in so doing. They fail to comprehend that "helping out" or "doing a favor" requires them to become a participant in the crime or action

---

[5] Not for Publication means the decision won't be published in the law books and Not for Citation means the decision can't be cited in any other action even if the unpublished decision can be located by an attorney.

through collusion. The temptation to help a cohort is overwhelming because the co-conspirator wants to bank a favor for future use.

The second flaw has nothing to do with friendship, but is related to conduct under the color of authority. They don't understand committing a crime for the purpose of "proving" someone else is a criminal makes the member of the justice system a criminal. A "sting" is a good example. A police officer sells drugs to an unsuspecting user. The police officer, the seller, is not prosecuted, the buyer, the user, is prosecuted. This kind of flawed thinking filters all the way up to and includes members of the Supreme Court. The member of the justice system should be prosecuted for his or her unlawful acts. What would be a better approach? In my opinion, it would be to change the law so the seller is engaged in a crime and the buyer is not. The officers could then track the buyers, which is what they do anyway, and arrest the sellers. It would take more time, there would be fewer arrests, but the results would be more dramatic and the law-enforcement officers wouldn't have to engage in criminal activities in an attempt to stop the illegal activities. The prisons could then be filled with those who initiate the criminal act. And the prison population would drop dramatically.

Understanding ligitimate law is easy. It's really just common sense. As an example, if you owe money to someone, that person will use the law to collect if you don't pay voluntarily. The other side must prove you owe the money and then must prove how much you owe. Again, if you harm someone, that person or his representative, the government, must exact punishment for the harm you've caused. The other side must prove you caused the harm and then must prove the extent of the harm. A price is then placed on the value of the harm. The price can be monetary, incarceration, or both. There are time constraints. There are time limitations placed on nearly all causes for litigation. The time restraint is called the statute of limitations. Different violations require legal action to be taken within different time frames. If you know how to read and know how to look up the definitions of words used by the legal community you can easily understand what's happening in any lawsuit.

What's the big deal about the legal system if that's all there is to it? People don't want to be held accountable, so they engage in a variety of techniques to limit or eliminate the damages. Fraud, deception, bribery, perjury, and collusion, are the usual means of avoidance. One attorney

*Judicial Deception*

in Anderson, Indiana, told me fifty percent of all litigants are liars. The liars can be on either side, or both sides, of the lawsuit and the attorneys and judges usually know the side that is lying because they talk to each other. So, why do the attorneys and judges go along with the liars? For money and favors, it's that simple.

If someone in the legal system decides to prevent another person from seeking proper redress through the courts, the person being denied is tagged a troublemaker, a crank, someone who's trying to misuse the system. Once a person with authority creates the tag, everyone else in the system goes along and the person tagged is finished. It's an easy method for a judge or attorney to cover up his or her transgressions.

The rule of law isn't functioning in the United States; in fact, the rule of law might function better in the courts in other nations. The difference between enforcing judicial decisions in other nations and the United States is that in the United States the courts have more command over the sheriff in criminal actions. The sheriff is more independent in civil actions. Why should the rule of law function at all? R. M. MacIver[6] said: "No union can endure where the units are above the law." If the judiciary is above the law our nation is doomed.

Why waste time going to court? Are courts necessary? Could we settle our disputes by rounding up six or twelve unrelated people to hear the dispute without the involvement of attorneys and judges? It's possible. The only rule would be that each party be allowed to plead his or her case while the other party remains silent. The party that refuses to remain silent automatically loses. Could we settle our disputes by simply putting various results in a hat and asking a stranger to pick out a selection on a folded piece of paper? In both situations the results could be more fair to all parties than the current judicial process. If the judge, jury, or your own attorney has been compromised, you're certain to lose. The hat process improves your odds.

This book chronicles a variety of methods used to deceive me in court. I'm not alone. Thousands of others have received the same treatment. If I happen to be the only person in the United States cheated by the judiciary, how and where did the attorneys and judges decide that I was selected for this special honor?

---

[6] The Web of Government, The MacMillan Company, New York, 1948. (p. 392.)

The possibility of anyone achieving success in court, based upon the facts and the laws, is remote at best. The process of the judicial system isn't what it appears to be. Decisions impacting the outcome of the case usually have nothing to do with the issues at hand. Litigants usually have no idea what's happening behind the scenes. You should stay away from court under nearly all conditions, unless you're willing to have your case decided by someone who's had sex with or made a payoff to a judge, attorney, or politician. Going to court means you're willing to allow someone who's pulling strings in the background decide the outcome; you're willing to roll the dice and allow the outcome to depend on chance, not truth, contracts, or obligations. Many judges don't understand business, finance, medicine, economics, engineering, or most other professional activities. Small claims courts in particular have a person issuing decisions from the seat of their pants. They deal with mundane and petty issues not requiring legal research. As a result, they seldom refer to the laws that require more advanced study than the study obtained in law school and they forget much of their legal training. The process becomes rote with little, if any, thought given to their judgments. If you sue in small claims courts your odds are still 50-50, but the decision maker will probably compromise which means you'll receive less than you're entitled to receive. In any event, you should never settle for less than a jury trial in criminal cases or any civil case that involves large amounts of money. Even then the odds are against you. You're guaranteed to lose if you don't have a jury trial. This is a book that outlines my experiences in the judicial system over the last forty years. Fairness and justice occur only occasionally. I don't advocate lawless behavior by the general public. I believe we should be a nation of laws. But that's a far distance in the future.

...........................................................................................

*From January 1968 through May 1973 a show named "Laugh In" was presented on NBC Television. One of the scenes had a courtroom with a judge, jury, the plaintiff, the plaintiff's attorneys, and the defendant's attorneys, all seated and waiting for someone to enter the courtroom. Finally, the defendant walked into the courtroom. The bailiff shouted "All rise." Everyone stood up, the judge, jury members, and attorneys, all except the plaintiff. After the defendant took a seat, all others took their seats. Welcome to the legal system in the United States.*

On January 27, 1947, I was living in St. Anthony, Idaho. St. Anthony is a few miles away from the Wyoming border and south of Yellowstone National Park. I had just turned 16 years of age. It was a cold, winter morning and I was walking to school. I met a couple of other boys who were ready to hitch-hike to Salt Lake City, Utah, and they asked me to join them. I was venturesome and agreed to go. Another student walked over to us and we asked him if he wanted to come along and he agreed. We received several rides for short distances and arrived in Idaho Falls in the early evening. Weather reports from the radio said a very cold snap and blizzard were approaching. The roads were being closed by the police, so we decided to stay in Idaho Falls for awhile to see if the storm would blow over. We hung out in pool halls and cafes until midnight to keep warm. None of us had any money. It wasn't possible to rent a room to spend the night in a motel or hotel. All of the business establishments closed at midnight and we were put out in the cold, 17-degree weather and a blizzard. There was a large parking lot in the middle of town with about fifty to sixty cars in the lot. One of our companions suggested we find an unlocked car and use it for shelter. He found one and we all got in. Then he discovered the key was in the car and he turned on the motor so we could use the heater. He checked the gas gauge and concluded there was enough gas in the car to get us to Salt Lake City and suggested that, instead of sitting in the car all night, we drive to Utah. We all agreed. We drove in the blizzard down the snow-covered highway, which was supposed to be closed to traffic. After we passed the Idaho-Utah border, the motor started to heat up. The car had been leaking oil, and the oil was now gone. The engine froze. We coasted into a very small town, got out of the car and pushed it to the side of the road. We searched for another car because the storm was now worse than when we started out. We found one nearby, but it was locked. Nevertheless, we tried to break in. As luck would have it, the car belonged to the sheriff and it was parked next to the jail. He was awake and immediately arrested us. We really didn't care because the jail was warm and we were cold.

The sheriff interviewed us and found we were from Idaho, now in Utah in a stolen car. This brought us under the jurisdiction of the Dyer Act, a federal law describing the interstate transport of a stolen vehicle. The sherrif notified the U.S. Marshall in Odgen, Utah. The marshall picked us up the next day and transported us to Ogden. The marshall's office contacted the car's owner in Idaho Falls, and he said he had no interest in pressing charges against us. We were later transferred to Boise, Idaho. We spent a couple of nights in jail in Boise. When we were released, we were advised we had been placed on probation and would have to report to a probation officer in St. Anthony after we returned home. I did as I was instructed. My probation officer told me if I joined the Army my probation would be terminated and the arrest record would be expunged if I received an honorable discharge. In June 1948, when I was seventeen years old, I asked my parents for permission to join the Army and they agreed. I enlisted for a three-year term. During that time, the Korean War broke out, which caused an extra year to be added to my enlistment. I remained in the service for four years, spending three of those in Panama, and received an honorable discharge

During my military service, my family moved to Salt Lake City. Shortly thereafter, my Father passed away as a result of a heart attack. When I was discharged from the Army in 1952, I moved to Salt Lake City and lived with my family for a short while. My first job after leaving the Army was digging ditches for a company that laid sewers. It was hard work, and I spent all day with a shovel or moving something heavy. My body and clothes were filthy each night after work. We didn't have any hot water at home, so I'd to take a cold bath every night. A couple of months of this kind of work were enough for me. I spent my next Saturday off looking for other work and found a job on the shipping dock at Sears Roebuck in Salt Lake City. After a couple of months, Sears moved me to the shoe department as a salesman. That's were I met Dorothy, who later became my wife. I talked to the store manager about the possibility of promotion, and he told me a person needed a college education to move into management. So I attended the University of Utah part time during 1953 and 1954. I stopped attending school, which meant my opportunities at Sears seemed to be limited. I changed jobs again. In 1955, I began selling hospital and medical insurance for a small, new life insurance company.

Individually owned medical insurance was a novelty. The insurance company took me to small and remote towns in Utah to work with a crew of door-to-door solicitors. The insurance company ran full-page ads in the local newspaper, and we used the ads as an introduction when we knocked on the door of every house in town. We would ask the resident if he or she had any interest in purchasing hospital or medical insurance. People needed the insurance but almost no one owned it. The monthly insurance premiums for a family of four averaged about $4.05 for both doctor and hospital coverage. A one-time policy fee was added to the cost, which brought the first month's premium cost up to about $20.00 with monthly payments of $4.05 thereafter. The salesman was paid most of the first month's premium and the fee, plus a percentage of any additional premiums collected in the future. It was possible to make between two and four sales each day. We were paid every Friday. We were required to pay our own expenses out of our pay. The income was adequate for a short time.

The company began expanding the sales force because sales were good. The company hired a new general agent who moved to Utah from Washington. I was assigned to him. We went to a small town in southern Utah and began selling medical insurance, going door to door without using a newspaper ad as a means of introduction. The second day on the job the general agent applied for life insurance with his new company and took a medical exam as part of the qualification process. He had been insured with his previous company and allowed that life insurance policy to lapse without value because he assumed he could purchase replacement coverage. At his physical examination, the doctor told my boss he had a fatal illness with only a couple of months to live. He had a wife in Washington, very little money, and now he had no life insurance. He was almost forty-five years old and about to die. That night he decided to get drunk. He quit working the next day and returned to Washington. He abandoned me in a small town several hundred miles from home without enough money to pay the motel bill and buy gas to get home. My only option was to sell insurance and collect some of the premiums in cash.

While eating lunch at the counter in a small café, an older gentleman sat down beside me and asked if I was the person selling hospital and medical insurance. I told him I was indeed that person. He thanked me. He said he owned the local hospital, and, if I sold a few policies, it would help keep his hospital solvent. That was nice for him, but I was trying to find a way to get back home. After making several sales, the buyers gave cash deposits or checks payable to me. Although several people were willing to pay me in this manner, others insisted on making the checks payable to the insurance company. By Friday I had enough cash to pay the motel bill, but not enough to buy the gas needed to get home. My last appointment was at 7:30 that night. The family purchased insurance and agreed to pay me in cash. It saved the day. On my way home it was clear that it was time to look for another job.

The next week I went to work for a different small Utah company called Reliance National Life Insurance Company. They had a couple of men selling life insurance door to door in Salt Lake City, so I worked with them for several months. We were selling $1,000 face amount Twenty-Payment Life policies with an average premium of about $20.00 per year. As the salesmen, we completed the medical questionnaire as well as the application, two pieces of paper. The process was simple; we would show the person the total premiums paid over twenty years and the cash available at the end of twenty years. We subtracted the cash value from the total premium paid; the difference, usually between $10.00 and $20.00, was the total cost of insurance. The presentation was easy, but cold calling was hard. Some people were nice, but others were rude, they slammed the doors and called us names.

Eventually, I worked with salesmen who were selling "Special Profit-Sharing" policies. These policies offered values to the buyer that didn't exist in most life insurance policies, such as cash coupons and extra dividends. The premiums on these policies ranged from $1,000 to $5,000 per year. This arrangement didn't work out for me. It didn't seem to me that anyone could afford to pay $5,000 a year in life insurance premiums. That was more money than I was earning.

Dorothy and I reached a day when we only had a can of soup left in the house for food. Dorothy hoped a friend of our daughter, Wendy, would ask Wendy to stay for lunch while I tried to earn some money. An organization was selling stock to the public in an attempt to form a new life insurance company. A friend of mine asked me to join him in trying to sell stock. We approached one of the owners of Southeast Furniture Company and he agreed to make a $2,000 investment. We took the check to the sales manager of the stock offering at about 6:00 p.m. and collected our commission. My share of the commission was $100.00. I brought groceries home at 7:30 that night. The next day I began looking for salaried work.

My next job was as a sales trainee at Equitable Life and Casualty Insurance Company in Salt Lake City, another small Utah domiciled company. They gave me a weekly guaranteed draw against commissions. Ray Ross was the agency director and my supervisor. Ray's father, "Doc" Ross, a chiropractor, was president, and Ray's brother, David, was secretary. Lewis Rich was the financial officer. Ray's son, Galen worked part time at the company while studying law at the University of Utah. Ray sent me to Hayden Lake, near Coeur d'Alene, Idaho, to work with a "specialty" policy salesman. I drove our ancient car up through northern Utah into Idaho and then to Montana and across the mountains back into northern Idaho. The roads were very curvy, vertically as well as horizontally. The car was having serious problems. It finally quit running in one of the deep gullies. Someone used their car to give me a push to the top of the next hill where I coasted into the next town and stopped right in front of an auto repair garage. The mechanic was willing to fix the car and send the bill to Equitable L & C. It's a good thing because I only had $10.00. Then I drove on to Hayden Lake. The salesman who was training me failed to make any sales for a week so I returned to Salt Lake City and began working as a clerk in the home office. Since the company was very small, it gave me an opportunity to become familiar with some of the home-office functions of a life insurance company. My job was to do anything Ray or Doc asked me to do, which was primarily clerical work.

Ray, David, and the Ross families would go deer hunting every year. The male employees at Equitable were requested to participate. I went with them once even though I didn't own a gun. Alcohol flowed freely during the hunt. Dave consumed more alcohol than most people under normal conditions. Hunting didn't interfere with his drinking. Dave and I were sitting in a car during the day while he was trying to unload a rifle. I was in the front passenger seat while he was in the driver's seat. I had opened the car door on my side. Dave had the gun on his lap with the barrel pointed in my direction. The gun went off. A bullet passed in front of me and through the car door. We both got out of the car. Dave walked around the car to look at the damage. We were facing each other. I asked him to give me the gun so I could unload it. He refused. He insisted there were no more bullets in it. He pulled the trigger to prove his point. A bullet went into the ground between my feet. I walked several hundred yards away and sat behind a rock for a while until I thought it was safe to go back to camp.

The next day Ray asked me to go about three fourths of the way up a small mountain peak. It was about 300 feet high from our location. He asked me to walk around the peak, a full circle, to chase the deer out. We talked very plainly about Ray shooting at the deer and not me. He assured me he wouldn't shoot until I came back down from the peak. Well, I got about 330 degrees around the peak when I heard gun shots and bullets went flying past me. I backed up and climbed down on the far side of the peak. When I confronted Ray about his shooting he said he wasn't aiming at me, he just didn't want to let the deer get away. That was the end of my lifelong hunting ventures.

The 1950's were a time that bred and promoted the incorporation of many different types of companies in Utah. Unregulated penny stock was sold in uranium mine companies and a host of other ventures. A filing with the Utah Corporation Commissioner and the purchase of stock certificates at a stationery store were all that was required. People would stand on the street corners downtown and peddle penny stock. They would sell 100 shares for $1.00 or 1,000 shares for $10.00. The people who created the companies would pay a ten percent commission to anyone who'd help them sell the stock. I tried selling the penny stock during my lunch hours. I didn't make much money, but I did learn a couple of things. One person sold stock in a uranium mine down by St. George, Utah. He raised enough cash to go to the St. George area and make his search. He actually found some uranium ore on the surface of the ground located by a small cliff. He went into town to rent a dump truck to carry the ore. He then hired a bulldozer operator to push the uranium over the cliff into the bed of the dump truck. He gave the dozer operator a map and directions to the location of the uranium and told him where he was going to park the truck at the bottom of the cliff.

The bulldozer operator got there before the person with the truck. The dozer operator assumed the truck was parked below because the truck could travel faster than the dozer. He pushed the uranium off the cliff without verifying the truck was in place. The truck wasn't there and the uranium was dispersed over a wide area. That was the end of that person's uranium find.

One owner of a uranium ore search company found his stock listed in the newspaper one morning. The company was a shell; he had no uranium and no present possibility of finding any. But the stock kept increasing in value from a penny a share to two pennies, then higher. Eventually it was trading in the dollars. He wanted to know why it was trading and who was making the market. After talking to all of the stock brokers in the city he learned the market in his stock was being made in New York City. The price of the stock kept increasing on a daily basis. The market value of his personal shares of stock was soon a little below $1,000,000. He put all of his stock certificates in his pocket and took a plane ride to New York. He went to the trading desk of the brokerage firm and asked if the broker would really pay the current share price of the stock. The broker assured him that was indeed the market price and he would indeed purchase stock at the market bid price. The owner's stock was currently valued at about $990,000. He decided to sell as soon as the value reached a million dollars. He sat down in the waiting room and watched the ticker. The price began dropping, rapidly. In less than an hour the stock had no value whatsoever. He went home and used his certificates to paper the bathroom wall.

There's a valuable lesson to be learned here. A stock broker could purchase 100,000 shares of stock at one penny a share, a $1,000 investment. He could sell a few shares at two cents, five cents, ten cents, etc. and ask his clients to watch the price of this particular stock. As the price moves up, more people would buy it on speculation knowing nothing about the company. An active market could be created. If the broker sells the balance of his holdings at only one dollar a share he's made a handsome profit on his investment. If he then drops the price rapidly there's little risk of having to repurchase any of the shares. The investors hold their shares while the price is increasing and they won't sell when the price is rapidly decreasing. If the stockholders hold their shares while the price is increasing the only person who profits is the stockbroker. Does this still happen today? Yes, it does, in one manner or another.

Silicon Valley in California became famous following the same process during the 1990s. Venture capital firms were successful prior to the 1990s when they backed new companies that had developed a business plan, created a product, tested the product on the market, found customers, and were then able to modify the plan and calculate the true cost of doing business. Venture capitalists would fund the start-up companies assuming nineteen out of twenty would fail. They would take the one successful start-up to the public with an initial public offering and recoup their entire investment in the twenty start-ups. All of these companies were composed of "penny stock" because the par value of the stock (the amount the original incorporators paid) was either one cent or even as low as zero. The difference between the Salt Lake City penny stock market and the Silicon Valley penny stock market is that the stock sold for its par value, one penny, in Salt Lake City, and the penny stock sold for $10.00, $20.00 or $25.00 in Silicon Valley. Those who purchased 1,000 shares for a penny a share in Salt Lake City lost $10.00 when the business failed. Those who purchased 1,000 shares for $10.00 a share in Silicon Valley lost $10,000.00 when the business failed. The market became so hot in the 1990s that Silicon Valley start-ups were only required to write a business plan before the venture capitalists would take the stock to the public. Most of the business plans were no more elaborate than the business plans of the old uranium stocks. The results were comparable.

In the late 1950s, stock was being sold in new life insurance companies in Utah. Life insurance companies are different than uranium companies. Insurance companies are required to maintain surplus, capital, and reserves. A stock broker in Los Angeles had promoted stock in Kansas City Life Insurance Company, ran up the price dramatically, and then wrote a book about the riches people received. Stock issues in new life insurance companies became easy to sell using that book as a reference. Stock was sold to the public based upon the long-term riches to be reaped through life insurance company growth. Several new companies were formed in Utah, which gave me the idea to start a company. I read several books on life insurance company management.

Then I analyzed the number of domestic companies in each state in the United States. I concluded California and Oregon had the fewest companies per population. I traveled to San Francisco, and asked the Corporations Commissioner about the possibility of forming a company. He said California required $1,000,000 in cash from the organizers prior to authorizing a public sale of stock. I didn't have $100.00.

I decided I would go to Oregon to form a life insurance company. I told Ray Ross about my plans. He thought I was crazy, but he gave me the name of a banker at the United States National Bank in Portland, and the name of a Deputy Insurance Commissioner, Clifford Ingham, in Salem. I traveled to Oregon and asked the banker if he would handle the stock sale escrow funds. He said he would. I also asked him to give me the name of some prominent person who might be interested in serving on the Board of Directors. He gave me the name of C. Edwin Francis, the owner of a Ford automobile dealership. Then I went to Salem and met Cliff Ingham. I asked Ingham if he knew an attorney who would help me. He introduced me to Thomas Churchill. Churchill agreed to do the legal work required to start the company. He agreed to wait for payment of fees until after the stock had been sold.

Now I had to find someone who would manage the sale of the stock. Lincoln Hanks had managed several life insurance company stock sales in Utah and later in several other states. I went back to Salt Lake City, contacted Hanks, and asked him if he would organize and manage the stock sale after enough directors had agreed to serve and the company was incorporated. He said he would. I decided on the name Insurance Company of America. I then placed a want ad in the newspaper asking for a $3,000 personal loan as risk capital to finance me in starting the company. Ray Potts responded to the ad and loaned the money to me on the spot. Dorothy and I quit our jobs and prepared to move to Oregon. We were both 28 years old. Dorothy was pregnant with our third daughter, Leslie. Since our oldest daughter, Wendy, and our youngest daughter, Cindy, were very young, we decided Dorothy and the girls would fly to Portland and stay at the Benson Hotel while I drove our car with some of our meager possessions. We shipped our furniture by truck. We left Salt Lake City in January in the middle of a very cold winter.

Our car was very old and completely unreliable, particularly in the wind and cold.  I decided to drive all of the way from Salt Lake City to Portland without stopping for the night.  In the late afternoon, I arrived in Boise and stopped at a bar and café for dinner.  A man about 40 years old asked me what I was doing and where I was going.  I said I was on my way to Portland.  He asked if he could ride along with me.  I told him OK, I needed company to help keep me awake.  On the way I asked my guest who he was and why he was traveling to Portland.  He said he was just released from prison in Idaho after serving time for murder.  He assured me he wasn't a threat, the murder occurred during a fight with one of his enemies.  He said he wanted to go to Portland to become a sailor.  He planned on going down to the docks, getting drunk, and going out towards a ship.  He was convinced he would be Shanghaied onto a ship as a hand and be on his way to the Orient.  We drove through Onterio, Oregon, to Baker, La Grande, Pendleton, The Dalles, and into Portland.  The car just barely made it to Portland in the early morning hours.  I dropped my guest off at the Portland docks and never saw him again.  By this time the radiator was falling off the car, but it lasted long enough for me to park it at the Benson Hotel.  Then I went up to the rooms and met Dorothy and the girls and got a few hours sleep.  The next morning I found some wire and wired the radiator to the body of the car and wired the door on the passenger side closed.  Then we ate breakfast and drove to Salem.  We were lucky to have the car hold together for the last leg of the trip.

The Willamette Valley was absolutely beautiful.  It was warm, lush, and green, in stark contrast to the dreary cold and snow in Utah.  We fell in love with Oregon immediately.  We thought we had just arrived in heaven.  Flowers were in bloom with a variety of lovely colors.  The flowers on the Rhododendron bushes were huge and beautiful.  The trees were filled with leaves, some green and some red; the green pine trees and the green ground cover were amazing to us.  Our feelings about Oregon have never changed.

Tom Churchill and his wife, Marian, located a house for us to rent and live in for awhile.  We settled down and tried to make friends with our neighbors.  Most of the neighbors were friendly, but one neighbor asked us how long we had lived in Oregon.  We told him we just moved from Utah. He said he would be willing to talk to us if we were still in Oregon ten years later. He said people weren't recognized as permanent citizens unless they have lived in Oregon for ten years or longer. The citizens didn't want strangers coming into the state because too many people might spoil the area. This attitude was pervasive in Oregon at the time.[7]

I soon met with the Oregon Insurance Commissioner, Dean Musser, to get from him the requirements to follow in organizing the company. He insisted I had life insurance policies developed, printed, and submitted to the state for approval, before he would approve the company charter. It would take an actuary to prepare the policies. The only actuarial firm in the area was in Seattle, Washington. I met with Stuart A. Robertson of the actuarial firm of Milliman and Robertson and asked him if he would develop the policies and wait until the company raised the money for his payment. He agreed.

Frank Healy was a blind attorney and, as Oregon Corporation Commissioner, he insisted the Insurance Commissioner approve the charter before authorizing the sale of stock. The Corporation Commissioner would not allow shares of stock to be issued to me, or any person, in exchange for the work of organizing the company. That meant everyone must pay cash for their shares. It made it difficult to find people who would serve as directors. I wanted eleven directors and at least eleven advisory directors. The directors needed to be located in different parts of the state to create a broad appeal for the sale of stock. The directors and advisory board members would contribute to the company growth by providing referrals for the sale of stock and life insurance. The stockholders would contribute to the company by purchasing insurance and also provide referrals for the sale of insurance. It took six months of traveling around the Willamette Valley to find

---

[7] For example; a few years later Governor Tom McCall invited Reader's Digest executives to Salem after the Reader's Digest printed color photos showing the beauty of the State. Governor McCall put them up in the Marion Hotel for a Saturday night, then joined them for breakfast on Sunday. He asked them if they knew why he had invited them to be his guests. They said they thought they did, but wanted to hear it from the Governor. McCall chastised the executives and suggested they never return and never print another story about Oregon. He said Oregonians didn't want outsiders to know about the beauty of the state.

the directors. The board was finally organized. It included my oldest brother, Harold (Hank). Hank had earned his Master's Degree at Columbia University. At the time he was working as a management consultant for the George S. May Company in Chicago, Illinois. He was ideal to be vice president of administration and corporate secretary because of his education and experience. I also believed he would be a stabilizing influence on me and the company. Hank was vital to the organization and development of the insurance company. He knew exactly what to do in establishing the budget, systems, controls and structuring the various departments. He became the backbone of the management team. He also became the center of communication between the board members.

Other members of the board, included myself as vice president and sales director; James Hatfield, a tall, well-proportioned man (a cousin to Gov. Mark Hatfield) who served as the company treasurer; Churchill, a tall, heavier and husky man who served as legal counsel; Hugh Earle, a small, feisty retired former insurance commissioner of Oregon in his late seventies who served as president; Bruce Herzinger, a CPA and bank board member; Ernest Hinkle, a stock broker in Portland who frequently smoked a cigar; Francis, the auto dealer in Portland, with many different silent investments; and Henry Buehner, an attorney with the firm of Buehner, Tilbury & Alexander in Portland.. Buehner served as chairman. He had a photographic memory; he could read a book and remember many of the words that were written on each page. Tilbury was a short man of average weight who appeared to care for his physical condition. Alexander was a tall, husky person. We later appointed Dr. Harmon T. Harvey, of Salem, to the board of directors.

In the 1950s Earle had served for several years as an Oregon collector of internal revenue. We were riding in my car one day when he told me how he collected taxes from houses of prostitution. He said he'd go to the houses in the early morning and count the soiled sheets. Then he'd assign one customer to each sheet and apply the tax to the result. He said the madams never argued or complained.

Lincoln Hanks came to Oregon and helped me complete the advisory board members. The advisory board included Robert Duncan in Medford, an attorney who was soon elected to the United States Congress; "Bun" Kelsay, a lumberman in Roseburg and member of the Oregon State Legislature; and several other prominent Oregon businessmen. Everything fell into place and the corporation commissioner authorized the sale of stock.

Hanks hired about 30 salesmen to sell the stock. Salesmen came from different parts of the Western United States. They were competent, straightforward and honest. The number of shares that could be purchased by any single buyer was limited so the company would have many shareholders dispersed around the state. The stock sale was completed in less than two months. Hanks' salesmen raised more than $2,200,000 from about 2,400 people. I sold some of the stock and used my commissions to purchase my original shares. By December 1959 Insurance Company of America was in business. Insurance Commissioner Musser issued our charter.

Hugh Earle began to assert authority after we were in business and caused friction among the other officers and employees. Jim Hatfield suggested we offer him a chance to resign in return for a $5,000 payment. He refused at first but then agreed after we called a board meeting to consider removing him. The board accepted his resignation and authorized the payment. The Board then elected me as president. I was just past my 29th birthday. My salary was $1,000 a month.

The actuarial firm of Milliman and Robertson had developed standard life insurance policies for the company; whole life and term. I wanted to sell policies reflecting the status of a new company. I asked them to create a policy with a series of endowment coupons attached. The coupons had both cash surrender value and additional death benefits. The coupons could finance the future payment of premiums so that the policies could be fully paid up in fourteen or fifteen years. The policies were also participating (dividend paying). The dividends could also be used to reduce the premium-paying period. These were not profit-sharing policies because they would not share in the profits of the company. They would share in the earnings from the coupon policy block of business, an important distinction. Developing the policies and obtaining state approval would take time.

We rented office space and hired staff, but without sales there was little to do. American Guarantee Life Insurance Company in Portland offered to sell its medical insurance business to us. We agreed on the price, purchased the business and used it to train the office staff in the procedures of managing premiums, claims and reserves. We hired several agents to sell new medical insurance policies we developed and they did a credible job. Health insurance is simply the prepayment of medical benefits using the insurance company to administer the business. The company pays a commission to the agents and retains a fee for its services. In some instances, insurance companies overprice the medical policies and in some instances the policies are underpriced, but the end result is the prepayment of medical benefits plus administrative costs and profits. That wasn't the purpose of our company. Our company's purpose was to sell life insurance. Selling life insurance would be more difficult and require a more competitive sales force.

We needed an accountant who was familiar with the life insurance business. William (Bill) Martindale in Los Angeles was recommended to us by an insurance company professional. We interviewed Bill and he agreed to move to Salem. The move was easy for him because he was single. He was very competent and enjoyed his work. He set up the department and organized the accounting to match the convention blank[8] requirements. The use of punch-card computers was just becoming popular. Bill constructed a punch-card computer system. He had to reconstruct a room to control the heat and air conditioning. His machines were very large but accomplished his goals. Martindale was with us for about five years. He was an ideal employee. He was honest, fair, trustworthy, and never complained about the hours of work he put in. His work was error free. About five years later he suffered a heart attack and died in his apartment at night. I was notified by a newspaper reporter about his demise. Bill Martindale was a credit to all of us.

The first stockholder's meeting took place in April 1960. There were about fifty people present. I had never been exposed to a stockholders' meeting and had no idea how to proceed and I was scared. I had no public speaking experience. I asked Hank to chair the meeting for me. He handled it very well. It moved smoothly and came to an end quickly.

---

[8] State required insurance accounting reporting form.

Soon after the insurance company was in business, Commissioner Musser called me, said he wanted a job and asked if he could be employed. I told him I was sorry, but we had a full staff. He found another company in Oregon that gave him a job and he resigned as commissioner. A new commissioner was to be appointed. Governor Mark Hatfield asked the President of Standard Insurance Company in Portland to convene a meeting of the presidents of all Oregon insurance companies, life and casualty, to select a nominee to be the new commissioner. Standard Insurance Company made its recommendation. I knew no one who would qualify for the post, I made no suggestions. The president of Insurance Company of Oregon made a suggestion and Oregon Auto Insurance Company made suggestions. The companies settled on Walter G. Korlann and he was then appointed by Governor Hatfield.

During 1960 and 1961 the Oregon State Legislature conducted hearings on the sale of hospital and medical insurance policies. Members of the public were solicited to submit complaints to a joint committee consisting of House and Senate members. The committee then conducted an investigation of the insurance business and sales practices. State Representative Monte Montgomery from Eugene was Chairman. I was called to testify about Insurance Company of America's medical insurance practices. We didn't have enough history to provide any valuable information. Several complaints were about policies issued by Equitable L & C. The committee assumed Equitable L & C had financed my work in establishing Insurance Company of America. The committee also believed Insurance Company of America would be merged into Equitable L & C in Salt Lake City. Our purchase of the block of medical insurance policies from American Guarantee Life seemed to add credence to their belief. If the two companies were to merge the distribution of shares would cause the shareholders of Equitable L & C to be the minority shareholders and the Ross family to lose control. The Ross family owned control of Equitable L & C and would never consider giving it up. The committee was really off base in their assumption. During the morning on the second day of the hearing, my testimony was before only the committee members. The committee members were vocal and rude. Their form of questioning was demeaning. During the afternoon, while I was still a witness, a group of high school students were guests to observe the legislature in action. The committee members were very considerate and courteous during the afternoon. It created the impression the entire hearing was only for show and no substance.

I was riding down an elevator with Churchill during a break in the hearings and one prominent State Senator, Mike Mahoney, and several of his friends pressed onto the elevator. Senator Mahoney said he controlled the investigation by the committee and he would terminate it if I paid him $10,000. I told him his request was something I couldn't honor. I told him I didn't have $10,000 to give him and I couldn't request the money from the insurance company. Was his motive to receive a few extra dollars for himself or was it for the purpose of trapping me into the payment of a bribe? I don't know.

Suggestions about how to pay bribes, who paid and received bribes, which companies held money in escrow for the payment of bribes, and a whole host of bribery-related issues seemed to come out of the walls after that. Several months later a stranger walked into my office with documents purported to be escrow funds held by Oregon Auto Insurance Company to be paid as a bribe to a juror in a lawsuit in Portland. He handed the papers to me and disappeared out the front door. I walked out the front door to see if I could locate him, but he was completely out of sight. I had never seen him before and I never saw him again. I had no interest in the papers and disposed of them. The hearings soon died with little results for the State of Oregon or anyone else.

One night in Portland after the hearings were over, I was having a few cocktails with acquaintances who were active in politics. They told me about a story that appeared in the newspaper that day. One of the candidates for state representative was found by police in a wrecked auto. The candidate was married with children but he had a prostitute in the car with him. What happened? Several of his "friends" took him out to several bars, made sure he was drunk, drove him to a major thoroughfare, ran his car into a tree, then placed him behind the wheel and hired a prostitute to sit in the car and wait while one of the "friends" called the police to report an accident. That man's political career was over. Politics can be just as cutthroat as the life insurance business.

In 1961, Insurance Company of America was forced by Insurance Company of North America to change its name. The new name became ICOA Life Insurance Company. In the same year when it was time for the second stockholders' meeting, I asked Hank if he would run the meeting again, but he refused. He told me it was my job so I'd better get used to it. When I rose to chair the meeting, my legs were wobbling, I was sweating, my voice trembled, and eventually I had to sit. It was a relief when it was over.

I knew I needed more education and instruction in business management, so in 1961 I joined the American Management Association (AMA) in New York. They would conduct meetings and educational sessions in different places in New York City as well as in other cities across the United States. The classes, which usually lasted one week, covered various management subjects. The AMA organized the President's Professional Association (later the President's Association) that same year and I became one of the incorporators. The class instruction was outstanding with instructors coming from the top ranks of every leading industry in the United States. I enrolled in several classes each year. Lawrence A. Appley was President of the AMA and his skills were really impressive. From time to time he'd use true stories to emphasize a point he was making. Following is a piece of advice he gave the members and one story he told at one of the classes.

The question came up from a class participant about how to select a successor president or CEO of a company and the advice Appley passed on was this: Imagine yourself as paralyzed and bed-ridden without the ability to communicate in any manner for a ten-year period. You must make sure the company and your family survives. The company employees are also part of your family. Find someone who will preserve the company assets and make them grow at about ten percent a year. Dividends will also grow at the same rate at the same time. The income of your employees and family will continue to grow along with the growth of the company. The company customers will continue to be happy and satisfied with the product or service offered, and the company will continue to increase its customer base. The person you select will do all of this for you and be paid for the effort. At the end of the ten years, when your paralysis terminates, the successor president will return management of the company back to you in better shape than it was in when you turned it over to him.

Appley also advised us about hard and fast company rules. The AMA had a rule prohibiting any business contact under any conditions with a person who was on vacation. His theory was that a vacation meant getting away from the business. One year Appley was on vacation in southern Florida. One of his vice presidents called him while he was there. Appley asked his vice president if he knew and understood the rule about no contact while someone is on vacation. The vice president said he did, but this was important. Appley asked him what could be so important that it would put his job in jeopardy. The vice president told him the AMA was out of money, they were broke. Appley asked him what he was talking about; the finances were in good shape when he left for vacation. The vice president insisted the AMA was near bankruptcy. Appley immediately returned to New York City and asked his Chief Financial Officer (CFO) to bring the records to him. When he concluded his analysis, Appley determined the AMA was indeed out of money. He asked the CFO what was going on and the CFO told him the accounting records didn't make any difference; the only important part about the records was to present a picture to management of robust corporate growth, that's what management wanted to see. Appley found another CFO immediately and set about returning the organization back to financial health. The moral of the story was hard and fast rules aren't always hard and fast. The CEO can't rely on his top managers to always be correct and the CEO must be ready, willing, and able, to monitor and test the information and results he or she receives.

The AMA distributed a survey it obtained relating to the theoretical actions of company presidents when honesty became an issue. A question submitted to company presidents, several thousand of whom responded, asked: If they knew their company was about to fail, but they could save the company from failure through deception or lying, would they lie to save the company? Sixty percent of the respondents said they would lie; forty percent said they would not. Attorneys and judges manage companies. Their company might be a one-man-operation, or it might employ several hundred people. Judges typically manage a crew of individuals and a substantial budget. Attorneys and judges are no different than the majority of the population when ethics come into consideration. They will lie to avoid embarrassment or exposure.

Taking management courses at the AMA wasn't sufficient for me. I needed specialized insurance-management guidance and found it in the form of a mentor, Clarence Tookey, of Pasadena, California. I needed someone with Clarence's stature, experience, and knowledge to help hone my rough edges. Clarence was an actuary and recently retired as Senior Vice President and board member of Occidental Life Insurance Company of California. Occidental Life was a very large California company that began business in 1906. Albert Giannini purchased the company through his Transamerica organization. Giannini was the man who started Bank of America in California. Giannini financed the growth of Occidental Life. Hank was responsible for my association with Clarence. Lincoln National Life Insurance Company in Ft. Wayne, Indiana, was the primary reinsurance company for Insurance Company of America. Insurance companies reinsure part of the risk on large policies so that any payout because of death will have very little financial effect on the company that sells and issues the policy. Robert Tookey was a reinsurance representative for Lincoln National. Hank was Robert's contact. Robert was Clarence Tookey's son.

Hank asked Robert if he knew someone who could help me. Robert explained to his dad we were a young company with young management and we could use some seasoned and experienced management help. Clarence was about to retire and he agreed to become my mentor after his retirement was official. Clarence was invaluable. He helped me in numerous important ways. One of the first questions I asked Clarence was about management. I asked him who should be president of a life insurance company from the standpoint of experience. He said the first president should be a salesman and promoter. He said that person should remain until sales and assets had increased to where business was steady and stable. He said the next person should be an actuary who would adjust the reserves and premiums to add to the long-term financial stability of the company. He said the third person should be an investment specialist. The excess interest earnings on investments will be the primary profit feature of any life insurance company in the long-term. Safe and secure investments that could be securitized and sufficient to meet the long-term cash needs would be vital to the future success of the company.

Our special life insurance policies were finally ready for sale. Hank's friend, Ben Rosen, of New York City, was skilled in design work and agreed to design the policies for us. Each policy type had a different color. The dividend-paying coupon policies had a brightly colored green cover with the letters ICOA placed in the center of a bright green sunburst. The coupons were green and embossed. The coupons looked like coupons on government bonds. The design and logo were outstanding. The term-life insurance policies were colored red to alert the buyer to the fact that term insurance doesn't last beyond the policy time limits. Other types of policies had different colors.

I had hired local salesmen to sell our medical insurance policies, but they had no experience selling life insurance. Our coupon policies required experienced salesmen who knew the rules and procedures of selling sophisticated policies. I placed help-wanted ads in various out-of-state newspapers and magazines throughout the West. Salesman came from Utah, Texas, Kentucky, Colorado, Pennsylvania and other states. They were experienced agents who knew the specialty policy business and were willing to sell the policies to the new stockholders. Many of the stockholders were grandparents who purchased policies as gifts to their grandchildren. The grandparents liked the idea of paying premiums for thirteen to fifteen years, which would give their grandchildren life insurance for the balance of their lives. Everything was a good match.

The salesmen were a non-conforming group. I found all of the salesmen to be unique and interesting. I enjoyed their company. They weren't typical life-insurance agents. One agent came from Texas, made a few dollars, returned to Texas for a vacation and purchased a small used airplane. I don't think he had a license, but the salesman showed him how to fly the plane and he flew it back to Oregon. It rains a lot in Oregon which means there are usually clouds in the sky. He was flying over the clouds and guessed he must be somewhere near Salem. So, he dove down through the clouds to see where he was. It happened he was out over the ocean just west of Coos Bay. He spotted a small airport near Coos Bay and landed to get instructions and directions to Salem and to fill up his plane with gas. He had no radio in the plane and the manager of the airport wouldn't let him fly again without purchasing a radio. The salesman called me on the phone at night and asked me to authorize his check. I OK'd it and he flew into Salem that night. He had no fear and really didn't understand the risks he was taking for himself and his wife who was in the plane with him.

Many life-insurance agents feel they are professionals who give advice to their clients. They don't believe they "sell" policies, they find solutions to problems. They expect the policies to sell themselves. Our salesmen were selling policies based upon the value and attraction of the policies. The need of the grandparents was the lifetime gift to the grandchildren and our insurance policy was the solution. The conflict between the stereotypes caused conflicts with insurance agent's organizations and competing insurance companies.

This is probably an appropriate place to explain a purpose of life insurance and how insurance policies serve that purpose. The primary purpose of life insurance is to replace the income of the deceased person. A parent or spouse usually contributes necessary and vital income to the family. The death of that person can cause great emotional and financial harm to the family. The income gap that remains must be eliminated with life insurance, otherwise the family can no longer be satisfied with its accustomed standard of living. Most life insurance sales are based upon the estimated sum of the future lost income of the insured. The insurance policy is designed to pay the present value of that sum. But that death benefit paid in cash can cause the beneficiary to feel rich even though the money might not last a lifetime. The real need is monthly income, not a large immediate check. Every life insurance policy contains a provision referred to as "Settlement Options." The settlement options include annuity payments based upon different needs and time spans. Annuities are payments that continue for a certain period, such as twenty years. If the annuitant dies prior to the end of the guaranteed period, payments will continue to the beneficiary for the balance of that period. However, if the annuitant lives longer than the guaranteed period the payments can continue for the balance of life if that continuation provision is included. The death benefit of a life insurance policy should be paid to the beneficiary as a lifetime annuity, which means the death benefit should be transferred to the appropriate settlement option or to the purchase of a new annuity if the payment is greater.

The majority of life insurance agents recognize an insured has a slim possibility of dying prior to life expectancy. Life insurance company underwriting practices are designed to eliminate persons who are in ill health or who live risky lifestyles. This is called eliminating adverse selection against the insurer. It means legal reserve life insurance policies, which accumulate large cash values are very practical; it's a forced savings arrangement. The amount saved in the policy can be used for retirement or emergency purposes. New insurance companies need to create lifelong customers and the best way to do it is to insure children who will live for many years. This creates a lifetime association and also gives the children an opportunity to learn how insurance works and how valuable it can be for them. Our specialty salesmen were now doing a great job. Sales were high, the men were making plenty of money, the customers and stockholders were happy, and the employees were busy.

In 1963, I negotiated the purchase of voting control of a small life insurance company in Minnesota, Security National Life Insurance Company (SNLIC). The company had two classes of stock, common voting and preferred nonvoting. The company had been organized by two life insurance agents who sold the stock to Minnesota residents. Rather than sell insurance after the company was in business one of the organizers gambled much of the money in Las Vegas. The SNLIC Board of Directors wanted to close this embarrassing chapter in their professional lives. After purchasing the voting stock, the Oregon Insurance Commissioner advised me that ICOA couldn't carry the stock as an asset. It would be necessary to convert all stock to common voting shares. We called an SNLIC shareholders' meeting, which authorized the exchange of preferred shares for common shares using a ratio that would leave ICOA with more than 50 percent of the common shares. The Minnesota Insurance Commissioner approved the offer. Several ICOA and SNLIC employees personally visited each preferred shareholder and obtained exchange-authorization signatures. Once the exchange was complete, the shares were listed as an ICOA asset. The original intent was to merge SNLIC into ICOA and continue operations. But Minnesota was too far away and the local shareholders were too disappointed with the former management and weren't inclined to help advance the sale of insurance.

A representative of Republic National Life of Texas made an offer to purchase ICOA's interest in SNLIC and I decided to meet with him. We met in a neutral location and I delivered the financial information to him. He examined the convention blank and told me the following story: "A blacksmith was preparing horseshoes when a dude asked him what he was doing. The blacksmith said he was the best blacksmith in the world and he had just finished making the finest set of horseshoes. The horseshoes had just turned black after being heated for shaping purposes. The dude said, 'Let me see one of those works of art.' So he picked up a horseshoe and immediately dropped it on the ground. The blacksmith asked 'What's wrong? Was it hot?' The dude said 'It wasn't hot, it just doesn't take me long to examine a horseshoe.'" The RNL representative said he'd examined a lot of hot company records but ours were not. The financials were very clean and accurate. The sale of stock was completed at a substantial profit to ICOA.

In 1963 I was introduced to Larry Crosby, singer Bing Crosby's brother and publicity manager. Larry was on the board of directors of a life insurance company in Montana. Larry supervised the annual Bing Crosby clambake and golf tournament at the Pebble Beach Golf Club in Monterey, California. Part of Larry's responsibilities were to provide the profits from the golf tournament as gifts to charitable organizations. Larry invited me to play in the tournament but I declined, feeling my golf skills were so poor I would delay and embarrass any group in which I was included. We ultimately asked Larry to join the Board of Directors of ICOA and he agreed. Larry arranged to give the city of Salem several charitable contributions on behalf of Bing.

Many of ICOA's medical-insurance agents wanted to be able to sell the coupon policies because they could see how much money the other salesmen were making. So I arranged for the specialty salesmen to take some of the medical-insurance salesmen with them on sales calls so they could learn the procedures. The medical agents became very successful. By 1963, we had more than 100 agents selling the coupon policy throughout the state of Oregon. There were several hundred life insurance companies operating in Oregon at that time. ICOA was second in new premiums written by domestic life companies and sixteenth in the state compared to all life companies. The company was progressing very nicely. We seemed to have a compatible team.

In early 1964 Henry Buehner told me he had made an appointment in New York City to talk to a stock broker about purchasing a company named BanLife. The company was more than 20 times larger than ICOA, but it had reached a stagnation stage, it was no longer growing and was only maintaining its current business. Buehner rented a four-passenger plane. He and I, along with Churchill and the pilot, flew back to New Jersey and then into New York City. We talked to the management of BanLife to make sure the company was for sale and to fix the asking price. They assured us it was for sale if we could come up with the cash. We then went into New York City and met with a stock brokerage firm. The firm liked the idea of creating a new stock offering and said it would raise the money for us if we could put the deal together. The brokers were impressed with the idea because they could earn a substantial commission. They said once they received our final 1964 financial results they would negotiate the transaction. We were scheduled to talk to them again in April 1965.

I wanted to review The Prudential Insurance Company of America's financial statement as long as we were in New York. Prudential was a mutual company and the largest life insurance company in the United States at that time. We went to the New Jersey Insurance Department and asked to see the Prudential convention blank. The insurance department was maintained like a fortress. The office personnel required a legitimate reason prior to delivering the financials. Finally, they escorted us into a secluded room and brought the financials to us. There was a notation in the file identifying a dividend-reserve deficiency. The deficiency exceeded Prudential's current surplus funds, which meant the company had no operating funds. Next was an insert which showed the New Jersey legislature approved granting an exception to the requirement that Prudential's deficiency must reduce surplus as required by law. It was a one-year exemption. I asked the insurance department deputy how often this special exemption is passed by the legislature. He told me it has happened every year since the dust bowl years in the Midwest in the 1930s. He said Prudential had made mortgage loans on farms in the dust bowl. The value of the foreclosed property at the time was so low that it reduced Prudential's financial situation to potential insolvency. This exemption was New Jersey's method of keeping Prudential operating until land values could erase the deficiency, but the deficiency hadn't yet been erased. As a result, the Board of Directors of Prudential was required to include members of the New Jersey state legislature to monitor the progress of the company.

The first four years of ICOA were fast-growth years. However, nothing seemed to deter our detractors. The opposition's goal was to dramatically reduce ICOA's sales. Our detractors seemed to stop at nothing in their attempts to harm the company. Our competitors believed the people who purchased insurance from us would buy it from them if they could terminate our sales. It was a false assumption because most of our buyers were directly and indirectly associated with ICOA as stockholders and relatives. Our goal was to expand from the stockholder base to family and friends of these same people.

Our first death claim was the result of two young children who died in a terrible accident. Other insurance agents told the parents of the children ICOA didn't have enough money to pay the claim. This cruelty placed additional pain and hurt on the grieving parents. When I visited with the parents and delivered the checks I tried to reduce their feelings of pain and suggested they set the money aside for the future benefit of their surviving children.

Some of the other insurance companies filed objections with the state Insurance Commissioner to the sale of the coupon policies. The beauty of the policies with their color and attractiveness startled and surprised other companies. Our competitors believed people were buying the policies because of their beauty. Some of our competitors complained because the coupons actually "looked like money." In fact, the coupons were money. They could be converted to cash on the day they matured, just like any coupons. But the coupons also contained the additional life-insurance benefits.

The Oregon Life Underwriters Association (OLUA) also opposed the sale of the policies and filed an objection with the Commissioner. Marshall Duncan, the president of the OLUA wrote an article for the National Underwriter, a trade magazine located in Ohio, complaining about our sale of "Profit-Sharing" policies. The sale of our coupon policies soon became a minor national insurance issue. During the next year, a lot of publicity was generated. The majority of the publicity was in Oregon. The publicity worked in our favor at first. Articles were printed discussing how the company was started, how it had grown, and the success that seemed to be achieved. A publicity attack on a company or person usually begins with a positive portrayal and then follows with negative comments. I didn't understand this at the time and was pleased with the original media coverage. Several years later it turned against us, because the public would rather read negative reports, not positive reports.

Continued opposition to our coupon policies forced the Insurance Commissioner to issue regulations prohibiting the sale of life insurance policies with coupons attached. On July 8, 1964, Commissioner Walter Korlann issued a NOTICE OF HEARING of the proposed regulations. The thrust of the regulations was to prohibit the sale of so-called "Profit Sharing" policies. ICOA's policies were not profit-sharing policies, but the opposition lumped profit-sharing and coupon policies into the same category. In reality, nearly all policies sold by mutual insurance companies are profit-sharing policies, because the profits of the mutual companies belong to the policyholders and those profits must be returned through dividends payments on the life insurance policies. Policyholder reserves must exceed potential death benefit payments for the purpose of securing the solvency of the company. If a company permanently ceases the sale of new policies, there will be money left over after the payment of the last death claim. A mutual insurance company faces the dilemma of what to do with the excess money if the company were to terminate operations. Mutual companies attempt to create fairness by setting up a terminal reserve death benefit payment. The terminal reserve is supposed to represent the deceased's share of the excess reserve that would exist upon termination of operations. Those excess reserves will be counted as profits at some point of time.

Commissioner Korlann had now attempted to put an end to the sale of the policies that were the lifeblood of our company. Yet, he called me on the phone and told me he knew I had several acquaintances in New York City. He said he was planning to make a trip to New York and wanted me to obtain several tickets to the hit Broadway show *A Funny Thing Happened on the Way to the Forum*. He expected me to obtain the tickets and to pay for them. I called someone I'd met at one of the American Management Association meetings in New York City and asked for his help. He obtained the tickets for me, but he demanded I forward the funds to him immediately. ICOA made out a check in the amount of the price of the tickets and sent the check to the person who helped me out. The tickets arrived shortly afterwards. Commissioner Korlann thanked me for the gifts.

Clarence Tookey strongly objected to the characterization by the National Underwriter of ICOA's policies to be profit sharing as evidenced by his letter to me dated September 2, 1964:

CLARENCE H. TOOKEY, F. S. A.
PASADENA, CALIFORNIA  91101

September 2, 1964

Mr. Reginald L. Jensen, President
ICOA Life Insurance Company
P. O. Box 2228
Salem, Oregon 97301

Dear Reg:

I've been following the press reports which Harold sent me regarding the controversy in Oregon and did not see anything to remark on beyond my recent letter to him. However in the August 29, 1964, issue of the National Underwriter I think you have something you might answer. You are quoted as stating that companies like yours will be stifled if regulations barring the sale of "profit sharing" policies go into effect. Now what do "profit sharing" policies mean? In the first part of the article they specifically mean policies sharing in the general profits of the company. If you read the article you will see a very good complete definition.

ICOA has never issued such policies and I feel that it is unfair to quote you as supporting issue of such policies. It is most unfortunate that coupon policies which carry guaranteed benefits are included in the same class as the policies which Mr. Dunkin so specifically defined.

I have not yet seen a clear exposition of the very wide distinction being made between such policies and par or non par coupon policies. I can't see why your participating coupon policy is not just as good as any policy issued by a mutual company in the State of Oregon. Any policy issued by a mutual company can be misrepresented by unrealistic dividend estimates. So far I've not felt that I needed to give you any direct help. I think however you might write a letter to the National Underwriter referring to this article and emphasizing that you do not support and that your company has never issued the type of profit sharing policy defined by Mr. Dunkin. If you wish to draft a letter and send it to me for suggestions as to content I'll be glad to do that.

Regards.

Yours sincerely,

Signed by Clarence Tookey

I took his advice and did write the letter. Included in my letter was a recommendation that the mutual companies should consider converting to stock companies. The surplus funds owned by mutual companies belong to the policyholders, but it's very difficult for a mutual company to credit the living policyholder with his or her proper share of that account. These excess reserves eventually return to the surplus account, but not to the surplus account of the insureds who created them. The terminal reserve is never sufficient. Nevertheless, participating life insurance policies can show a better financial result for the insured than nonparticipating policies. Twenty-five years later, many of the large mutual companies did convert to stock companies. The managers of some of these companies anticipated benefiting themselves through grants of stock and stock options issued at the time of conversion or at a later time. The Prudential Insurance Company of America and Metropolitan Life Insurance Company were two of the largest companies converted.

ICOA decided to take the offensive and filed suit against the Insurance Commissioner claiming his regulations went beyond his authority. Our position was the coupons were life-insurance units and that the Commissioner didn't have the authority to prohibit the sale of life insurance. The action was *ICOA v. Insurance Commissioner,* Marion County, Oregon, No. 57339 (1964). The OLUA soon reversed its position and decided to remain neutral in the controversy. One of its officers told me the members were afraid of being sued. There were other insurance companies selling policies similar to ICOA's but none of them were willing to get involved in the fray. We were the lightning rod.

Dave Robb had been named Agency Vice President for ICOA. In late 1964, he and I were driving through Oregon visiting the agents in the field. Robb was driving. We were traveling down Central Oregon on a little-used road when he began to speed up. He got the speed of the car up to about 90 mph then slammed on the brakes, crossed the highway and pulled into a service station. Another car pulled in behind us. The driver was red-faced, angry and scared. Robb said the man was following us. We just ignored him from then on and went about our business. After we returned to Salem, I did some investigating to find out who and what had an interest in following us around. It turned out he was with the United States Securities & Exchange Commission (SEC) Investigations Division, which had been monitoring all of our activities. The government was attempting to build a case against ICOA for the unlawful sale of securities. It was the position of the SEC that the coupon policies were securities.

Mrs. Peg Drager was ICOA's office manager. She invited me over to her house one day in 1964 while the legislature was in session. Her husband was hosting a poker game in the living room, but he wasn't a player. These games were held periodically at different locations. All of the players were state representatives or state senators except one gentleman who was a lobbyist for the Weyerhaeuser Lumber Company in the state of Washington. Bun Kelsay was one of the players. As it turned out, the lobbyist proved to be a poor poker player. He lost, big. The members of the state legislature won big and were always anxious to get into a game. I was told the lobbyist entered many poker games over the years, but never seemed to win; for him, it was just the fun of playing.

In December 1964 I received a letter from Robert J. Wright, one of ICOA's life-insurance agents in Eugene, Oregon, demanding the delivery of a list of ICOA's stockholders. I took the letter to Hank to ask him what it meant. He said Wright was fronting a proxy contest. This opened up a brand new learning experience for me. I had no knowledge of proxy contests and wasn't even aware of the term. The officers met and had a lengthy discussion about our procedure in responding to the demand. Churchill told us we could delay in responding to the demand, but eventually we must comply. Hank suggested we register our stock with the SEC. His position was the registration would require stricter rules, make it more expensive and give management the advantage. We called a special Board meeting, authorized the registration, and began working with the SEC in preparation for the proxy contest. In the meantime we allowed Wright to review the list, but we prohibited him from making copies. Wright brought a tape recorder to our office and started reading the names, addresses and numbers of shares into the recorder. It took him about 10 days to complete his work. Then he needed to transcribe the recordings.

After receiving Wright's demand, several insurance agents brought some of Wright's selling tactics to my attention. One of his errors was traveling to the state of Washington to sell a policy even though he wasn't licensed in Washington. He also used sales material that had not been provided by ICOA. So, I terminated his agent's contract based on the license infraction and his misrepresentation in his sales of the insurance policies. Wright used this opportunity to file suit against ICOA claiming commissions due and payable. The action was *Wright v. ICOA Life Insurance Company*, Lane County Circuit Court Cause No.

74854. Wright was represented by Buehner's partner, Roger Tilbury. A successful suit by Wright would make all renewal commissions payable to him immediately, rather than having to wait until future premiums were paid.

It was my belief Wright represented Buehner and his cohorts, but I wanted to know for certain, so I hired a private detective to follow him to find out how he spent his time. I informed the board of directors about my decision and it approved my action. The detective placed a monitoring device on Wright's car so he could keep track of the car at all times. The detective kept me informed of his activities and I informed the board. Wright was immediately able to identify the detective and he knew the exact location of the monitoring device. His attorney contacted me and demanded that I remove the investigator. Obviously, someone on our board of directors passed the information on to Wright. The knowledge gave him more information that could be used to attack the company. Wright later filed another suit against ICOA claiming invasion of privacy; this action was *Wright v. ICOA Life Insurance Company,* Marion County (Salem) Number 59458. Wright was again represented by Roger Tilbury.

In late December, shortly after Wright finished recording the names and addresses of stockholders, the Willamette Valley had an unusually heavy snowstorm. The weather changed within a day and it became unusually warm. The melting snow caused flooding in Salem. The flood waters filled the ICOA parking lot. Henry Buehner had been in Salem the day the flooding occurred. He stayed across the street at the Marion Hotel overnight. The next day Buehner told me he was isolated in Salem, his auto wouldn't run, and he needed immediate transportation. I talked to Jim Hatfield and he agreed to lend one of his autos to Buehner until Buehner's auto was back in service. The following morning the water was drained from the lot and we discovered an auto that was immersed but we weren't sure who the owner was. The auto was unlocked, so we drained the water and removed the contents, which were a file of papers lying on the passenger's seat. We took the papers into the board room and laid them on the table to dry. After the papers dried we could see they belonged to Buehner. We checked the registration on the auto and found it belonged to a stranger.

The papers told an interesting story of a United States National Bank (Oregon) loan of $300,000 to a lumber company, then the transfer of most of the money through several other companies. The money eventually disappeared. Buehner borrowed the money from the bank on July 9, 1963. He had other loans with the bank and eventually all of the transactions wound up in court. The case became *Investment Service Company (Oregon) v. Columbia Softwood Lumber Company, Buehner Lumber Company, Vulcan Mountain Lumber Company, Thelin Lumber Sales, and Henry A. Buehner*; Multnomah County (Portland), cause number 299776, filed March 31, 1964. Investment Service Company was owned by the bank. The law firm representing the bank was Rockwood, Davis, Biggs, Strayer, & Stoel. Dean Alexander represented Buehner and the other defendants. Judge Charles W. Redding presided. Judge Redding's orders were always favorable to the bank and its law firm.

I recalled that Buehner had asked me several years earlier how much it would cost to finance a proxy contest against management. I'd said it would take about $300,000. I made copies of the papers because the connection seemed to be there. When Buehner returned to the office with Hatfield's auto I gave him the papers and told him I made copies. He said he didn't care about my copies. I asked him about the auto in the parking lot and he said he'd borrowed a friend's auto in Portland and it was the friend's auto that was water damaged. He arranged to have the auto towed to a repair shop and then asked Hatfield to drive him home.

In early January 1965, Jim Hatfield was called to appear before the criminal grand jury in Portland. We drove to Portland together because I wanted to know what it was all about. Hatfield said he had no idea why he was subpoenaed. After he testified and as we were returning to Salem he explained the questions and his answers. He said he wasn't sure of the direction of the questions but it had something to do with his automobile. Hatfield said the grand jury seemed to be investigating prostitution in Oregon. He was surprised by any suggestion he was involved. He did remember Buehner was using his auto during the time period in question.

As soon as we returned to the office, I phoned Buehner and asked him if he would come down to Salem and talk to us. He was there in about an hour. Hank, Jim, and I then began asking questions. Hank listened for a short period of time and then went back to his office. I asked the questions: Why was Jim's car being photographed by the police? Who was in his car when Henry wasn't driving? Why was the car photographed throughout Portland and in other parts of the Willamette Valley?

Buehner began to open up. His first comment was he didn't want to hurt us, so he'd resign from the board if we asked him to. Then he said he controlled a prostitution operation in Oregon. He said he operated out of the University Club in Portland. He said he loaned his car, and the cars of his friends, to prostitutes so they could make their rounds. He said he had loaned Hatfield's car to several prostitutes and the investigators had taken pictures of them. He said a lawsuit for promoting prostitution had been filed against him in Portland. But, he said there was no reason to worry. He said in addition to providing prostitutes for businessmen, politicians, and the general public, he had furnished prostitutes for every judge in Oregon and possessed photographs of each judge with a prostitute. He said he had placed the photos in the court files in the clerk's record room. He said it would be treated as part of the discovery process. All of the pictures were subject to review by the plaintiffs or the public at any time. Now all of the evidence implicating the judges was secured in the clerk's offices, and he would make the evidence public if the suit wasn't dropped. He said he was confident the suit against him would be dropped. He said there wasn't a judge in Oregon who would preside over the case and no pro tem judge would permit the regular judges to be embarrassed. I told Buehner I would like to have his resignation. He wrote it out and signed it immediately. As it turned out, he was right. Nothing ever came of the prostitution investigation. (In 2007 the Multnomah County (Oregon) court records clerk told me no record existed of the criminal charge against Buehner. Several months later, I talked to the police records office and was told promoting prostitution is a misdemeanor and that all of those records are destroyed after several years and no records existed regarding Buehner. Several months later, the Multnomah County District Attorney's office told me no criminal records are ever destroyed, but the public isn't allowed to see those records and I couldn't search the records.)

Buehner then told me he and the others in opposition to the re-election of board members had found Wright to be a perfect front man. Buehner said he had met and talked with different ICOA agents around the state and centered on Wright because Wright was aggressive and without reservations in approaching and challenging people in authority. He said Wright would put up a worthy battle in the proxy contest. Wright was promised the job of supervising the sales force. Wright, with Buehner's assistance, moved to the front. Buehner's law background, attorney friends and partners, and his influence over judges, made life easy for Wright.

After Buehner resigned, we asked Larry Crosby to serve as board chairman and he agreed.

It was clear ICOA would face a proxy contest for control of the company fronted by Wright acting on behalf of Buehner, Francis, Herzinger, and Hinkle. All of this activity brought an end to the prospects of selling stock to purchase BanLife. Buehner and his group had planned the BanLife purchase to be a coup on their part once they took over management of ICOA. The problem they would have faced was one of management. None of the board members would have any knowledge of the insurance business and would then be required to find someone with the knowledge and experience. Qualified insurance-company management personnel are few and far between. The managers in New Jersey were prepared to resign once the sale of the company was completed; none were interested in moving to Oregon. Insurance-company management is a key factor for stock brokers in selling stock to sophisticated investors and its unlikely the brokerage firm would have any interest in handling a stock issue after a management change. This would be especially true with the acquiring company being less than one-twentieth the size of the company to be acquired. In any event, the concept of acquiring BanLife came to an end.

Hank had suggested ICOA file a registration with the SEC so that the proxy solicitation would be conducted under strict rules. The Board agreed and instructed Churchill to prepare the registration. Registration was a very complicated process, but Churchill's unique ability allowed him to learn the massive rules in short order and complete the registration in a timely manner. The attorneys representing the opposition had fewer skills than Churchill and they were placed in a disadvantageous situation.

In early 1965, a trial was held concerning ICOA's suit against the Insurance Commissioner based on the insurance regulations. Jim Hatfield knew all of the judges and was very close to the chief judge, Val Sloper. It's pretty clear the other judges in the county believed Jim Hatfield and I were aware of Buehner's extra-curricular activities. None of them wanted to handle the case. Since no sitting judge would handle the case, Governor Mark Hatfield appointed Loren Hicks to a vacant judge position. Judge Hicks was of average size and build, a little slender and healthy looking. He was about 40 years old. Governor Hatfield was about age 40 and all of the appointed individuals surrounding him were in the same age group. Judge Hicks was then directed to preside over the case. The Insurance Commissioner believed the judge had been instructed to rule in his favor. Several comments coming from members of the department were that their case was a slam dunk. I felt the same at the time. The commissioner asked us to withdraw our suit. I felt enough damage had been done, which forced us to fight it out and refused.

Judge Hicks took testimony at trial. We had two witnesses testify, our full-time actuary, David Bothum, and Clarence Tookey, both expert witnesses. Bothum testified that the coupon policies were, in fact, life insurance policies. Tookey's testimony was clear and convincing. His testimony included the fact that dividends and coupons in life insurance policies are simply single-premium life insurance units. Dividends (single premium life insurance units) and the coupons have additional life-insurance benefits. Both the dividends and coupons have immediate cash values each year. The insurance company will issue a check to the policy owner if the owner surrenders the dividend or the coupon, otherwise the insurance benefit will increase every year. Prohibiting the sale of coupon policies would be the same as prohibiting paid-up life insurance units purchased with policy dividends. The Commissioner's position was that the law prevented coupons from being inserted into life insurance contracts. However, the Commissioner had previously approved the policies.

On April 6, 1965, Judge Hicks drafted his ruling and, on April 7 he held a bench conference in his courtroom where he first read his decision before giving copies to the parties. The courtroom was large and nearly empty. The judge was at the bench and there were two tables for the attorneys and several wooden chairs at the back of the courtroom next to the door. Tom Churchill and I were present along with the attorney, Peter Herman, from the Commissioner's office. We were all standing while we listened to the judge read his decision. Judge Hicks ruled in ICOA's favor. His ruling said "It is the opinion of the court that the Commissioner is without authority to make such regulations of prohibition and limitation, and that they therefore are invalid and unenforceable." Judge Hicks could see clearly through the maze of publicity and rhetoric. As a newly appointed judge, Hicks maintained his integrity. After Judge Hicks read his decision someone in the courtroom who had been sitting in one of the chairs near the door came over to me as I approached the door. He said he represented the SEC and that I was lucky, he had an indictment in his hand ready to deliver to me for violation of the 1933 and 1934 SEC acts. Soon afterwards Judge Hicks left the bench and returned to private practice.

ICOA's annual meeting was held April 19, 1965, just twelve days after Judge Hick's ruling. If the ruling was against ICOA, it would have been used in an attempt to remove me and the other officers from the Board of Directors and our positions as corporate officers. Buehner and Francis, et. al. would then have the company to do with as they saw fit.

Wright used attorney Melvin Goode of Albany, Oregon, as his attorney in the proxy contest, which got underway in February 1965. ICOA had completed its registration with the SEC and solicited proxies under the rules. Wright's group solicited second. Wright's group outlined a number of problems they believed existed with company management. The first statement was that the Insurance Commissioner had attempted to prohibit the sale of our policies, which meant we must be doing something illegal. Wright's group captured a majority of the votes with their proxy solicitation. We mailed a second solicitation, which countered all of the opposition claims beginning with the decision in our favor issued by Judge Hicks. Our theme was "Wright is Wrong."

We recaptured a large majority of the votes. The opposition group was either unprepared to mail a second time or were counting on a positive decision from Judge Hicks in the suit against the commissioner. Since the judge's ruling was adverse to them they relied on the votes they believed they had in their pocket.

The meeting was held in the Marion Hotel ballroom across the street from our office. The meeting was tense and exhilarating. There were more than 500 stockholders present. Wright set up a booth in one corner of the meeting hall where he made his presentation in an attempt to capture more proxies. Those in attendance weren't about to change without listening to management's presentation. This was my trial by fire of being in charge of a contested election in front of a large group of people. I was well-prepared this time and kept the meeting under control and well-organized. Everyone was given a chance to speak and to present arguments and ask questions, both pro and con. At the end of the meeting, those in attendance were given a chance to affirm their prior vote or to recast their ballots.

Voting was cumulative, which meant all votes could be accumulated and cast for one candidate or for any group of candidates. If there are three candidates, then one share of stock could accumulate the three votes and cast three votes for one person or cast one vote for each of three persons. When the proxies were tabulated the results showed Wright's group could elect one board member. Wright's group elected Goode as its representative. ICOA's slate lost one candidate. However, there were three open seats on the Board so ICOA's losing candidate was appointed to the vacant position. The opposition never attempted to declare those three seats open.

After the proxy contest several of the agents told me about being recruited by Buehner and Francis to take part in defeating management in the proxy contest. One agent from Bend, Oregon, told me Francis had sent an emissary to tell him he could use a new automobile for at least a year as a free gift if he gave support to the opposition. Another agent told me he had been introduced to prostitutes by Buehner. One of the prostitutes told him she was servicing a client in bed in a motel when, during intercourse, the client had a heart attack and died. She was startled and frightened. The client was a heavy person and it was difficult for her to remove his body from her. She finally extricated herself, got up, dressed, and covered the dead client with blankets. Then she left the motel, phoned the manager and asked him to check on the health of the man in his room. It seemed like the management of ICOA knew less about what was happening prior to and during the proxy contest than anyone else.

In May 1965, Commissioner Korlann held a hearing on Wright's license termination. He didn't rule immediately, but eventually ruled in favor of Wright retaining his license. The Commissioner told me he just couldn't bring himself to prevent another person from earning a living.

Nearly all of ICOA's life-insurance sales were in Oregon. The proxy contest received considerable publicity in the Salem newspapers and minor publicity in the Portland paper. The concentration on the proxy contest meant the agency force was ignored. Sales began to drop off. There seemed to be unusual dissention in the ranks of the sales force. I interviewed the agents to find out what could be done to satisfy them and to get sales back off the ground again. They told me other insurance companies had financed some negative sales activities against ICOA. We had hired a former Northwestern Mutual Life Insurance Company (NML) agent who later admitted to me he was being paid by NML while he was in ICOA's employ. He said he was taking money from both companies. He said he was instructed to demoralize our salesmen. I never heard from him again after he left my office.

The concentrated effort to put ICOA out of business came from many different directions. Lincoln Hanks returned to Oregon and formed another company named Oregon National Life Insurance Company. Many of the same people who opposed ICOA were members of the board of that company. Hanks came over to my house one evening and suggested we merge the two companies. He proposed that Oregon National would pay me $750,000 to resign. He suggested the combined company would then engage in reinsurance arrangements with several other Oregon companies, and perhaps others from out of state, so the sale of one policy could be reinsured four or five times. He thought that would allow each company to take credit for the insurance, creating four or five times the original value, and make it look like all companies were tremendously successful. I told him I didn't think it would work and refused to take it to the board of ICOA. Oregon National was never able to create a business plan and was never able to hire a sales force. Oregon National changed its name to Farwest American Assurance Company in 1975. Universe Life Insurance Company in Idaho purchased the policies of Oregon National in 1990. In 1998 Universe Life was liquidated by the Idaho Insurance Department and its policies were assumed by several other companies.

Wright, using Roger Tilbury, Buehner's partner, was able to press his contract suit against ICOA in the fall of 1965, in Eugene. The verdict was in Wright's favor. The jury awarded him about $56,000. Wright filed a slander suit, *Robert J. Wright v. Reginald L. Jensen & ICOA Life Insurance Company*, Marion County Cause Number 59635, claiming the "Wright is Wrong" pamphlet used by management during the proxy contest damaged his reputation. Buehner gave Tilbury all of the information he needed to prepare for the suit. Since Buehner was no longer on the board, he received all the information he needed from Francis, Hinkle, or Herzinger. Wright's slander suit went to trial in Salem later in the winter before a jury with Judge Douglas Hay presiding. I was dropped as a defendant because I wasn't the person who signed the letter claiming "Wright is Wrong." Judge Hay lived in my neighborhood, his daughter played with our daughter, but he had never been to my house, nor had I been to his. We had no association with each other. Judge Hay allowed the case to go to the jury and Wright was awarded about $50,000. Judge Hay came over to my house after the trial on the same day at his own invitation and had a couple of cocktails with me and my wife. He asked how I felt about the verdict. I told him I was stunned. He told us Wright hadn't proved his case. He said he should have dismissed the action but he let it go to the jury because he was certain the jury would find in favor of ICOA. Judge Hay and I never met or talked again. The invasion of privacy action was settled out of court with a payment to Wright.

Wright's relationship with Buehner and the other backers of the proxy contest allowed him to do many things with impunity. Wright went back to many of his clients and told them he had misrepresented the policy sales to them and he wanted to help them get their money back. However, he told the policyholders he was entitled to a percentage of the money they received. He collected a commission on the sale of the policies and now he would collect a commission on the rescission of the policies. He began acting as an attorney on a contingency-fee basis preparing and filing lawsuits on behalf of policy holders claiming sales misrepresentation by ICOA. He filed between ten and twelve lawsuits. He never produced any evidence, only his declaration that the policies violated Oregon insurance law. He also claimed some sales material he used, but never developed by ICOA, was sanctioned by management.

One case went to trial by judge in Roseburg. The plaintiffs (husband and wife) wanted their money back. The judge prohibited Wright from representing the plaintiffs in court. The plaintiffs were required to represent themselves or be represented by a licensed attorney when presenting their case. An attorney did come to their rescue and the case proceeded. Several years had passed since they had purchased the insurance policy and the cash value was less than the total premiums paid. The only evidence presented to the court was newspaper publicity and negative statements by competitors. The trial lasted one day. During a break in taking testimony, Jim Hatfield and I were standing in the hall of the courthouse when a couple of men came into the hall just a few feet away from us and told another person they were sent by Governor Mark Hatfield's office to talk to the judge handling the case against ICOA. They were escorted into the judge's chambers. After the break, the judge took my testimony. He asked questions that were limited to the cost of term insurance and home-office expenses per policy. He then immediately ruled ICOA must refund all premiums in excess of those costs. No appeal was taken and the plaintiffs were paid according to the Court's order. One husband and wife policyholder decided to visit with me in my office and asked for settlement on the same basis as the court-ordered settlement, a refund of the amount in excess of the term insurance cost. I agreed to pay them on the condition they keep the settlement confidential.

After each suit was filed, the courts told Wright he needed to find an attorney to prosecute the case. That was never done until a case was set for trial. The rest of the cases eventually died for lack of prosecution. Wright was never prevented from acting as an attorney, the courts (including the Oregon Supreme Court) simply advised him to stop. The advice went unheeded and the courts did nothing about it.

In the summer of 1965, I met with Henry Buehner again to find out about his part in the proxy contest. Buehner never backed away from any question and his answers always seemed to be correct. He said he and Francis were partners from the beginning, when ICOA was created. Buehner and Francis were both members of an exclusive club in Portland and that's where they hatched their plan before all the directors were selected. After all the directors had been appointed, Francis and Buehner enlisted the support of Herzinger and Hinkle to take over the company. They believed the count was four (Buehner, Francis, Hinkle, and Herzinger) to four (Me, Hank, Churchill, and Hatfield). Hugh Earle was the odd man out. Earle resigned and Dr. Harvey was appointed to the board. With Earle gone, the outside directors would only be required to eliminate me, which seemed simple, and to add one new member to the board. They believed they could eventually neutralize one of the management board members. But things changed along the way. With Buehner off the board they now had to elect more than one new member. After the proxy contest, they had Melvin Goode as a compatriot, but they needed to do more.

Buehner said he arranged the financing for the proxy contest. He said he and Dean Alexander were the primary partners in that transaction. He said the $300,000 loan papers I had found in the auto the night it was flooded in the ICOA parking lot told the story. He said he filled out papers to borrow $300,000 from the United States National Bank in Portland on behalf of a shell lumber company. The shell lumber company had borrowed a substantial amount of lumber from an unrelated company and listed it as its own asset on the loan application. He and several other attorneys took an executive vice president of the bank out drinking and partying that night. They kept the banker out until nearly 6:00 a.m., drove him home and let him out of the auto. They had an appointment with the banker at 8:00 a.m. in his office. Buehner and his friends went somewhere for breakfast, then Buehner met the banker at the appointed time. The banker had just arrived and was still blurry-eyed and hung over. Buehner asked the banker's secretary to bring the loan papers in for the officer's signature, which she did. The banker signed the papers and Buehner took the papers over to another person to obtain the funds. Buehner deposited the funds into the account of the shell corporation. He subsequently transferred the money to another bank and then returned the borrowed lumber except for lumber valued at $10,000, which his shell company purchased. He transferred the purchased lumber to a lot in Las Vegas, Nevada, and made one payment on the $300,000 loan. Buehner and his cohorts had $290,000, minus one bank-loan payment. Then he transferred the money several more times until it was no longer attachable by the bank. Now the money was available for use in the proxy contest against ICOA. The loan went into default, the bank seized the lumber in Las Vegas but had no recourse on the balance of the money. The banker was subsequently transferred and demoted.

Ed Francis wanted to get out of the auto business and into the financial-services business. His goal was to be President of ICOA and eventually become a board member of the United States National Bank. He felt ICOA could be a stepping stone onto other boards of directors. In early 1966, he sold his Ford dealership and asked me to step down as president, become vice president, and ask the board to elect him as president. I refused. His knowledge of the life insurance business was too limited for him to be effective in managing a small, new life insurance company. His position was that anyone could manage any kind of company, it was the management skills that counted, not knowledge of the industry.

Several months had passed when Francis called me on the phone and asked me to meet him in Portland. At the meeting, Francis said he and several other people had purchased a computer for about $300,000. He said he wanted to lease it to ICOA for $150,000 a year on a three-year lease. ICOA would have the right to buy the computer for $150,000 at the end of the three years (their investment return would amount to about 38 percent per year compounded). I said it would be a great arrangement for him and a serious mistake for ICOA. ICOA could buy its own computers when and if it found it necessary. Spending $600,000 for something that we could buy for $300,000 wasn't my idea of prudent management. Francis was very upset.

*Judicial Deception*

ICOA's independent auditing firm, Peat Marwick Mitchell & Co. (PMM), decided to help us out about this time. They worked with a small insurance company in Portland that was controlled by an attorney. PMM suggested to us that we might be able to work out a profitable merger agreement with the Portland company. Hank and I met at the Portland company with a PMM employee and the attorney. PMM gave us a proposed-merger document, which was just a rough draft of a form used as a guideline for serious discussions. Some of the paragraphs had been crossed out, some of the blank sections had penciled in figures, and some of the blank spaces had no entries. It seemed to me it was really a haphazard presentation, hastily created, with little consideration for their audience.

The attorney said, after the merger of our company into his, he wanted to be the majority owner and sole decision maker. I met with him in his office for a few minutes. He agreed to tell me how he got involved in the management of the company. He said the company was owned by one of his clients, a widow in New York City, who knew nothing about insurance and had no interest in learning. He said he had an opportunity to purchase the company for about ten cents on the dollar. He expected to arrange the purchase of the company and merge ICOA with his company at the same time so he could use ICOA's surplus to pay the widow. It seemed to me it would be a pretty good trick if he could pull it off. I didn't give the merger offer any serious consideration. (It's my understanding the attorney did eventually complete the ownership transaction and soon converted the company to a group accident and health insurer. His company did survive for a few years as a health insurance provider.)

Bun Kelsay was Vice President of Hult Lumber Company in Eugene, Oregon. He wanted to be a member of ICOA's Board. He was being considered for an appointment. I had a lot of respect for Bun and would have welcomed him on the board. ICOA had scheduled a board meeting and invited Bun to attend. He had been attending a function near Coos Bay and wanted to be in Salem the next morning to attend the meeting. He was driving through the mountains at night in a rainstorm when his car went off the road and the accident was fatal to him. I was home in bed when it occurred. (It was later brought to my attention that Bun was an advocate of the faction supporting Buehner and Francis.)

As an advisory board member, Bun was insured in the amount $50,000 under ICOA's group life plan, which was purchased from an insurance company unrelated to ICOA. After his death, his wife, Betty, filed a suit against the insurer requesting compensation exceeding the $50,000. Her suit made no sense to me because she had been offered the entire amount of the death benefit. Betty's attorney took my deposition. The direction of his questions seemed to imply I had some responsibility for her husband's death. The lawsuit failed to produce any results, was soon dropped, the insurance company paid the claim, and mailed the check to me for delivery. I delivered the check to Betty at her home in Roseburg. She met me at her front door and took the check from me without letting me enter her house. She said she had little interest in the money. I asked her why. She told me she had been to the bank where Bun had a safe deposit box and there was more cash inside than she would need for the rest of her life. When I was driving back home, I wondered why she filed the lawsuit.

About this time I was discussing business and personal problems with a psychiatrist. He suggested it's possible for a person to fight very intensely with an enemy yet, at the same time, be able to sit down at a meal with that person. Soon afterwards, my wife's parents who were born in Germany prior to the First World War explained their experiences with the enemy during that conflict. They were in their middle teens when Germany went to war and were able to converse with German soldiers from time to time. My wife's mother said the soldiers on both sides would shoot at each other during the day but would get out their meals at night and sit with the enemy soldiers to eat. Then they would go back to their bunkers and foxholes to sleep before renewing the battle the next day. Throughout the rest of my life. I found this tactic worked very well. Talking directly to an adversary often bore fruit.

Wright led a second proxy contest in 1966. This time the faction hired attorney Clarke Brown of Salem. Brown was a good showman but he wasn't detail-oriented. Brown made a tactical error when he failed to read or understand the corporate articles and by-laws. There was a provision in the by-laws that required the names of candidates for the board to be submitted to the corporate secretary 60 days prior to the annual meeting. The opposition group not only missed the day but they never submitted any nominees prior to the meeting. They attempted to nominate their slate at the opening of the meeting. I simply read to those in attendance the provision of the by-laws that required nominations to be submitted to the board sixty days prior to the annual meeting. None of the opposition nominees were eligible to serve and they received no qualifying votes. Brown showed his disdain for the benefit of his group and then went his separate way.

I'll return to ICOA but first I'll finish the Wright episode. Wright lost interest in ICOA and now had bigger fish to fry. He had developed a close relationship with the Oregon Corporation Commissioner, Frank Healy. He once told me Commissioner Healy would give a good recommendation about him if anyone called and inquired of his character. He was moving in different circles and felt as if he could influence many people. One of his activities from the middle 1960s through the middle 1970s was practicing law in Oregon. Wright decided he could act as an attorney for anyone he thought he could help. His experiences with Buehner and his friends gave him the confidence he needed. He was free to wander about the state, like Diogenes, searching for people who would let him file lawsuits. He filed a variety of lawsuits against a variety of people and companies on behalf of a variety of people. And he moved on to other projects he had already developed. He was selling jumbo certificates of deposits that were being marketed by different savings and loans around the country. The savings and loans were paying commissions of up to one percent to any representative who could initiate the transactions for any deposits of $100,000 or more. He found a few people with money who would purchase the CDs, which earned a few extra dollars for him.

By the end of 1970, I was no longer living in Oregon so the information I have about Wright after that time is only anecdotal. The Oregon State Bar was active in trying to put an end to Wright's legal practice, but the judges had no serious interest in banning his activities. Prior to 1977, he was sued by the Oregon State Bar because he was practicing law without a license. He fought that suit and, in 1977, it was carried to the Oregon Supreme Court in a case titled *Oregon State Bar v. Wright*, 573 P.2d 283. Wright believed the Bar committed a host of errors in pursuing the case. He advanced those errors in the appeal. The Oregon Supreme Court answered 17 assignments of error put forth by Wright and then concluded:

> For all of these reasons, the decree of permanent injuction as entered by the trial court is affirmed, except as modified so as to the extent that it shall be amended so as to provide that defendant "may appear as counsel as defined in ORS 9.310 in any civil *or criminal* case in a justice court or as counsel in the civil *or criminal* case in any municipal court which authorizes such appearances by city charter or code.

Immediately following that case is *State of Oregon ex rel. Oregon State Bar, Respondent v. Robert J. Wright, Appellant.* Or. 573 P. 2d 294. The Lane County Circuit Court had found Wright in contempt of a temporary restraining order banning him from engaging in the practice of law. *The Oregon Supreme Court found the evidence was insufficient to support defendant's violation as willful and with bad intent.* Wright's unlicensed practice of law in Oregon for more than ten years brought him a tap on the wrist from the highest legal authority in the state. The highest court in Oregon said the tap on the wrist was too restrictive and violent. The injuction meant nothing to him because it left him an opening to continue his practice. If one of his clients wanted to proceed in a court where the injuction applied he would claim he was working on his client's behalf, not the court's behalf. Wright's working on a client's behalf shouldn't be considered bad intent. It takes a lot of time, work, and effort to do competent research in the field of law. It seems to me he would need to be pointed in the correct direction to achieve any degree of success when acting on his own or for the benefit of others.

Wright practiced law either as a sideline or as his primary activity for a number of years. He also continued his activities in selling jumbo savings and loan or bank certificates of deposit, which was perfectly legal and truly helpful to some people until the savings and loan crises commenced in the late 1970s. He seemed to be successful and active from 1977 to 1985. He created a unique and interesting way of raising money. He found several new careers and was attempting to capitalize on them. It seems he was having a great time and enjoyed a lot of success in his new-found ventures. Somehow or another he became active in challenging the United States government and the Internal Revenue Service (IRS). It seems as though he concluded the collection of income taxes was illegal and he filed a claim against the IRS for billions of dollars. Then he transferred that claim to the *Oregon Evangelical Trust*, which he had created. Apparently, the trust became a vehicle for him to accomplish greater good. It gave him a lot of leverage and the opportunity to do business in other states.

Wright comes into the picture again in 1985 in Iowa. An article appeared in the Indianapolis Star[9] referring to Robert J. Wright of Lodi, Oregon, using Senator Charles Grassley's name in an apparent scheme to swindle credit-starved farmers in Iowa. Iowa is quite a distance from Oregon and Senator Grassley spends most of his time in Washington, D.C. Wright was reported to be under investigation by the Iowa Attorney General's office. Wright claimed to be a Trustee of the Oregon Evangelical Trust, which claimed to own an asset of $100 million dollars due from the federal government.

Wright had created and became the Trustee of the Oregon Evangelical Trust as the successor to Trans-Pacific Enterprises with authorized capital of 10 million shares. He then claimed the Farmers Home Administration was the owner of sixteen thousand shares of the Trust. He also demonstrated that others were also owners of shares in the trust. Various other reports stated Wright claimed either the trust or Trans-Pacific was due several billion dollars from the IRS. I have no idea how he arrived at any of those numbers, but it must have made him feel good.

A person must travel through Idaho, Wyoming, and Kansas to get to Iowa from Oregon. Wright was still active in Oregon during that time period and it leaves the impression he was active in other states as well. How and why he worked in Iowa and attached Senator Grassley's name to his projects has never been publicly revealed. If he believed he had the funding of hundreds of millions of dollars or even billions of dollars from the United States government, it's easy to see he was having a field day. A person has to wonder why Wright was concerned

---

[9] May 23, 1985, (p. 65)

about the farmers in Iowa when he had that kind of money to occupy his time. In any event, the state of Iowa wanted to protect its farmers and set about trying to convince him to find other fertile territory.

Something about the activities in Iowa attracted the attention of the Oregonian. The Oregonian reported[10] Iowa Attorney General Tom Miller obtained a temporary injunction against Wright. Miller's suit asked for the return of any land or money the farmers had lost. On May 23, 1985, the Attorney General for the State of Iowa filed a petition in the *Iowa District Court for Polk County*, No. CE 023 13125, outlining the following acts, some of which were improper:

> **Wright** lives in Noti, Oregon;
>
> **Wright** is providing services to farmers which are experiencing serious financial difficulties;
>
> **Wright** represents he is experienced in helping these farmers;
>
> **Wright** has misrepresented his background, business activities, and his net worth through the Trust (Oregon Evangelical Trust);
>
> **Wright** is the trustee and the Trust claims to have assets of up to $6 billion.
>
> **The Trust** issues stock to the farmers in return for title to the farm;
>
> **The farmer** then tenders the stock to his creditors to satisfy all obligations;
>
> **The farmer** can repurchase the farm for 25 percent of the original purchase price;
>
> **The farmer** pays the trust $300 per month interest while the farmer leases the farm from the Trust;
>
> **Wright** issues "United States Treasury Department Obligation Checks" allegedly under "Title 12 U.S.C. §

---

[10] May 24, 1985, (p. 4M)

248 (m) noting that "a bank holding obligations of the United States Treasury Department is exempt from the above-cited law," and that "the obligation referred to is in excess of one hundred million dollars for 10 million tons of Uranium Ore;"

**Wright** says the Trust's stock is fully guaranteed;

**At the time** of the payment of debts owed by the United States government the Trust will pay a "six hundred million dollar tax lien."

**Wright** claimed his law firm is "planning an extensive audit" of the records of a bank which has refused to accept Oregon Evangelical Trust stock certificates as payment in full for debtor obligations.

**Wright** has concealed the fact that the claims of the Trust are subject to an action before the court of claims and the United States Court of Appeals for the District of Columbia;

**The case** has been before the Court of Claims since March 1979 and the Court found Wright's position to be "remarkably unrevealing, unresponsive, confusing, incoherent, conflicting and incomprehensible;"

**The Court** found a persistent and bad faith course of conduct;

**The Department** of Treasury has never heard of Wright and will not honor the Trust obligations.

**All of the claims** are false, deceptive, and misleading.

**All of the claims** were made with the knowledge they were false, deceptive, and misleading.

**Residents of Iowa** relied on the claims.

**All in violation** of the provisions of §714.16(2)(a) of the Iowa Consumer Fraud Act, 1985 Code of Iowa.

**The Court** is requested to ban Wright from any further acts in violation of the Iowa Consumer Fraud Act.

**Signed** by Tom B. Ormiston, Assistant Attorney General, Hoover State Office Building, Des Moines, Iowa, 50319 ((515) 281-6634. Attorneys for the Plaintiff. (Various documents were submitted as evidence.)

It's possible that Wright's activities expanded well beyond Oregon and Iowa. It's uncertain where Wright was located when he became involved with the United States Court of Claims. The United States Court of Appeals in Washington, DC, was very tolerant of Wright for more than six years, from 1979 to 1985, yet no decision or conclusion had been reached. It seems as though the court of appeals was waiting for Wright to submit evidence and support for his claims. Normally, evidence and support is submitted in the district or trial court and new evidence isn't accepted in the court of appeals.

How did the IRS respond? It appears as though the IRS had no real objection to Wright's claims. During the six years the case was being held by the United States Court of Appeals there seems to be no objection delivered to Wright asking him to stop using the IRS or federal government as part of his dog and pony show. No federal agent stepped in to put an end to his activities, they left it up to the states of Iowa and Oregon. There's no record of Oregon ever objecting to Wright's claims of billions of dollars due to him. So, Iowa was left on its own. Wright was ultimately required to stop his practice in Iowa and return the deeds to the farmers. He did that and returned to Oregon. Was this another slap on the wrist, or would a slap on the wrist be too severe of a discription?

Life was still good for Wright. The bountiful hunting grounds of Oregon continued to beckon. Oregon provided more freedom of action and better protection. In 1989, four years after his sojourn in Iowa, he was again enjoined from practicing law and the Oregon Supreme Court upheld that decision in *Oregon State Bar v. Robert J. Wright* 772 P 2d 1366. But that still didn't deter Wright. He still had more work to do. The Oregon State Bar attempted to file criminal-contempt charges against Wright. The Oregon Supreme Court held in *Oregon State Bar v. Robert J. Wright*, 785 P2d 340 that the criminal contempt charges should be reversed and the case should go back to determine whether the statute of limitations barred the action or if additional charges should be filed.

Wright continued his normal practice in Oregon, and elsewhere I presume, until Henry Buehner died in 1991. Thereafter, the courts began to impose their will on him. In the Circuit Court of the State of Oregon for Lane County (Eugene), the *Oregon State Bar v. Robert J. Wright*, Cause No. 76-1522 (221), Judgment and Sentence filed December 14, 1994, the authorities finally jailed Wright. Based on his stipulation that he will no longer practice law in Oregon they reduced his jail sentence to time served, 88 days. Buehner gave him a free ride for a long time, a twenty-six year run (1965-1991), helping the citizens of Oregon and other states with their legal and financial problems. Wright is the same man Insurance Commissioner Korlann didn't want to deprive of his ability to make a living. He's the same man who said ICOA was misrepresenting its policies, not Wright himself. He didn't need an insurance license. He didn't even need a license to practice law. He didn't need a license for anything while he was in Oregon. He was free to do anything he wanted to do until 1991.

Leaving Wright for good and coming back to the summer of 1966, I was in a restaurant having lunch when someone pointed out the new attorney working for the insurance department sitting with Commissioner Korlann and one of his deputies a couple of tables away. A few minutes later the attorney walked over to me and told me he believed the actions proposed by the insurance department designed to damage ICOA were unethical. He said he refused to allow it to proceed and would have no part in it. He apologized for what they were doing and left. It was a brief conversation coming from someone I'd never met. He never explained what he meant by the insurance department actions and he went into no more detail. He left the restaurant and soon resigned from the department.

Governor Hatfield had two primary assistants. One was Warne H. Nunn and the other was Travis Cross. Nunn was the primary contact with the business community and Cross was the primary public relations man. Cross had a rare and unusual knack for remembering people's names. He could recall the name of just about everyone he'd ever met. He was always with the governor and, when someone approached them, he would whisper the person's name into Hatfield's ear. Several weeks after the insurance department attorney talked to me about the department's improper approach towards ICOA, I was in the bar at the Marion Hotel in Salem when Cross came over to talk to me. He said he was sorry for all of the problems he and the governor's office had caused me and the company. He never explained any further, just a simple apology. Cross later found another job in southern California and left Oregon. Governor Hatfield served two terms and then was elected to the United States Senate. Nunn went back to Washington, D.C., with Senator Hatfield, but only remained for a short time. He returned to Portland and became employed as a vice president with the Pacific Power and Light Company.

In 1966, I had negotiated a merger with a Montana company that was to be acquired by ICOA. It would have been beneficial to ICOA and the other company to consummate the merger. The president of the Montana company wanted to do something else. He said he had an opportunity to work with or for Senator Mike Mansfield. The Montana company had no person available who could take his place. However, the opposition board members of ICOA fought the acquisition because several of their group would be required to resign. A new board make-up would terminate any effective challenge to control. The merger was never consummated.

In 1967, it was a different story. That year, one of the largest and most-influential law firms in Oregon; Davies, Biggs, Strayer, Stoel and Boley, led by Hugh Biggs, was retained to conduct the third proxy contest. This was the same law firm that represented the United States National Bank in its suit against Buehner and the lumber companies (it had changed its name). Neither Biggs nor the bank ever obtained the stockholder list from me. The bank was the transfer agent and probably used that list. Biggs called me on the phone and asked what was so important about a small insurance company in Salem that required the services of his firm. His comment was just a dodge, but his firm was powerful. As an illustration, at a later time I hired Biggs to form a corporation on my behalf. In the process, Biggs needed an approval by the Oregon Corporation Department on a different matter and he asked me to take it to the State Capital offices in Salem. I talked to a deputy Corporation Commissioner who said he hadn't seen the document but would approve it. I asked him how he could approve a document without reading it. He said Biggs's law firm knew more about the law than the corporation department, and the state asked Biggs's law firm for advice, not the other way around, therefore, he knew the document was covered by state law. I took the document to the department and the deputy signed it.

Biggs' opposition committee consisted of unrelated people from different areas around the state. It was obvious none of the committee candidates for the board had the intent, finances, or skills to lead a proxy contest. Yet, the committee used every available means of solicitation. Many of the solicitations appeared to be in violation of federal law. Many stockholders reported receiving requests for proxies from unknown solicitors over the phone and in person. It was a massive and well-organized solicitation. It appeared as though we had no opportunity of obtaining even a modicum of the votes. However, we redoubled our appeal to the smaller stockholders. When the votes were counted, the opposition only gained three seats. Hugh Biggs was elected; Claude Key, a small businessman in Eastern Oregon, and George Higgins, a rancher in the middle of Oregon, were also elected. The management group still had control of the company.

The new board members knew nothing about the insurance business and really had no interest on serving on the board. They could offer nothing and didn't understand the language and financials. They felt like fish out of water. Crosby did not intend to continue as chairman of the board, so we elected Biggs as chairman. He graciously accepted. The board members weren't paid for their services. There was no obvious reason why Biggs would contribute his valuable time to the matters of our company without compensation. I'm convinced he was paid, but not by ICOA. Later, Higgins told us how and why he became a member of the opposition group. He said he had no interest in getting involved but was forced into it by some "friends" he wouldn't identify. Key said the United States National Bank instructed him to become an opposition candidate. Key said he told the bank he had no interest, but the bank said it would call all of his loans if he refused to participate. He said the bank wanted representation from different areas in Oregon and he was selected from Eastern Oregon. I told Biggs about the conversations. Biggs wasn't pleased with what was said, but he never denied it. The proxy contest was expensive, and it's my impression the United States National Bank financed the greatest majority of the costs including the legal fees.

ICOA had reached a stalemate after the three proxy contests. Sales of new life insurance had pretty much come to an end. Ongoing expenses continued. The company could rest for several years and show profits from investment income as well as a return on renewal premiums, but the continued friction on the board prevented us from developing a cohesive plan for the future of the company. It would take at least three more years before a completely new board could be organized. It would also require the termination of proxy contests. Several board members were so entrenched in their battle another contest was likely. The only agreement the board could reach was to bring in a consultant who would analyze the situation and offer a new plan of action.

The board wanted to select a consultant who would not be influenced by management. The board agreed to follow the advice of the consultant. We had to find someone who wasn't associated with any current employees, management, or consultants. Tom Bowles, an actuary with Bowles & Tillinghast, based in Atlanta, Georgia, seemed to be a good candidate. He had a good reputation, none of us had ever met him, and Atlanta was about as far away as it could get. Biggs was assigned the duty of interviewing Bowles. After the interview, Biggs assured the board Bowles was and would be independent. He was retained. He spent several weeks in Oregon studying the company, its management, and interviewing the individual members of the board. He never discussed his conclusions with me prior to the board meeting where he addressed all members. His conclusions surprised the dissident directors. He made two recommendations. One was for the dissident directors to resign and let me run the company. The other was to merge the company into some other insurer. The dissident directors were stunned. They were fully convinced Bowles was about to recommend my termination and a search begun to find my replacement. The dissident directors refused to resign. So, we began a search for potential merger candidates.

The United States National Bank suit against Buehner had dragged on for several years. Biggs's law firm had submitted all of the documents to the court it needed to collect on the loan, including the note, checks, and drafts against the account, along with a complete accounting. It was cut and dried. Alexander filed an answer on behalf of Buehner and later filed amended answers. I believe there were seven amended answers. Most of the answers said the same thing with minor alterations to make it look like there were changes, along with a couple of red herrings for diversion. The bank and its law firm also filed amended complaints. The bank filed a series of requests with the court in an attempt to simplify the issues and the judge granted its requests. Judge Redding consistently ruled in favor of the bank and against Buehner. I accidentally met Alexander one day while the lawsuit was still in court and he told me he developed cold feet and withdrew as Buehner's counsel. Buehner brought in Harry Osborn to represent him for a couple of months. Then a series of trial dates were set but none of them came to fruition. Osborn withdrew and Roger Tilbury re-entered the picture as Buehner's attorney in July 1967. At the same time, Judge Alfred T. Sulmonetti replaced Judge Redding. Tilbury filed a couple of documents that were supported by Judge Sulmonetti. The parties had previously agreed to a trial by judge, but Tilbury demanded a trial by jury, which was granted. On December 5, 1967, Tilbury demanded to take the deposition of E.C. Sammons, the president of the bank, along with the depositions of two bank managers, Howard Fox and Ronald Schriber. The depositions were set for December 19, 1967, but were never completed. On December 20, 1967, the bank agreed to a judgment of nonsuit[11] against the bank with prejudice and without costs to either party. Neither Buehner nor any of his lumber companies ever came up with any money. The end result was that the loan became a gift to Buehner.

ICOA had made a commitment to merge. The next step was to find a suitable partner. We started looking for companies that would be good candidates for a merger. I received offers from eight companies. Hugh Biggs obtained offers from two companies. The companies

---

[11] A nonsuit is a judgment against the plaintiff for failure to comply with court rules or failure to respond to the defendants.

recommended by Biggs felt ICOA's negotiating position was low and, as a result, offers of stock-exchange ratios were less than desirable. Most of the companies I talked to had the same approach. First Executive Corporation (FEC), a holding company for Executive Life Insurance Company of California (ELIC), was anxious to make an acquisition. Otto Forst, president of both companies, made a realistic stock-exchange proposal and an offer of employment to me, Hank and Jim Hatfield. The merger would include placing two ICOA directors on the board of FEC. Jim Hatfield and I were named as FEC board members. The board members representing the last dissident stockholder group, other than Biggs, insisted that, in exchange for their vote in favor of the merger, they be allowed to be reimbursed for their out-of-pocket proxy solicitation costs, which amounted to a couple of thousand dollars. The ICOA board and FEC's board agreed to submit to the stockholders the merger agreement, which, if approved, would allow the dissidents to be reimbursed. The merger was submitted first to the ICOA stockholders. The merger was approved by ICOA stockholders in January, 1968. The merger proposal was then submitted to and approved by the FEC stockholders. I was elected vice president of sales for the State of Oregon for ELIC.

In the spring of 1968, ICOA was merged into ELIC with ICOA stockholders receiving shares in FEC. ICOA ceased to exist. The merged company had $13,000,000 in assets and $3,300,000 in capital and surplus. The dissident directors had forced the company out of business without ever achieving their goal of taking over the company. Nor were they part of the surviving organization. Their only achievement was the destruction of the insurance company. That's what normally happens to organizations where the individuals place their personal needs and desires above that of the common good.

Otto Forst had been negotiating the purchase of Executive Life Insurance Company of New York by FEC. The purchase required $10,000,000 in cash. FEC's only asset was the stock in ELIC, no cash. ELIC had $3,300,000 in surplus funds available to be used for any proper insurance purpose. Forst wanted to cause FEC to borrow $10,000,000 to purchase the New York company. If FEC borrowed $10,000,000 there wouldn't be enough earning potential from the insurance company to pay the interest on the loan. ELIC would have to pay dividends in excess of $1,600,000 per year to FEC to meet the interest and principal payments to the bank. Those payments would have to come from the profits on premiums and excess interest earnings. (Overall, the majority of premium payments are assigned to the reserve account for the benefit of policyholders. The reserves include most of the interest earnings on the assets.) The company's earned surplus, which includes only excess interest earnings, amounts in excess of three-percent interest in this case, plus a small amount of the premium income, would be insufficient to meet the demand. Even if ELIC earned a million distributable dollars each of the next several years the principal and interest on the loan would accumulate a deficit that would cause serious financial difficulties in the future. Repayment of principal and interest from insurance operations seemed impossible to me.

Forst prevailed over the board of directors with his loan request. Two of the FEC Directors were also Union Bank (California) Directors. The Union Bank authorized the loan. FEC purchased ELICNY. I asked Forst how he was going to repay the loan and he said he had no idea. He said he would find a way in the future. The only practical method of repayment of the $10,000,000 would be through the sale of common stock. The bank loan agreement placed restrictions on the sale of common shares, but FEC could sell preferred shares. Preferred shares would require cash-dividend payments. Those cash dividends would reduce the real value of the common stock. Selling preferred shares didn't seem practical to me. FEC now had to find some method to repay the loan. I decided to change directions and resigned from the board in 1969.

Meanwhile, FEC had a problem to solve. FEC used investment income and insurance profits to meet the first one or two interest payments on the loan. But the option of having sufficient income to continue the interest payments soon disappeared. By 1974, the loan had ballooned to $15,000,000 with the addition of unpaid interest. The company was losing money, Otto Forst was asked to resign and was offered about $500,000 to leave. The board then hired Fred Carr as President. Carr was a former mutual fund manager and was friends with other mutual fund managers. He was also a friend of Michael Milkin. Milkin advocated the use of junk bonds by many companies and he earned a few dollars with his project. Milkin became known as the Junk Bond King. Milkin helped Carr gather up some money, but that money required interest payments, too. Carr arranged for FEC to sell preferred stock to mutual funds. The mutual funds then distributed the stock directly to the funds' shareholders, which kept the stock out of the funds' portfolio. It also avoided the necessity of delivering prospectuses to the real purchasers of the stock, the individual fund investors. Carr was able to convince some of his friends in the stock-brokerage firms to sell single-premium, deferred annuities on behalf of ELIC. The annuities paid high interest rates, which were tax deferred. Promised interest rates were between 11 percent and 14 percent per annum. This brought in enormous amounts of money for ELIC. Carr's operation produced so much annuity business Executive Life accumulated several billion dollars in assets. These transactions allowed FEC to repay the bank loan. It also incurred continuing obligations in the form of interest due on the annuities. But interest rates began falling and this created severe problems for ELIC. The combination of reserve requirements for the annuities and falling rates caused ELIC to try to create surplus using creative accounting practices. Eventually, ELIC's surplus was depleted and the company assets were sold to a foreign owner. The stockholders lost their investment. ELIC became the largest insurance-company failure in U.S. history up to that time. (Failed life insurance companies aren't bankrupt; they simply run out of operating funds and fall into receivership.) The policy owners were protected through policy reserves and contributions from other U.S. life insurance companies to cover the deficit in the ELIC policyholder reserve account. That is how owners of legal reserve life insurance contracts are secured. The policyholders never suffered any principal losses, but they were paid interest amounts that were lower than the promised rates. There's been at least one book written on the adventures of FEC and ELIC.[12]

---

[12] See: Schulte, Gary. The Fall of First Executive The House That Fred Carr Built. New York: Harper Business. 1998. Schulte quotes Peter Lynch, Magellan Fund manager, in Barron's, February 2, 1987, (page 165) "I'd rather have Fred Carr running my company than the people who run General Motors."

I'll finish with FEC. In 1989 it was revealed that Credit Lyonnais of France had purchased the junk bonds owned by ELIC in violation of California law. Credit Lyonnais and its principal officer had earned a substantial profit on the bond purchase. The California Insurance Department took exception to this transaction and tried to have it corrected. Negotiations continued for a long time.

On May 22, 2001, an article appeared in the Wall Street Journal saying a proxy constest for control of Credit Lyonnais had begun. At the same time the French government asked the United States government to intervene in the ELIC problem to make it go away. The United States Justice Department refused to back off, mainly because the California Insurance Commissioner, John Garamendi, demanded to pursue the case. The Credit Lyonnais problem continued for several more years. In 2003, France's central bank chief, Jean-Claude Trichet, was scheduled to stand trial for his actions during a government bailout of former state-owned bank Credit Lyonnais a decade ago. Credit Lyonnaise and the French government were advised they would be fined up to $600 million.

The Economist on January 13, 2003, and the Wall Street Journal on July 10, 2003, outlined how Credit Lyonnais realized several hundred million dollars profit on the junk-bond portfolio it and private individuals managed to spirit out of the former ELIC. The California Insurance Department finally took the parties to court. The Insurance Commissioner stuck to his guns and finally brought the matter to a conclusion after federal indictments were brought against the French. The name of ELIC had been changed and the company is now dormant. It seems like attempts by directors to steal money from the insurance companies had now run full circle.

Returning to 1968; after opening a sales office in Portland for ELIC the negative publicity ICOA had received made it difficult to convince other insurance agencies in Oregon to sell insurance for ELIC based on my recommendations. The Oregon Life Underwriters were not my friends. My solution was to create a group permanent life insurance policy where part of the employer's premium was applied to a permanent policy owned by the employee. The employee could increase his cash value in the policy by the amount of the term insurance premium.

Those insureds who didn't die while insured would have more money at a later date and those who died would have more insurance through the dividend growth. One of the Directors of FEC arranged for me to meet with an insurance agency in Los Angeles to present the plan. The agency agreed to help present the idea to an employer with 500 employees. But they wanted me to move to Los Angeles to do the work. Forst wanted me in Oregon, so the plan was never sold. I decided to concentrate on passing the National Association of Securities Dealers (NASD) Principal's exam in preparation for the sale of securities. A person with a Principal's license is allowed to own a stock-brokerage firm and to supervise securities salesmen. Technically, all security sales are completed by the Principal, the salesmen merely recommend the transactions and submit them to the Principal for execution. This was a new area and I had a lot to learn. Later in 1968, I traveled to San Francisco to take the exam. After finding the building it turned out there were only two people who were there to take the exam, myself and one other. It was written, not multiple choice, where we had to explain the laws, company accounting methods, and financial results for annual-reporting purposes. We were required to analyze company financial statements and find various clues to the intrinsic value of the stock in the company we analyzed. It was a tough exam. When I left the offices and walked down the streets of San Francisco, it took me awhile to recognize where I was. I was completely disoriented. Several weeks later, the NASD notified me that I had passed, earning a grade of "B."

I wasn't contributing to the growth and development of ELIC, and, several months later, Otto Forst offered to buy out my employment contract for $65,000. I agreed. That ended my tenure with FEC and ELIC.

In 1968 the Chairman of Merrill Lynch Pierce Fenner and Smith had announced the stock market was too hot and his firm expected it to cool off. Nevertheless, in 1969 I decided to open a stock-brokerage firm using the name Normandy Securities, Incorporated. Churchill completed the legal requirements and arranged for my stock to be issued under IRC Sec. 1044. It meant, for tax purposes, that I could write off the cost of the entire amount of my original investment against ordinary income if Normandy Securities closed business with no gain. I opened an office in Salem. There were three employees, myself, a salesman, and an accountant. I had the names of more than 6,000 individuals who had purchased stock in the past. I mailed notices to all of these people offering to make securities trades on their behalf. Only one person had any interest in completing a transaction. My commission on the trade was less than $100. I then tried telephone direct marketing. That produced no results. I noticed the entire securities industry was recording failures in record numbers. Securities firms in New York City, which had 4,000 employees one day were closed the next. I believe more stock-brokerage firms went into bankruptcy in 1970 than in any other previous year. From the end of 1968 through the end of 1974, the Standard & Poor's 500 Index dropped 36.7 percent in market value. It was a long dry spell for the securities industry. MLPFS was right; I picked the wrong time to start a firm.

Normandy Securities was a profitable personal learning experience but it consumed all of my money. It was time to find another job. I was now forty years old. I hired an executive search firm in San Francisco, California, to help me. The search firm asked me to obtain letters of recommendation from different people to use in my job search. All of the letters were to be addressed and mailed to the search firm. I asked several people, including James R. Faulstich, the Oregon Insurance Commissioner at the time, for letters of recommendation. Positive letters of recommendation came in, but Commissioner Faulstich wrote a false and damaging letter. The search firm refused to give me a copy. My agent claimed the letter was their property. He got up and left the room for a few minutes leaving the letter on his desk. I assumed he left me an opening to take the letter but, since his position was that the letter was their property, I left it with him.

 The search firm helped me prepare a resume in the form of a letter outlining my history and qualifications. Then the letter was mailed to about 500 life insurance companies throughout the United States. I received thirty-seven responses from companies that had an interest in meeting with me. Seventeen companies had openings for agency sales manager. The other twenty wanted regular insurance agents. Those looking for agency sales managers were small companies located in states from Arizona to Pennsylvania. I asked the search firm their recommendation concerning the companies I should respond to since the companies were thousands of miles apart. I felt I should concentrate on those located in the West. The search firm advised me to visit all of them. They believed an offer from one company could be used as leverage when talking to another. I agreed to follow the search firm's advice and made appointments with the presidents of seven companies. My schedule called for me to travel to South Dakota, Indiana, Pennsylvania, Missouri, Arizona (two cities), Utah, and back to Oregon, in that order.

I first met with the president of a small company in Rapid City, South Dakota, in late November 1970. He showed me around the company home office, which was very small. It was the time of year when dust blows constantly throughout the area. The floor, desks, and equipment were covered with dust. The president told me it was impossible to keep the offices clean at that time of year. He reviewed the company finances with me. The company had limited assets and no sales force. I explained my schedule and that I wouldn't make a commitment until my return to Oregon. We kept negotiations open as I left for Indiana.

I then met with James Eckman, President of First Equity Security Life Insurance Company (FESLIC), a small company in Anderson, Indiana, on the afternoon of December 1. We talked briefly that day. It was warm with the temperature reaching into the mid-60s. I stayed at a Holiday Inn motel, which had a glass window as the entire wall facing the parking lot. That night the temperature went down to about 10 degrees. It was impossible to keep warm. The heater in the room wasn't working properly. The ice cold wind blew right through the glass window and kept the room temperature around 40 degrees. I slept for only about two hours.

We met the next morning and continued discussing employment and the task to be accomplished. He needed a sales manager immediately and hadn't found anyone capable and willing to take the job. The size of the company should have allowed him to handle the role himself in addition to functioning as president. But neither he nor anyone else in the area had the ability or the desire. There was another life insurance company in Anderson, Laymen Life Insurance Company, and it had no sales management either. FESLIC had three salesmen whose production at the time was less than satisfactory. Their total production was less than $2,000 in annualized premiums during the month of November. Their total production was less than $20,000 in annual premiums for the entire year. It wasn't even remotely possible to finance salesmen, the officer's salaries, the costs of home-office personnel, rent, heat, lights, and all of the state fees and taxes that were required based upon current sales. FESLIC's operating surplus was less than $200,000, enough to remain in business for one more year unless it increased sales dramatically without increasing expenses. The company was in serious financial trouble. It couldn't afford to postpone the acquisition of new business. Only substantial new life insurance premiums could keep the company alive.

There was the strong possibility FESLIC would fail in spite of my efforts. That meant I was negotiating with a small company in a remote town in the Midwest, 2,300 miles from home, with the prospect of near-certain failure. I had a lot to lose. I'd be moving my family with the risk of looking for work again at the end of 1971. I had no interest in working for FESLIC and told Eckman I'd talk to him again after I returned to Salem. Since I had an appointment with another company in Pennsylvania and had to leave it was time to move on. He insisted we talk longer. He asked me to stay another day or two. Eckman said I could name my terms. It seemed to be worth the challenge. I called the other companies and rescheduled my appointments.

The next day it was my proposal that if FESLIC would agree to pay me $25,000 per year plus expenses along with 5 percent first-year commission and a 2.5 percent renewal commission on all new business from whatever source written by the company in the future—whether or not I was employed—then I'd take the risk. If the company survived, we'd all be rewarded. It seemed to me that, with success, it would be foolish for the company to terminate our relationship. If the company failed there would be no new commissions and no income for me. I would have to start over after working at a failed company. The problem for FESLIC was that it had already spent several years searching for someone who could handle sales management and it might not find another capable person in the time it had left. The company's risk was that it would be required to pay commissions to me on sales that occurred in the future after I was no longer with the company if the required new business was produced. The benefit for FESLIC was that a successful sales operation would bring in enough new premiums to allow the company to continue in business with a solid base for future growth. It didn't seem to me that Eckman would accept the agreement and I could get on with my travel schedule. To my surprise, he said he would sign the contract if we excluded credit life insurance from the commissions. There was no interest on my part in credit life insurance so that adjustment was just fine.

We sat up that night and drafted the contract. The language was revised several times until we were both satisfied. Then, at about 11 p.m., we placed our signatures on the agreement. The next day, Eckman presented the contract to the executive committee of the board of directors. The executive committee consisted of a bank president, Richard Doermer, of Fort Wayne, Indiana, who was also an attorney and the board chairman; Thomas A. Gallmeyer, another practicing attorney in Fort Wayne, who was the corporate secretary; and Eckman. I did not expect the executive committee to approve it, but, to my surprise again, it did. I called Dorothy and told her I had signed a contract and I wouldn't be home for several months. I went to work immediately.

Was it an unrealistic agreement? In 1976, Ozzie and Dan Silna agreed to terminate the operation of the ABA team Spirit of St. Louis in return for one-seventh of the TV revenue given to the four ABA teams that merged into the NBA. The Silnas had been paid $168 million so far.[13] Lifetime contracts do exist and most of them were crafted based on the risk being taken by the parties at the time.

Eckman wanted the salesmen he had employed prior to hiring me to remain as sales supervisors. That was all right with me. I hired several new men and placed them under the direction of the supervisors and then monitored how they did their work. They sat in motel rooms all day long making phone calls asking people to buy life insurance. They weren't making any sales. I took them out of the motel rooms and showed them how to make personal calls on people at home during the day to make appointments for the evening. Then I showed them how to make the sales presentations in the evening. The policies being sold were plain

---

[13] San Jose Mercury News reported August 1, 2006, page 2D,

ordinary life insurance policies just like the policies I sold when I first entered the business. The average premium was between $15.00 and $25.00 per month, paid on a monthly premium plan. The prospective insureds were shown they would pay about $4,800 in premiums over twenty years. At the end of twenty years they could borrow about $4,400 against the cash value or surrender the policy for the same amount. Thus, the cost of insurance was only about $20 per year. I took each new salesman on three or four sales calls with me so they could witness how it was done. Even though I made the sale I would put the new agent's name on the application along with mine as a fifty percent agent so that he would earn immediate income and feel rewarded for his time. Once the salesmen learned the process, it was easy for them to follow through. FESLIC guaranteed them $100 a week, but they all earned from $400 to $600 per week. The commissions they earned while accompanying me always exceeded the first week's guarantee. They were happy and the work was easy. The supervisors caught on quickly and they were earning fifty percent more than their agents.

It was time to clear up the issue with Faulstich, the Oregon Commissioner, and his derogatory letter. I withheld my last payment to the San Francisco employment search firm. They sued me in Chicago, Illinois, to collect the payment. I hired an Illinois attorney and asked the attorney to make an offer where I would agree to make full payment if, in return, the search firm would give me the Faulstich letter. My attorney demanded the letter through the discovery process. The search firm said they wouldn't deliver the letter without a judge's order. That meant we had to go to court. We were required to go to the Chicago courtroom to take delivery of the letter and to make final payment. While sitting in the courtroom waiting for my case to be called, I noticed how the judge handled the litigants. His calendar for the day was filled with only contract issues. There were about fifty different litigants in the courtroom waiting for their cases to be called. This judge had a reputation for honesty and speed (in Illinois mind you). He certainly demonstrated his reputation was accurate while I was present. He would give each attorney 30 seconds to present their position, he then immediately ruled. One attorney was representing a well-known football player in a contract dispute. The player wanted to avoid being held to the contract. The judge gave the attorney 30 seconds and told him he could read the contract as well as he, the judge, could read it. His ruling was the language controlled. The attorney said his client was in the courtroom and he needed more time to impress his client. The judge gave the attorney two minutes to talk, measured the time, shut him off when the two minutes were up, and ruled the contract language held. When my case came up to be heard, the California search firm gave the letter to me in return for my payment. There was no need for the judge to rule. They only forced me to go the entire nine yards.

When my attorney read Faulstich's letter, he offered to file and finance a suit against the State of Oregon and Faulstich using his own money. It seemed to me that, since I now had the letter, there was little chance of it ever getting into someone else's hands. The search firm had assured me they did not retain a copy, so, rather than pursue the matter, I decided to destroy the letter and go on with my life.

In January 1971, James Eckman told me he decided to create a new corporation. He said I was to be the incorporating officer and director. He said 1,000 shares of stock would be issued to me. He said I was to endorse 800 shares over to him using assignments separate from certificates. His stated purpose was for the corporation to be paid commissions on the sale of insurance by FESLIC. He said he wanted to use the commissions to purchase stock from various FESLIC stockholders. The market value of the stock was down substantially from its original issue price and he thought many stockholders would be willing to sell. He said he was afraid the low stock price might cause the stockholders to revolt with a proxy contest for control and he would lose his job. He wanted me to offer to buy shares from any stockholder who was willing to sell. He would control all finances and the corporation from his position as 80 percent shareholder. I wasn't familiar with Indiana law, nor with his relationship and obligations to the board and FESLIC. I said I doubted if such a plan would work. He assured me he had cleared the transaction with the board. Based upon his assurances, I agreed to participate. He took me to see Joseph Ketner, one of his attorney friends. He explained to Ketner what he wanted done and arranged to pay him. Ketner created Anderson Agency, Inc. Eckman prepared a commission contract between Anderson Agency and FESLIC that provided for 100 percent first-year commissions on all life insurance policies issued by FESLIC after the date of the contract and during the term of the contract. Eckman kept the commission contract, eight stock certificates representing 100 shares each, which I had assigned to him, consisting of eighty percent of the stock. He also kept the corporate documents, the articles and bylaws. He gave me two stock certificates representing 100 shares each, or twenty percent of the stock.

Indiana had a law that prohibited the employment of insurance agents who had been convicted of a felony. Even though I had never been convicted of any crime, I was concerned about the record from the stolen car incident in 1947 so I wrote to the FBI office in Boise, Idaho. That office turned my letter over to the probation office. Coite E. Cloninger, the chief U.S. probation officer in the Boise office, wrote back to me saying I'd never been convicted and no records were available. The letter is below.

> February 22, 1971
>
> Mr. Reginald L. Jensen
>
> 315 Citizens Bank Building
>
> Anderson, Indiana 46016
>
> Dear Mr. Jensen:
>
> Your letter of February 12, 1971, to the Clerk, U. S. District Court, Boise, concerning a stolen car violation back in 1947 has been referred to this office for reply. The clerk reports he has no record of a charge against you.
>
> Since the case is so old, our records have been sent to the records storage center in Seattle, Washington. A statistical card record in our office indicates prosecution was deferred by the United States Attorney on the condition that you complete a period of probation without getting into further trouble. In that event you probably never even appeared before the judge

in the courtroom. Upon completion of the period of probation, the United States Attorney dismissed the charges and you were never convicted.

Sincerely yours,

Coite E. Cloninger

Chief U. S. Probation Officer

CEC:rst

My probation was completed in June 1948, when I joined the United States Army. The record was supposed to have been destroyed in 1952 because it was a juvenile offense. I dropped the issue.

I hired about 12 men for FESLIC within a couple of months. Sales increased quickly. Soon, there were more than 35 salesmen in the field. The sales organization was now working in the northwestern Indiana territory. Eckman gave me a partial list of stockholders in that area. During my spare time after my normal work had been completed, I talked to a number of stockholders. The investments of the stockholders in FESLIC were small and of little concern to them. None of them had any interest in selling.

One stockholder owned a few shares of stock with a market value of less than $50.00. But he owned a FESLIC annuity contract with a cash value of about $850.00. He was planning on getting married in a couple of days and needed money for his wedding. He wanted to surrender his annuity for its cash value. I offered to purchase the annuity from him immediately for the full policy value at that time. He agreed. He assigned the contract to me and I gave him a personal check. Upon returning to Anderson that Friday, I brought Eckman up to date on the transaction and had the assignment recorded at the home office.

In March 1971, Eckman told me there would be a meeting of the FESLIC Board of Directors and he wanted me to attend. I attended as a guest and sat in a chair about fifteen feet away from the board members. Gallmeyer, board member and secretary, read the entire December 1970 contract, word for word. At the end of his reading, there was a call for questions regarding the contract language and purpose. There was no discussion and the contract was ratified. I was excused from the meeting.

FESLIC sold a participating Savings Expansion Contract (life insurance policy) that had a deferred annuity purchase option.[14] At the end of each year, the policyholder received cash dividends on the policy. The policyholder could use those dividends to purchase a deferred annuity. The policyholder could also add additional cash amounts to the annuity purchase and thus increase his investment. The immediate cash value of the FESLIC annuity was 92 percent of the premium paid and the annuity earned 8 percent guaranteed compound interest each year. (Normal interest rates since the beginning of our nation have averaged 4.0 percent.) The annuity investment for the owner produced tax-deferred profits after the first year. Tax law at that time allowed the annuity principal to be withdrawn tax free up to the amount invested; the interest could remain in the contract tax deferred. After a few years, the policyholder could withdraw all principal and allow the interest earnings to continue to increase the remaining cash value. The policy was very attractive from a long-term savings standpoint. It had a lot of potential and by the month of June the salesmen were being trained to properly market this product. By the end of May 1971, sales of the ordinary life insurance product were at a rate that would reach $400,000 in premiums by year end. June sales remained steady.

In June, I traveled back to Oregon for the first time since December and met Dorothy and the girls to complete our move back to Indiana. Wendy was attending the University of Oregon. Cindy and Leslie enjoyed their friends and they fit in well at school in Salem. It was an emotional time for Dorothy and the girls. Dorothy had no desire to leave Salem. They all wanted to stay where they were. We loved our home. It was the first house we owned. Tom Churchill had introduced us to Jack Beck, a professional interior decorator who really knew how to match colors and styles to personalities. It had been decorated exactly to our liking. Dorothy had planted all of the flowers and shrubbery.

---

[14] An annuity is a contract which promises to pay an amount certain over a period of years which exceed one year. Payments can continue for a fixed period of time, or for life, or for both. An annuity can be immediate (payments begin now) or deferred (payments begin at some later date).

We had lived in the house for more than eight years. Still, it was up to Dorothy to sell our house because I wasn't there. After finding a buyer she held a garage sale and sold many of our personal items with the express intention of reducing the moving costs that would be billed to FESLIC (my contract required the company to pay our moving costs). We loaded our furniture on a moving van and sent it on its way to Indiana. We spent the night in a motel in Salem and then left for Indiana in Dorothy's Buick station wagon the next day.

Dorothy and the girls had been in Anderson for only a month when Eckman told me FESLIC now had enough new-premium income for the company to survive and he didn't need me anymore. He fired me. He said according to his calculations he would earn less money from the life insurance company than I would. He said my future commissions would exceed the future value of his stock. He said he couldn't allow that to happen because he started the company, the company was his. He handed me his 800 shares in Anderson Agency and destroyed the assignments. He also gave me the corporate documents and the Anderson Agency commission contract. He said he didn't need them any more. I said his actions were fine with me, but just to be sure to pay the commissions provided by my December 1970 contract. He said I'd get nothing, to clear out my things and get out of the offices. He had no intention of honoring our agreement. I took my property and left.

I needed to find an attorney who would help me enforce the contract. At the same time I needed to get another job. Money was short, we were in strange territory, and time was limited. Finding work and enforcing the contract was going to be difficult.

Eckman was secretary of the Madison County Democratic Party. The Democrats controlled the County. All of the judges, commissioners, and the Mayor, were Democrats. I talked to a number of attorneys but most of them didn't want to handle the case because of their party affiliation. One attorney agreed to take the case but he died over the weekend. Another attorney suggested Walter Dietzen might take the case. I contacted Dietzen and explained the situation to him. Dietzen said he'd let me know in a day and asked me to return. *When I returned, he said he had talked to Eckman and he'd have no problem working for me.* He agreed to become my attorney. He was a Democrat who had hopes of becoming a judge. He was up for election in 1972 and would rely on the Democratic Party support to be elected. He felt the conflict between me and FESLIC would be settled before the elections.

He first filed suit against FESLIC based on the December 1, 1970, contract. The suit demanded specific performance of the contract rather than claiming damages due, which meant FESLIC would only be required to pay to me overriding commissions on premiums actually paid to the company. The original judge was Paul Shrenker, a close friend to both Dietzen and Eckman. Attorney Walter Riebenack with the firm Rothberg, Gallmeyer, Fruechtenicht, and Logan in Ft. Wayne, Indiana, (Gallmeyer was FESLIC's corporate secretary) filed an appearance along with FESLIC's answer to my claim. Attorney Martin Fletcher with the same law firm filed an appearance shortly thereafter.

How does an attorney proceed with a lawsuit? Criminal actions and civil actions have different forms of pleading. In a criminal action, the prosecutor makes allegations of violations of the law and the defendant must respond to each paragraph in the complaint by either admitting or denying the charges. If the defendant neither admits nor denies a charge, a denial is automatically entered on the defendant's behalf. The prosecutor must then prove the allegations are true. In civil actions, the plaintiff makes the allegations and the defendant must admit or deny each paragraph. If the defendant fails to deny a claim or paragraph, an admission is automatically assumed by the court. The defendant also has the option of filing an affirmative defense, which means the plaintiff has no right to complain. The defendant can also file a counterclaim, which is used to offset the plaintiff's claim. In a contract action, the plaintiff must then prove the contract exists, the plaintiff has performed, and that the defendant has failed to live up to the contract. The defendant's denial of the plaintiff's claims in a civil action establishes what is to be litigated. At trial, the plaintiff submits the contract into evidence, demonstrates performance by the plaintiff, and proves the amount of money the defendant has failed to pay or how the defendant has otherwise failed to perform. The defendant then must prove he did perform or is not required to perform because of the actions of the plaintiff. If the plaintiff proves his case to a jury or judge, a judgment will be entered by the court in favor of the plaintiff. Can this all be done within a year? Yes, it can, unless the legal system decides otherwise.

Now I needed to work for a reputable company, so I again began sending out letters to insurance companies in Indiana, Ohio and Illinois. Several replies were received from companies in each state. I met with the president of each company but was refused second interviews. However, the president of Franklin National Life Insurance Company in Ft Wayne, Indiana, did give me a second interview. He said he didn't want to proceed. I was baffled. Why didn't he want to proceed? He said that in Indiana the law requires every insurance company to investigate the background of potential agents. Most companies nationwide do background investigations anyway, but in Indiana, it was required by law. He asked me if I had checked with Retail Credit Company to review my background. I said I had not seen any background report. A federal law, the Fair Credit Reporting Act, had been passed October 26, 1970, requiring background investigating agencies to make the results of their investigations available to the person who was being investigated. He said "Go look at the file. You should review the report before contacting any other insurance companies."

The main Retail Credit Company office was in Atlanta, Georgia. The local Retail Credit office was in Muncie, only a few miles from Anderson. I went to Muncie, identified myself and asked to review any and all reports they had in their possession that referred to me. One of the managers took me into her office and read their report to me, which contained an interview with James Eckman. The report was outrageous. It was replete with falsehoods and misrepresentations. I couldn't believe my ears. It said in substance that I had a poor work record, did not develop the insurance agency, had a poor record of developing insurance-agent recruits, wrongfully split commissions with other agents, created confusion in the office and in the field, that the firm of First Equity Security Life Insurance Company of Anderson, Indiana, had several complaints concerning me, that I used crude language in the presence of my fellow employees, and that I had a poor reputation in getting along with my fellow agents and employees.

I asked the woman to give me a copy of the report but she told me they weren't required to give me a copy, just to tell me what it said. I wrote down notes covering what I heard and then went back to Anderson and talked to Dietzen. He accompanied me to Muncie to hear the report himself. The Retail Credit employee read the report to him slow enough so he could take notes. Dietzen and I returned to his office in Anderson where he drafted a complaint for slander naming FESLIC and James Eckman as defendants. The action was *Jensen v. James Eckman and First Equity Security Life Insurance Company* Cause #S72-697, filed in the Madison County Superior Court on July 28, 1972, alleging the slander occurred July 21, 1972. Martin Fletcher appeared as attorney for Eckman and FESLIC. Eckman's and FESLIC's answer was a denial of the allegations.

Dietzen subpoenaed the documents from Retail Credit. When the papers were to be delivered, Retail Credit's attorney, Marshal Hanley, met with Dietzen and me in the Muncie Courthouse and asked to delay delivery. The reason Hanley gave for the delay was to allow him to earn more fees. Dietzen acquiesced for a couple of days, then he took possession of the documents. The documents showed two additional slander transactions. Hanley and Stephen Murphy appeared as attorneys for Retail Credit. It was seven years later when I learned the primary law firm for Retail Credit was Barnes & Hickam in Indianapolis. They stayed in the background and didn't file an appearance until 1979 (This is highly irregular. Legal counsel should identify themselves immediately). The documents contained the exact words spoken, the dates the words were spoken and to whom. Dietzen now had everything necessary to proceed to trial. All that was left was to interview the Retail Credit Company employee(s) who took the information from Eckman.

How is a slander or libel suit litigated? It's a civil action. The plaintiff alleges he was slandered (spoken words) or libeled (written words) in the complaint. The defendant must either admit or deny the slander or libel. If the defendant denies the allegations, the plaintiff must prove the words cited in the complaint were false and damaging. Once proven, the defendant becomes liable to pay damages. If the defendant admits the words spoken or written, he can file an affirmative defense of truth. The defendant claims the words are true and thus not damaging. The plaintiff loses if the words are true. All involved parties are usually named as defendants so that one unnamed person can't take responsibility for the actions, which would absolve the named parties. Once the plaintiff has the evidence of the libel or slander in some manner the only thing left to do is locate and interview the witnesses and go to trial. It isn't complicated and it too, can be completed within one year.

In late 1971, I filed a request with FESLIC to borrow the cash value of the annuity contract. Eckman denied my loan request with the comment that I had no rights under the contract. I gave the annuity contract to Dietzen and asked him to force FESLIC to make the loan. Dietzen also filed suit for me based on the Anderson Agency, Inc. contract demanding payment of commissions due. By now I had four separate issues to be litigated with Eckman and FESLIC. The first was the December 1, 1970, contract. The second was the January 1971, contract. The third was the annuity contract. And the fourth was the slander action.

Forrest Drudge came to work for me as a salesman for FESLIC. Drudge lived in northwestern Indiana. Drudge was a member of the Teamsters Union, but had joined a splinter group that wanted to oust Teamsters' management. Drudge introduced me to some of his friends in the splinter-group movement and showed me the results of some of the bitterness between the two groups. One person's house had been burned. Others had their lives threatened. At one point in time, the Teamsters truck drivers and the splinter group members were shooting at each other along the freeways and highways in Illinois, Indiana, and Ohio.

Drudge took me to one of the splinter group meetings. Members of the FBI were quartered in a room above the meeting room with peep holes in the floor (ceiling of the meeting room) so they could watch the activities. Teamsters members favorable to management were also there for the purpose of breaking up the meeting. Some Teamsters had blackjacks under their sleeves and some were reported to have guns under their coats. Several of the members of the splinter group got up in front of the meeting and tried to address the group so they could discuss their grievances, but the management Teamsters members began to boo and hiss the speakers. They made so much noise no one could hear what was being said. After about 45 minutes, the splinter-members gave up and left the meeting hall.

Drudge told me about a disagreement the splinter group had with one union secretary. The secretary was responsible for the finances of a local affiliate. Drudge said one day the local members called for an audit of the funds. Drudge reported the auditor claimed $1,000,000 couldn't be accounted for according to his analysis. The members asked the secretary to explain the discrepancy. The secretary said he didn't know what happened to the money. He's reported to have said he was counting government bonds on his desk and he probably accidentally brushed a bond worth $1,000,000 into the waste-paper basket and the janitor emptied the basket. He said the money was just gone but he couldn't accuse anyone of stealing it. The union accepted the explanation; the secretary kept his job and no one was ever prosecuted.

Several companies were willing to give me a contract to sell insurance as an agent on a brokerage basis, but not on a supervisory basis. I met with the sales manger of Layman Life Insurance Company. He gave me several rate cards and a few application forms so I could sell for his company. I asked Drudge if he would take me around to some of his friends to sell insurance. He agreed and we sold between fifteen and twenty policies. Shortly thereafter, Drudge went to Anderson and talked to Eckman. Drudge returned and told me Eckman said I was a crook and he should have nothing to do with me. We never saw each other again and all of those policies lapsed.

The contract cases were venued in late 1971, from Anderson to Muncie, Indiana, in Delaware County, before Judge Alva Cox. The December 1, 1970 contract was numbered S71/1083 and the January 1971, Anderson Agency contract case was numbered S71/1084. Even though the cases had two different numbers, they were consolidated and the docket sheets stopped carrying the activity separately. Thereafter, the court record was entered only on one docket sheet. This is a good example of how two related actions can be merged into one unless one of the parties prefers to have them tried separately.

Dietzen concluded we needed an actuary, as an expert witness, to calculate the commissions due. I found an actuary who would handle the work, Daryl J. Dean, FSA (Fellow of the Society of Actuaries), who worked at the Howard Nyhart Company in Indianapolis. He wanted assurance of payment. Dietzen said he would guarantee payment if I would assign my December 1970, contract to him. He said he would take 33 percent of any award and I would keep the balance. Payment of all costs would come out of my share. The assignment was prepared. He and I signed it. Dietzen gave me a copy and kept the original. Dean then entered the FESLIC offices, obtained the sales records and calculated the premiums and commissions due to me.

Dietzen decided to take Eckman's deposition in the contract case. Dietzen arranged the time and place for Eckman's deposition and also arranged to take Dean's deposition to create a record of the money due under the contracts just in case something happened to Dean. Dietzen took Eckman's deposition in April 1972. Present were Dietzen, myself, Eckman and FESLIC's attorneys, Walter Riebenack and Martin Fletcher. After the deposition, I went home and Riebenack and Fletcher went back to their office in Ft. Wayne. Riebenack later withdrew from representing Eckman and FESLIC and Fletcher took over as counsel. Fletcher remained for the balance of the actions.

After Eckman's deposition was completed, I thought Eckman and Dietzen went their separate ways. But, several days later, FESLIC mailed a check to me in an amount of about $340.00. I took the check over to Dietzen and asked him if he had any idea why the check was mailed to me. He said he did. He said he and Eckman had agreed upon a settlement of the suits. I asked what he was talking about. He said he and Eckman went over to a bar after Eckman's deposition, consumed a couple of highballs, and agreed that FESLIC would pay me a commission on premiums only on ordinary life policies written only during my tenure with FESLIC. I told Dietzen he was crazy, I would never authorize such a settlement. I asked him why he reached that agreement. He said Eckman agreed to help him get elected judge, so he made a trade.

I reaffirmed I would never agree to such an arrangement. I asked him what to do with the check since 33 percent belonged to him. He said to keep the money for the time being because he didn't need it right now. He said to endorse the back to clarify cashing the check was not an acceptance of any settlement. Small checks continued to arrive each month until the first trial in Muncie, which was scheduled for October 1972. I handled them all the same way, endorsing them to indicate I was not accepting the money as a settlement of the action. Meanwhile, Dietzen took Daryl Dean's deposition, which established FESLIC's debt to me.

Dean calculated the amount due me as of April 30, 1972, to be $222,157.66, less any commissions previously paid and excluding commissions for premiums due after April 30, 1972, and excluding commissions for policies issued and to be issued after April 30, 1972, and excluding interest on said amount. Dean then signed an affidavit to that effect. His affidavit is below. Dietzen was trading commissions due to me of more than $222,000, plus renewals and new business for a current check paid to me of about $340 a month. The so-called settlement was a good deal for Eckman and FESLIC and it might have been a good deal for Dietzen if he were to be elected judge. Dietzen was willing to trade $74,000, his share of $222,000, for a judgeship. It was a bad deal for me no matter how you slice it.

| | | |
|---|---|---|
| STATE OF INDIANA | ) | IN THE DELAWARE CIRCUIT COURT |
| | ) | 1972 Term |
| DELAWARE COUNTY | ) | FILED |
| | ) | |
| | ) | DELAWARE CO. INDIANA |
| | ) | |
| REGINALD L. JENSEN | ) | |
| | ) | CAUSE NO: 71/1083 |
| VS | ) | |
| | ) | CLERKS OFFICE |
| FESLIC SECURITY | ) | Garland G. Miller |
| | ) | CLERK |
| INVESTMENT CORP. ET AL | ) | MAY 10, 1972 |

## AFFIDAVIT

Comes now Daryl J. Dean being duly sworn upon his oath deposes and says that:

In the matter of Reginald L. Jensen vs First Equity Security Investment Corp. et al that subject to a final audit and based upon instructions given me by the counsel for Reginald L. Jensen and by Reginald L. Jensen, individually and pursuant to Court order of the Delaware Circuit Court, the current monies due the Reginald L. Jensen by First Equity Security Life Insurance Company and First Equity Security Investment Corp. as of April 30, 1972, is Two Hundred Twenty-two Thousand One Hundred Fifty-seven and sixty-six cents ($222,157.66) less any commissions previously paid. Said amount excludes commissions for premiums due after April 30, 1972, and excludes commissions for policies issued and to be issued April 30, 1972, and excludes interest on said amount.

Signed
Daryl J. Dean, FSA

Subscribed and sworn to before me this 10$^{th}$ day of May 1972
Signed
Notary Public
My commission expires January 7, 1975

Dietzen and I were walking past a carnival that came to town in the summer of 1972. He said there were a lot of con games going on in the carnival, but the owners would send several woman to Anderson a couple of days before the arrival of the carnival. He said the girls would visit several judges and provide them with sex. Then, when the carnival arrived, it had no trouble with the police. The carnival would stay for just a few days and then move on.

The state and national elections came up in November. Richard Nixon was running for President of the United States on the Republican ticket. The Democratic organization in Madison County believed it had control of the election outcome. A substantial majority of registered voters were Democrats and the county always voted Democratic. Dietzen was sure he would be elected judge. I assumed he would be, too. We discussed what would happen to my lawsuit when he became judge. He said he didn't know what would happen. He knew he couldn't continue to represent me if he was elected. What would happen to the assignment of my contract? Would it be invalidated? Would it be transferred? Would Dietzen have an effect on other judges? Nothing was settled except the first trial. Trial was finally set before Judge Cox in Muncie in early December 1972.

In the elections that November, Nixon and the Republicans swept Indiana, including Madison County. All the Republican candidates in Madison County won, Dietzen lost. He was so infuriated he went into his office and tore up some of the records of my cases and threw the scraps about his office. He then went over to the courthouse and threw all of my court papers around the clerk's office. My records had been thrown to all corners of the room and on various different shelves like they'd been ravaged by a tornado. I went into the clerk's office the next day to review my files and couldn't find them. It seemed as though none of the file clerks paid any attention to the files and documents. I gathered up all of the papers I could find and placed them back into their proper file jackets. I went back to Dietzen's office and asked him what he thought he was accomplishing. He said he made all of his plans centered upon becoming a judge. I tried to convince him Eckman had no effect on the outcome of the election, it was a Republican sweep, but he didn't listen to me. He was still noticeably upset. I left his office and waited until it was time for trial in Muncie.

Dietzen and I rode over to Muncie together on the morning of the trial. Eckman was nowhere to be found. It left me with the impression FESLIC was going to admit the contracts without objection and would admit the testimony of Daryl Dean without objection. If so, it meant the judge would only be required to rule on the evidence without a defense. He'd have the contract and the amount due. There would be nothing remaining except to issue an order requiring adherence to the contracts. Dietzen opened the case by placing me on the stand, identifying both contracts, termination documents, and verifying my performance. Next, he placed Daryl Dean on the stand taking his testimony as to the amount due. He then closed his case.

Fletcher jumped up like a bullet shot out of a rifle and moved for a judgment in favor of FESLIC because Dietzen never entered the contracts into evidence. The correct process is to mark the evidence, have it identified, offer it into evidence, and the court receives it into evidence if there's no objection. Fletcher cited the procedural steps taken by Dietzen and Judge Cox confirmed Fletcher's position. Dietzen completed only two of the four steps. The contracts were only marked and identified. Dietzen's procedural error had failed to present a case for consideration by the court. Eckman's presence wasn't necessary to either affirm or deny the contracts and my performance. It was my conclusion Eckman knew the plan in advance and had better things to do with his time.

Judge Cox recessed the case until the following morning to give Dietzen a chance to research the law to see if he could find a reason for the judge to grant permission to reopen his case for the purpose of offering and receiving the contract into evidence. Dietzen, several other attorneys, and I spent the next 10 hours trying to find a similar historical case. We found none. The next morning Judge Cox said he would permit Dietzen to reopen for the purpose of entering the documents to preserve appeal. He then ruled in favor of FESLIC, dismissed the case with prejudice[15] and wrote his order on one docket sheet. The other docket sheet was left blank.

---

[15] With prejudice means a case can't be refilled.

*Judicial Deception*

We drove back to Anderson. When we arrived at Dietzen's office, I said to him I was going to Indianapolis to find a new attorney. He said he had no objection and he could understand why I wanted new counsel. The next day I went to the tallest building in Indianapolis and into the largest law firm in the building. I explained my situation to an attorney and asked him to represent me. He said he didn't have the time but he knew another attorney who might be able to take on the cases. He said he'd call me after talking to the other attorney. Later in the week, he called and asked me to contact attorney James Tuohy with the firm of Schortemeier, Eby & Wood (later Wood Tuohy Gleason & Mercer). Tuohy was a partner in the firm. Wood was a former judge.

I called Tuohy's office the next day to make an appointment. When we met I explained my situation to him. He said he understood my predicament, he had talked to the other attorney, and he agreed to take the case. Tuohy was intelligent, competent, influential, and a feared adversary. Tuohy was chairman of the Indianapolis Judicial Nominating Commission, an organization that helped select and approve attorneys for nomination to the bench as judges. Tuohy's brother was president of one of the largest banks in Indiana. Tuohy controlled a flow of political contributions to the various judges. John Herrin was an attorney employed by Tuohy and who did most of Tuohy's leg work for him in handling my cases. On December 12, 1972, even though he had Dean's affidavit, Tuohy prepared a contract for me giving him 40 percent of all receipts with all costs and expenses and taxes deducted from my share. The contract required me to accept a gross settlement of $100,000. I signed the contract. Tuohy entered his appearance in the slander action in Anderson on the same day. I went back to Anderson and told Dietzen what I had done and picked up all of my papers. I took the papers into Tuohy's office the next day and left them with the secretary. Then Dietzen was notified that Tuohy was entering an appearance. Tuohy now had all of the Retail Credit reports, dates of slander and libel, breach of contract, and every document Dietzen ever had. Tuohy said he was going to re-file one case at a time. He said he was going to re-file the January 1971, contract first, resolve it, and then re-file the December 1970 contract.

Several days later Tuohy drove to Muncie, entered his appearance and talked to Judge Cox. He convinced the judge to change the dismissal from "with prejudice" to "with prejudice as to the theory of specific performance only," which meant the cases could be re-filed demanding damages only and a new trial could take place. The two cases had been consolidated, but still carried separate cause numbers: 71-1083 and 71-1084. Judge Cox had written "Dismissed with prejudice" on the 71-1084 docket sheet. However, he wrote "Dismissed with prejudice as to the theory of specific performance" on the 71-1083 docket sheet. The two docket sheets had conflicting orders. The order book entry had the correct sequence of events and the correct status.

I saw Dietzen on the street in Anderson a couple of days later and he told me he had just finished a phone conversation with Tuohy explaining my lawsuits and my character. I later found out Dietzen told Tuohy that I wasn't entitled to anything of substance. He said I wasn't slandered and my demands exceeded my contractual rights. Tuohy never mentioned receiving the call, but he should have told me, explained the comments he received, and asked me for my comments. Tuohy now had to decide whether Dietzen simply made a mistake at the trial, was incompetent, or deliberately lost my case.

Tuohy had the ability and sources of information to decide whether or not he wanted to continue to represent me. He represented several insurance companies in Indiana. He had contact with the state insurance department from time to time. The current insurance commissioner was a Democrat and the employer of one of FESLIC's Board members. The National Association of Insurance Commissioners (NAIC) meet from time to time to discuss various issues. Many members of the insurance industry attend these meetings for lobbying or other purposes. Tuohy was the type of attorney who would use every means to investigate his clients before becoming committed to representation. It would be a simple and natural process for him to make inquiry about my background after hearing from Dietzen. He could make a phone call to the Indiana insurance department, which could make contract with the Oregon department to obtain my history. He also obtained information from Retail Credit Company in the process of discovery. Retail Credit had recorded my Oregon conflict with the Oregon commissioner and Wright and the proxy contests, although their interpretation of events was inaccurate and biased. Tuohy had a direct line into my background. If he had reservations he should have confronted me to hear my version of events or withdrawn as counsel immediately. He did neither.

Tuohy set another appointment with me for several days later. When I arrived, he gave me a piece of paper and a pen and asked me to sit down in his lobby and calculate the commissions that were due to me. He gave me insufficient data and documents to work with; I was supposed to do most of it from memory. I started to write down some numbers, but then got up and reminded him an actuary had already done all of the calculations, the additional work by me was a waste of time. He said he wanted to know if I knew how to do it. I left his office and decided to wait and see how he performed. I had signed a contract with him and I wanted to see if he understood what his contract meant. He had every means to bring my claims to fruition in short order.

I had initiated an exercise regimen in 1967 that included jogging and weight lifting. The YMCAs around the United States had all of the necessary facilities for me to use. I joined the Anderson YMCA immediately after signing the contract with FESLIC in December. Eckman also jogged at the Y from time to time, but not on a regular schedule. I went into the Y in Anderson in the afternoon in early January 1973. Eckman happened to be in the locker room at the same time. We talked for a few minutes. He laughed at Dietzen's loss of the contract case in Muncie and told me how he thought Dietzen was stupid and foolish. He said Dietzen had a win in his hands that would have paid him a lot of money and he threw it away. He said the elections were over and that Dietzen wouldn't have been elected judge even if he, Eckman, tried to help. He said Dietzen should have kept his eye on the ball. He gave me the impression he was trying to distance himself from Dietzen.

The law in Indiana allows for a six-month delay by an insurance company in granting policy loans. That didn't bother FESLIC, they simply would not grant my annuity policy loan request. I took the letter Eckman had written to me saying FESLIC would not allow me to borrow the cash value of the annuity to the Indiana Insurance Department. A deputy for the department said FESLIC was required to permit me to make the loan. He then wrote a letter to FESLIC demanding the company execute the loan. Eckman still refused. I went back to the deputy's office and asked him how he was going to enforce his demand. He said my only recourse was the courts. I asked him how the insurance department could protect policyholders if it could not force a company to comply with a contract that contains the language the insurance department requires by law. The insurance department had the power to revoke FESLIC's license. Still, he said my only recourse was the courts. A total of 21 months had passed when Tuohy advised me FESLIC was making payment to me in return for surrendering the annuity. He agreed to settle the annuity dispute by surrendering my annuity contract. I reminded him that I didn't want to surrender the annuity; I just wanted to borrow the cash value. He said he'd agreed to the settlement and there would be no change in his agreement. He handed me the check representing the surrender value. His decision was more important to him than properly representing his client. His two accomplishments thus far were to arrange to have the contract dismissal changed from "with prejudice" to "with prejudice as to the theory of specific performance" and the surrender of the annuity contract.

Tuohy told me in January 1973, he was going to amend the slander suit, S72-697, in Madison County. At that time there seemed to be no reason for an amendment but he said it should be done. Tuohy did re-file the January contract suit on April 25, 1973, in Madison County as *Jensen v. First Equity Security Life Insurance Company*, and then had it venued to Henry County as 73-C-185, Judge Wesley W. Ratliff, Jr. presiding. The Henry County seat is New Castle. The amount of commissions due on that contract was $181,139.53. Daryl Dean calculated $196,139.53 as total commissions due with $15,000 subtracted for monies advanced to agents by FESLIC. Tuohy amended the suit, once. I waited for about six or seven months before I contacted Tuohy again. I asked him how he was proceeding on the lawsuits. He said that he was trying to work out a settlement. On September 24, 1973, he wrote a letter to me saying he *"was proceeding against FESLIC and Eckman in the slander case inasmuch as the law around the country is overwhelming in favor of Retail Credit's being able to claim a "privilege" in producing such information."* He intended to drop Retail Credit as a defendant.

I was now in a difficult financial situation. During 1973, we had to sell our house organ to raise cash to pay the rent. We had to turn the keys to our car over to the bank because we couldn't make the payments. I arranged to pay off the balance of the loan after the bank sold the car at wholesale. Dorothy had to find work to help meet our expenses. I applied for work at the Y as a locker-room employee at $2.00 per hour but didn't get the job. There were two people more qualified than me. I also worked part time at Sears for $2.00 per hour. I had parked my life insurance and securities licenses with Transamerica Insurance Company of California, a company controlled by Occidental Life of California. I was selling insurance part time, but I had no enthusiasm for the work.

I needed work where I could earn enough to pay the bills and keep the family together. I saw an ad in the newspaper looking for someone who could sell radio advertising. I went to WHUT radio station and met with the manager, Charles Dunn. WHUT was owned by Eastern Broadcasting Company of Pennsylvania. Dunn talked to me for a few minutes and hired me on the spot. Lou Shapiro was the sales manager. Dunn called Shapiro into his office and told him I had just been hired as Shapiro's new salesman. Shapiro objected saying he had been told he would make the decision. Dunn told Shapiro the decision had been made and to get me started on the job. Shapiro was a gentleman, took me back to the sales office space and explained my work to me. Shapiro was an excellent sales manager; he knew how to manage a small team and did a good job of it. Dunn's wife was the bookkeeper. The assistant manager was David Butler. Dunn was a member of The Church of Scientology based in southern California. Several months later, he and his wife quit the station and left for California to work full time for the religious organization. Butler took over as manager. Butler was one of Eckman's close friends.

I was given an account list with two or three accounts that advertised regularly on WHUT and with the names of some small, one- or two-person businesses and some addresses of closed businesses and empty lots, which seldom or never advertised. It was my responsibility to create an account of regular advertisers out of this list. I was given a temporary draw of $600 a month, but was expected to create commissions that exceeded the draw within three months.  The commission earnings from current advertisers on my list were about $100 a month.  The job was a challenge at first but it turned out to be the easiest job of my life.  I organized the list and my daily routine so that I was able to meet personally with each business decision maker on a weekly or monthly basis depending on their business needs and capability to advertise.  There was plenty of time during the day to locate and create clients who seldom or never advertised on the radio in the past.  I quickly turned my clients into regular advertisers.  Within nine months, my commission earnings were averaging about $1,700 per month.  The maximum earnings would reach $2,300 per month.  By this time it wasn't possible to increase sales by adding more customers because all of the potential customers in the territory were being contacted.  Earnings could be increased only by increasing the costs to advertisers.

WHUT was an AM station.  Soon after my being employed, Eastern Broadcasting obtained the license for WLHN, an FM station.  Butler hired a new salesman, a man who had once managed another radio station.  Butler expected sales to increase dramatically with WLHN now in business.  He looked to the sales force to increase income by 50 to 100 percent.  Most advertisers didn't have the funds to double their radio-advertising budgets, they simply selected one station versus the other.  Some advertisers would use both stations by increasing their budget slightly and splitting the commercials.  The sales were restricted to the Madison County area and the fringes of Marion County (Northeastern Indianapolis).  My work was organized so that working an average of two hours a day allowed me to make contact with every possible client.  I could have handled 100 percent of the sales for the stations in an eight-hour workday.  My sales for both stations had reached a peak within the first two years of my employment.  For several years, I still worked at Sears part time and continued selling life insurance part time.

The schedule and routine gave me the opportunity to spend time at the law library and the county library.  For the next four years, I spent an average of 3 hours a day at the law library and an hour a day at the county library.  With only disappointment occurring in the lawsuits I needed to find out how and why the attorneys and judges could rationalize destroying an individual's legitimate claims in court.  It seemed to me it might be beneficial to have the understanding of how the court and justice system works.

Nyhart billed Dietzen $3,575 on August, 15, 1972. In 1974 Nyhart sued me in Marion County (Indianapolis), *Nyhart Company v. Reginald L. Jensen*, Cause # S74-506, demanding payment. I took the lawsuit papers into Dietzen and asked him what he wanted to do about it. Robert York was a new attorney in Dietzen's office. Dietzen said York worked for him and that York would take care of it for me. Dietzen introduced me to York and then walked out of the office. York filed an answer of denial although he objected to doing so because he felt I owned the money to Nyhart. I told him about the assignment to Dietzen, but York wouldn't accept that. He said an assignment to an attorney wasn't possible because it was illegal. York said he would not proceed as my attorney and I was forced to represent myself in the defense. It would be awhile before this came before a judge.

Seven more months went by without any action or effort by Tuohy. Tuohy was still listed as the attorney of record in the contract case. I became frustrated with his lack of action and failure to communicate with me. I finally called him and expressed my dissatisfaction. Tuohy and Herrin then drove to Anderson and met with me at Frisch's Big Boy restaurant across the street from the courthouse. We had a bitter argument about his work progress and his perception of my conduct. Tuohy said he believed I duped Eckman into creating the Anderson Agency contract. I asked him how it was possible for me to convince the president of an insurance company who had just hired me under a different contract, where I had not yet proven my ability to produce, to provide me with a second contract paying me 100 percent of the first year premiums on all new business written for the company? I also asked him why I hadn't been paid any commissions under the contract between January and July 1971, after the contract was signed? If any commissions were paid, they were paid to Eckman, not to me. I said Eckman maintained possession of the Anderson Agency corporate documents, the commission contract, and eight of the ten stock certificates.

Tuohy didn't make any sense. Tuohy assumed Eckman would cause FESLIC to pay that money to me while I was employed. He assumed Eckman would stand by and watch the company go out of business. The general agent's (manager's) commission, plus the agent's commission, plus my overriding commission, came to almost 90 percent of the first year's premium. Add another 100 percent to that and the insurance company would be paying out 190 percent of the first year's premium, which would have consumed more operating money than the company possessed, it would have guaranteed the company's demise in 1971. Richard Doermer controlled the assets, nearly 100 percent of which were held by his bank. Most of the assets were held in a safe under joint lock and key with the Indiana Insurance Department holding one of the two keys necessary for entry. The assets in Doermer's bank couldn't be paid out without Doermer's and the Insurance Department's consent. Eckman controlled the company's daily operating account. The only value of the January contract to me at this point of time was to force Eckman and FESLIC to bring the litigation to an end. I explained to Tuohy that my primary interest was to force FESLIC to honor the December contract as written. That's why Dietzen sued demanding specific performance of the December contract rather than demanding liquidating damages. Under specific performance the insurance company could possibly grow and prosper, which would have benefited everyone involved. Yet, I would still be at risk because the company could easily fail. Tuohy didn't believe me; his impression of me was fixed and his mind was closed.

We were not on the best of terms when we separated. He had no confidence in me, and I had none in him. He took no further action. Because of his prior statement that the slander case needed to be amended, I asked him to amend that case and then withdraw as my attorney. He agreed. He said John Herrin was taking care of the amendment and Herrin would call me so we could file it with the court together. On June 25, 1974, Tuohy did withdraw from the January 1971, contract case in New Castle. On the same day Herrin mailed a motion for permission to amend the slander complaint to the court in Anderson. The stated reasons were: *discovery found Eckman had full authority to make the slanderous statements; Retail Credit Company misattributed statements in its report, and made false allegations concerning the plaintiff, such allegations not coming from James Eckman; necessary to make additional allegations and name additional parties; and that justice requires First Equity Security Life Insurance Company and Retail Credit Company be joined as defendants.* The motion contradicted Tuohy's statement that Retail Credit could claim privilege as a perfect defense and that he was going to drop Retail Credit as a defendant. Herrin didn't do anything without Tuohy's knowledge.

On July 19, 1974, Herrin came to Anderson and filed the amendment. The amended complaint said the date of the slander was July 14, 1972 (more than two years had passed from July 14, 1972, thus time barred according to the amendment. In reality, the date must be within two years of the date of filing the original complaint, which it was.) He gave me a file-stamped copy. I asked Herrin how he could make such an obvious mistake. He said the papers in his office were on the chair away from him and the dates were hard to read. The amended complaint changing the dates gave an opportunity for the judge to release FESLIC and Eckman as defendants because of the two-year statute of limitations. Since Tuohy and I were at loggerheads, it appeared to me that Tuohy decided to create problems for me after he withdrew.

All of the defendants moved for a dismissal on the theory the date of slander in the amended complaint occurred beyond the statute of limitations. On October 9, 1974, Herrin filed both a Notice of Filing a Second Amended Complaint and a Second Amended Complaint naming First Equity Security Life Insurance Company and Retail Credit Company as additional defendants. The dates of the slander were amended to include July 14, 1972, and August 2, 1972, and that the slander was published July 21, 1972, and in January 1973. (Eckman spoke the words to Retail Credit on July 14 and Retail Credit published them to Franklin National Life on July 21.) The August 2 date was a publication to a company in Ohio. Tuohy possessed all of these other dates of slander and libel and withheld the evidence from me, his client. He concealed the information from me prior to his agreement to withdraw from the case. He filed them with the court giving the defendants a chance to argue the statute of limitations had expired. If I had known about these other dates, I could have attempted to apply pressure on Tuohy earlier or I could have demanded return of my files and either filed the amendments myself or tried to find another attorney who would file the amendments. Tuohy had assured me he would file the amendment in a timely fashion and then return my documents to me and complete his withdrawal. I had every reason to believe he would turn the cases back over to me without harming me in court.

Retail Credit, FESLIC, and Eckman moved for a dismissal of the Second-Amended Complaint in the slander action. Tuohy never appeared and I was left on my own to argue against the dismissal motions. Judges assume a party to an action is in the wrong if the attorney representing that party withdraws and leaves the person to proceed *pro se*.[16] *On September 30, 1974, Judge Schrenker sustained the motions to dismiss filed by Retail Credit and FESLIC, but had second thoughts. He crossed out his dismissal entry and disqualified himself on November 4, 1974.* He had remained the judge from the commencement of the action for two and one-half years. The reality of being disqualified as judge on the first day of the action as well as two-and-one-half years later didn't mean anything to him. On January 3, 1975, Judge George B. Davis assumed jurisdiction of the slander action.

Tuohy and Herrin knew exactly what they were doing and so did the defendant's attorneys. They all knew the rules and knew the motions to dismiss were inappropriate. Tuohy said Retail Credit could not be held liable because of the defense of privilege, yet Retail Credit would be the only remaining party if the judge granted the motions to dismiss.

I still needed to earn more money while all of this was going on and a new opportunity came up. The law, which is now referred to as ERISA, The Employees Retirement Income Securities Act, was passed by Congress in 1974. I wrote to one of the Indiana senators and requested a copy of the law. The senator mailed a copy of the act to me. It was a long, complicated document; it was really a book. I read it several times until it made sense. Section 408 provided for Individual Retirement Accounts (IRAs). It took the financial community awhile to fully understand the meaning of section 408. Soon the insurance companies began selling life insurance policies and annuities and banks set up savings accounts that could be used for IRAs. ERISA originally only provided for government bonds, savings accounts, and annuity contracts. Life insurance policies were prohibited because the

---

[16] Representing himself, with no legal counsel.

policies had low or no first-year cash surrender values. Annuities were acceptable investments because they were both deferred savings vehicles and income vehicles when the monies were withdrawn. Most annuities at that time had cash values that were only about 50 percent of the first-year premium or savings amount. The primary purpose of an annuity was to provide guaranteed income, not savings. The cash in the bank savings accounts was substantially more than the insurance company annuities in 1976. The banks paid between 3-percent and 5-percent interest on the IRA certificates of deposit. There was a lot of potential for the sale of IRAs by insurance companies as well as by banks, but insurance companies would have to create more-competitive products. FESLIC's annuity fit the required pattern perfectly and most other insurance companies adopted a similar contract. The first-year cash values became 92 percent of the premium paid into the contract and the interest earned was the current interest rate of eight percent.

Insurance Company of North America (INA) owned several life insurance companies. Life Insurance Company of North America (LICNA), a subsidiary of INA, decided to offer annuities with a 92-percent, first-year cash value and a first-year interest rate of 8 percent. This made the LICNA annuities competitive with the banks. The cash values of the annuities equaled the bank CD values by the end of three years and exceeded the bank CD values thereafter. LICNA wanted to set up sales agencies using the IRA annuities as introductions to their other life insurance policies. They hired an employment search firm to recruit agents. The search firm in Indianapolis contacted me and recommended me to LICNA. A LICNA officer flew in from New York City to Indianapolis for a first meeting with me and other prospective agents. I applied to be contracted as a personal producing general agent. We made an appointment to meet one week later at a hotel to sign the contracts. I went to Indianapolis the next week to meet with him at the appointed time. He avoided meeting me. I finally found him in the hotel bar. He said he would sign the contract with me but there would be no payments to me except earned commissions and I was prohibited from hiring agents. We both signed the contracts and I returned to Anderson. It was obvious LICNA had obtained a investigative report from Retail Credit, FESLIC, or Eckman, or all three.

I continued to work for Eastern Broadcasting but started selling IRA annuities for LICNA part time. I made quite a few sales, but after a year, LICNA told me I must sell their life insurance policies to retain my contract. I examined their life insurance policies and found them to be noncompetitive. The buyer would pay a higher price for average protection than would be available from many other companies. I decided not to sell their life products. Eventually LICNA terminated my contract.

I notified the court in New Castle I would be proceeding pro se. FESLIC, through Fletcher, immediately asked for a dismissal of the contract cases and Judge Wesley Ratliff set a hearing date for February 7, 1975. I had talked to at least a dozen attorneys about representing me, but no one was interested. Dietzen saw me in downtown Anderson a couple of days before the hearing date. He asked me how I was doing on the law suits, and I told him I was trying to find a new attorney. He knew the date of the hearing and said he'd help me out until I could find someone. I had no idea how to present my case before a judge or jury, so I accepted his offer. Dietzen said he would ask York to pick up my files from Tuohy's office. Dietzen called the court clerk in New Castle and asked her to send copies of all of the paperwork to him and the clerk obliged.

I had reviewed the docket sheets and the file in Muncie after Tuohy told me he had arranged to have the dismissal changed from with prejudice to with prejudice as to the theory of specific performance only. I wanted to verify it was actually done. The Delaware County (Muncie) docket sheets were unique in size and shape. Most of the court papers, including the docket sheets, were on 8.5" by 14" sheets of paper. The Delaware County sheets were closer to 12" by 20". The order book had the correct entry. But, one docket sheet, 71-1083, had the dismissal written on it to show it was with prejudice as to the theory of specific performance only. The other docket sheet, 71-1084, showed the dismissal with prejudice.

On February 7, 1975, Dietzen and I traveled together in his car to the courthouse in New Castle. It was time for the pre-trial hearing before Judge Ratliff. Fletcher was to meet us in the courthouse. On the way over, Dietzen told me Tuohy was still in control of all of my cases. I asked Dietzen how Tuohy could be in control after he had been dismissed and he had withdrawn as counsel. Dietzen said he couldn't answer, but that's the way it was. After we arrived at the courthouse, Dietzen and Fletcher were alone in a room where they carried on a discussion. I could see Dietzen through the doorway showing documents to Fletcher. I could hear Dietzen offer to help Fletcher and could see Dietzen showing Fletcher different entries on the papers. It was easy to notice Dietzen pointing out the inconsistencies in the dismissals on the Muncie docket sheets because those pieces of paper were so unique. Fletcher asked Dietzen, "Why are you doing this?" but I couldn't hear Dietzen's answer.

Both attorneys appeared before the judge. I could watch from the hall outside the courtroom. The docket sheet with "with prejudice" written on it was shown to judge Ratliff by Dietzen. Fletcher offered Exhibit "A," which was a transcript of the proceeding in Muncie before Judge Cox. The transcript showed Judge Cox had dismissed "with prejudice." Fletcher moved to dismiss the complaint. Dietzen supported the motion to dismiss because, he said, the litigation must come to an end. Judge Ratliff took the motion under advisement. Dietzen and I returned to Anderson.

The next morning I drove back to the courthouse in New Castle and asked to see the court files on the case. The clerk showed me the complete file. It confirmed what had happened. Dietzen didn't file Judge Cox's order of dismissal with prejudice as to specific performance only. The clerk affirmed Dietzen did not oppose the motion to dismiss and said the judge would issue the order of dismissal in a couple of days.

I immediately drove over to Muncie and obtained certified copies of both docket sheets plus Judge Cox's amended order of dismissal with prejudice as to specific performance only. I took them back to New Castle and filed the documents with the clerk. The clerk gave me a receipt identifying each document.

While I was in New Castle, I went to the Henry County prosecutor's personal office and explained my situation to him. The prosecutor maintained a private practice in addition to his county duties. I asked him to represent me. He asked me why Tuohy had withdrawn and I told him Tuohy and I didn't agree on any of the aspects of the case. He said every attorney in Indiana knew or knew of Tuohy and because of Tuohy's influence in the state it would be difficult to find someone to represent me. Several days later, he called me on the phone and said he wouldn't represent me.

On *May 22, 1975,* Judge Ratliff mailed letters to me, Dietzen, and Fletcher, saying he was preparing the order overruling the motion for summary judgment and affirmed a trial date of September 4, 1975. He also said the record reflected I was without counsel at the time. He said he'd presume I would obtain counsel in sufficient time to be prepared for trial. On May 23, 1975, Judge Ratliff issued a decision overruling FESLIC's motion for a summary judgment in 73-C-185 and clarified the issues for trial. The judge mailed copies of the order to me, Fletcher, and Dietzen. Judge Ratliff's findings and order said in part:

> A. Defendant's entered Exhibit "A" into evidence, which is a transcript of the proceedings in Causes number 71/1083 and 71/1084 in Delaware Circuit Court in Delaware County, Indiana.
>
> B. The actions were a demand on defendant to make payment to Jensen according to the contracts.
>
> C. The action was for specific performance and resulted in an order of involuntary dismissal as to the defendant as to the theory of recovery by way of specific performance of contract only, as reflected by the entry of said Delaware Circuit Court on January 27, 1972, entered on the docket sheet of that court in cause number 71/1083, signed by Judge Alva Cox. *(My comment: this docket sheet was entered into evidence by me, not by Dietzen or the defendant.)*
>
> D. That there is a genuine issue of material fact as to whether or not the cause of action sued upon in this action is the same cause or claim as the one sued upon in the Delaware Circuit Court.
>
> E. That there is a genuine issue of fact and law as to whether or not the disposition in the Delaware Circuit

Court, wherein the cases pending between the parties in that court were dismissed as to the theory of specific performance of contracts only, includes the complaint for damages which is the basis of the action now pending in this court.

Immediately after receiving Judge Ratliff's letter, Dietzen called me into his office, gave me all of my papers and admitted his fraudulent conduct. He said he would give me the name of his malpractice insurance company if I intended to sue him. I was having trouble finding an attorney who would represent me in my current actions, how would I find an attorney who would also sue another influential attorney? And who were my witnesses? They were Fletcher and Judge Ratliff. I had enough lawsuits going on at the time and didn't need another one.

On May 22, 1975, Herrin mailed a request to the court for his firm to withdraw as my counsel in the slander action, along with a copy of a letter addressed to me enclosed for the court to read, but the letter was never mailed to me by Herrin. The letter attributed the reason for Tuohy's law firm withdrawal as a result of my past actions, but without explaining my past actions. I obtained a copy from the court files. It's highly improper for an attorney to send derogatory or inaccurate information to a court or to send such information to anyone without submitting it to the client. Attorney-client privilege is supposed to apply. Herrin's letter said he understood Dietzen was now representing me. (I often wonder what goes through the minds of attorneys. Herrin must have visualized me walking into Dietzen's office asking him to engage in malpractice on my behalf one more time.) Dietzen hadn't filed an appearance in New Castle. He certainly wasn't about to file an appearance in the slander and December 1970 contract action. I had not contacted Herrin or Tuohy after the pre-trial conference in New Castle and gave no indication to them that Dietzen was representing me. My only association with Dietzen was his agreement to help me with the contract action on February 7. His fiasco in trying to obtain the fraudulent dismissal of the contract action brought our relationship to an end. Herrin's letter also included an acknowledgement that I had requested them to withdraw on March 4, 1975. My request to Tuohy included a request to file the amended complaint he felt was necessary prior to withdrawing and to file it in a timely manner because time was becoming critical. Herrin never mentioned that, of course.

It's my belief the timing behind Judge Ratliff's letter of May 22 and Tuohy's withdrawal from the slander action on the same day was not coincidental. It's my belief Judge Ratliff called Judge Cox and Tuohy to ascertain any facts that would help him. Judge Cox's dismissal was in his handwriting, and Tuohy had filed the lawsuit. Judge Ratliff had documents in front of him that were supposed to be official court records, but they conflicted. Someone was lying. The duration from February to May gave the judge enough time to confer with the court in Muncie and to compare the Muncie records with the records in his possession. He also had time to check with Tuohy to find out about his involvement. Tuohy was in a position to say he arranged with Judge Cox for the dismissal to be changed from with prejudice to with prejudice as to the theory of specific performance only. Tuohy could also say he had withdrawn from this case and explain his reasons for withdrawing. He could also say he didn't know what was going on with me and the other attorneys. That information would prepare Judge Ratliff to enter his ruling.

On May 30, Tuohy's and Herrin's withdrawal was approved by the court in Madison County. Herrin mailed a letter to me dated June 6, 1975, saying he had been advised by the court that his (and Tuohy's) withdrawal of appearance had been approved. He asked me to pick up my files. He also said he received a copy of an entry on June 4 concerning the resetting of the June 27, 1975, arguments on the motions to dismiss. He said either my counsel or I should be there.

I wrote to Tuohy and demanded he file an appeal in the slander action based upon the original complaint having been timely filed. *The law in Indiana says that filing a complaint is "notice," and the notice commences the action.* The defendants had been put on notice within one week after the slander occurred. The time for appeal begins to run from the date of the dismissal. I had no idea how to file an appeal and it seemed to me the only persons who could do so within the time limit and at the lowest cost would be Tuohy and Herrin.

Judge Davis held the hearing on the motions to dismiss the slander action on June 27, 1975. I appeared on my own behalf and counsel for the defendants appeared to argue their motions. The judge took the motions under advisement.

On August, 26, 1975, Judge Davis dismissed defendants FESLIC and Eckman. The judge held Retail Credit answerable for the alleged delivery of the slanderous report in January 1973. *The only remaining defendant was Retail Credit and the only remaining date of slander was January 1973.*

Judge Ratliff advised me there would be a trial on September 4, 1975, in New Castle on the January contract. Judge Davis held the hearing on the dismissal motions in the slander action in Anderson. I had no idea what the next event would be like.

I decided to file a complaint against Tuohy with the Indiana Disciplinary Commission. The commission mailed the complaint to Tuohy and asked for his response. He told the commission he would pay me all of my damages. The commission accepted Tuohy's word and dismissed the complaint. He never paid and never offered to pay.

In 1975, FESLIC moved from its Anderson offices to the office of Underwriters National Assurance Company (UNAC) in Indianapolis. FESLIC sales were negligible except for credit life insurance sales arranged by Doermer. It had the same number of home office employees, yet it rented double the amount of space at UNAC for triple the rent it paid in Anderson. UNAC was in receivership and under supervision of the court. Judge Michael Dugan, an Indianapolis Democrat and friend of Tuohy and Eckman, controlled UNAC.

My search for a new attorney continued. York had moved out of Dietzen's office and I had no interest in locating him. I had talked to nearly every attorney in Anderson and none would handle my cases. My search continued in Indianapolis and discussions were held with several attorneys. One large law firm agreed to review my files and asked me to come back in a week. When I returned, the attorney had placed my files on a table in a conference room for me to pick up. While sitting at the table, he said he had talked to Tuohy and would have nothing further to say. He asked me to take my files with me. I asked him a couple of questions, but he just sat in his chair with his mouth closed and wouldn't speak. The Sphinx was more loquacious. I picked up my files and left. My search continued in Indianapolis by walking into offices and explaining my situation. I talked to four or five attorneys a day for about a week. Each attorney called Tuohy to get his views on me and my cases. None would take me as a client. One young attorney walked me outside and talked to me on the sidewalk. He told me I would never get anyone to represent me if they ever contacted Tuohy. He advised me to pick someone who needed work and who had a tarnished reputation and thus would not contact Tuohy. He directed me to Daniel Friedland. Friedland had a reputation of taking cases he wasn't qualified to handle.

I talked to Friedland in late August. He said he'd talk to Fletcher and let me know if he'd represent me. Friedland called Fletcher. Fletcher told Friedland that FESLIC would pay $15,000 to settle all cases. I told Friedland the offer was unacceptable. Friedland then said he had only a week to prepare to meet the judge in New Castle and he didn't have time. He said that if he could settle the New Castle case for $15,000 he would take $4,000 and use the money to finance my other cases. He said he would not ask for any additional money to take both the slander action and the December 1970 contract action to trial and appeal to the state supreme court if he didn't reach a settlement or jury verdict in my favor. He said the $4,000 would apply to his percentage and any costs I wasn't required to cover myself. My real interest was in the December 1970 contract and the slander case. The January contract case was being used as leverage. I accepted Friedland's terms. Based upon our agreement, Fletcher mailed checks to Daryl Dean and the Howard Nyhart Company in the amount of $3,000, which was a partial payment on their fees and was not included in the one-third percentage to Friedland; to the IRS on my behalf in the amount of $3,397.08; and $8,602.92 payable to me and Friedland. Friedland took $4,000 and the balance was paid to me. After we completed the settlement of the January 1971 action, Friedland drafted a contract between us on his stationary, which we signed. The entire language is below:

M. Daniel Friedland
*Attorney at Law*
Suite 811
415 N. PENNSYLVANIA STREET
INDIANAPOLIS, INDIANA

October 17, 1975

TO;  Mr. Reginald Jensen
     4511 Columbus, F39
     Anderson, Ind.
     649-1634

FEES FOR SERVICES RENDERED
Fee agreement : 1/3 on settlement out of court
40% at trial
50% in case of appeal
This agreement shall hold in all cases involving Mr. Jensen's claims.

Reginald L. Jensen           M.  Daniel  Friedland
  (Signature)                     (Signature)

Friedland did re-file the December 1, 1970, contract in Madison County on October 28, 1975, as *Jensen v. First Equity Security Life Insurance Company*, Madison County Cause No. S-75-828. On the same day he filed a Motion To Correct Errors in the slander action, which was quickly denied by the judge. Fletcher filed Defendant's Motion To Correct Errors And To Strike Or Overrule Plaintiff's Motion. Friedland then filed the Plaintiff's Memorandum In Opposition To Motion To Strike Or Overrule Motion To Correct Errors in the slander case. Then the defendant requested oral argument on pending motions in the same case. Arguments on the motions were set for January 16, 1976, at 1:15 p.m. Finally, on December 1, 1975, Friedland filed his appearance in the case. On December 22, 1975, Defendant Retail Credit filed an answer. Then FESLIC filed a Motion To Strike The Pleadings Under Trial Rule 11. On January 7, 1976, Plaintiff's Memorandum In Opposition To Strike Pleadings Under Trial Rule 11 and Memorandum

In Opposition To Motion To Strike Or Overrule Motion To Correct Errors was filed.

I met with Friedland in his office once more and he objected to me about continuing with the case because it "had whiskers." He didn't want to proceed because he had his money and didn't want to do any more work. We discussed his agreement with me. He had no interest in returning the money, so he tried to find different methods of accommodating me without doing any work himself.

On January 16, 1976, attorney Eric Sivin, Friedland's New York City friend, was visiting in Indianapolis and agreed to go to Anderson and represent me at the hearing as Friedland's stand-in. He wasn't licensed to practice in Indiana. He still appeared on my behalf in front of Judge Davis and said he was in the process of making application to practice in the state. Judge Davis allowed him to proceed. Sivin's argument was that Judge Davis should remove the prior dismissal and allow the trial to go to a jury. It was an emotional appeal without citing any law or rule. Fletcher appeared on behalf of Eckman and FESLIC. Fletcher argued the case had been dismissed and the dismissal should stand. No attorney appeared on behalf of Retail Credit. A new judge in an action will seldom reverse a previous judicial order, that's the purpose of the appeal process. The new judge usually picks up from where the last transaction took place. He listened patiently to Sivin and Fletcher then took the motions under advisement. Sivin and I left the courthouse and got into his car. Sivin said he wanted to be paid for his efforts, so I asked him to stop at a liquor store. I bought a quart of whiskey and gave it to him along with ten dollars for gas money so he could drive back to Indianapolis. He seemed to be satisfied. A couple of days later he returned to New York. To my knowledge he never became licensed in Indiana.

Judge Davis overruled Sivin's motion to correct errors on January 22, 1976. On February 20, Friedland filed a notice of appeal and praecipe[17] for the record of proceedings with the court. The trial record is supposed to be delivered to the requesting party within 60 days of the filing of the notice and praecipe. The notice and praecipe were completely ignored by the court, the clerk of the court, and by all

---

[17] A notice to issue a writ (a writ is a command to a person to perform) specifying the contents, the court records in this case.

attorneys, including Friedland. *Tuohy had refused to appeal the dismissal and now Friedland refused.*

During the next six months, Friedland did nothing whatsoever. He moved from his office and left it up to me to locate him. When I found his new office, I went in to see him. He asked me who I was and what he had agreed to do for me. I jogged his memory. He said he'd get right to work and do what he'd promised to do.

I had transferred my Principal's license to Transamerica. Since LICNA had cancelled my contract I needed to find another company to represent. It was necessary to continue earning some extra money. Transamerica's general agent in Indianapolis explained the annuities they were offering as IRA investments. The Transamerica annuities were substantially the same as the LICNA annuities. So, I began selling IRAs for Transamerica Life exclusively.

I decided to follow up on my search for my 1947 arrest record and wrote a letter to the FBI in Washington, DC. A letter signed on behalf of Clarence Kelly, the director, which was mailed to me on December 9, 1975, said it would take a long time to search the record and they needed my notarized signature. In mid-1976, the FBI provided me with a copy of the arrest document along with a redacted copy of the arrest report completed by the officers involved. I put those papers in a file in a storage room in our apartment in Anderson.

In 1975, I talked to an editor at the Indianapolis Star about my being slandered. He introduced me to reporter Carolyn Pickering and asked her to follow up. I gave her copies of the Retail Credit report and Tuohy's malpractice. She said she'd look into it and did write a story, which was published on June 3, 1976, headlined "Attorney Fees Seen Forcing Liquidation Of Insurance Firm" discussing Judge Dugan's attempted reinsurance[18] of UNAC's assets. Judge Dugan held an emergency hearing and awarded $300,000 in legal fees to be paid by UNAC to various attorneys. The emergency existed because Judge Dugan was going on vacation. A Chicago firm was paid $167,362.50; A Virginia firm was paid $64,237.50; Dillon, McCarty, Hardeman and

---

[18] A transfer of a future right to assets in return for current cash.

Cohen (Dillon was the former Democratic attorney general for Indiana) was paid $17,887. Dillon and Gregory Hahn, treasurer of the Marion County Democratic Central Committee, were appointed by Judge Dugan as local counsel for the out of state firms, which means Dillon and Hahn were involved in total payments exceeding $230,000. The firm of Tuohy, Gleason and Mercer was paid $48,960. Tuohy was paid even though he had no records of time spent and didn't perform any legal functions on behalf of the company. Tuohy said he represented the stockholders, but he submitted no proof and no stockholder ever verified his claim. The amount Tuohy received was about the same amount he would have received as his share of my claims against FESLIC and Eckman. It was also an amount that would approximate the extra rental income paid to UNAC by FESLIC during its first year in the UNAC offices. One attorney who observed what was happening said it was outrageous and really gross. He thought Judge Dugan was being buffaloed. (I don't believe any reinsurance in the traditional form took place, because UNAC remained an entity with the reserves still intact. A merger took place a few years later, but reinsurance of the assets would have transferred the assets out of Judge Dugan's control.) Reporter Pickering then mailed all of my records back to me and left the newspaper. The Indianapolis Star said she became a real estate agent. None of the attorneys returned any money. Judge Dugan continued to manage UNAC. Eckman later came into the Y in Anderson and said FESLIC intended to buy the UNAC building and assume management of the UNAC policies. Either or both transactions would place more cash under Judge Dugan's control. Neither ever happened.

Around this time I was serving on the board of directors of a service club in Anderson. Another attorney and two judges, Dennis Carroll and Thomas Newman, Jr., sat on the same board. Judge Carroll said they handle cases that come before them differently; he said they pay attention to the cases involving large sums of money and pay little attention to the cases that seemed minor to them. About the same time, a former client sued a different attorney for malpractice. The attorney admitted to the other attorneys involved in the case that he was guilty of the charge. I talked to one of the attorneys representing the attorney being sued. He had moved for a dismissal of the action based upon unfounded grounds. I asked him why he would make such an unconscionable motion. His answer was you never know what will happen in court, the judge might dismiss the case. That's exactly what happened. The plaintiff's attorney then recommended the dismissal not be appealed and that's what happened. The attorney got off scot free from being held responsible for harming his client.

It was during this time frame when Butler talked to me in the sales office of WHUT for a few minutes and explained he was Eckman's friend and he would do whatever he could to help Eckman.

In 1976, acting pro se, I sued Tuohy and his firm for malpractice. This was my first real attempt to represent myself. The action became *Jensen v. Tuohy,* Marion County (Indianapolis) cause number *S276-735*, before Judge Webster Brewer. Tuohy's attorney, Stewart Irwin, was a respected and competent attorney and a hero who returned from the wars. He taught me a couple of new tricks in the legal business. He would mail papers to me with my correct address on the letters or documents in the envelope but with an incorrect address on the envelope itself. I would never receive the mail. A postman remembered my name and showed an envelope to me that had the wrong address. I checked the court file and found the same letter with my correct address. There were other letters in the court file that I had never received. He would file his papers in court and certify he had mailed copies to me. It was necessary to visit the court periodically to be certain I had all papers that had been filed and all notices mailed by the court. Irwin soon moved for a dismissal on the theory *there hadn't been a final entry* in the slander action. He also claimed the *slander case was on appeal* and that the appeal could reverse the dismissal. (The two positions are inconsistent, an appeal can't be filed except based upon a final entry.) I obtained a certified copy of the dismissal of the slander action and offered it to the court. I obtained a certification from Billie R. McCullough, Clerk of the Indiana Appellate Court, stating no action regarding the slander case had been filed. The legal effect of the argument was that the entries in the slander case were final and not on appeal. Irwin argued I could still pursue Retail Credit Company, which would absolve Tuohy. I offered Tuohy's own letter saying Retail Credit's actions were privileged and they were not liable. Irwin countered saying Tuohy might be wrong, maybe Retail Credit could be held liable. No real defense existed to my suit against Tuohy, but that didn't bother the defendants, their counsel, or the judge. Judge Brewer was happy to dismiss my case.

The hearing ended after 5 P.M. The clerk had closed the office and reset the date on the court file stamps to show the following day. Tuohy, Irwin, and Judge Brewer spent five minutes resetting all of the stamps and entries to save one day. They did it to reduce my allowed time to file an appeal. I left the courthouse and drove back to Anderson. The flagrant manipulation of the judicial system was really hard for me to stomach. I was so upset on the drive home I had trouble seeing the road. While driving down the freeway, I shifted the car into reverse in an attempt to stop the car, rather than just applying the brakes. I was lucky I didn't strip the gears. I was able to stop the car and pull over to the side of the road and just sat in the car and tried to collect my composure. Finally, I drove back home to Anderson. The next morning it was painfully apparent to me that I still had no idea how to file an appeal and couldn't find an attorney to help me anyway, so I just let the dismissal stand. Several weeks later, Dietzen saw me downtown and again told me Tuohy still controlled all of my cases.

The Nyhart Company wanted the balance of the money it had earned. It arranged a motion for a summary judgment in front of a judge in Indianapolis in 1978. The attorney for Nyhart met me in the office of the judge, not in the courtroom. The judge sat at his desk: the attorney and I sat in chairs in front of his desk. It was my position Nyhart had sued the wrong person; it should have sued Walter Dietzen because I had assigned my contract to Dietzen and Dietzen hired Nyhart. The attorney asked to see the assignment. I told him it was at home. The judge told me it wasn't possible for me to have received an assignment because it's unlawful for an attorney to take an assignment of a contract in return for services. The judge said he would enter judgment for plaintiff. The attorney left the office and I remained. The judge and I talked for a few minutes. *He said that I should hire an attorney who has an office in one of the tall buildings downtown because those attorneys know the law better than he does and he just takes their word for whatever position they present in court.* He said any attorney who comes into his court who operates out of his home or in a one-man office will always lose. This is a good indication of how most judges work. The judge becomes subservient to (the employee of) the respected attorney. Respect comes from personal contact and favors received. I never told him I had received some valuable experience from several of those terrific attorneys he respects, who have offices in those tall buildings downtown. I thought to myself "What a thrill, I'm learning more about the justice system every day." This judge was probably the most open and straightforward of all judges I met by revealing how he managed his affairs. As a practical matter it isn't possible for a judge to do the necessary research and comprehend all of the varied issues that come before him/her. There are too many laws, the issues are too diverse, and, often, deliberately convoluted for the purpose of confusing those involved. Quite often it requires an unbiased expert to sort out the issues. Over time the attorneys learn the judges who will accept their arguments and the judges learn the attorneys who they will rely upon. And, of course, there are always political, financial, and social favors to repay. I left the judge, went back to my apartment in Anderson and located my copy of the assignment. I made a copy and mailed it to the Nyhart attorney. I never heard from that attorney again and Nyhart made no further attempt to collect on the judgment.

Friedland was in the middle of a battle with the Indiana Supreme Court. They wanted to put him out of business. Friedland's problems with the Supreme Court continued to escalate. He managed to have a loud vocal confrontation with one of the justices in the office of the justice. Friedland thought he was being picked on and was demanding the Supreme Court get off his back. The Indianapolis Star published an article on the shouting match.[19]

Friedland also was having problems with the other attorneys where he shared offices. They decided to increase each attorney's rent to an amount beyond Friedland's ability to pay. He was finally forced out and opened his own office at 45 N. Pennsylvania St. in Indianapolis. I called Friedland on the phone several times. He did his utmost to avoid contact with me. When we did meet he always had many excuses as to

---

[19] Wilcox, Oqden & DuMond represented Friedland when he lost his liscence.

why he had done nothing. I had paid for the legal effort and I believed I was entitled to receive it.

Nothing happened on the slander action from early 1976 to mid-1978. In 1978, I was pressuring Friedland about continuing with my cases. He said he had offices in New Jersey and Indiana and he would soon be moving to New Jersey. He was providing office space to Stephen Laudig, a young new attorney who had just passed the bar exam. Friedland asked Laudig to work with me as an assistant.

The next time I made a trip to Indianapolis to try to get Friedland to do his work, he wasn't there, he had moved to New Jersey and I only saw him one more time after that. So, I tried to get Laudig to follow through on the request for the appeal of the slander action. Laudig attempted to pacify me by pretending he was doing his job. I helped him prepare a new document demanding the court proceed with the appeal requirements. He would type the proposed order and motion and then he'd make copies so he could cut and paste the words to restructure the document. His copy machine didn't work very well, so he asked me to take the papers down to the lobby of the building and make copies on a Xerox machine at ten cents each. After several days, the documents were finished. He placed the documents into a sealed envelope and said he'd mail it the next day. A couple of days later, I went into his office, but he wasn't there. The envelope was still on his desk. He hadn't mailed it, so I picked it up and mailed it for him. Later in the day, he called me and asked me if I knew what happened to the envelope. I said I mailed it. He was very upset. He said he didn't want to mail it yet. As a result he drove to Judge Davis' office (in a different county) and retrieved it. Judge Davis then withdrew from the contract case and Judge Brandon Griffis in New Castle was appointed to take over.

The next time we met I asked Laudig if he was engaged in deception and his response was, "You found us out." Now what to do! Friedland was somewhere in New Jersey. I was working with a young attorney who didn't seem to know what he was doing. Neither one had any interest in pursuing my cases. It was time to take a different approach. I decided to continue working with Laudig on a weekly basis. I started paying him additional money at each meeting. I'd give him whatever money I had in my pocket. Sometimes it was $3.00 sometimes $5.00,

$10.00, $25.00, once in awhile $50.00 or more. At one point in time he told me he needed to set up an escrow account for witness fees and needed $100.00. I gave him a check for that specific purpose. I wrote on the back of the check "Witness Fees, escrow account." He deposited the check in a witness fee escrow account with that endorsement above his signature.

Laudig asked me if I had any history that could affect my claim in the slander action. He said, if I had ever been arrested it could come out at trial, he wanted to be prepared in advance. I took him to my apartment and showed him the papers I'd received from the FBI relating to the 1947 arrest and then put the papers back into the file in the storage area. Sometime during the next year, those papers disappeared. The maintenance manager for the apartment complex came to our apartment and talked to my wife and me about his having been discharged from his job. He said there were allegations of pilfering and he wanted to make it clear that, even though he had been in various apartments from time to time while the renters weren't home, he never took any property that belonged to the renters. The only thing ever missing from our apartment was the FBI documents, and I could see no reason for him to have any interest in those papers.

As Laudig and I continued to meet, he complained pressure was being applied by me while he was engaged in what he called voluminous lawyers' legal work. To provide the reader with some insight as to what constitutes lawyers legal work the following is a list of most of the filings recorded on the docket sheet with the court in the slander case prior to Laudig's entrance in the case and then beginning with the time Laudig came into the picture. This list is being presented now to illustrate how the legal fraternity can manipulate a party to an action. All of the court filings by Laudig came about because we met, which caused him to take some action on the lawsuits. We would sit in his office and go through the same routine of typing, copying, cutting and pasting. Motions, responses, supplemental responses, supplemental responses to the responses, objections, ad infinitum, were filed. Keep in mind that the case was ready for trial in early 1973. (*Laudig later signed an affidavit saying all of these lawsuits could have been completed in one year.*) Lost in the fog is the issue of whether FESLIC and Retail Credit had been dismissed and no appeal had been filed. They would have been out of the lawsuit if in fact they were dismissed in 1974 or 1975.

The majority entries prior to April 19, 1978 are:

July 28, 1972, Complaint for Slander filed by Dietzen against Eckman assigning the date of July 21, 1972, as the date of occurrence. Judge Paul Shrenker assumes jurisdiction.

April 25, 1973, James Tuohy appears for Plaintiff Jensen

July 19, 1974, Tuohy files Amended Complaint naming Eckman, FESLIC, and Retail Credit
assigning July 14, 1972, as the date of occurrence.

September 30, 1974, Judge Shrenker dismisses FESLIC and Retail Credit.

October 9, 1974, Tuohy files the Second Amended Complaint naming the same parties, but including other dates prior to October 9, 1972, and January 1973.

October 21, 1974, FESLIC and Eckman file motion to dismiss.

October 24, 1974, Retail Credit files motion to dismiss.

(Unknown), 1974, Judge Shrenker dismisses the Second Amended Complaint.

December 4, 1974, Judge Shrenker crosses out his dismissal of the Second Amended Complaint, disqualifies himself and resigns.

April 23, 1975, Judge George B. Davis assumes jurisdiction.

May 23, 1975, Jensen, pro se, files Third Amended Complaint.

August 26, 1975, Judge Davis dismissed the Third Amended Complaint against FESLIC and Eckman. Retail Credit's motion to dismiss is sustained as to July 21, 1972, but overruled as to January 1973. (Retail Credit remains a defendant.)

December 1, 1975, Friedland appears for Jensen.

January 22, 1976, Motion to correct errors is overruled.

February 20, 1976, Motion to correct errors and praecipe of the record filed by Friedland.

No judge ever signed an Order of Dismissal, there were only entries on the docket sheet, which is an indication to the prevailing attorney(s) to prepare the ruling and order. None of the defending attorneys ever prepared an order of dismissal.

Eckman and FESLIC have been dismissed and Retail Credit is the sole defendant. In reality, Eckman and FELIC should be the defendants and Retail Credit should have been dismissed.

DOCKET ENTRIES OF THE FILINGS INITIATED BY LAUDIG

April 19, 1978, Laudig mailed interrogatories to Retail Credit.

April 21, 1978, First Equity filed an <u>objection</u> to the plaintiff's petition to file a third amended complaint.

April 26, 1978, Plaintiff filed a <u>petition</u> for leave to file a third amended complaint.
*(How and why FESLIC was able to file an objection to a petition which had not been filed is beyond me. The petition was mailed to both parties and the court at the same time.)*

May 4, 1978, The petition to file third amended complaint was <u>granted</u>.

May 23, 1978, Retail Credit filed a motion to vacate the order and to strike the third amended complaint.

May 26, 1978, Judge Davis resigned and Judge Paul Johnson was appointed.

June 7, 1978, Judge Paul Johnson assumed jurisdiction.

June 8, 1978, Plaintiff's opposition to motion to vacate and strike was filed.

June 9, 1978, Defendant's supplemental memorandum in support of defendant's motion to vacate order and strike plaintiff's third amended complaint was filed.

June 11, 1978, Hearing on motion to vacate set for July 3, 1978, at 3:00 p.m.

June 15, 1978, Appearance of Stephen Laudig filed.

June 23, 1978, Plaintiff's reply to defendant's supplemental memorandum in support of defendant's motion to vacate order and strike plaintiff's purported third amended complaint.

June 25, 1978, Motion for continuance of hearing July 3, 1978, filed. Petition for certification to the Supreme Court for selection of special judge pursuant to Indiana Rule of Trial Procedure 79 filed. Petition for order to compel responses to interrogatories filed. Motion for default judgment against all defendants filed.

July 3, 1978, Comes now the Court and sustains Plaintiff's motion for continuance of hearing herein. Plaintiff's petition for certification to Supreme Court is now overruled. Defendant Retail Credit's motion to vacate order of May 4, 1978, is now sustained and Plaintiff's third amended complaint is now stricken subject to hearing on Plaintiff's petition for leave to file third amended complaint. <u>Plaintiff's motion for default judgment is overruled</u>. Plaintiff's petition to compel answers to interrogatories is sustained as per written entry.

July 6, 1978, Defendant's James Eckman and First Equity Security Life Insurance Co.'s response to motion for continuance of hearing of 7/3/78 filed together with said <u>defendant's response to plaintiff's motion for default judgment</u>.

July 12, 1978, Cause assigned for hearing and for argument on Plaintiff's petition for leave to file third amended complaint and on defendant's objections thereto 3:00 p.m. August 17, 1978.

August 1, 1978, Defendant Retail Credit's answers to interrogatories filed.

August 11, 1978, Plaintiff's request for production of documents by defendant Retail Credit Co. filed.

August 15, 1978, Plaintiff's motion to compel production and motion to apply sanctions filed together with presentation of the issue and facts and plaintiff's interrogatory #4, #5, #8, #9, and authority for order and for imposition of sanctions, and exhibits.

August 17, 1978, Comes now Plaintiff in person and by Counsel and comes also Defendant Retail Credit by Counsel. Cause submitted on Plaintiff's petition for leave to file 3$^{rd}$ amended complaint. Statement and argument of counsel heard. Cause taken under advisement.

August 22, 1978, Plaintiff's supplemental memorandum in support of his motion for leave to amend complaint.

August 28, 1978, Defendant James Eckman's memorandum in opposition to plaintiff's motion for leave to amend complaint.

September 15, 1978, Defendant Retail Credit's response to plaintiff's request for production of documents filed.

September 23, 1978, Renewed motion of plaintiff's to compel answers to interrogatories and for the application of sanctions filed.

October 11, 1978, Defendant's request for hearing filed. Notice of Special Judge Johnson in this matter.

October 17, 1978, Comes now the Court and sustains plaintiff's motion to file third amended complaint and plaintiff is ordered to file same on or before 10/27/1978. Cause set on discovery motions at 2:00 p.m. on November 1, 1978.

October 27, 1978, Plaintiff's third amended complaint for slander and libel filed.

November 1, 1978, Comes now the court by Special Judge Johnson and he being detained in his own court, the court now continues this matter to November 28, 1978, at 3:30 p.m.

November 14, 1978, Comes now the court and orders that the hearing on motion to compel and sanctions scheduled for November 28, 1978, at 3:30 p.m. be held in the Boone Courthouse in Lebanon, Indiana. All per written order. Written appearance of Martin T. Fletcher, attorney for defendants James E. Eckman and First Equity Security Life Insurance, filed together with said defendant's motion for more definite statement and memorandum in support of said motion, and move to strike, and motion to dismiss with memorandum in support of motion to dismiss.

November 27, 1978, Plaintiff's reply and response to defendant's various motions filed with memorandum in three sections attached.

November 28, 1978, Defendant Retail Credit's motion to make more specific and motion to strike filed together with motion to dismiss with memorandum attached.

November 29, 1978, Comes now the court and reassigns this cause for hearing and/or argument on plaintiff's discovery motion, defendant First Equity's motion for more definite statement, motion to strike, and motion to dismiss; and defendant Retail Credit's motion to make more specific, motion to strike, and motion to dismiss, all of which are now set for hearing on January 9, 1979.

December 8, 1978, Plaintiff's supplemental reply and response to defendants Eckman and First Equity's motions.

December 14, 1978, Plaintiff's supplemental authority in opposition to defendant Eckman's and First Equity Security Life Insurance Co. filed.

December 19, 1978, Notice of deposition filed.

> *(My deposition in the slander action in the Andeson court house began in December 1978 and was completed in 1980. Present at the start of the deposition were Laudig, Fletcher, and Steven Murphy representing Retail Credit. During the deposition, Fletcher continually asked me questions I didn't feel I needed to answer. Some of the interrogatories delivered to Eckman had never been answered, so I refused to answer based on the theory I was entitled to an answer from Eckman first. Fletcher told me that if I didn't answer, he would go out and get a judge to force me to answer. I said to Fletcher I saw a judge out in the hall a few minutes ago, and I'd go get the judge for him. I stood up and headed out the door. Fletcher told me to come back in the room and sit down. The deposition continued for about five hours. Then the deposition began again in 1980 with Laudig, Fletcher, and Johnstone representing Retail Credit, present. Johnstone was with the firm of Barnes and Hickam in Indianapolis. It continued for another five hours. This was his first appearance at any event, although his firm was the lead attorney from the very beginning of the slander trial. His firm's representation was withheld from me.)* Steven Murphy borrowed the typed deposition and had not returned it to the court prior to 1984.

December 21, 1978, Motion for default judgment against defendant Retail Credit filed.

December 28, 1978, Corrections to the Plaintiff's "Supplemental Reply and Response to Eckman and First Equity Motions to Dismiss" filed.

January 9, 1979, Comes now all parties by respective counsel and cause is submitted pending matter. Cause taken under advisement.

March 27, 1979, Comes now the court and being duly advised now overrules the motion to dismiss filed by Eckman and First Equity on November 14, 1978, and now sustains said defendant's motion to strike. Motion for more definite statement filed by defendants Eckman and First Equity is now sustained and Plaintiff is ordered to amend rhetorical paragraph 10 by interlineation on or before April 13, 1979. The court being duly advised now overrules defendant Retail Credit's motion to dismiss, motion to make more specific, and motion to strike heretofore filed on November 28, 1978. All defendants are now given until May 4, 1979 to respond to plaintiff's third amended complaint.

April 17, 1979. Motion to withdraw appearance filed by Stephen Laudig, attorney for plaintiff, requesting withdrawal of M. Daniel Friedland as counsel of record herein. Motion granted.

April 18, 1979, Plaintiff's amendment by interlineation of paragraph 10 of third amended complaint pursuant to court order, filed.

May 4, 1979, Defendant Retail Credit's answer to plaintiff's third amended complaint filed.

May 9, 1979, Defendant's answer to plaintiff's third amended complaint for slander and libel filed.

May 18, 1979, Plaintiff's first set of interrogatories to Defendant First Equity Security Life Insurance Company filed along with Plaintiff's first request for production of documents to Defendant First Equity Security Life Insurance Company filed.

June 8, 1979, Plaintiff's first set of interrogatories to defendant Retail Credit (Equifax) on third amended complaint filed. Plaintiff's first request for production of documents to defendant James Eckman filed. Plaintiff's request for production of documents by defendant Retail

Credit (Equifax) based upon third amended complaint filed. Plaintiff's first set of interrogatories to defendant James Eckman filed.

June 14, 1979, Defendant First Equity's motion for extension of time filed.

June 18, 1979, Defendant First Equity's motion for extension of time granted and said defendant is given to and including July 29, 1979 in which to file a responsive pleading. All per written order.

June 27, 1979, Plaintiff's notice of correction filed.

July 11, 1979, Defendant Retail Credit's motion for leave to file amended answer filed together with said defendant's response to plaintiff's request for production of documents and answer to plaintiff's first set of interrogatories.

July 17, 1979, Plaintiff's motion to compel responses to plaintiff's interrogatories and requests production. Motion to strike and for relief filed and granted.

July 18, 1979, Plaintiff's motion to strike or deny defendant Retail Credit's motion for leave to file an amended answer filed.

July 23, 1979, Amended response of defendant Retail Credit Co. to plaintiff's request for production of documents filed together with said defendant's response to plaintiff's motion to strike and supplemental answers to plaintiff's first set of interrogatories.

July 31, 1979, Defendant Retail Credit's supplemental answers to plaintiff's first set of interrogatories filed.

August 6, 1979, Defendant James Eckman's answers to interrogatories of plaintiff filed together with response to request for production and interrogatories and objections to request for production. Defendant First Equity's answers to interrogatories filed together with response to request for production, objection to interrogatories and objections to request for production filed. Request for hearing filed by Defendant Eckman and First Equity Security Life Insurance Company.

August 21, 1979, Notice of defendant Retail Credit to take deposition of plaintiff filed.

August 29, 1979, Plaintiff, by counsel, files motion to strike answer and enter judgment against defendant Retail Credit. Cause set for hearing on Plaintiff's motion and on defendant's objections at 2:00 p.m., September 18, 1979.

September 10, 1979, Defendant's (First Equity Life Insurance Company) first request for production of documents filed.

September 12, 1979, Motion of plaintiff's to compel defendant James Eckman to answer interrogatories and for further relief filed.

September 14, 1979 Plaintiff's motion to compel defendant First Equity Security Life Ins. Co. to answer plaintiff's interrogatories and to strike certain answers and for other relief filed.

September 18, 1979, Defendant Retail Credit's memorandum in response of said defendant to plaintiff's motion to strike answer and enter default judgment. Parties appear by counsel, cause submitted on all pending matters, arguments heard. Cause taken under advisement.

October 10, 1979, Plaintiff's response to defendant's first request for production filed. Defendant's supplemental memorandum on pending matters filed.

November 9, 1979, Defendant's supplemental memorandum on pending matters filed.

November 26, 1979, Plaintiff's motion for extension of time to reply to defendant's supplemental motion on pending matters filed.

November 28, 1979, Plaintiff's motion for extension granted, all as per written order.

December 14, 1979, Plaintiff Reginald L. Jensen's motion to strike defendant First Equity's supplemental memorandum on pending matters filed.

January 4, 1980, Motion for pre-trial conference filed.

January 8, 1980, Plaintiff's motion for pre-trial conference is sustained and cause is assigned pre-trial conference at 3:00 p.m. on March 20, 1980, all as per written order.

March 20, 1980, Plaintiff's motion to strike First Equity memorandum is overruled. Plaintiff's motion to strike answer and for default judgment against Retail Credit is overruled. Plaintiff's motion to compel answers to interrogatories is overruled. Defendant Retail Credit's motion for leave to file amended answer is overruled. *Cause assigned for trial by jury commencing at 9:00 a.m. on October 27, 1980.* Parties directed to complete all discovery, including depositions, interrogatories, production and exchange of final witness and exhibit lists by August 18, 1980.

April 2, 1980, Defendant Retail Credit Company's supplemental to its answer to plaintiff's interrogatory #4 filed.

April 24, 1980, Plaintiff's second set of interrogatories to defendant First Equity filed.

April 30, 1980, Plaintiff's requests for admissions to defendant First Equity filed.

May 19, 1980, Defendant First Equity's objection to request for admissions No. 22 filed.

May 28, 1980, Response of First Equity to plaintiff's request for admissions filed.

June 13, 1980, Plaintiff's motion to compel answers to plaintiff's second set of interrogatories to defendant First Equity filed. Motion granted and defendant First Equity is ordered to answer the interrogatories submitted to them through their attorney on or before June 23, 1980, and serve copy of same on plaintiff's counsel. All as per written order.

June 17, 1980, Defendant First Equity's request for extension of time filed.

June 20, 1980, Comes now Robert P. Johnstone and Charles E. Bruess, attorneys, and file written appearance for defendant Equifax, Inc. (formerly Retail Credit Co.) *(The Indianapolis firm of Barnes and Hickam finally filed their appearance in the action.)*

June 25, 1980, Defendant First Equity's answers to Plaintiffs' second set of interrogatories filed.

July 17, 1980, Defendant Retail Credit's motion to reconsider and motion for leave to amend answer filed.

July 21, 1980, Defendant Retail Credit's motion to reconsider and motion for leave to file amendment granted and Retail Credit granted leave to file amended answer. All per written order.

July 23, 1980, Amended answer of Defendant Retail Credit Company to plaintiff's third amended complaint filed.

August 4, 1980, Defendants Eckman and First Equity Security's motion for partial summary judgment and memorandum in support of said motion filed together with defendant First Equity's supplemental answer to plaintiff's interrogatory #22. Plaintiff given to and including August 22, 1980, in which to file responsive pleading to defendant's motion for partial summary judgment.

August 15, 1980, <u>Defendant's motion to strike jury demand</u> and brief in support of said motion together with appendix to brief in support. Plaintiff's motion for relief of entry of 9/30/74 filed together with plaintiff's response to defendant's First Equity and James Eckman's motion for summary judgment, cross motion for default judgment, and motion to publish depositions of James Eckman and plaintiff's interrogatories to Retail Credit Corp. Comes now the court by Special Judge Johnson and sets this matter for hearing on all pending motions on September 5, 1980, at 1:00 p.m.

August 18, 1980, Plaintiff's motion for relief of entry of August 26, 1975 filed.

August 20, 1980, Witness list of Retail Credit filed together with exhibit list.

August 21, 1980, Defendant's First Equity and James Eckman's list of exhibits and witness list filed.

August 26, 1980, Plaintiff's petition for extension of time to submit lists filed. Plaintiff's witness list and exhibit list filed.

August 28, 1980, Defendant's reply to motions for relief from entry filed together with plaintiff's response to pending motion for summary judgment and response to cross-motion for default judgment (H.I.).

August 29, 1980, <u>Plaintiff's motion to strike or deny defendant's motion to strike jury demand.</u>

September 4, 1980, Defendant's reply brief in support of the motion to strike plaintiff's jury demand.

September 5, 1980, Plaintiff's supplemental submissions in support of plaintiff's opposition to motion for summary judgment filed. Come now the parties, by respective counsel, cause submitted for argument on defendant's motion for partial summary judgment, plaintiff's response thereon, plaintiff's motion for default judgment and defendant's motion to strike jury demand. Argument heard. Cause taken under advisement. Parties directed to file any trial briefs or proposed preliminary instructions prior to trial.

September, 8, 1980, Plaintiff's witness list filed.

September 15, 1980, Answers and objections of Retail Credit Company to plaintiff's interrogatories 21 through 26 filed.

September 17, 1980, Affidavit of plaintiff's personal service of subpoena filed.

September 24, 1980, Comes now the Court and being duly advised now sustains Defendant's motion to strike jury demand, overrules defendant's motion for partial summary judgment, overrules plaintiff's motion for default judgment.

> *(Robert Johnstone asked to strike the jury based upon a ruling in Jameson v. McCaffry, 300 NE 2nd, 889, 891, 892. This case says a party waives his right to a jury if the request isn't filed within 10 days of the filing of the suit. A jury trial was requested by me immediately after filing the suit, within the 10 day period. Johnstone said that didn't apply since the case was dismissed and the complaint was amended. It was still the same lawsuit with the same court file number. Laudig presented the same argument to Judge Johnson that was offered by Robert Johnstone, using McDonald v. Miller 242 NE 2d 39 (1968) at 42. Page 42 (2) says, "A demand for trial by jury may not be withdrawn without the consent of all parties." This case did not extend to the withdrawal of the right of a jury trial. Jameson superseded McDonald. Laudig made a false argument by referring back to the case that had been superseded and not arguing that the original jury request still applied. Neither case applied because amended complaints don't require new jury demands each time an amendment has been filed. Judge Johnson knew Laudig was working against my interests. Judge Johnson had authorized amending the complaint)*

September 29, 1980, Written appearance of plaintiff pro-se as co-counsel herein filed together with plaintiff's additional exhibits and witnesses list. Subpoenas issued to various persons.

October 2, 1980, Affidavits of service of subpoenas and supplemental witness lists filed.

October 3, 1980, Affidavit of service of subpoenas.

October 6, 1980, Defendant Retail Credit's notice of taking testimony deposition of J. L. Eckman filed.

October 7, 1980, Plaintiff's notice of withdrawal of appearance of plaintiff, pro se, filed by Laudig.

October 10, 1980, Defendant James Eckman's motion to quash subpoena duces tecum[20] filed. Defendant Retail Credit Co's notice of taking testimonial depositions filed.

October 15, 1980, Defendant Retail Credit Co's notice of taking testimonial depositions filed.

October 20, 1980, Defendants motion to withdraw defendant's motion to quash subpoena duces tecum filed.

A "trial" is about to begin.

It's time to go back to October 28, 1975, when Friedland re-filed the December contract case in Anderson. It became *Jensen v. First Equity Security Life Insurance Company, Madison* County cause number S-75-828. There was a ten year statute of limitations on contract actions in Indiana, so it could be re-filed any time up to 1981. Nothing happened from March 1976, to March 1977, even though everything necessary was ready for trial and presentation of damages. The contract, the calculation of commissions, and the expert testimony, were all ready. The only thing needed was an estimate of the value of commissions on the annuity contracts. Remember, the case did go to trial before Judge

---

[20] A command to a witness to produce documents. A writ or process of the same kind as the subpoena ad testificandum, including a clause requiring the witness to bring with him and produce to the court, books, papers, etc., in his hands, tending to elucidate the matter in issue.

Cox in 1972 when Dietzen failed to enter the contracts into evidence. The case was ready for trial each and every year thereafter. The judge could determine damages by adding up the premiums and calculating commissions because no facts were in dispute. The only thing that needed to be done after Tuohy had convinced Judge Cox to correct the dismissal from with prejudice to with prejudice as to the theory of specific performance was to set a new trial date and properly present the accounting to the court. All Friedland needed to do was set the trial date. This would probably be the easiest lawsuit he would ever handle. Yet, he did absolutely nothing.

In 1978, I continued to pressure Laudig to take action on the contract case. Laudig refused to demand setting a trial date. He drafted a motion which he said would force action. His motion only set the stage for more motions and arguments for the courts to handle. Fletcher filed his own motions for change of judge and a summary judgment. Now we went through the same routine that we went through in the slander case. There are pages and pages of entries on the docket sheets showing the court filings. I won't repeat everything here because you've seen part of the slander docket sheets. The docket sheets in the contract case were just as full and cumbersome. There were motions to produce, responses, motions to compel, two motions for summary judgment by FESLIC, and motions for extension of time. Judge Davis resigned from the contract action on March 15, 1978. Judge Hays was then appointed to serve as special judge. Judge Hays refused to serve and never assumed jurisdiction. The Supreme Court next appointed Judge Mario Pieroni of Delaware County (Muncie) as the Special Judge.

Pieroni was blind. He had a secretary who would read all of the papers to him and he relied on the attorney's verbal arguments before ruling. On July 21, 1978, Judge Pieroni held a hearing on a motion to determine the span of time my contract would cover for commissions to be paid on policies issued by FESLIC. Fletcher was attempting to reduce and restrict the commissions on the contract even further. Fletcher and Laudig met privately in the judge's chambers. Laudig came out and told me he had acceded to Fletcher's demands. Judge Pieroni issued an order limiting the contract commission dates to commencing December 1, 1970, and ending on December 19, 1971. I was furious with Laudig. I insisted over and over again that the contract should be enforced according to the terms beginning with the first word on the first page and ending with the last word on the last page. The contract was clear and approved by the board of directors. Laudig said he agreed to the restriction because he wanted to bring the case to conclusion. Now what could I do? Friedland was somewhere in New Jersey, Laudig was caving in to Fletcher, and it seemed impossible for me to find another attorney who would represent my position.

Judge Pieroni reaffirmed my right to a jury trial and affirmed all issues were now settled except damages. On October 11, 1978, he caused to be written in the order book "It appearing that this cause is now at issue and ready for trial by jury, except for pretrial conference, but that the judge's calendar is already crowded with settings, so that it will be impossible to dispose of this matter prior to January 1, 1979,..." and then he withdrew because he was retiring and he soon left Indiana.

Daryl Dean had calculated the amount due, including renewal commissions, on the ordinary life policies only. Credit life and accident commissions were excluded by the contract, but annuities were not. Dean never calculated the commission value of the annuities because of the speculative nature of the annuity contracts. He could make a reasonable estimate, but he said he would do that only upon order of the Court. (Based upon my calculations the annuity commissions covering the identical time span had the potential to exceed $500,000. All options in the annuities would have to be exercised for this amount to be due. The same lapse assumptions used for the life policies, which were high, could be applied to the annuity contracts. Those assumptions would mean the amount due from annuities were approximately $300,000.) In any event, Laudig's interests were not compatible with my interests and no one paid any attention to the actuary's professional work.

In November 1978 I met with an employment placement firm in Anderson, gave them my work history and said I wanted to make a change from the radio station, perhaps to a station in Indianapolis or another large Indiana city. They advised me to return to insurance full time. I had no interest in returning to selling insurance full time until my problems with FESLIC were settled. They said a large insurance company needed agents and would make me an attractive offer and suggested I at least hear what the company had to say. I agreed to listen. Roger Warrum was a district manager for Massachusetts Mutual Life Insurance Company (MassMutual) in Anderson. Warrum was about my age or a little younger. He was my height, had a ruddy complexion and broad shoulders. He had a quick mind and he was an excellent salesman. (He was later elected to the Anderson City Council.) He had requested the placement firm to search for potential insurance agents. I met with Warrum and told him about my current employment with Eastern Broadcasting Company and my desire to find other employment, perhaps in the radio business in some other town. I explained my history and background in the insurance business, including the fact I had been president of a small life insurance company in Oregon and that I was engaged in several lawsuits with a life insurance company in Anderson. I explained I had no interest in joining another insurance company until the controversy was settled. My meeting with him was only at the request of the placement firm. Warrum said to me it was the policy of MassMutual to promote from within. He said the current president of the company was a former agent and general agent in Indiana who had worked his way up. He said I could also be promoted to the home office and eventually be considered for senior management and it was possible to even become president. I asked him what was necessary on my part to be advanced to the home office and he said I would have to produce enough business to validate my contract and demonstrate that I was trustworthy and responsible. He said my previous management experience was a plus.

I decided to look into the arrangement a little further. We went to Indianapolis and met with the Indiana General Agent, Tom Garrison. Garrison was a tall, broad, and heavier person. He was also a couple of years older than me. He seemed to have a lot of self-confidence. The Indianapolis Agency was located in Northeast Indianapolis in an area known as Keystone Crossing. MassMutual rented a large office area with the staff workers placed behind a counter as a person enters the room. The agents had offices to the right of the counter and down a hall. Garrison had a large corner office to the left of the entry. Garrison and I had a lengthy conversation in his office about my background and history and the potential with MassMutual. He affirmed the current president of MassMutual was a former agent from Indiana. He said this was an agents' company, the agents moved into upper management so that it would always be driven to support the policyholders. He said since the president came from the Indiana agency force, I would have an opportunity to advance to the home office in Springfield, Massachusetts. He said for my part, as a start, I would have to come up with at least 300 names of people I could contact for the purpose of discussing life insurance. If so, I would be hired under Warrum's jurisdiction. I went back to Anderson and completed the list of 300 people. Warrum and I then went back to Indianapolis and met with Garrison again. Garrison hired me, effective January 1979.

MassMutual was required to research my background as the other companies had done. They were required to check with Eckman and FESLIC, Transamerica and any other employer. The background check would have been ordered through Retail Credit Company (which was now named Equifax) because it was by far the largest character evaluation company in the United States. The records it possessed on individuals were probably three times more extensive than its nearest competitor. The normal process would be for the home office in Springfield, Massachusetts to complete the evaluation and to relay the results to Garrison. A copy of the investigative report would be made available to Garrison and be placed into my personnel file. No one at MassMutual provided me with any information they received regarding my background.

After signing the contract with MassMutual, I advised Butler and Shapiro that I was leaving EBC. When I met with Butler I asked him to pay me whatever commissions I had earned. He said he would. My final check included only the commissions on commercials that had been aired up to the date I left. I told Butler I thought I was entitled to commissions on any contracts I had obtained that were signed and in force. My records showed the radio stations still owed me $3,000. He didn't agree. He said I was only entitled to commissions on commercials that had aired up to the day I left. Laudig agreed to file suit on my behalf against EBC demanding payment of $3,000 in commissions. Using the discovery process he obtained the WHUT and WLHN records showing the commissions they had recorded as belonging to me. They abruptly stopped showing credits to my account right in the middle of February, during the month after I left. Their records showed they owed $3,000 to me covering only part of the contracts I had obtained for the stations. Those commissions were assigned to my name.

The Indiana Supreme Court appointed Judge J. Brandon Griffis of Wayne County Superior Court Number 1 (Richmond), to take over the contract case. Judge Griffis assumed jurisdiction on November 9, 1978. He set a pre-trial conference for February 20, 1979. On February 22, 1979, he set trial for May 10, 1979. On March 1 he severed the issues and set a hearing by the court for May 10 as to the issue of the interpretation of the word policies. Judge Pieroni had already settled this issue. Martin Fletcher wasn't satisfied restricting the contract commission dates; he wanted to eliminate the annuities from the commissions payable by requesting the judge to decide annuities are not policies. Annuities issued by insurance companies have always been, are now, and always will be policies. The word policies means contracts. The only policies excluded were credit life and credit accident and health. More motions and requests were filed by Laudig and Fletcher.

Judge Griffis used May 10 to hear motions and other arguments in the courthouse in Anderson. After the hearing he set a new trial date for July 23. On July 23, 1979, Fletcher said he'd agree to a jury trial if the annuities were removed. I refused. The annuities were the only reason for a jury to determine values. Even if Fletcher honestly believed the annuities were to be excluded, that would be a fact issue to be presented to a jury. Fletcher and Laudig then agreed to another hearing before the judge. Laudig came out of the hearing and asked me again if I would remove the annuities from consideration. I refused again.

Judge Griffis decided to have a hearing on the issue of whether or not an annuity is a policy. When it came time to call witnesses, the money I had given to Laudig for the witness fee escrow account wasn't there. He had converted the funds to his own personal use and couldn't come up with $100.00. I had to find additional funds for subpoenas and witness fees. That hearing began August 13 and lasted until August 15, 1979. Both sides presented witnesses. An actuary other than Dean represented me and swore annuities were policies. Fletcher offered no proof or any other evidence that the annuities were not policies. His main argument was Eckman didn't intend to pay commissions on the annuities. Judge Griffis made sure every document, deposition, and piece of paper available was entered into the record. The file record for appeal now consisted of thousands of pages. Laudig told the judge the case could probably be settled without trial if the annuities were withdrawn from the commissionable policies. With that concession, Judge Griffis issued a finding that the annuities were not commissionable.

By now the words written on the contract meant nothing. The life insurance policies issued between December 1, 1970, and December 19, 1971, were the only policies to be included in the commission calculations due to me. The net effect of Judge Griffis' ruling was to eliminate the jury requirement and leave the issue to be resolved as the amount due to me from First Equity. Daryl Dean had calculated that amount to be $114,056 in 1972. Dean's sworn statement and all of his detailed accounting had been in the hands of Fletcher, FESLIC, and my attorneys since 1972. All Laudig needed to do now was to demand payment, plus interest. I told Laudig to take Dean's affidavit to Fletcher and collect the money. Laudig said Fletcher didn't believe Dean, so he, Laudig, wouldn't pursue it. I reminded Laudig that Dean is an actuary and his testimony had more value than Fletcher's, but my words fell on deaf ears. Laudig told me Fletcher maintained a consistent position that the entire amount I was entitled to receive was $10,000. There was a huge gap between what Dean had calculated and what Fletcher insisted was due to me.

Laudig now felt he was entitled to any fees that might be paid as a result of any settlement. He said he should be paid $4,000 if settlement was for $10,000. He claimed he could get FESLIC to settle for $15,000, which he thought would earn $6,000 for him. He also wanted to reach a compensation agreement with me directly and to abandon Friedland. Friedland had already been paid $4,000 and he had done no work on the settlement of the Anderson Agency contract. I reminded Laudig the payment was an advance for future work. If Laudig arranged a $10,000 settlement and was paid $4,000 that would be in addition to the $4,000 I had already paid. It's easy to see why Friedland had no interest in doing any additional work; he could see no benefit to him if Fletcher was correct as to the amount due. I told Laudig the only arrangement I would make would be to recognize him as an attorney who assumed the Friedland agreement. He agreed and said he would obtain a release from Friedland. He then proceeded to remove Friedland as my counsel.

Laudig and I debated whether or not he really understood the law and if he really knew what he was doing. It seemed to me I had been doing an inordinate amount of research compared to his research. After awhile, it seemed to get his goat. He took me to the law library at the Indianapolis courthouse, which was reserved for attorneys only, and asked me to wait for a few minutes while he went back into the stacks of law books. He returned about an hour later with more than a dozen books citing relevant cases on slander issues. He wanted to demonstrate to me he did know what he was doing. That raised the question in my mind over again. If he knew how to practice law, why didn't he do it?

The dramatic changes in our lives created serious strains on the relationship between Dorothy and me. Dorothy was receiving no attention or the recognition she was entitled to receive for her contribution to the family. She was ignored by me because I had placed the lawsuits in a position of higher need. I was spending all of my time working, reading law books, or managing our budget, because our money was so tight. Cindy's college costs needed to be solved and we didn't have any extra money. Cindy was financing a large part of her college and living expenses at Purdue University, but we also contributed to her support. All of my extra money was being paid to Steve Laudig or in legal expenses. Every penny had to be accounted for, even down to the pennies used in the parking meters. Dorothy told me in January 1979 she was returning to Salt Lake City, alone. She said she would leave in June 1979. She was sick and tired of the lawsuits, the fraud and deception we were dealing with and the strain it caused on our marriage. She had enough and wanted to get away from it. I asked her to stay in Anderson for one more year to help me with finances; she agreed.

In December 1979 I expected a substantial commission check, but there were charge-backs against my account that had not been revealed to me by Garrison. I received no payment from Mass Mutual that month. I borrowed against my credit cards to buy food, pay the rent, and buy presents. We had $18.00 available from all sources on December 15, 1979. There were very few presents and Christmas was miserable. That was a month I'll never forget.

All through 1979 Garrison acted in a duplicitous manner. He would send me letters of commendation on MassMutual stationery and would send me negative remarks in personal notes. I finally told Warrum I had no interest in talking directly to Garrison. Warrum said he would act as the intermediary. Just before Christmas 1979, Dorothy and I received a postcard from Garrison that said in large red ink "Merry Christmas to you and to all a good night. Let this be the first card & the last you ever get from me. Tom" Dorothy and I wondered about the nature of the people I was working for.

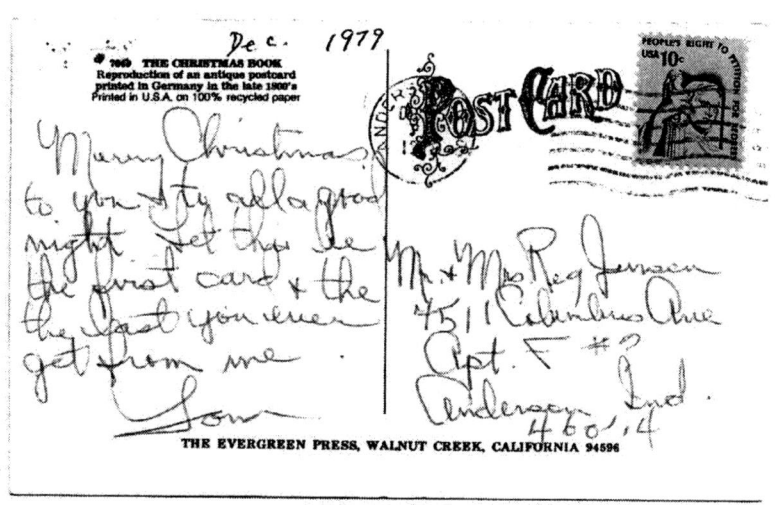

On January 9, 1980, Garrison mailed a letter to me closing with "Your anniversary gives me the opportunity to tell you at least once a year how pleased I am to have you represent our company and the agency."[21] Then again on February 1, 1980, Garrison mailed a letter to me with the closing "Keep up the good work – you have a great future ahead with the Mass and this agency." He said I was entitled to be paid my extra compensation and he was sending it to me. I had to wonder what was wrong with this man. It seemed as though he found it impossible to be straightforward with me.

---

MASSACHUSETTS MUTUAL LIFE INSURANCE COMPANY
SPRINGFIELD, MASSACHUSETTS 01111

THOMAS C. GARRISON, C.L.U., GENERAL AGENT
SUITE 260
9000 KEYSTONE CROSSING
INDIANAPOLIS, INDIANA 46240

(317) 844-7711

February 1, 1980

Mr. Reginald L. Jensen
Anderson, Indiana

Dear Reg:

You wrote to Lee regarding payment of your TAS. She brought the matter to my attention because she knew I would want to take this opportunity to tell you that I am well aware of the fine job you are doing and am proud of you.

For this reason, I am happy to tell you that I have sent the formal request to Home Office to release your TAS -- both the TAS "A" which has been held in reserve and "B" as it becomes available.

Perhaps Roger didn't tell you, but we could not request payment to you of the accumulated TAS "A" until the end of your first year of financing. Your financing started on February 1, 1979. I anticipate we will receive this in time for it to come through on your next check.

Keep up the good work -- you have a great future ahead with the Mass and this agency.

Cordially,

Thomas C. Garrison, CLU
General Agent

TCG:lh

cc: Roger J. Warrum
    District Manager

---

[21] On September 2, 2009, attorney Dorothy Varon said that MassMutual refuses to allow me to use any MassMutual information in the book and that they would vigorously defend any negative comments.

Then on March 28, 1980, Garrison complains about my production even though he had recently admitted I was ahead of schedule in sales and earnings. He completes his complaint saying "We are counting on you to devote your time to this business — not the business of 10 years ago."

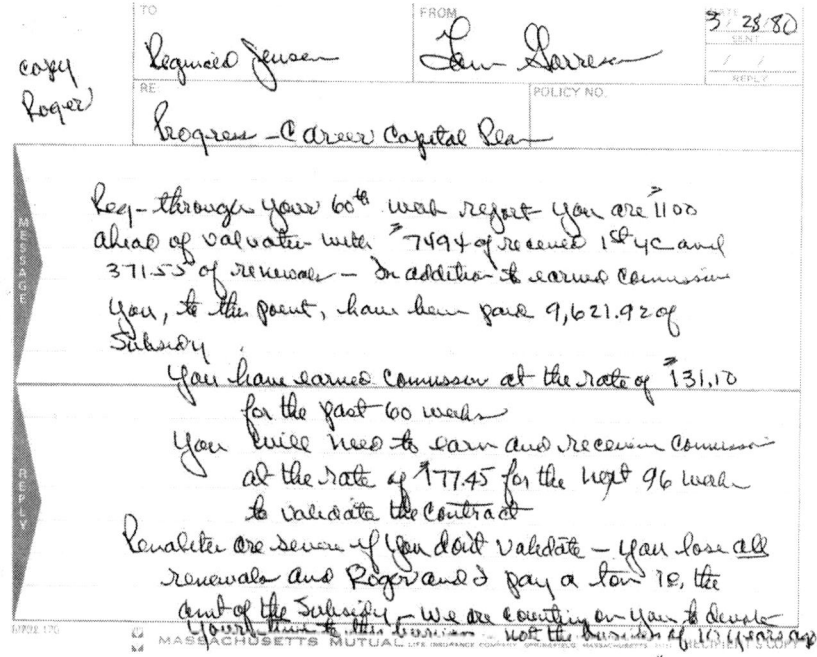

First, Garrison insults me and my wife and suggests he hopes I disappear into the woodwork. Then he says I'm doing a great job. The "great job" I did for him was during 1979, before he mailed the Christmas card to me and my wife. Finally, he says he wants me to work harder for him and to forget what's happened to me in the last 10 years. What benefit would it be to him if I dropped the lawsuits? But will he ever keep his commitment to me?

Judge Griffis held another hearing on May 16, 1980. Fletcher, Laudig and I met in Judge Griffis' courtroom in Wayne County Superior Court in Richmond, Indiana. It was a very large room. The attorney's tables were a long way from the judge's bench. It felt like we were in an empty chamber. Fletcher argued strongly that his accounting process should be accepted. Laudig said nothing. It was my argument that an actuary had already calculated the amount due and he, Judge Griffis, and Fletcher still had all of the records in their possession. It was my position the actuary's records would be more reliable than Fletcher's. Fletcher insisted he wouldn't accept Dean's calculations because the results were too high. Judge Griffis asked me to accept Fletcher's offer because he and Fletcher were just trying to bring the litigation to an end. *(Judge Griffis recognized his error and instructed the court reporter to remove his comments from the record, which she did.)* I told Judge Griffis he was mistaken and that, even if I accepted Fletcher's offer to calculate the amount due using his own calculation methods, FESLIC still wouldn't pay. Frustrated, Judge Griffis told us to work it out. He said he might not set another hearing or trial for several more years, if ever.

In June 1980, I drove Dorothy to Salt Lake City, Utah. She moved in with her parents in their small, two bedroom home. Dorothy bought a car with the retirement account money she received from her employer, the Madison County Department of Public Welfare. She found a job in Salt Lake City and went to work while living with her parents.

October 27, 1980, trial in the slander action begins before Judge Johnson. Laudig introduced evidence of slanders occurring on September 23, 1971; October 12, 1971; October 22, 1971; January 24, 1972; and July 14, 1972. *Laudig enters only information as to slander dates that had been dismissed previously and made no mention of preserving "relation back" provisions for dates that are concerned with the amended complaints.* Laudig then closed his case in chief.

*Laudig did very little discovery because Tuohy did nearly all of it. The Statute of Limitations on any slander that occurred prior to July 1973 had already expired by July 1975 based upon the Amended Complaint. Claiming the slanders occurred on September 23, 1971; October 12, 1971; October 22, 1971; and January 24, 1972, was making the claim nine years after the events occurred. Only one of these dates was cited in any of the complaints filed in court and that was July 14, 1972. Each publication or new publication is a new cause of action. Tuohy discovered those events. He should have told me about them. He should have included them in the Amended Complaint and be prepared to prove the date of discovery. The additional occurrences are important because there could be difficulties with witnesses in one or more events. I only had to prove I was slandered once and that I sued within two years of the date of the occurrence. The other dates show a pattern of conduct. The July 14, 1972, date was certainly within two years of the filing of the complaint on July 28, 1972. The July 14 date is the date Eckman gave the information to Retail Credit. July 21 was the date Retail Credit passed it on to Franklin National Life. No attorney ever introduced evidence or even a statement as to the date of discovery of any occurrence of slander or libel. July 14, 21, and 28, 1972, needed to be tied together, but never were.*

*Laudig never advanced the argument the dates presented at trial were within the statute of limitations based upon the filing of the original complaint. He never argued the original suit should not have been dismissed and thus submit evidence that would apply on appeal. He failed to submit evidence as to the slanders and libels that occurred August 2, 1972, (filed in the second amended complaint), or in January 1973, both of which were within the statute of limitations based on the second amended complaint. Every single slander occurrence presented at trial by Laudig was beyond the statute of limitations based on the July 19, 1974, filing of the Amended Complaint. His entire case-in-chief applied only to issues that were not before the court based upon the previous dismissals that had been entered. It was simply a bogus trial.* Canon 7 (EC 7-23), of the Indiana Canon of Ethics for attorneys said "The adversary system contemplates that each lawyer will present and argue the existing law in the light most favorable to his client." This Canon meant nothing.

October 31, 1980, Plaintiff rests. Defendants move for involuntary dismissal. Motions taken under advisement.

November 17, 1980. Judgment entered for all defendants.

*Judge Johnson ruled all of my claims against First Equity and Eckman were barred by the statute of limitations.* <u>*Judge Johnson ruled the slander action was filed on July 19, 1974, not July 28, 1972.*</u> *Amendments never change the date the action was filed in any court. If the date of the amended complaint was the critical date of filing a complaint then the date of the last amendment would be the date the action was filed. The last-amended complaint was filed on October 27, 1978. The conclusion that a complaint is filed on the date an amended complaint is filed is ludicrous. Nevertheless, that's what the defendants argued and that's how the judge ruled. Judge Johnson issued a separate ruling that Retail Credit didn't perform the slander, only that they acted as an agent for First Equity and Eckman. Judge Johnson ruled Retail Credit did nothing to damage me. He ruled Retail Credit had a qualified privilege to publish the reports. This was Tuohy's original position. He also ruled the statute of limitations barred my action against Retail Credit.*

More motions had been filed by both parties in the contract action over the balance of the year and they were all ignored by Judge Griffis. We were at a stalemate in the contract action by December 1980. Laudig had lost the slander action and he was totally incompetent in his management of the contract action.

During this time, I would leave the Y or the spa after exercising and walk through the alleys on my way back to my car. Sometimes it would be light outside and sometimes dark. I had no concern about encountering someone who might be threatening to me; in fact I often hoped I'd meet up with someone who would threaten me. I was ready, willing, and able, for a fight to the death. It took many years for these feelings to ease.

There are two reasons why lawsuits are dragged out over time. The first reason is so the plaintiff will lose. The second reason is so one or both attorneys will be paid more money. The percentage of cases that can be completed within one year of filing is very high. Complicated cases are hard to find. Nearly every lawsuit can be reduced to one or two simple issues. If the issues haven't been reduced prior to trial, the pretrial conference is used to make that reduction.

*The courts don't take slander and libel suits seriously.* The courts don't believe a person should be compensated because that person's reputation has been damaged. They believe the spoken or written words will somehow fade away with no permanent damage done. The courts seem to believe the best thing to do is to dismiss the suits and let the parties fight it out somewhere else. It can be a duel on the East Coast or a gunfight at a corral out West. I read an article about people who are involved in libel and slander suits regarding their job performance, where their ability to earn a living is involved. The article pointed out that a very large percentage, approaching fifty percent, of those damaged by slander or libel that affects their ability to earn a living die before the suit has been resolved. The strenuous pressure applied by the persons or organizations doing the harm, for the purpose of avoiding payment, creates the result that the harmed person may never be able to obtain work for which he or she is qualified. These kinds of lawsuits bring out the fight-or-flight response in everyone involved.

After Judge Johnson dismissed the slander action I called Laudig and asked him if he was going to appeal. He told me there was no reason to appeal because there was no possibility of winning on appeal. Laudig said the judge zapped me and an appeal would be a waste of time. He said I had lost and I should try to get whatever I could out of the contract. He said I'd be lucky to get $9,000. It seemed to me Laudig didn't want to appeal the slander action because it might have been reversed and it might have exposed his conduct. Dietzen's position that Tuohy was still managing the suit seemed right on target.

I met Laudig in his office a few days later, on December 8. Upon entering his office I could see neatly placed boxes all around the walls of the office. I asked him what the boxes represented and he told me a person with a company in Texas, on the advice of Robert Johnstone (Retail Credit Company's counsel in the slander trial), asked him (Laudig) to sue a client of Johnstone's firm, Barnes & Hickam. Laudig said Johnstone represented the firm's client. Laudig said all he had to do was submit the papers to the court and the case would be settled. He told me the case was settled in 30 days and he was paid $5,000. He told me the $5,000 was more than he would ever receive on any settlement of my claims against FESLIC. He said he used that money to go to Chicago and spend an exciting weekend on the town.

I advised Laudig that, since he had decided there was no reason to appeal the loss of the slander action, I wanted to take over the case and file an appeal on my own. I gave a letter to him to memorialize our separation. He accepted the letter and didn't object, but said he wanted a chance to settle the cases before he officially withdrew because he thought he could earn a fee. We discussed what his role would be and the conditions of any settlement. He thought he could get a few dollars out of Retail Credit and he thought he could get Fletcher to make an offer. He said he could get $12,000 from FESLIC to settle the contract action and $3,000 out of Retail Credit if I do not appeal the slander action. I agreed to give him one more week and told him I would pay the full percentage referred to in the contract between Friedland and myself, when the actions were finally terminated, on any offer he received, whether or not I accepted the offer. It would be a full payment without regard to the amounts I had paid him in the past and without regard to the amount I had paid Friedland. He agreed. He immediately tried to call Fletcher on the phone but wasn't able to reach him. We agreed to meet one week later.

On December 8, 1980, I filed a withdrawal of appearance of counsel for plaintiff together with written appearance of myself, pro se, and a motion for mistrial, a motion to correct errors, and a certification to the supreme court for change of judge. My motions for mistrial and to correct errors were each respectively overruled.

When I returned to Laudig's office the following week, he said he had an offer to settle from EBC for $1,000 and that was the only offer he was able to obtain. He said he had no offer whatsoever from Fletcher on behalf of FESLIC and/or Eckman and no offer from Johnstone for Retail Credit. He said Johnstone told him I owned money to Retail Credit for costs. I had already paid Johnstone's firm the amount of money billed to me and saw no reason to pay any more. I agreed to send a check for $333.33 after receiving the money from EBC, we agreed we had now terminated our arrangement. I picked up my files and left. When I returned to Anderson I called EBC's attorney Miller and said I'd settle for $1,000. He agreed and arranged for me to receive payment.

On December 22, 1980, Laudig filed his motion for leave to withdraw appearance as my counsel. The motion was granted and his appearance was immediately ordered withdrawn. The judge prepared and signed the order.

On December 29, 1980, I filed a praecipe of the record in the slander action for the purpose of appeal. The clerk began the process of photocopying the record, which now consisted of thousands of pages of documents. It was a toss-up between the slander action and the contract action as to which had the greatest number of pages. It's normal for attorneys to agree which papers would be proper for appeal of a decision, but there would be no possibility of that happening in my situation. Any appeal that excludes what the Court of Appeals or the opposing attorney considers relevant will automatically be lost. So, every piece of paper had to be included.

Our daughter, Leslie, moved to Florida in 1978, and returned to Anderson in December 1980 to live with me. Shortly thereafter, Leslie said she would like to move to Salt Lake City and live with her mother. Dorothy agreed to a temporary arrangement. In January 1981, Dorothy found an apartment and waited until I brought Leslie and some of our belongings to Salt Lake City. I rented a truck and put all of our belongings in it except a chair, an old TV set, a cot to sleep on, and all of the files relating to the lawsuit. Some of the furniture wasn't worth shipping so I gave it away. We drove across the plains, over the Rocky Mountains, into Utah and Salt Lake City. We unloaded the household items at Dorothy's apartment. When we arrived, it was obvious Dorothy was much happier and felt more in control of her life. I stayed with them for a couple of days and then flew back to Indiana.

In January 1981, EBC delivered a check to attorney Miller. Miller met with me so I could sign releases and take the check. As soon as I received the money, I mailed a check to Laudig in the amount of $333.33.

The slander case files were being copied for appeal purposes; Judge Griffis had all but abandoned the contract case; no attorney would represent me; Fletcher wouldn't budge; Tuohy was still intent on my losing everything; money was even more scarce; my wife now lived in Utah; and I lived in a nearly bare apartment working for a general agent whose integrity had been brought into question. The bills, at a dollar a page, were adding up quickly with the court copying the papers for appeal, and there was no money to pay. The clock was running with the time for filing the appeal rapidly approaching.

Richard Roby, owner of Roby's Plumbing & Heating in Anderson, had purchased life insurance from me. Richard was shorter in height than me, a little heavier, several years younger, and he always had a smile on his face. But he was precise with money and individual responsibility. His mother, Frances, was a very nice woman who owned a small bathroom accessory store. She had purchased radio commercials from me on occasion. Richard's older brother, Daniel, was an attorney in Ft. Wayne, Indiana. I asked Richard if his brother might represent me. Richard said he would introduce me to his brother, but he didn't know whether or not Dan would be willing to work for me. Dan was older than Richard, taller, and a little more athletic appearing. I met with Dan and asked him to try to negotiate a settlement with Fletcher and FESLIC. Dan Roby said he would meet with Fletcher and report back, but he refused to become an attorney in the case. He made an appointment with Fletcher and met with him in Ft. Wayne. Fletcher showed Roby his own calculations of commissions due to me from FESLIC. Fletcher's calculations came to $10,000. Roby reported back to me that Fletcher would only offer $20,000. I told Roby the amount of money owed to me was much greater and that I wouldn't accept $20,000. That was the extent of his involvement. My reputation with attorneys in Anderson and some parts of Indianapolis was now at an all time low. I'm sure every attorney in Anderson and many in Indianapolis had heard about my various lawsuits and the inability to bring them to a close. My options were really limited.

Warrum had rented a large office in downtown Anderson and had rented some of his office space to his close friend Steve Clase, who was an attorney. Clase had a partner, Charles Braddock. Clase and Braddock were about the same age. Clase was slender and professional in appearance. Braddock was heavier and appeared to have more physical strength. They were both about six feet tall. The offices were on the main floor of a small building with each office placed next to each other going from front to back in a single row. The attorneys' offices were up front with Warrum. I shared a space with two other salesmen in the back. I asked Braddock to try to settle with Fletcher on my behalf. Braddock refused. It seemed to me that if Braddock refused, Clase would also refuse.

In the middle of January 1981, it was time to apply a different tactic, so I called Fletcher on the phone from my office. I asked him if he would discuss settling the cases directly with me. His response was that he had no interest in talking to me, he hated me, my actions had caused him and FESLIC much harm and undue litigation, and he would never talk to me about settlement any at time, any place, under any conditions. He said he couldn't stand to be in the same room with me. I asked him to forget for a moment that he hated me and to pretend he liked me and to try to approach talking to me as if I was a stranger who had never worked with him before. He should think of me as someone who could and would be reasonable if we could sit down together. He said it wasn't possible. I mentioned again that I was a reasonable person and I thought it was in our best interests to bring the litigation to an end. I asked him to think it over and I'd call him back in a day or two. I did call back a couple of days later. He was still reluctant to talk, but after awhile we were speaking to each other in a civilized manner. He agreed to discuss settlement and we made an appointment to meet several days later in his office.

In the meantime, Laudig came back into the picture again and wrote the following letter to me on February 3, 1981:

> Mr. Reginald L. Jensen
> 4511 Columbus, #F-39
> Anderson, IN 46014
>
> Dear Reg:
>
> Thank you very much for the Three Hundred Thirty Three Dollar and Thirty Three Cent check which was my part of the agreed upon settlement of Eastern Broadcasting Corporation's suit.
>
> If you will recall, prior to the first trial, it is my recollection that First Equity offered Twenty Two Thousand Dollars to settle that matter. It is my firm belief that they would offer Thirty Thousand Dollars for dismissal, both of the appeal in the defamation action and to settle the contract suit.
>
> My advice to you would be that rather than represent yourself which in all frankness, I believe that you are not competent to do, I suggest that you attempt to settle it on those terms. This is offered with the best of intentions because I believe that it is in your interests to get whatever you can out of this suit.
>
> Again, the best of luck.
>
> Sincerely yours,
>
> Stephen Laudig

SL/df

In his letter he tells me to settle for $30,000. It seemed strange to me that an attorney who could never get an offer to settle above $10,000 now advised me to obtain a settlement of $30,000, because I'm incompetent. He considered himself superior to me. It also seemed strange for the same attorney who conducted a bogus trial in the slander case now had my best interests at heart. Laudig had already said an appeal of the slander action had no value. If he were to engage in settlement negotiations he would need to prepare an appeal. There would be no reason for FESLIC or Retail Credit to negotiate a settlement of the slander action if they knew there would be no appeal of the loss. Why would an attorney tell his former client to settle for an amount which was three times the amount the attorney himself was never able to obtain, and to settle a possible appeal that he said had no value? To my knowledge at that time, FESLIC never offered $20,000 or $30,000. Laudig said at various times he could only get a $10,000 or $12,000 offer and now he says he once had an offer of $22,000. Why didn't he spend a little more time obtaining an offer from Fletcher for somewhere between the $22,000 and $30,000 which would have meant money in his pocket? I wondered if Laudig was sane. If he was sane, the $30,000 figure was given to him from someone who knew it to be reliable.

The 90 days permitted to file the appeal were running out. I checked with the Madison County Clerk to see how much of the file had been copied. She said she was only about half way through. I asked her what a party does if it takes more than 90 days to copy the file. She told me to ask the Court of Appeals for an extension of time. I called the office of the Clerk of the Court of Appeals and asked how to proceed. They said I should file a motion requesting an extension of time. On February 10, 1981, I filed the motion. The motion was granted and the time was extended to April 13, 1981. This gave me a few more days to try to figure out what to do when the court clerk gave me the bill for copying the files, which would be many thousands of dollars more than I had or could borrow.

Several days later I drove to Ft. Wayne and met with Fletcher in his office. His office was medium sized with ample room for clients to sit in front of his desk and talk to him. His desk was in the middle of the office with his back against the wall. We talked calmly for a few minutes. After about fifteen minutes we agreed to each personally calculate the amount due to me using his formula and including only the policies he selected. We would complete our calculations by ourselves. He insisted that all annuities and that all Special Expansion Contracts would be excluded from the calculations and that we would only include commissions on policies written up to the middle of December 1971. We jointly wrote out the formula to be used. Fletcher agreed to pay and I agreed to accept the final result. We agreed to meet the next week to confirm the results. I returned to Anderson and completed my calculations which brought the total amount due to more than $97,000. The following week we met in Fletcher's office. Fletcher asked me about my results and I gave him my results. His results matched mine. Fletcher said he couldn't believe it. He said he had calculated the amount due to me on his desk blotter back in 1972. The blotter was still on his desk. The amount he previously arrived at was $10,000. He said he now found errors in his blotter math. He had used his blotter results to successfully contradict my actuary's results when he confronted all of my attorneys. My attorneys accepted his erroneous calculations rather than the actuary's calculations.

Fletcher then said he wouldn't pay. He was going back on his word. I was stunned. I asked him why. He said he had told the FESLIC Board of Directors that their obligations amounted to only $10,000 and that he would be embarrassed to tell them differently now. I said "OK, let's do something different. Let's write settlement figures on slips of paper, such as $0, $25,000, $50,000, $100,000, $500,000, $1,000,000, then fold the papers, put them in a hat, go out in the street, and let a stranger pick the settlement out of the hat." He wouldn't agree.

I asked him what we could do now. He said he would be willing to change the formula and exclude some more policies, then recalculate, and pay that result. The problem with the Clerk in Anderson copying the files was lurking in the background with the meter running, so I agreed. We did the calculations ourselves once again and met a few days later. The result was in excess of $76,000. He refused to pay again. I was devastated. We talked some more and made one more adjustment in the calculation method and he agreed to pay this third result. I returned on February 27, 1981, with the result of $63,850.23. He absolutely refused to pay this third time.

I left his office feeling like the world's biggest fool. After returning to Anderson I wrote a letter to Judge Griffis, with a copy to Fletcher, explaining I offered to settle the lawsuit using Fletcher's own formula and that he still refused to settle. I reminded the judge of my statement to him making that very point. Fletcher countered by immediately mailing to Judge Griffis a motion and entry of Summary Judgment in his favor for the judge's signature. Several days later when I returned to my apartment there was a letter from Judge Griffis in my mailbox. I had no confidence whatsoever in Judge Griffis and had to either find some sort of solution or give up the fight after all these years. I sat down and read the letter expecting the worst. The judge denied Fletcher's summary judgment attempt, but he did set a trial date. The slander action files were still being copied. Would it now be possible to find an attorney who would and could help me in a trial of the contract action?

On March 3, 1981, the Indiana Supreme Court made a change in their case law regarding suing attorneys for malpractice. The case was *Shideler v. Dwyer*, 417 N.E. 2d 281 (Ind. 1981). It decided that the two year statute of limitations applies to legal malpractice. It said a cause of action for legal malpractice accrues, and the statute of limitations begins to run, before a determination is made that the attorney's services failed to have their intended effect. The time begins to run as of the date of the malpractice act. Robert D. MacGill (I believe he was Tuohy's son-in-law) analyzed the *Shideler* case for a law review article.[22] When is there a determination by the courts that the attorney's action didn't have the intended effect? According to *Shideler* it's after an appeal has been perfected and decided in the original suit which gave rise to the cause of action against the attorney. If the appeal results in a decision that the loss was a result of the attorney's conduct then the client has a cause of action. But the suit must be filed BEFORE this appellate determination. If a suit is filed against an attorney before the original suit has been decided by the appellate court the attorney's defense is that the suit is premature, it isn't ripe. The court will grant a dismissal in favor of the attorney defendant. Appeals take time, usually too much time. If more than two years has passed before the appellate determination is

---

[22] MacGill, Robert D., Comment. *Legal Malpractice*. The Indiana Law Review, Vol. 14:927. (1981)

made then the statute of limitations bars an action against the attorney. Attorneys engaged in malpractice in Indiana were absolutely protected. In other words, don't sue an attorney; you'll lose either in trial court or on appeal. You'll be filing your suit either too early or too late.

On March 9, 1981, my meetings with Fletcher were over. He had failed to keep his word three times. I had lost every lawsuit, was broke, depressed, alone in an apartment with no furniture, and deeply in debt with the debt increasing by the minute. There was no money to pay the court costs for copying the slander records for appeal purposes. This was in a town that produced nothing but misery, fraud, and deception, for me to deal with. I just sat in the apartment wondering what to do next. The next morning I went to the Court of Appeals in Indianapolis to find out what an appeal looks like and how to prepare one. No one in the Court of Appeals offices would tell me the procedure. They only showed me copies of briefs. The rules concentrated on the minutia, such as the size of type, the spacing, the location of specific sections, and other details. There was nothing about what kind of information that should be included and how to present it. It gave me no information on how to proceed and there was very little time left to learn. I would lose the appeal based on procedure. The Court of Appeals had granted an extension to April 13, 1981, and that date was fast arriving.

A couple of days later, on March 11, 1981, I received a large white envelope in the mail from Fletcher. It had an offer of settlement to pay me $50,000. I couldn't believe it. I called Fletcher and told him I'd accept the offer if it was $55,000 and if FESLIC would pay my remaining obligations based upon the lawsuits. He said OK. He said to just white out the 0 and change it to a 5, then sign it and send it back. I returned the acceptance letter to Fletcher. I still owed Daryl Dean's firm about $4,000. I called Dean and brought him up to date. I advised him to hold firm on the total amount due because Fletcher had agreed to pay it. Dean said he would. Money was also due to Dan Roby and several others.

When we met in Fletcher's office in Ft. Wayne on March 25 he presented an extensive settlement agreement for me to sign and delivered a $55,000 check. The amount being paid to Dean was less than the amount due. I asked Fletcher why there was a difference and he said

Dean agreed to come down in the amount. I explained to Fletcher what I had said to Dean. Fletcher's reply was that he likes to negotiate people down and he was successful. Fletcher now knew that if the case goes to trial FESLIC would probably receive a decision against them of at least $97,000, because that's what he calculated the amount to be. But I didn't give any thought to his position or any comparative results on my side. I was just glad to get out of the lawsuits with a little skin left. The agreement contained a confidentiality provision and it included each and every person against whom I might have a claim and who might have a claim against me. Confidentiality goes both ways. There's no sense in a requirement that I maintain confidentiality if anyone on the other side could reveal the agreement terms to those outside of the agreement.

I drove back to Anderson and called the Madison County Clerk to find out how much of the copying work her office had completed. She said they were still only about half way through. I asked her how much money was due if the case was settled and there was no need for her to proceed any further. She said nothing would owed if they did not deliver the entire file. I asked her to stop for the time being and said I'd call back if there was a reason to proceed. She agreed. The Clerk's office had completely ignored requests to copy the files for appeal purposes several times in the past. Were they really copying the files this time? This raised interesting questions for me. Suppose they were not able to complete copying the files by the April 13 date. What would happen then? Would the Court of Appeals grant a second extension?

It seemed to me that one of the most bazaar legal episodes conceivable had finally come to a close. The fraud, deception, collusion, and incompetence, by a total of 34 attorneys and judges designed to prohibit my recovery of any damages, and to prevent me from ever being reemployed in insurance company management, had accomplished most of the goals which were established by James Eckman in 1971. Some of the attorneys and judges had been well paid by someone; others only granted favors for their friends which appeared to me to be fraudulent conduct; several didn't take the time necessary to examine the pertinent facts. It seemed as though all of the legal battles were finished and I could go on with my life; perhaps put our marriage and family back together. My immediate plan was to move to California. But the most unique and unbelievable series of events lay ahead. Judicial deception, in all of its glory was about to raise its ugly head much higher than I believed to be possible.

On April 3, 1981, Laudig's partner and new member of the bar, Linda Zook, mailed a letter to me demanding $22,000 to be paid to Laudig as his fee for his settling my lawsuits. I wrote a letter to Zook stating that Laudig had not settled nor caused a settlement and that if he sued me I would file a counterclaim against him for malpractice. *This was the only document I ever created which contained the language saying I would file a counterclaim against Laudig for malpractice if he sued me.* Laudig then filed a lawsuit, *Laudig v. Jensen,* Madison County No. S581-260, against me on April 22, 1981, demanding $22,000 (40 percent of the settlement), plus quantum meruit.[23] The quantum meruit amount was based on 500 hours of legal work at a cost between $50 and $100 an hour. The total he demanded was more than $55,000. Linda Zook also filed a request in court to shorten the time for me to answer the complaint and she submitted interrogatories to me. I have no idea why Laudig wanted to shorten my time to answer, but no ruling on that motion ever happened. On May 27, 1981, Laudig filed liens against me in Madison County Circuit Court claiming $22,000 due. Judge Johnson struck the liens.

Assume for a moment that Laudig had arranged the $55,000 settlement. Our verbal agreement was that if he arranged any settlement I would pay him the amount specified in the agreement with Friedland. That percentage was one-third because the contract case never went to trial. There was a determination of the interpretation of words in the contract, but there was never a trial on the amount due. The slander action went to trial, but the result was a loss and Laudig never filed an appeal. Since Laudig had withdrawn from the slander suit it was a clear signal to Fletcher that Laudig had no intention of appealing that loss. The contract specified 40 percent at trial, but 40 percent of nothing is nothing. The only logical position could have been based upon a settlement. The correct dollar amount would have been one-third of $55,000 or $18,333.33. The only real issue for settlement discussions at this point by Laudig was the contract action which Fletcher set at $10,000 in the settlement agreement. If any settlement discussion between Laudig and Fletcher exceeded the $10,000 figure it would only

---

[23] A demand for payment based upon the merits of his performance.

be an amount which included the value to FESLIC for terminating the litigation. Fletcher won every point in court, so terminating the litigation wasn't much of an incentive to him.

This lawsuit was thrust upon me by unscrupulous attorneys. My options were to give Laudig $22,000 and hope that he wouldn't demand more; or to defend the suit and either lose everything or pay him nothing. I decided to fight. It seemed to me that I need not be present for most of the legal process in preparation for trial. My intent was to let the attorneys handle the lawsuits and move to California. I had gone through enough pain and suffering in Indiana.

I advised Garrison of my desire to move to California and transfer to a MassMutual Agency in that state. I had earned enough commissions to completely repay the total financing commitment. The financing started at a high level the first three months of employment with Mass Mutual. The financing amount reduced every three months until it equaled zero at the end of the third year. The general agent and Mass Mutual share the risk. The amount of financing to the agent is the amount of the payment that exceeds the commissions earned, but the amounts advanced are returned to the company and the general agent in the form of renewal commissions if the sales remain on the books. Earned commissions must exceed the three year financing requirement if my contract was to validate. I completed my requirement nearly one year ahead of schedule and had no further financial obligation to the Indiana agency. But Garrison insisted the language of my contract with him required me to remain in his agency for three years in any event. He didn't want me as an agent, he wanted the override money from my sales. My reading of the contract left the impression that the language was vague in this regard. Garrison said he'd ask the Home Office to interpret the contract. His letter to me on April 16, 1981, said:

> We now have a response from the Home Office, relative to the possibility of terminating your financing plan as a "completer." I learn, and would have understood had I thought about it more, that there is no way the Company (sic) is willing to do this. Let me explain; the plan is designed to run the full three years. It is anticipated that there will be "completers" prior to the end of the full

week experience, and it is the renewals of these people in part, which are owned by the Company (sic) should they subsequently terminate, which help subsidize the entire plan. There would be a disadvantage to you in terminating, you would not receive the additional TAS payments, amounting to 10% during the third and final year, and so, an early termination would not seem to be to your advantage in any case, since with your contract continuation, all renewals, service fees, and career contract benefits will continue to be paid on this business, the renewals of which are owned by the Home Office.

There is an alternative way to accomplish a short term completion, which is simply to terminate the financing agreement. If that would be the case, your account balance of $14,645 (the amount paid you in excess of received commissions) becomes a loss and we, as general agents, would be responsible for your share – some 65%. There are exceptions to this rule, but only two. In the situation where we have a "completer (sic) who the General Agent wishes to appoint to a staff position; or alternatively, where we have a "completer" who is accepting a Home Office position of some sort or another.

I hope this answers your question. If you have others, please write or call.

Cordially,

Signed
Thomas C. Garrison, CLU
General Agent

TCG:jr

Cc:   Mr. Roger J. Warrum
      District Manager

MassMutual never offered a Home Office position to me. Since I had signed the contract, I made sure I would honor it. I remained in Indiana. (Later, other General Agents for MassMutual said they considered Garrison's representation to be false.)

Braddock knew I had some money in the bank. He became aware of my settlement when he found out about Laudig's actions. Braddock was a little upset with himself for not representing me and obtaining a substantial amount of the settlement in return for very little work. The suits were settled within a very short time, less than a month, after I asked him to represent me. Now he agreed to represent me in response to Laudig's demand. I asked Braddock to file a malpractice counterclaim against Laudig and outlined all of the instances of malpractice. He refused. He said he wouldn't sue another attorney for malpractice until he was personally convinced he would win the suit. He said the malpractice complaint could be filed at a later time or as a separate action. It was my position the malpractice issue be filed as a counterclaim, but he still refused.

Since my settlement agreement with FESLIC was to be held confidential, I wanted to know who told Laudig about the settlement. I wrote to Daniel Roby on April 7, 1981, asking if he was the person who told Laudig. On April 14 Roby replied, saying he'd never spoken to or written to Laudig in his life. I phoned Fletcher and asked if he told Laudig, and Fletcher said he hadn't. He said he had no communication with Laudig after the end of December 1980.

On April 30, 1981, I filed a complaint against Laudig with the Indiana Supreme Court Disciplinary Commission citing Laudig's conversion of $100.00 in trust funds for witness fees to his own use. Theldon Brestow, executive secretary of the disciplinary commission, responded favorably to my complaint on December 21, 1981. His letter is below:

CERTIFIED MAIL NO. P31 4654689

Mr. Stephen Laudig
Attorney at Law
1810 East 62$^{nd}$ Street
Indianapolis, Indiana

Dear Mr. Laudig,

Pursuant to Indiana Supreme Court Rule A.D. 23, Section 10(b) this is to advise that the grievance of

Reginald L. Jensen against you has been reviewed along with the preliminary investigation, and it has been determined that a substantial question of misconduct exists. Therefore, pursuant to the above rule the grievance has been reclassified as a misconduct and docketed. You may make whatever additional responses you deem necessary.

If you have any questions concerning this matter, feel free to inquire. Thank your for your cooperation.

Very truly yours,

Signed
Sheldon A. Breskow
Executive Secretary

SAB:jl

Cc: Indianapolis Bar Association
    Mr. Reginald L. Jensen

    Breskow later dismissed the claim without a hearing taking place. Immediately thereafter, he became an executive with the Legal Services Organization in Washington, D.C., a nice promotion. It was obvious to me someone other than Laudig made a trade with Breskow. It was my conclusion Tuohy helped Laudig again.

    On June 15, 1981, Braddock filed an answer in Laudig's lawsuit against me, denying any debt existed from me to Laudig and demanded a jury trial. At the same time, he filed an affirmative defense saying Laudig had been fully compensated for all services he performed for me. He also requested a change of venue from Madison County. Trial by jury was granted by the Madison County judge on June 18, 1981.

    After reviewing the evidence, Braddock finally filed a malpractice suit on October 26, 1981, against Laudig on my behalf in Madison County, venued in 1982 to Marion County (Indianapolis) as *Jensen v. Laudig, Cause No. S582-1389*, with Judge Michael Dugan presiding. This was the same Judge Dugan who was involved with UNAC, Tuohy, and Eckman. Laudig filed his appearance, pro se, and asked for an extension of time to respond. Ann Wilcox of Wilcox Ogden & DuMond, in Indianapolis, later filed an appearance as Laudig's attorney. Wilcox was one of Tuohy's friends.

Laudig wanted to get his money fast. Various motions were filed by both sides requesting documents and other discovery. This lawsuit wouldn't take 10 years; the attorneys and judges wouldn't allow it to take that long. It would go to a jury, because the attorneys would want it to go to a jury. But there was nothing that could be done other than follow the course of events. In May, 1982, Zook resigned as Laudig's attorney in *Laudig v. Jensen* and took a job with the federal government in Indianapolis. Ann Wilcox became Laudig's new attorney.

Braddock took Laudig's deposition on June 3, 1982. In answer to a question in his deposition he said he spoke with Martin Fletcher in early December of 1980, in which he proposed settlement in the amount of $55,000. He said he spoke with Fletcher on the telephone.

The deposition questions and answers are below:

Q. All right, did Mr. Jensen ask you to appeal S-72-697?
A. We discussed it....I decided that I would not be willing to represent him on appeal because I thought the appeal to be lacking in merit.

Q. How were you being compensated for the work you performed for Mr. Jensen, if you were being compensated?
A. OK. I, I believe that by that time Mr. Jensen and I had agreed to adopt as our attorney-client fee arrangement the agreement that he had with Mr. Friedland.

Q. And what was that agreement?
A. That there was a contingency arrangement where Mr. Jensen would pay the expenses, that one-third (1/3) of a recovery prior to trial would be attorney's fees, that should the matters go to trial, it would be forty (40) percent, and should they go on appeal, it would be half.

Q. You initiated the settlement talk? When did you initiate the settlement talk?

A. I spoke with Martin Jensen, I'm sorry, with Martin Fletcher in early December of 1980 in which I proposed settlement in the amount of $55,000.

Q. Did that result in the actual settlement?
A. I don't understand the question.

Q. Did that discussion with Mr. Fletcher in December of 1980 result in the settlement?
A. I can't, I can't answer that question. I don't know what you mean. I don't understand the question.

How can an attorney not know the reason why he filed a personal lawsuit against his former client? Laudig said in his suit that, in December 1980 he made an offer over the phone to Martin Fletcher to settle my lawsuit with FESLIC in the amount of $55,000 prior to resigning as my attorney. He made the same statement in his answer to interrogatories. I knew Laudig hadn't spoken to Fletcher when I was in Laudig's office, because Fletcher wasn't able to answer Laudig's phone call. I thought Fletcher might have later called Laudig back. Cause number S-72-697 was the slander action. The settlement paid $45,000 towards terminating the appeal of the slander action. If he thought the appeal of the slander action had no merit and he wouldn't represent me on the appeal, how did he justify to himself that he settled the slander action for $45,000?

Laudig was asked numerous times about who told him of the settlement agreement. Wilcox continued to object and Laudig didn't answer. Braddock could have demanded an answer that could have later been stricken by the judge, but he didn't do that.

In Laudig's suit against me there were several discussions between Braddock and Laudig's counsel over discovery, depositions, admissions, etc. Braddock finally requested a change of venue in Laudig's suit against me because of the influence of Dietzen and Eckman in Anderson. That case was venued to Tipton County on January 29, 1982. Change of venue is normally approved immediately but about nine months had transpired before the change was granted. Laudig knew the change was going to be granted because he filed a motion to have the Madison

County Court resume jurisdiction on January 26, 1982, three days before the venue change was granted. His motion was entered in the court record February 2nd, four days later. The Judge denied his motion February 16. On March 8 the case files were transferred to the town of Tipton. Judge Pearce was presiding in Tipton at the time of transfer. I drove over to Tipton to see the courthouse. The courtroom was very large, situated on the second floor of the old historical building in the center of the small town. The wood stairs to the second floor entered the room to the left middle section. The courtroom floor was wooden and a little squeaky. The ceiling was very high and there were very large, uncovered windows on the right side and back of the room. The judge's bench was a high, imposing structure. The attorney's tables and chairs were ancient. There was a large law library to the left of the courtroom. Left and right are measured while facing the judge's bench, which faced south.

Wilcox soon withdrew from the *Jensen v. Laudig* case. Laudig needed a new defense team. Tuohy arranged for the law firm in my suit against Laudig to be lead by a former Governor of Indiana, Matthew Welsh, of Bingham, Summers, Welsh and Spilman. It's my understanding that Tuohy's daughter, Sue Tuohy MacGill, was an attorney in the Welsh firm. David Campbell handled the case. Donald J. Graham and David C. Campbell filed an answer and affirmative defense. The affirmative defense claim was that my suit should have been filed as a compulsory counterclaim in the *Laudig v. Jensen* case in Tipton. Campbell moved to dismiss my suit. Braddock had assured me it wasn't a compulsory counterclaim. However, he became very concerned and nervous when the powerful legal team offered that defense. Braddock could see he made a mistake in not filing a malpractice counterclaim against Laudig as I had requested. He now wanted to get out of the lawsuit.

I wrote to Fletcher and asked him to respond to Laudig's claims. Fletcher called me and asked the amount of money Laudig demanded and basis of his claim. When I told him what Laudig said in his suit, Fletcher said it was outrageous! Fletcher replied by letter on August 12, 1982, and again in an affidavit on December 16, 1982, that Laudig never made any offer or suggestion about settling for $55,000. Fletcher said the highest offer ever suggested by Laudig was $20,000. Fletcher said the highest offer ever proposed by him to Laudig on behalf of

FESLIC and Eckman was $10,000. He said he suggested to Laudig on September 30, 1980, that there was a standing offer to discuss settlement, not a formal offer, which amounted to $22,597.06. Fletcher said that on July 28, 1977, he suggested $20,000 to Friedland. Fletcher thought he could get the Board of Directors of FESLIC to pay that amount if there was an agreement to accept it as full settlement. His suggestion remained the same until September 30, 1980. Neither Friedland nor Laudig ever mentioned the $20,000 or $22,597.06 amounts to me.

This is a good place to go over the accounting from my attorney's point of view. In 1977 Friedland apparently had a suggested offer of settlement from Fletcher to pay the amount Fletcher believed was due on the contract, $10,000. Fletcher apparently proposed an additional amount of $10,000 on the slander. The results:

| | |
|---|---|
| Settle for | $20,000 |
| Due Friedland | 6,667 |
| Advance to Friedland | 4,000 |
| Net to Friedland | $ 2,667 |

The extra $2,597.60 offered by Fletcher (above) amounted to interest on the $20,000 offer.

It's easy to see why Friedland lost interest in working on my cases. He could see where the disputes had continued for the last six years and the only payment to me up to the time we met was $15,000. One case, perhaps both, would have to go to trial before determination. He had no intention of working on my cases for another six years for payment of $2,667. If he paid any attention to Dean's calculations, he would have been entitled to receive a minimum of one-third of $114,056, the commissions due on the ordinary policies only. His share would have been $38,019, less $4,000, or a balance of $34,019.

Carry the same accounting over to Laudig, who was employed by Friedland. I doubt if Friedland ever paid Laudig anything more that office space. Laudig had free office space for about two years and then he had to find someone else who would allow him to share space. Laudig eventually assumed my agreement with Friedland. Laudig also discounted Dean's calculations. I don't believe someone is going to put in several years of work with the total payoff available in the amount of $2,667; not even if that person has a law degree. Keep in mind Laudig lost every court encounter with Fletcher and each concession meant he would earn less money. Later, Laudig would give me the number of hours he said he worked on my cases.

I called Fletcher in Ft. Wayne and said his testimony would be needed at trial. He agreed to testify on my behalf. He said Laudig was totally incompetent and entitled to nothing on quantum meruit. During our phone conversation, Fletcher continued to say Laudig's errors at trial were his failure to put Eckman on the stand and his failure to move to have the libelous Retail Credit investigative reports included in evidence against FESLIC and Eckman. *He said the records had been entered against Retail Credit but the link between Retail Credit and Eckman was never completed as a matter of evidence.* He said he gave Laudig several opportunities to complete his case but Laudig rested. Fletcher called this gross incompetence and malpractice. This was the same type of "mistake" made by Dietzen in 1972. It was also a follow through on Tuohy's position Retail Credit could claim absolute privilege as a defense. Tuohy's filing of the amended complaints, which gave the judges an opportunity to dismiss FESLIC and Eckman and leave Retail Credit as the sole defendant, was carried through by Laudig.

I had sold many group-permanent life insurance policies and was beginning to work in the split-dollar life insurance arena. Split-dollar life insurance is where the premiums, cash values, and death benefits of a life insurance policy are split between two parties, usually an employer and employee, which resulted in substantial tax advantages to the employee. Garrison traveled to MassMutual's home office in Springfield, Massachusetts in 1982 and talked to attorney Gerry Ouelette. When Garrison returned, he said he asked Ouelette to keep in touch with me and report any of my infractions back to him. Ouelette agreed. Garrison picked up about 50 of Ouelette's business cards and gave them to me. I threw them away. But I did take advantage of the new contact. Ouelette and I developed an extended relationship over the next 10 years analyzing split-dollar life insurance and nonqualified-deferred compensation. It gave me an opportunity to become an expert in the application of these two products. I learned more about the application of split-dollar than Ouelette because he taught me everything he knew, yet he didn't understand the configurations of life insurance policy values and had no interest in learning. Combining the split-dollar policies with nonqualified-deferred compensation gave small-business owners an opportunity to set aside additional money on a tax-deferred basis for their personal retirement. It also provided a satisfactory source of income for me over the next eighteen years.

I was standing in the lobby at the general agency offices about this same time when Garrison passed by, slapped me on the butt, and said "Reg, I'm afraid of you." He never explained his antics. But later he called me into his office and told me that the awards he passed out to agents for exemplary performance are biased. He said he only gave awards to those he selected and he deliberately excluded me from any recognition I should have earned. He never explained his reasoning, only his actions. I assumed he was rationalizing his behavior. The production of all agents was posted in the office and given to each agent. We all knew where we stood in relation to each other. My response was that as general agent he could do whatever he wanted and any awards from him made no difference to me. Recognition was always forthcoming to me from the MassMutual home office.

Garrison asked Sam Huston, a general agent with a different life insurance company, to become his co-general agent. Huston's brother was a partner in a large legal firm in Indianapolis and he had a long list of clients. Huston accepted the offer. It never made any sense why Garrison made the change, because he had a son he brought into the business and he had the opportunity of transferring the agency to his son. It also meant Garrison would share the total agency commission overrides with Huston. Garrison was taking a pay cut.

It was time to change attorneys again. I advised Braddock it was time for me to search for new counsel. He was relieved. His primary concern seemed to be that I would sue him because he failed to file the malpractice claim against Laudig as a counterclaim. He had been paid for his services up to that day. He did some sort of an accounting and decided he owed me several dollars. He sat down and immediately wrote a check. I picked up the two files relative to the lawsuits, which were now in process, and left the balance of the files with him and began searching for a new attorney.

During this same time period I was in the insurance agency in Indianapolis when Garrison called me into his office. He asked me how my lawsuit was coming along. I said I needed a new attorney. Garrison said he knew an attorney who had sold insurance in the past. He said he'd introduce me to him and that maybe this attorney could help me out. He telephoned Al George who had an office in a northeastern Indianapolis suburb. We made an appointment for February 3, 1983. I met with George for two hours in his office on that day. George asked Robert York to come into the office. York was now associated with George. This is the same attorney who had been associated with Dietzen in Anderson. York had been in the same offices with Friedland and Laudig on Washington Boulevard in Indianapolis, but he wasn't associated with either one. York said he wanted to make sure I understood he wouldn't be involved in my cases because he felt it was a conflict of interest. Obviously, Garrison had filled George in on some of the legal history.

I continued explaining the *Laudig v. Jensen* and the *Jensen v. Laudig* cases. George said he believed he understood what was taking place and asked me to leave the files with him so he could study them. He said if he handled the cases he would want $2,000 advance and he would charge $85.00 per hour. The hours he worked would apply towards the $2,000. He said he would have to hire local counsel in Tipton at extra cost to me. I agreed to pay his charges with the clear understanding he would do everything in his power to get the legal fees returned to me from Laudig. It was my position Laudig had filed a false and fraudulent suit against a non-attorney and if the attorney-plaintiff as well as the defendant's attorney are both aware the suit is false, then the action is a scam. I gave him most of the pleadings, Laudig's deposition, my deposition, Dean's deposition and affidavit, Braddock's charges, the disciplinary commission documents and exhibits, plus Fletcher's affidavit and letter. He now had everything he needed to make a decision. He said he would call me on Wednesday, February 9, 1983.

On February 9 Garrison called me into his office and said George talked to him for a long time on the phone explaining that I had a good case, York had a conflict of interest, and that he, George, did not have the time to get into my cases right now. George said I needed someone who had the time to begin in the Tipton County case and to get started in the Marion County case. On February 10 I talked to Al George on the phone. He said my case was a good case and he would like to handle it but he didn't have time. George said he wanted to help me find legal counsel and had talked to four attorneys: Mike Farr, Mr. Hobbs, Dave Quigly, and Ron Byal, all of Tipton. Byal was a former prosecutor and was willing to review the file. George said Byal had no objection to tangling with other members of the legal profession. When I went to George's office the next day to pick up my files, he told me he'd never lost a case because he doesn't take cases where there's a chance of losing.

On February 11 I talked to Byal on the phone. He said he had talked to George and he was interested in the case. We made an appointment for Tuesday, February 15 in his office in Tipton. He was a little younger than me, much shorter, and perhaps my weight. But he had a heart condition and wore a pacemaker. He listened intently and looked at me with piercing, inquisitive eyes. His practice was a one-man operation. He worked out of a small, brown office with a small law library. A secretary worked for him on a part-time basis. We discussed all of the events leading up to the current cases. We discussed Braddock's position and why Braddock had proceeded as he did. When we finished talking, Byal said he wanted to review the files on the current cases. He said he'd contact me at the end of the week.

At the end of the week Byal called back and set an appointment for February 25 in his office at 4:30 p.m. He agreed to handle the cases. He prepared a contract outlining his duties and my obligations. He was to be paid $50 an hour for non-court time and $100 an hour for court time. He wanted a $1,000 retainer, which I paid him immediately. Byal then said if I want to talk to Barnes & Hickam (Robert Johnstone's firm representing Retail Credit) and offer to settle for $4,500 they would probably pay me. (Braddock and Johnstone were co-counsel or opposing counsel in one or more suits.) I asked Byal how Johnstone and Barnes & Hickam would be in a position to settle a case for Laudig, but he never explained. He just said it was something he'd heard via the grapevine. I never pursued his suggestion in any event.

A couple of days later, Braddock returned my files to me and completed his withdrawal from both cases on March 1. Byal entered his appearances the following day.

The next time we talked, Byal said Judge Pearce would be assigned to the case, but Pearce was about to resign from the bench because a wealthy farmer just died and the judge was to be the executor of the estate. Pearce believed his new duties would take all of his time. Dane Nash was to be appointed to replace Judge Pearce. Byal said the proposed new judge had not practiced law, had just passed the bar and he was about 40 years old. Judge Nash had earned his law degree working his way through law school much later than most students. He was a tall, slender, and conscientious gentleman. My case was one of the very first on his docket, both as judge and as a practitioner of the law. I believe this was to be his first jury trial.

Byal outlined his concept of the current situation and the lawsuits. He said a summary judgment was possible, which could force Laudig to appeal if he desired. He was apprehensive about the malpractice action. He said every attorney is reluctant to sue another attorney. However, he said he'd try to have the Marion County suit merged into the Tipton case. Then if the cases were merged he would ask for separate trials. He also said he would request a summary judgment on the *Laudig v. Jensen* suit based upon the statute of frauds. He said a contract for more than $500 must be in writing in Indiana, which meant the quantum meruit demand could be a fraudulent demand. He said as far as my contract with Friedland is concerned, which Laudig now said he had assumed, Laudig breached the agreement when he refused to appeal the dismissal. As far as Laudig being entitled to payment based upon the settlement with FESLIC, he said an attorney only expects to claim completing or being part of a settlement if his signature is on the agreement. *He also said he wanted to leave all of the attorneys' errors out of the Laudig v. Jensen case.*

On March 9 I called Byal's office and told his secretary I was in my office and available if needed. She said he went to Anderson to get some papers signed and pretrial was scheduled for the next day, March 10, 1983. On March 14 I received a letter from Byal stating pretrial had been held. The judge ordered the plaintiff to answer previously issued interrogatories, which he had never answered. Other actions were taken by Byal including a motion for summary judgment in my favor. The Court set March 24 at 10 a.m. for the next hearing. Judge Nash was moving ahead with the case in an attempt to prevent unnecessary delays.

At the hearing on March 24 Byal's summary judgment motion was denied. The court allowed interrogatories and further discovery to continue for 45 days. The trial date was to be reset. Byal asked the judge to allow the suits to be amended to include Laudig as a defendant on my counterclaim for malpractice, theft, and deceit, but Laudig and his attorney, William DuMond (Wilcox's partner), advised Judge Nash that my suit is not a counterclaim. DuMond said my suit was being pursued in Indianapolis. Based upon DuMond's and Laudig's representation, Judge Nash denied Byal's motion to amend. The issues were now closed.

Motions, interrogatories, and responses were filed by both parties. Byal acquired new information for his benefit, but nothing was achieved by Laudig, he already knew everything about me and the lawsuits. On April 7, 1983, Byal called and said he received interrogatories from Laudig's attorney for the Tipton case. He said he would send them to me. Among other things, Laudig provided his notes on his phone calls to me. This was another record that made no sense to me. Laudig produced his phone bills, which confirmed his calls, but showed most of his calls were made to WHUT radio station. He never left any messages and never left a call-back number. Why call if there's no reason to talk or no information to be exchanged? Perhaps he was calling just to see if I was still living in Indiana.

I wanted to verify Herrin was the source of Laudig's knowledge of the settlement agreement. I hadn't heard anything by April 4, 1983, so I mailed a letter to Byal reminding him to depose Herrin and maybe Tuohy too. Byal said he would arrange to take John Herrin's deposition on either May 5 or 6. He couldn't confirm Tuohy would agree to be deposed. It seemed like Tuohy was immune from all legal processes.

Byal had served interrogatories to Laudig on January 14, 1983, which he answered on April 12. The first question was "How did you acquire knowledge of the settlement between defendant and FESLIC." His answer was "I believe I received this information during a phone conversation with John Herrin." So, now it finally came out. Laudig knew the information would eventually be disclosed. Why did he wait so long? He was protecting Herrin for as long as possible but he was also trying to conceal his association with Herrin and Tuohy. Tuohy was in the stratosphere of the legal and political hierarchy and Laudig was on the lowest rung.

May 5 and 6 came and went and nothing happened on the request for depositions of Herrin and Tuohy. It seemed to me Byal needed a clearer picture of how some of the attorneys and judges conducted their affairs, at least those who have been involved with me in the past. On May 10 I mailed to Byal a copy of the Indianapolis Star newspaper article written by Carolyn Pickering outlining the transfer of money from UNAC to Tuohy and the other attorneys arranged by Judge Dugan. I explained in the letter that FESLIC wanted to buy the UNAC building and take over the management of the UNAC policyholders. In my letter to Byal, I asked him to request a change of venue from Judge Dugan. Byal forwarded to Judge Dugan's court the first of many requests for a change of judge.

Laudig immediately asked me to pay him $7,500 to settle the two cases. My response was that, instead of me paying Laudig, I would accept $1,600 payment from Laudig. That's the amount I had paid in legal fees to Byal thus far. Laudig was incensed. He threatened to sue me for abuse of process for filing the disciplinary complaint against him regarding the $100 trust-fund money. He must have believed I was afraid of attorney's threats and lawsuits. All of this turned out to be nothing more than posturing. In the meantime, I moved into a small apartment in Speedway, Indiana, an Indianapolis suburb, across from the Indianapolis 500 racetrack.

Byal did whatever he had to do to convince Herrin to finally agree to be deposed. The deposition was set for May 18, 1983, at 1 p.m. in Wilcox's office in Indianapolis. The offices were on the fourth or fifth floor of an old office building in downtown Indianapolis. I went into the law firm offices a little early and sat in the lobby waiting for the others to arrive. There were about three separate offices with a waiting room and a small conference room. The conference room is where the deposition was to take place. Wilcox came out of her office, looked at me in the waiting room, and returned to her office. Byal and Herrin showed up on time, but Laudig wasn't there. Ogden handled Herrin's deposition for Wilcox. I talked to Ogden for a few minutes while the court reporter was setting up. He said he specialized in appeals. He said there are seldom any errors by attorneys that give cause for a successful appeal. Ogden said attorneys never or rarely make mistakes in pleadings and procedure. He said errors are either deliberate, wrong statements by clients, or the wrong application of law.

During the deposition, Herrin said Tuohy received the settlement papers from Fletcher and gave them to him. He said he knew there was a confidentiality provision in the agreement and that Laudig was not included for payment purposes. Herrin admitted giving the settlement information to Laudig. He said he phoned Laudig on or about March 31, 1981, and told him he was glad he was paid for the settlement. Herrin later gave Zook a copy of the settlement agreement, and Laudig was given an opportunity to review the document. On April 24, 1981, Laudig filed his suit against me.

After the deposition, Herrin and I talked for awhile outside on the street. He told me Tuohy had to replace Zook as Laudig's attorney because she wasn't capable of handling the case. He said Tuohy arranged for Zook to be employed by the federal government in Indianapolis. Zook's new employment prevented her from engaging in the private practice of law. He said Tuohy arranged to bring in Wilcox as Laudig's attorney. This conversation made it clear to me that Tuohy had arranged this lawsuit against me. Herrin gave me the impression Tuohy had encouraged Laudig to write the letter to me dated February 3, 1981, suggesting I settle for $30,000. First, Dietzen told me Tuohy was still in charge of my lawsuits after Tuohy had withdrawn; now Herrin seemed to confirm Tuohy was still in charge. Eckman and FESLIC could have reached a point in time when they wanted to bring the litigation to a close, but Tuohy wasn't at that point yet.

Several weeks later, Herrin came into the Indianapolis Olympia Super Spa when I was there to do my running and exercising. That was the only time I had ever seen him in the spa, and I asked him how often he used it. He said he came in all of the time. I mentioned Laudig's conversion of my trust-fund money to his own account and asked him how he and Tuohy could become partners with someone like Laudig. Herrin said "A person does what he has to do." With that, he went into the shower area, cleaned up, dressed and left.

Wilcox decided she didn't want to remain in the lawsuit and withdrew as counsel. She soon decided to move to Denver, Colorado. It seemed to me she wanted to get out of any current local controversy.

In late May, I flew to Salt Lake City for a visit with Dorothy and our families. On May 27, 1983, Wilcox, Ogden and DuMond filed a motion to withdraw from representing Laudig, which was done with Laudig's consent. On the same day, Byal called me while I was in Salt Lake City and said Laudig offered to settle by dismissing his case if I dismiss mine, no money either way. I said I would settle if Laudig would pay my legal fees up to that point of time. Laudig refused.

Laudig searched around for a new attorney and found William Fatout who was willing to take DuMond's place. It was said Fatout had an office in the basement of his home. He obviously had nothing to do with Tuohy and his compatriots. It appeared as though Tuohy decided to let Laudig find his own attorney for the trial phase and Tuohy would handle any problems on appeal if Laudig lost at trial. Still, none of the attorneys really seemed to believe Laudig would lose at trial. They all seemed to believe he would be awarded some compensation in addition to the amounts he'd already been paid. In doing some research, I found no attorney in Indiana who sued a client claiming unpaid fees and who lost at the trial stage had that loss affirmed on appeal. The appellate court always awarded damages to the attorney no matter what happened in the court below. Even if Laudig lost, all he had to do was file an appeal and he'd win. But usually, the trial judge will reverse the jury verdict and award money to the attorney.

On June 1 I wrote a letter to Herrin saying I knew about his firm's political involvement with Judge Dugan and that I had an action against Laudig in Dugan's court. I also said if I need witnesses in either action I would subpoena him and Tuohy and submit evidence involving his firm and their prior actions, which would include his late filing in the slander action, the law firm's failure to appeal the slander rulings, the mistakes in New Castle, and Laudig's bogus trial in the slander action, including Laudig's submission of evidence only as to the dates of slander, which had previously been dismissed, his failure to present evidence against FESLIC or Eckman, his failure to place Eckman on the witness stand, and his submission of evidence only as to the time-barred dates relative to Retail Credit. Herrin didn't respond. A few days later I wrote a letter to Tuohy with the same information just to make sure he received it.

Byal filed a motion in the Marion County action to strike the defendant's answer because it was late. On June 8 a hearing was held on that motion. Laudig opposed the motion on the theory the motion to strike should have been filed within 20 days of the answer. Judge Dugan didn't preside. Pro tem Judge Irwin Levin out of Dillon's firm (Dillon, Hardaman & Cohen), Tuohy's and Dugan's Democratic compatriots in the UNAC legal fee mess, presided. The motion to strike was denied.

After Judge Dugan refused to withdraw from the case, I talked to Susan Headden, a reporter at The Indianapolis Star. Headden was a slender young woman who seemed to be alert to her responsibilities. I explained to Headden what was happening in the case. I left documents with her so that she could recognize something was wrong. She had an interest. She told me she had heard there were irregularities in Dugan's court. What I didn't know at the time was she and two other reporters, Patrick Traub and Mary Balika, were in the process of investigating Dugan's purported acceptance of bribes and kickbacks.

MassMutual decided to get into the mutual funds sales business along with the sales of life insurance. The home office in Springfield, Massachusetts, was acting as a broker-dealer. Several years later, it decided to create its own stock-brokerage firm, MML Investors Services, Inc. (MMLISI) in early 1981, which became registered with the NASD. Since MassMutual operated in every state in the United States, MMLISI began operating in every MassMutual insurance agency. If the insurance agents were to be licensed to sell mutual funds, they would be required to pass a securities exam. The exam is a Representative's exam. The Representative's exam is easy to pass and the national undertaking to have the agents licensed was massive. It was difficult to find persons who could serve as Principals. The Principal's exam was very difficult. Many who took the exam didn't pass. In fact, there were very few Principals working for MassMutual in any office at the time. Each separate office of a stock-brokerage firm was required to have a Registered Principal in charge of sales operations in that office. I was the only person in the Indianapolis agency with such a license. In 1983, MassMutual and MMLISI asked me to file a new registration form with the NASD. I completed all of the paperwork and provided them with a new copy of my fingerprints. My Principal's registration was transferred from MassMutual to MMLISI. Later in the year, Garrison told me that I would only be allowed to sell mutual funds. I didn't know if that was his decision, MassMutual's decision, or MMLISI's decision. It was never explained to me and I didn't pursue the matter at that time. I was concentrating on the *Laudig v. Jensen* issues. The Indiana stockbrokerage operation of MassMutual continued to do business without the required supervision.

Trial in *Jensen v. Laudig* was set for September 6, 1983, in Indianapolis. Trial in *Laudig v. Jensen* was set for October 13 in Tipton. Byal had another motion before the court for a change of judge in Indianapolis. Laudig's attorneys in the Indianapolis case had filed a motion for continuance and a motion to retain Judge Dugan as the trial judge. Campbell said the affirmative defense of "compulsory counterclaim" required a ruling in Tipton before the case could go to trial in Indianapolis. If I should lose in Tipton, it would mean the jury found Laudig should receive additional compensation, an expression he had not engaged in malpractice thereby presaging a loss for me in my suit against him. Byal filed a response insisting Dugan resign and allow a new judge to preside. Byal suggested to Campbell and Graham that they move to consolidate the two cases. Campbell refused and insisted the cases be tried separately. As a result, the Indianapolis trial date was postponed and Judge Dugan remained.

Settlement was discussed again. Laudig's attorneys insisted we both drop the lawsuits and pay no money either way. I countered that we both drop the lawsuits and Laudig pay my legal fees. He refused. I decided the settlement discussions were a waste of time since there was no movement on such a small amount of money. So, I suggested Laudig drop his suit and pay me $75,000 for dropping my suit. Attorneys don't understand negotiations where one of the parties demands a higher amount after the first round of negotiations fails. Their normal routine is to constantly whittle one side down and the other side up from the previous offers until they reach a figure somewhere in between the original amounts discussed. My suggestion fell on deaf ears in any event. By now their misuse of the judicial system had really raised my ire. I was ready, willing and able to fight them to the very end. Apparently, they were, too.

On July 9, 1983, Byal again requested a change of judge in the Indianapolis case. He prepared the motion and I took it in to the court myself. Judge Dugan continued to refuse to withdraw, and Laudig's counsel continued to insist Judge Dugan remain. Judge Dugan was going to rule and that was all there was to it. Everything going on in Judge Dugan's court was legal double talk and it convinced me the fix was in. On August 9 Judge Dugan denied Byal's latest motion for a change of judge or, as an alternative, a request for voluntary disqualification. On August 12 Byal and I met in his office for awhile and then went to Indianapolis to file a reaffirmation of the change of judge motion. That motion was ignored; the judge was super-glued to the bench. Trial was set for May 22, 1984.

Byal took the depositions of several of my previous attorneys with the intent of introducing the depositions at trial in Tipton. On October 7 Byal requested copies of my legal fees and expense sheets showing payments to or on behalf of my previous attorneys in the slander and contract cases. Fees were paid to Friedland, Sivin, and Laudig totaling $6,120. $4,000 was paid to Friedland, and $2,110 to Laudig in amounts of $5; $10; $20; and $50; not counting the $100 "Witness fee" money. And $10 paid to Sivin. My direct expenses amounted to an additional $3,119. The attorneys were supposed to be working on a contingency basis, which meant they receive nothing unless they obtain a settlement or win a lawsuit. The $2,110 paid to Laudig was an advance just like the payment to Friedland. Byal now had all of the information necessary to demonstrate Laudig had been fully paid and that his representation of me in the two lawsuits was gross malpractice.

A jury trial was going to happen in Tipton. Jury trials in the United States are a thing of the past. There might be minor nuances in methods and procedures among different attorneys and judges, but the results are substantially the same nationwide. Jury trials are granted in only 1.8 percent of all litigation. That means most litigation is determined by dismissals of the complaint by a judge, by summary judgment, or by agreement of the attorneys. In all of those dismissals, the attorneys and judges have prevented jury consideration and have controlled the decision as to who wins and who loses. An independent examination of dismissals will most certainly show politics and the distribution of favors are the prime motivators.

During this period, a Public Broadcasting System television program originating out of Chicago had several attorneys discussing how they financed their practices. They agreed the most-effective method was through bank loans. They would pledge their potential earnings from clients based upon a percentage of the client's claims. One attorney said he would be willing to sell all of his cases to any willing buyer for five percent of the value of the claims determined from his client's positions. It can easily be seen that the attorneys have an obligation to repay the bank loans and must find ways to bring litigation to an end or to otherwise extract money from their clients. So, the outcome of their litigation depends more on their commitment to their lenders than on the merits of their cases. It also creates a relationship with the banks where the attorney will protect his source of borrowing or income. If an attorney sues the bank that carries his paper the bank might retaliate, call in the loans, and suspend the business relationship.

I asked Byal to issue a subpoena to Judge Johnson who presided over the slander trial in Anderson. Byal was opposed to the subpoena but issued it upon my insistence. Byal said he wouldn't remain in the room while I interrogated the judge. Judge Johnson appeared in Tipton at the courthouse several days before the trial. Byal introduced me to the judge and then left the room. Judge Johnson asked me what I had in mind for his appearance. My only real question was why he dismissed the slander case. He answered "I just thought it was the best thing to do." With that, I thanked him, shook his hand and he left. It seemed to me he seldom appeared as pro-tem judge in Madison County after that.

    I was grateful this was Judge Nash's first jury trial. As the courtroom was being set up, we walked around the ancient room and tested the chairs and tables. One of the chairs was in need of repair so I took a few minutes and fixed the legs so it wouldn't fall apart. Judge Nash came over and thanked me and mentioned the county didn't have enough funds to maintain the furniture. I mentioned to him that if the trial went against me I wouldn't have the funds either. That would put me and the county in the same position.

October 13 showed up on schedule and the jury trial began. Tuohy and Herrin were subpoenaed. Tuohy absolutely refused to appear. Since he was under subpoena, he was required to be there and could have shown up at any time during the trial. Herrin was present the morning of October 14 but had other things to do and wouldn't come back. Neither Tuohy nor Herrin can ever claim they didn't have a chance to rebut or refute testimony and evidence. If they'd been present, they could have challenged anything that was said about their legal performance that might have been derogatory.

Laudig was the first to testify. He said he put in more than 750 hours of time on my lawsuits in two and one-half years. He never maintained a record of his time; he only estimated. He testified his primary sources of records for calculating the time he spent on my cases were his telephone log and the court docket sheets. He said he usually called the WHUT offices. I kept a record of the times he called me and compared his notes to mine:

|      | Laudig's phone log | My notes |
|------|--------------------|----------|
| 1978 | 16 times           | 8 times  |
| 1979 | 44 times           | 3 times  |
| 1980 | 6 times            | 2 times  |

His phone bills amounted to $148.06.

The docket sheets showed every entry by Laudig on my behalf had a counter entry by Fletcher on Eckman's or FESLIC's behalf and Retail Credit attorneys on Retail Credit's behalf. This simply means that if Laudig put in time preparing a motion or some other document that would result in an entry on the docket sheets, at least one or more counter motions or documents would result in entries on the docket sheets. Time put in by Laudig should have been balanced by time put in on the other side.

On October 14 Laudig finished his direct testimony. Byal began his cross examination. But Laudig's testimony was interrupted so Fletcher could testify and return to Ft. Wayne. Fatout went to elaborate lengths to explain this interruption in testimony.

I had never asked Fletcher about his motives for his testimony. When I asked him to testify, he said he would explain at trial what transpired between him and Laudig. Although Fletcher had explained how he felt about Laudig's claim, I never asked Fletcher what he was about to say. There was no pretrial witness preparation. He waited to explain everything to the jury. What he had to say was as much a surprise to me as it was to everyone else in the courtroom, particularly Byal and Fatout. His testimony follows in its entirety because it gives a clear explanation of how the judicial system works. The exhibits have not been inserted. The exhibits consist of Laudig's notarized affidavit saying he made an offer to Fletcher to settle the litigation for $55,000; another Laudig affidavit saying both the contract case and the slander case could have been completed within one year; Fletcher's letter to Roby stating Fletcher would continue with the litigation in court and that Roby was out of the picture; Fletcher's letter to Judge Griffis in New Castle requesting a trial date; Roby's release; the letter to me from Fletcher offering to settle the litigation; the complete settlement agreement; and the docket from Madison County (Anderson) Cause # S-75-828 (the December 1, 1970, contract action).

## DIRECT EXAMINATION OF MARTIN FLETCHER QUESTIONS BY RONALD BYAL:

Q   Would you state your name for the Court, please?
A   Yes, my name is Martin Fletcher.
Q   And, what is your occupation, Mr. Fletcher?
A   I'm an attorney.
Q   And how long have you been a practicing attorney?
A   Since 1969.
Q   Would you give the Court and Jury a brief summary of your employment history and your legal education?
A   Well, I went to law school at Indiana University in Bloomington, and I graduated in June of 1969, Since that time I've been with the same law firm in Fort Wayne, Indiana, a firm called Rothberg, Gallmeyer, Frichtenick and Logan. I've always been there. So, I guess that's fourteen years.
Q   And do you hold a license from the State of Indiana to practice law?

A  Yes.
Q  Are you licensed in any other jurisdictions?
A  No.
Q  Do you belong to any professional associations?
A  All the standard ones. State and local bar associations, American bar. I guess that's all.
Q  Are you familiar with the Defendant in this case, Reginald Jensen?
A  Yes.
Q  Are you familiar with the Plaintiff in this case, Stephen Laudig?
A  I'm acquainted with him, yes.
Q  Are you familiar with a corporation known as First Equity Security Life Insurance Company?
A  Yes.
Q  What is your involvement with First Equity Security Life Insurance Company?
A  First Equity Security Life Insurance Company is a life insurance company here in Indiana and it's a client of our firm and has been for as long as there's been a First Equity Security Life Insurance Company. To my knowledge anyway, twenty years or so, they've been a client of our law firm.
Q  Mr. Fletcher, are you familiar with a law suit known as Reginald Jensen versus First Equity Security Life Insurance Company, Incorporated, known as Cause Number S-75-828, in the Madison Superior Court?
A  Well, I'm familiar that there are law suits by Mr. Jensen against First Equity. I cannot identify the numbers as between the slander case and the contract case and so forth. The numbers don't mean anything to me.
Q  Did you represent First Equity Security Life Insurance Company in defending two actions by Reginald Jensen? Three actions?
A  Well, there were three distinct law suits, as I recall.
Q  And were you the only attorney representing First Equity?
A  No, not throughout the whole history of the litigation. Initially, when the litigation started, one of my then partners, Mr. Walter Riebenack, had some initial involvement and in a firm like ours you always have younger people who help you with — yes, now the younger people — who help you with the work as it goes along.

So other lawyers in the firm would have worked on it from time to time but I followed through on ninety-five percent of it.

Q  And your firm was the only firm involved in defending First Equity in those actions?

A  Yes.

Q  Did you have occasion during the time period that you were involved in the actions to participate in adversarial proceedings with Stephen Laudig?

A  Yes.

Q  Approximately how long was Mr. Laudig involved in those litigations?

A  Well, Mr. Laudig became involved in the — I think the best I can do for you is the late seventies as a person identified as the opposing counsel. He may have been involved earlier when Dan Friedland was involved in one of the cases. He may have been assisting or something like that, I don't know. At least by the late seventies Mr. Laudig was involved in the law suits that then existed and that continued down until sometime in early December of 1980, whatever that span of time is. Two or three years.

Q  Directing your attention first to the slander case that you refer to. Through what stage of the proceedings did you have Mr. Laudig as an adversary in that action?

A  Well, again, I can't — I can't sit here and recall after all those years when the slander action was started. At least, if not from the beginning, at least very shortly after they were filed until the law suit was tried and over with. And then, for some brief period of time after the trial when I understood him to still be counsel for Mr. Jensen. So, basically, throughout most of the history of the slander case he was the opposing counsel.

Q  Do you recall what year that case started in?

A  No, I don't. It seems to me, again, that it was July or August of, uh, the early seventies that it started. Mid seventies. I'd have to look at the pleadings to tell you when it actually started.

Q  In any event, Mr. Laudig came into the case in the latter part of the seventies?

A  I think that's basically correct. At some point he showed up as counsel. The case was not initiated, as I recall, by Mr. Laudig, but

by a different lawyer, Walter Dietzen. At some point after that, I think after the trial, of the first contract action, Mr. Dietzen dropped out and Mr. Friedland and/or Mr. Laudig show up in the cases. I don't recall when that was.
Q Did that slander case go to a trial?
A Yes.
Q And, was that trial in front of a court or a jury?
A It was — the case was, of course, tried in a courthouse, in front of a judge, without a jury.
Q And, did Mr. Laudig participate in that trial?
A Yes, he did.
Q Did you have occasion to observe his performance in that trial?
A Well, I defended, so I was present throughout the trial from beginning to the point where we left, just before the end of the trial.
Q And why did you leave the trial?
A Well, at the end of the Plaintiff's case, my client in that case, which was First Equity Security Life Insurance Company and James Eckmand, were dismissed from the law suit on a Motion for Dismissal at the end of the Plaintiff's case. The case then continued as to Equifax or Retail Credit for some brief period of time after we were out of the law suit by virtue of the Court having decided that we were out of the law suit.
Q And, during the time that Mr. Laudig presented the Plaintiff's case, did you observe his performance?
A Yes.
Q And are you familiar with the standards of performance for trial attorneys in the State of Indiana?
A Well, based upon my experience and doing litigation, I think I am familiar with the standards of performance for the trial of a law suit, yes.
Q At this point in time, at that trial, approximately how many trials had you personally tried or been involved with?
A Aside from saying "too many", I have no idea. I have done litigation work exclusively since June 1, of 1969. I don't keep track — I don't pay any attention to how many cases that is. I don't know.
Q A considerable number, would you say?

A   Oh, dozens and dozens.
Q   And, have you had occasions during those trials to observe the performance of other attorneys in the State of Indiana?
A   Yes. At a trial there is always some attorney on the other side. I've seen dozens and dozens, and I don't think I'm yet at the point where I'd say hundreds, but I've dealt with many, many attorneys in many, many trials for a long time.
Q   And, based upon your experience as a trial attorney in the trials that you've been in and your observations of other trial attorneys in the State of Indiana, did you form any opinions regarding the performance by Mr. Laudig?
A   In the trial of the slander action?
Q   Yes, sir.
A   I would have an opinion concerning it.
Q   Would you tell the Court what that opinion was, or is?

MR. FATOUT: I would object to that. I would think that that is irrelevant and immaterial to the proceedings and the issues in this case.
BY THE COURT: How so, counsellor?
MR. FATOUT: It may be a matter of affirmative defense which is not pled. I certainly would not want that to be — evidence to be presented on an affirmative defense which is not pled.
BY THE COURT: You maintain that your client should be compensated for services rendered, is that correct?
MR. FATOUT: That's correct. But if there is a defense that the quality of the performance did not meet the standards, that smacks of an affirmative defense which is not pled in this case. If not, indeed, a compulsory counter-claim
BY THE COURT: Isn't it true that a standard — that part of the manner in which the value of his services are going to be measured is how good they were?
MR. FATOUT: Well, the question is not value of services at this point. The question is whether he meets some sort of intangible standards, which have not yet been defined. They only exist in this gentleman's mind by virtue of his experience.
BY THE COURT: The objection is overruled. The witness may answer the question, if he knows.

A   Well, I'm not sure, Your Honor, where we are in terms of the question.

BY THE COURT: Very well, counsellor, would you repeat the question for the witness?

Q   Mr. Fletcher, can you give the Court what your opinion was of the performance of Mr. Laudig at the slander case trial while you were present?
A   *It was, in my candid opinion, substantially incompetent. It was — I've searched words as I knew I would be asked that question — it was, it was terrible. That's in a nutshell, my opinion.*
Q   Now, Mr. Fletcher, after the Court in that slander action had dismissed out your clients, did you have any discussion with Stephen Laudig regarding settlement of the contract action?
A   Well if by discussions you mean, all — the slander action was tried, as my memory serves me, very late in October. There was some communication between Mr. Laudig and myself about the remaining pending contract action after the Judge directed a verdict, a decision in favor of my client in the slander case and at some point in early December of 1980, we did communicate about it. Letters and so forth.
Q   And do you recall the dates of those communications?
A   As I sit here from memory without looking at my time records and so forth I can recall the dates of some of those communications that occurred, yes.
Q   And in the period of early December, 1980, had you made any settlement offers to Mr. Laudig?
A   No.
Q   Had he made any settlement offers to you?
A   Not as I recall.
Q   Mr. Laudig testified in this Court that he had a telephone communication with you on what he believed to be either December 8th, 9th, or 10th of 1980. Do you have any recollection as to communication with Mr. Laudig on those days?
A   I did not have any telephone communication with Mr. Laudig on the 7th, 8th, 9th or 10th of December.

Q Did there come a time in December of 1980, that you became aware that Mr. Laudig was no longer representing Reginald Jensen?
A Yes.
Q And, when did you become aware of that?
A It would have been on perhaps a day or two earlier than December the 12th, 1980. What I'm saying is, I knew it for sure by December 12th. My recollection seems to be that I knew it a day or two in advance of that, but I certainly knew it by December the 12th.
Q And, after you had learned of that situation where Mr. Laudig was no longer representing Mr. Jensen, did you then have any further communication with Stephen Laudig?
A I had no communication with him subsequent to December the 12th, 1980, about this case. I have seen him, spoken to him since then, but I had no communication with him about the Jensen situation, the Jensen litigation after December the 12th, 1980.
Q Mr. Fletcher, did you have any communication with Mr. Laudig on December 12th of 1980?
A Yes, I did.
Q And what type of communication did you have with him?
A It was a telephone call between him and I. I have no recollection whether he called me or I called him, or we left word, but we did have a telephone conversation on the morning of December the 12th, 1980.
Q And would you relate to the Court and Jury, to the best of your knowledge, the substance of that telephone conversation?
A He called and indicated he was calling about the Jensen matters. I indicated to him I was surprised at that because I had heard at that time, in fact that day, that he was withdrawing as Mr. Jensen's lawyer. He then indicated that while that was correct, he was withdrawing as Mr. Jensen's lawyer, not representing him, he felt he still had enough control or influence over the client that he could get a settlement of the contract action for my client and I, First Equity Security Life Insurance Company, if we wished to pursue that. It is my recollection that my response to that was that I would not have pursued those discussions with a person who did not technically represent Mr. Jensen anymore, and that that was the end of the conversation.
(LONG PAUSE)

*Judicial Deception*

Q  Mr. Fletcher, I'm going to show you what has been marked as Defendant's Exhibit #8, consisting of two pages, and ask if you would look at that, please? (WITNESS REVIEWS DOCUMENT)
A  Well, I've read and finished Exhibit #8.
Q  Okay. Mr. Fletcher, directing your attention to paragraph number three of Defendant's Exhibit #8, is that a true statement?
A  (reviewing exhibit) The statement that services rendered by the Plaintiff could have been performed within a year is certainly a true statement, in the sense that it could have been done within a year. I don't want to speak out of line, but basically what it says is that it is theoretically possible, or it is possible, and it is not unusual for cases to arise and be resolved within a year. That could have happened in this case. It did not. I think the statement is true, for what it says.
Q  And, also, Mr. Fletcher, directing your attention to paragraph number five. Would you examine that and tell us whether that is a true statement?
A  Well, I of course, have no knowledge as to the statement that Defendant breached the agreement by discharging. I have no knowledge one way or the other about that. The second sentence of the paragraph, it states that "just prior to his discharge by the Defendant Jensen, the Plaintiff, Mr. Laudig, made an offer of settlement of Fifty Five Thousand Dollars". No such offer was made to me for Fifty Five Thousand Dollars. That statement is not true.
Q  Thank you, Mr. Fletcher.

MR. BYAL: At this time. Your Honor, we'd offer into evidence Defendant's Exhibit #8.
BY THE COURT: Let me see it just a minute counsellor. Isn't that already part of the Court record?
MR. BYAL: Yes, Judge.
BY THE COURT: Very well. Do you desire to see this exhibit?
MR. FATOUT: No, I don't need to see it. No objections to admissability.
BY THE COURT: Defendant's Exhibit #8 is accepted into evidence without objection.
  Whereupon Defendant's Exhibit #8 was admitted into evidence:

*Reginald L. Jensen*

*(My comment: A discussion ensued which has not been included regarding attorney Daniel Roby who attempted to represent me for a day or two. Roby was paid $375.00)*

## CONTINUED DIRECT EXAMINATION OF MARTIN FLETCHER, QUESTIONS BY RONALD C. BYAL:

Q  Now, Mr. Fletcher, after you ceased your communications with Mr. Roby, did you then enter into any communications with any other persons regarding the settlement of Reginald Jensen's claims?
A  After Mr. Roby ceased to be involved as counsel, a period of time went by and then the settlement discussions and negotiations were conducted between Mr. Jensen and myself.
Q  And, do you recall what day you first met with Mr. Jensen?
A  I cannot recall with absolute certainty, but certainly by very early in March of 1981, he and I were in communication. I believe we met early in March, 1981, in the sense of being in the same room to sit down together. We may have corresponded earlier than that. I'm sure we did correspond, because at that point in time he was acting pro se, for himself, without counsel in the contract action and I was, therefore, obliged to deal with him whenever I filed something with the Court — corresponded with the Court — he would have received copies of those, and the same on his part. So, I'm sure we were in correspondence. I believe we met for the first time to sit down and work on the numbers that led to the settlement, early in March.
Q  How many meetings did you have with Mr. Jensen?
A  After that point in time?
Q  Yes.
A  It would have been three or four actual meetings. That is, sit downs in my offices in Fort Wayne from the first of March down to and including the final execution of the settlement documents on March 25th. Three or four times.
Q  And during those three or four times what did you and Mr. Jensen discuss?
A  Settlement of the law suits which then existed.
Q  Did that involve the making of any computations?

A   Yes.

Q   And were the computations similar to those that you discussed that you had with Mr. Roby?

A   Yes.

Q   And did you and Mr. Jensen reach a figure as to those computations? Let me rephrase that. That was a little vague. During the time that you and Mr. Jensen sat down and made computations, did you arrive at a figure that the two of you reached a consensus on?

A   Well, again, I don't mean to be difficult about this, but we never agreed on the underlying figures in their totality. We ultimately arrived at a number of dollars and cents that we offered and he accepted and which did settle the law suits.

Q   And how did you reach that one figure that you offered and he accepted?

A   Ultimately, the last step of it was, I wrote a lengthy letter to him and sent him a separate written offer. It was finally a formal, written offer to compromise all the litigation, and he responded to that suggesting some changes and those changes were then incorporated into a final settlement agreement, which he signed and my client signed, or I signed on their behalf. So it was a matter of I finally made him a formal offer. He proposed slight variation in terms of the number of dollars. We accepted that variation and reduced it to a formal settlement agreement, which was then signed by the parties March 25th, 1981.

Q   Mr. Fletcher, I'll show you what's been marked as Defendant's Exhibit #10, and ask if you would identify that, please?

A   This is a letter dated March the 11th, 1981, from me to Mr. Jensen and this is what I indicated earlier I sent to him as a formal offer to settle on March the 11th, with one exception. That exception is that in the second paragraph the figure that appears — Fifty Five Thousand Dollars, was not the original figure that was in the first communication sent out. This was simply, as I recall, whited-over or changed. I mean that's the point at which the change was. The original of the March 11th, 1981, letter would have said Fifty Thousand. He wanted five grand more, we gave, and we simply then changed the figure of fifty to fifty-five. That final step. I had already executed, he then executed and returned it to me.

Q And does that Defendant's Exhibit #10, is that then a true and accurate copy of the agreement that the two of you reached? Mr. Jensen and yourself?

A No. I think I would characterize that this way; this is a true and accurate copy of a letter from me to Mr. Jensen, which he and I worked on that figure, and which became the basis for a much more formal settlement agreement. This letter simply says these are the parameters, the framework within which we will settle, and we will work out the language of the releases and a formal settlement document and execute an even more formal document than this one, which we then did, after he signed and returned this to me.

Q Now, does Defendant's Exhibit #10 spell out the parameters as to what would be paid in settlement of the slander case as well as the contract case?

A The document. Exhibit #10, the letter signed by Mr. Jensen and I, shows a compromise of both the slander action and of the contract action. It does not make a specific breakdown between — of the Fifty Five Thousand Dollars -- between the slander action and the contract action, but it does set a minimum number of dollars that must be allocated to the contract action.

Q And what was that minimum figure for the contract action?

A Not less than Ten Thousand Dollars out of the Fifty Five Thousand Dollars we required to be allocated to the contract action.

BY THE COURT: Counselor, will both counsel please approach the bench.

CONTINUED DIRECT EXAMINATION OF MARTIN FLETCHER
QUESTIONS BY RONALD C. BYAL:

Q Mr. Fletcher, I'll show you what is marked as Defendant's Exhibit #9, and ask if you would examine that and identify it, please?

A (Witness reviews document) Okay. Defendant's Exhibit #9 is a true and correct copy of an Agreement dated March 25th, 1981, between Mr. Jensen and my clients. First Equity Security Life Insurance Company, First Equity Security Investment Corporation and James Eckman, all of the past former officers, directors. It is the — it is the formal Agreement to compromise and release all claims between Mr. Jensen and my clients, of March 25th. Appended to this are the various documents that are required to be executed by the parties in order to carry out that agreement. There is, for example, just to run through them, a Release Agreement required by the General Agreement between Mr. Jensen and the law firm of Wood, Tuohy, Gleason and Mercer. There's a copy of the Release Agreement between Dan Roby and Mr. Jensen that was earlier received in evidence. There was then a Release, mutual Release between Mr. Jensen and the Howard E. Nyhart Company, who provided actuarial services or assistance in the law suit. There was then attached to it a waiver on the part of Mr. Jensen of his right to appeal from the slander action and the waiver of any rights he had to appeal from that action was gotten because it was in the process — the first Appellate steps had been taken, and he also had to waive his rights to appeal as well as release the underlying claim. As best I can tell without reading the settlement agreement in detail, this as a package would represent the final formal settlement documents in their totality.

Q   And does Exhibit #9 carry your signature in any way?
A   I'm sure it got in here somehow. Yes. I signed on behalf of First Equity Security Life Insurance Company.
Q   Is that an original signature?
A   Looks like it is an original signature on this copy. I would judge it to be, yes.
Q   Does it also bear the signature of Mr. Jensen?
A   It does.
Q   Are there any other signatures on that document?
A   My secretary, Lisa Coombs, signature appears as the Notary Public where required. And there are then either original or xerox signatures for Mr. Roby, for a representative of the Howard Nyhart Company and, again my secretary notarizing the waiver of rights.

MR. BYAL: At this time. Your Honor, we would offer into evidence State's Exhibit #9.
BY THE COURT: Defendant's Exhibit #9.
MR. FATOUT: Preliminary question, Your Honor?

BY THE COURT: You may.

## PRELIMINARY QUESTIONS TO MARTIN FLETCHER
## QUESTIONS BY WILLIAM R. FATOUT:

Q   Mr. Fletcher, as a part of Defendant's Exhibit #9 — well, strike that. Is Defendant's Roby Deposition Exhibit Number "D" a part of Defendant's Exhibit #9?
A   Yes, it is.
Q   Beg pardon?
A   Yes, it is.
Q   Okay.
A   In a sense that it's an attachment to that exhibit.
Q   Okay. And indeed there is a page in this packet of Defendant's Exhibit #9, which is that prior exhibit?
A   Yes.

MR. FATOUT: Plaintiff has no objection to the admission of Defendant's Exhibit #9.
BY THE COURT: The record will show Defendant's Exhibit #9 is accepted into evidence without objection.

Whereupon a series of documents marked for identification as Defendant's Exhibit #9, was admitted into evidence:

## CONTINUED DIRECT EXAMINATION OF MARTIN FLETCHER
## QUESTIONS BY RONALD C. BYAL:

Q   Mr. Fletcher, I'll show you what has been marked as Defendant's Exhibit #11, and ask if you would identify that?
A   (Witness reviews documents) Well I can in part and I cannot in part. I know what it is and I recognize the handwriting of the vast majority of the two pages as being, indeed, my handwriting. There's a small portion of it that is not my handwriting.
Q   Okay. Would you explain to the Court and Jury what handwriting you have placed on that document?

A   Well, all of the handwriting on the document appears to me to be mine, except in the center and slightly to the right where it says "M period Fletcher said he would advise his client to settle for this amount," and the date, "2/27/81." That is not in my handwriting. The rest of the document, which is a lapse projection, if I can call it that, is in my handwriting.

Q   Do you know who the other handwriting belongs to?

A   I cannot be sure. It — I would be reluctant to testify who that was -- who's handwriting it was. It's certainly not mine.

Q   And how would you identify that exhibit, as to what it is?

A   What this is, is a — one of the factors involved in computing how much money was due Mr. Jensen under his contract concerned the amount of renewal commissions and commissions he would receive on premium income First Equity Security Life Insurance Company received in the future. In order to determine what that is; in order to guess or arrive at what we're going to receive in the future, we had to assume that a certain number of insurance policy holders would cancel their policies or die or otherwise allow those policies to lapse, so that the pool of policies will, over time, shrink and that shrinkage of the pool of policies is called lapsing. They lapse because people die, or don't pay their premiums, or some other problem develops, and this is a projection of lapses on what are called SEC and other policies. And, it is a projection of how rapidly the pool of policies on which Mr. Jensen was to receive commissions over the ensuing thirty-five years would decline. And then it computes his commissions, shows amounts paid, plugs in an interest factor and then shows amounts due. So, this is — I have no idea when this came into existence. I — because the dating at the top is not in my hand. But this is one of the kinds of things that we did when we talked about projecting the underlying numbers, is to take current premiums and project them thirty-five years in the future and determine how much we owed Mr. Jensen, if these assumptions were correct.

Q   Thank you, Mr. Fletcher. Mr. Fletcher, earlier in your testimony I asked you questions regarding the slander case. Now, if I might direct your attention to the contract case. Were there any trials held in that cause?

A  Well, there were two causes.

Q  Let's — what I would identify as Cause Number S-75-828 in the Madison Superior Court with Judge Griffis. Do you recall that?

A  Well, I cannot at this time identify those cases by case numbers or particular judges. They had different numbers as they moved from County to County and different judges. The original — there was an original contract action brought on both contracts which came to an end, and then the contract actions were re-started. Once re-started there was never a full trial on the merits of the contract action involving the December contract. The January contract was settled. The December contract was never fully tried. Bits and pieces of it were decided over time.

Q  And during those bits and pieces that were decided, did you have occasion to observe the performance of Stephen Laudig?

A  Yes.

Q  During the bits and pieces of that December contract that had been tried, were any of those issues resolved in favor of Reginald Jensen?

A  I don't believe that any of them were ever decided in his favor.

Q  And, do you have an opinion as to the level of performance that Stephen Laudig had in those issues that were decided against Reginald Jensen?

A  In the contract action now?

Q  Yes, sir.

A  Well, I thought he did better in the contract action in terms of arguing things and research and so forth, than he did in the slander action. But he lost. The fact a lawyer loses doesn't mean he's done a bad job. It means he's got a bad argument or the law's against him. So I did not consider that he did a particularly bad job in the contract action as I did once we had a full-blown trial in the slander action. So, we never got -- it never got to a full-blown trial. The slander action was the only one that actually went to trial. I did not think he did as bad in the contract actions when we would argue motions for summary judgment or things like that.

Q  Did his level of performance reach that standard which you are accustomed to seeing in trial attorneys in central Indiana?

MR. FATOUT: Preliminary question. Your Honor?
BY THE COURT: You may.

[PRELIMINARY QUESTIONS TO MARTIN FLETCHER
QUESTIONS BY WILLIAM R. FATOUT:)

Q   Mr. Fletcher, did you say there were not trials in that case?
A   Well, there were — in the contract — the contract action, to the extent Mr. Laudig was involved in it, never had a formal trial. There were a variety of motions for partial summary judgment, and other proceedings, as a result of which bits and pieces of the issues would be resolved. But, there was never a formal trial where we actually had a trial as you're having here today, where all the issues were submitted. There was such a trial in the slander case. We did not get to that point in the suit over the December 19th, whatever, contract.

MR. FATOUT: Your Honor, I will object on the basis that the question asked him for an opinion as to trial skills, standards of performance at trial. He has said there was not such a trial in that case. For that reason he cannot testify as to an opinion.
BY THE COURT: Mr. Byal, will you repeat the question for the Court, please?
MR. BYAL: I believe my question was something to the effect, Your Honor, whether or not the performance observed by Mr. Fletcher of Mr. Laudig in the contract action reached that standard of performance that he was accustomed to seeing with trial attorneys in central Indiana.
BY THE COURT: That's my memory of the question too, that you didn't ask about -- the objection is overruled. If the witness has an answer he may put it to the Jury.

A   In my opinion, it did not comport with the standard I would expect in the conduct of those kind of proceedings prior to trial; did not measure up to the standard I would expect of a lawyer.
Q   Mr. Fletcher, in the course of your representation of the First Equity Security Life Insurance Corporation, did you keep records of the amount of time that you put into defending those cases?

A  Yes. Yes, we keep time records.
Q  And, did you keep time records for those periods when Mr. Laudig was your adversarial opponent?
A  Yes, we keep time records always.
Q  In the course of this trial Mr. Laudig has testified that he spent between seven hundred and seven hundred and fifty hours time on behalf of Mr. Jensen in the contract case and the slander case together. Do you have an opinion as to whether or not that would be an accurate assessment of the amount of time involved in this case?
A  By him?
Q  Yes.
A  Well, I do not know whether he or did-not put seven hundred or seven hundred and fifty hours into the case. It is possible to do that since there are seven hundred hours in a year. It's possible.
Q  Did you have a figure comparable to seven hundred or seven hundred and fifty hours?
A  I don't think we did, no.
Q  Would your figure of time been less than that seven hundred?
A  Yes.
Q  And, how much less?
A  Well, we don't deal in the aggregate with this particular client, so we don't ever sit down and add up. But this was a three hundred or three hundred and fifty hour operation for us over all those years.
Q  And how many years were you in these cases?
A  If I think back correctly, I got up towards eight and a half, nine years, we did this.

MR. BYAL. Is Exhibit #9 over here?
BY THE COURT: Exhibit #9, counselor?
MR. BYAL: No, #10.
BY THE COURT: Here's Exhibit #10.
MR. BYAL: Has that been offered and admitted?
BY THE COURT: Yes, it has been.

Q  Mr. Fletcher, I believe when you identified Exhibit #9, you identified a portion of that which was a waiver of rights regarding an appeal in the Indiana Court of Appeals, is that correct?

A   Yes.
Q   Did you defend First Equity Security Life Insurance Company in an appeal by Mr. Jensen?
A   The case didn't reach that point. The appeal process was initiated and, therefore, a number was assigned to the matter by the Court of Appeals as a result of some document filed. But, the appeal of the slander decision never reached a point where my client was required to respond in the Court of Appeals by way of appearance and Brief and so forth. Again, when the case then settled, here we've got a number assigned to it, we want to clean up everything, so we get a waiver of his right to perfect that appeal to clear up the record in the Court of Appeals so that nobody thinks there's an appeal going on. And again, it was as Mr. Laudig characterized it earlier, it was necessary to do that, in my judgment, to eliminate any questions that that case was over.
Q   And who initiated that appeal?
A   It's my recollection that Mr. Jensen attempted to initiate that appeal on his own.
Q   He had no attorney, is that correct?
A   Not at the time he was attempting to initiate the appeal of the slander action.
Q   At the time that you and Mr. Jensen negotiated your settlement of matters pending and his claims against First Equity Security Life Insurance Company, did you assign a value to that appeal?
A   Did I personally assign a value to it?
Q   Yes.
A   *I thought it had a value, yes.* In my own opinion, the judgment was the getting rid of the appeal or preventing the occurrence of perfection of the appeal was worth some of my client's money, yes.
Q   Okay. Thank you.

MR. BYAL: That's all we have. Judge, of this witness.
BY THE COURT: Thank you, counselor. It's an appropriate time for a short break. I'm not going to keep you here until midnight but I might keep you here until close to six o'clock. We'll take a ten minute break.

(JURY ADMONISHED AND EXCUSED) (OFF THE RECORD) (RECESS)

(ON THE RECORD)

(JURY ENTERS AND IS SEATED)

BY THE COURT: Trial is reconvened in 82-C-66, Laudig versus Jensen. The witness is advised that he is still under oath.
MR. FLETCHER: Yes, sir.
BY THE COURT: The direct examination has been completed. You may cross examine, counselor.

CROSS EXAMINATION OF MARTIN FLETCHER QUESTIONS BY WILLIAM R. FATOUT:

Q Thank you. Your Honor. Mr. Fletcher, referring to the trial of the slander case, I believe you testified you left the trial at some point and the trial was not concluded?
A I don't believe that's what I said. What I said was, my client and I left when we were dismissed at the end of the Plaintiff's case on Motion for Involuntary Dismissal. We were out. Retail Credit was still in. They were not dismissed out. So we left and Retail Credit stayed there and presented their defense. We never got to the point of having to put on a defense.
Q Did the trial continue?
A Yes, it did.
Q Were you present for the remainder of the trial?
A No.
Q All right. Were you in a position to render any kind of an opinion as to the competency of the performance of Mr. Laudig in representing Mr. Jensen for the rest of that trial after you were gone?
A Once I left, of course, I did not observe his conduct. I would have no opinion as to it.
Q Thank you. Do you recall what the grounds of granting your motion to dismiss at the end of the Plaintiff's case were?
A Yes.

Q   What were those grounds?
A   *There was a total and complete failure to prove that my client had had a communication that was defamatory within two years of the filing of the final pleadings. They sued us for slander and didn't prove it.*
Q   Sir, was there a problem with the statute of limitations, as you understood the grounds?
A   *Yes, there certainly was.*
Q   All right. Was that the majority of the grounds for dismissing your clients at that point?
A   *It was — it was certainly a very strong factor in the dismissal because the Court had already ruled in earlier proceedings that the allegations that we had committed slanders on various dates were barred by the statute of limitations, and the difficulty was to prove that we had any communications about Mr. Jensen by my clients, about Mr. Jensen, subsequent to the dates the Judge had already ruled were barred by the statute of limitations. There was not one iota of evidence that we made any communications. There was nothing.*
Q   So, in essence, the judgment in your favor — the granting of the motion to dismiss in your favor meant that there was no proof that slanderous statements had been made within the statute of limitations period in the case?
A   *Well, again, I don't want to get too technical for these proceedings, but, basically, the Judge ruled that there was absolutely no evidence that my client said anything about Mr. Jensen, defamatory or otherwise, subsequent to the dates which the Judge had already decided were barred by the statute of limitations. So, while they had those allegations of the earlier dates in there, that was the problem, it was improperly pleaded going into the trial, and they were unable to prove any communications by my client; which is an essential ingredient of a slander case, that were barred.*
Q   All right. What pleadings were improperly pleaded?
A   *Well, the -- if you're asking me to refer to specific pleadings, it was a matter of the Complaint, the Amended Complaint, the Second Amended Complaint, the Third Amended Complaint, were incorrectly done by the lawyers or lawyer submitting them.*
Q   Every one of those pleadings that you refer to, or to some of them?
A   *In my opinion, every single one of them was a mistake.*
Q   All right.

A   *Or had a fatal mistake in it.*
Q   Beg pardon, sir?
A   Had a fatal mistake in it.
Q   *And the fatal mistake was what?*
A   *They kept alleging the date upon which they accused my client of committing the slander, and they kept getting the date wrong. By the time they got around to filing a pleading that had the correct date in it, it was more than two years from that date and the Court ruled they were barred by the statute of limitations.*
Q   Okay.
A   As to those specific dates. And, then —
Q   The pleading with the proper date was finally filed but it was too late?
A   Yes.
Q   What pleading would that have been?
A   *Well, one of the amended complaints finally did get the correct date in it but it was too late then and a pleading was filed which said "if it didn't occur on one of these three dates, it was some other time within the period of limitations". It was only on that general allegation that we were obliged to go through the trial, to see if they could come up with any evidence of any communications subsequent to the specific dates, and they never did. And they never got a single one of Retail Credit's documents into evidence against my client which would have been a way to solve the problem, but they were never properly offered into evidence against my client, by Mr. Laudig.*
Q   All right. You're saying that there was a fatal mistake in the case, in that it was not properly plead so as to get beyond the fatal problem with the statute of limitations. Is that in essence what the granting the motion to dismiss was all about?

MR. BYAL: I'll object to the question, Judge. I think it's a misstatement.
MR. FATOUT: Well, I'm asking whether it's a statement or not.
MR. BYAL: He's already said that part of the problem was the failure to properly offer and admit evidence. That's been left out of this question.
MR. FATOUT: Well, I'm not asking that question. My question has to do with the pleadings.

MR. FLETCHER: The — I can answer the question, if you wish.
BY THE COURT: Counselor, I don't remember your question. Would you say it again, please?

Q *All right. I was asking whether the fatal mistake of the case had to do with the pleadings?*
A *That was one of several fatal errors made in the handling of the law suit.*
Q All right. Was Mr. Laudig responsible for that particular fatal mistake?
A Well, he was responsible for some of those. As I said —
Q (Interrupting) I'm asking you about the particular ones having to do with the pleadings and the statute of limitations. Was Mr. Laudig responsible for that fatal mistake?
A Yes.
Q How so, did he prepare and file all those pleadings?
A *You don't understand what I said. What I said was, each of several pleadings repeated the same, to me, fatal pleading mistake of alleging specific dates. I don't think Mr. Laudig was responsible for the original one. That was other lawyers. He may not have been responsible for the second one because I don't remember the timing of his entry, but once he was in the case that persisted. There was a persistence. There was yet another amended complaint. And, finally, in effort to solve the thing, he simply alleged that we had slandered him on unspecified dates within the period of limitations. But it wasn't originally, the very first one was not his, I don't recall who. It was some other lawyers.*
Q Would you say that there were pleadings filed in that case by other attorneys which fall in the category of what you would call a fatal mistake?
A Yes.
Q All right. Were you familiar with the facts relating to all the conversations, that sort of thing, whether they were plead at the trial at not?
A *Was I familiar with what conversations?*
Q *The allegedly slanderous conversations or communications?*
A Well, I was familiar with my client's version of those and I was familiar with the pleadings of Mr. Jensen's evidence and First Equifax's evidence of those communications. Yes, I was.

Q   Did you think that your client's version of the case, if it were shown to the Jury, or the Judge — excuse me — would the Judge have rendered a verdict in your client's decision, if he knew your client's version of the case?

MR. BYAL: I'll object, Your Honor. It calls for a speculation.

MR. FATOUT: I don't think it's speculation, Your Honor. This man is a learned, experienced trial attorney. He makes such judgments all the time and renders such opinions all the time.

BY THE COURT: I have no doubt that this man is a learned trial attorney. I have serious doubts that he can properly testify to what some judge would have done. The objection is sustained.

MR. FATOUT: All right.

Q   *Do you have an opinion as to what the outcome of that case would have been, were it properly -- were proper evidence presented?*

MR. BYAL: I'll again object to the question. It calls for speculation and is, therefore, irrelevant and immaterial.

BY THE COURT: I'll overrule the objection. If the witness has an answer he may express it.

MR. FLETCHER: Well, could I have the question again? Do I have an opinion as to what would have happened to the case had it been properly prepared and presented?

MR. FATOUT: Uh-huh.

MR. FLETCHER: *Sure. I have an opinion.*

Q   *What is your opinion?*

A   It *would have gotten settled before it ever went to trial.*

Q   Well, that was not my question if you recall. If it were — if proper evidence were presented at the trial, what would have happened?

MR. BYAL: I'm going to object, Your Honor. That was not the question.

BY THE COURT: Thank you counselor. I believe your question has been answered counselor.

MR. FATOUT: All right.

Q  You were familiar with the — would you be familiar with any possible appealable issues which arose out of the decision in the slander case?
A  Yes.
Q  *Do you think that there would be any merit and any possibility that an Appellate Court would reverse that decision?*

MR. BYAL: Let me place an objection, Judge. That calls for speculation by this witness.
MR. FATOUT: Your Honor, this is no more speculative than predicting the outcome of litigation. And this gentlemen, I'm sure, has had much experience with Appellate Courts and knows a reversible error when he sees one.
BY THE COURT: I concur. The witness may answer the question.

A  *Yes. I was very concerned that the case would be reversed on appeal on at least two independent grounds.*
Q  What were those grounds?
A  The original — we were sued within a week of the speaking of the alleged defamatory words, and as a result of the series of pleadings — a suit for slander is to be filed within two years of the speaking of the slanderous words. *We were sued within a week of the speaking of the slanderous words. And, as a result of a series of pleadings, the date kept changing, until the date ended up being more than two years from the last pleading. We argued to the Court and the Court accepted the proposition that, therefore, they were barred by the statute of limitations and the doctrine of relation back under Rule 15(A) would not be applicable. I had serious doubts, although I advocated that position, that I could sustain it in the Court of Appeals. I think the Court of Appeals would have said in light of the series of pleadings that had been made and the filing of the suit within a week of the speaking of the slanderous words that the Judge's original decision knocking out the actual dates upon which we had had communications claimed to be defamatory was erroneous. Secondly, I think that there was serious doubt as to the basic evidentiary ruling that the Court had made that caused Mr. Laudig to fall into a pattern of not offering*

*the Retail Credit documents against my client. I was concerned that while I had made the objection and the Court had found in my favor on the objection, I was concerned that that ruling by the Court was questionable. So, I think on those two basis, I was in trouble if the case - went to the Court of appeals. Of course, that presumes that the case properly gets to the Court of Appeals, and there are many things that can happen along the way. But, I think that, yes, there was grounds — good grounds to worry about that case in the Court of Appeals.*

Q. Okay. But you're saying that the granting of your objection to certain of the Retail Credit documents — did that contribute to the fact that Mr. Laudig did not present enough evidence to get past that motion to dismiss?

MR. BYAL: I'll object to the question. Judge. I don't think there's been a proper foundation laid as to what happened at that motion to dismiss.

MR. FATOUT: I think there has been. Your Honor. He's saying insufficient evidence and some other fatal errors. I'm pursuing a different one of the fatal errors. Why did it happen? He just alluded to it and I'm asking him.

BY THE COURT: At the risk of appearing dull, assuming I haven't already appeared dull, I confess I'm not sure I understand the question. Would you repeat it or rephrase it for me?

MR. FATOUT: All right, Your Honor. I'm asking whether the granting of the particular objection to the offer of certain evidence which I understand related to documents of the Retail Credit people at that trial — the gentleman said that objection was sustained. He has serious doubts that while he has a — he feels there is some risk that the Appellate Court would reverse that decision on the evidence — I'm asking him whether that evidentiary ruling contributed to the fact that the motion to dismiss was granted.

BY THE COURT: And your objection, Mr. Byal?

MR. BYAL: I think at this point in time my objection is, I don't understand the question.

BY THE COURT: Well, that doesn't matter. I understand the question, and if the witness understands the question and has an answer, he may speak it.

A  I do, and my answer is, I do think it contributed very strongly to the Judge's decision to a directed verdict in favor of my client.

Q  Thank you. Your testimony was that in early December, 1980, there were no offers made to Mr. Laudig by you to settle the contract case. Is that correct?

A  That is correct.

Q  Had there been any offers to settle that case and/or the slander case prior to that date?

A  Yes, there had been, from time to time, offers to settle.

Q  All right. Can you recall when some of those offers might have been made and in what amounts?

A  I recall early on — and I think Mr. Laudig alluded to this — that we had offered at one time to settle for seventeen or eighteen thousand dollars. Another time the figure went to twenty-two or twenty-three thousand dollars. I seem to also recall, perhaps, a figure in the low thirties that was mentioned. I don't mean to overemphasize this point, but in settling law suits there is constant talk, whether or not that amounts to an offer. But those kinds of numbers were discussed and mentioned and they were never an acceptable basis for a final settlement document.

Q  All right. But, for the contract case, you on behalf of your client were extending offers of seventeen, twenty-two and maybe thirty?

A  *Low thirties. Thirty-two seems to be the number that comes to mind at some point in the nine or ten years there.*

Q  Would it have been during the time nine or ten years that Mr. Laudig represented Mr. Jensen?

A  *Yes. I'm sure that there was discussion of settlement and I'm sure that some of those offers at least, were made around the time that -- or when Mr. Laudig was involved.*

Q  All right. Moving to your testimony about the dates of December 7th, 8th, 9th and 10th, 1980, I believe your testimony was you did not have telephone communication with Mr. Laudig on any of those dates?

A  That is correct.

Q  Okay. Is that a bit of recollection that you have and you're sure of it?

A   Yes, I'm absolutely certain of it.

Q   Sir, I'll hand you what has been marked Plaintiff's Exhibit "G" and ask if you can identify that document?

A   (Witness reviews document) Yes. This is a letter which I wrote on August the 12th, 1982, to Mr. Jensen in response to the letter he wrote to me of August 9th, asking some questions of me concerning my communications with Mr. Laudig.

Q   All right. Does the letter bear your signature -- a copy of your signature?

A   It does. Well, yes, that's my scrawl. But it says "dictated but not read" and is initialed by me which means I would have dictated it and my secretary would have typed it, scrawled my initials or name where it says "name", and I see that there's attached to it Mr. Jensen's letter of August 9th to me.

Q   I didn't mean to include that.

A   Yes, I just wanted to clarify.

Q   With your permission, I can remove that. My error.

Q   I would direct your attention to page three of this letter and ask you whether, in paragraph four, you would like to reconsider whether it's possible you talked to Mr. Laudig or whether it's impossible you talked to Mr. Laudig on December 7th, 1980?

A   (Witness reviews document) Now, what was your question, sir?

Q   My question is, do you still assert that it's impossible that you talked to Mr. Laudig on December 7th, 1980?

A   Yes, I do.

Q   Is there a possible way to read that paragraph that you might have talked to him on that date?

A   Is it possible to read it?

Q   Yes, is it possible at all to read the paragraph that you might have talked to him on December 7th?

A   It is possible that you can read this paragraph to say that. That is not in fact what occurred.

Q   Why did you say in this letter written more than a year ago that you didn't have a conversation with him on December 7th? Has your memory improved in the last year?

A   Yes, it has.

Q   Why is that?

A   It has improved because Mr. Jensen wrote and inquired of me based upon my memory as to whether or not I had talked with him December 7 -- you know, in the early part of December. And, I responded in the letter that I did not talk to him on the 8th, 9th and so forth, but I had a recollection I had talked to him in December, and I said in the letter that it was possible it was earlier than that. I knew it wasn't those dates because I was down in Indianapolis trying the electric heater case and that was my birthday. It stuck in my mind. My birthdays always do anymore. The question is, what I said in the letter was it might have been before the 8th or it might have been after the 8th. Since that time, based upon my review of my daily time records of what I do for First Equity Security Life Insurance Company, I can now account for that conversation. I know that that conversation occurred on December the 12th and not on December the 7th. So, to that extent my memory is improved because I refreshed my recollection by looking at my time records. I have a record of a phone call on December 12th and nothing on December the 7th and I now know where I was on December the 7th, which was also in Indianapolis. On that case I had been in Indianapolis on December the 6th, 7th, 8th, 9th, and so forth, in trial.

Q   All right. How did you celebrate your birthday on December 9th?

A   My partner, who was with me, and I went out carousing.

Q   Did that include consumption of spiritous beverages?

A   It certainly did.

Q   Did that affect your performance the subsequent day, December 10th.

A   No. I would never do that. In light of the result, $300,000.00 in favor of my client, I think I performed rather well the next day.

Q   I understand that. Here at the top of page three, the first complete sentence. Would you review that and tell me whether you believe you were affected by your birthday celebration?

A   I said "I celebrated my birthday party with my usual vigor and abandon. I subsequently paid the price the following day, December 10th, in the Court room for having engaged in the celebration for

I had one splitting headache." And, I still did a good job because my client won $300,000.00.

Q Well, is it true that a bad result is not necessarily the result of a bad job, is a good result necessarily the result of a good job?

A No. Cases tend to make themselves.

Q Now, I believe you testified fairly clearly that you were first aware Mr. Laudig was discharged by Mr. Jensen on December 12th, 1980.

A No. I testified that I was sure I knew that by that date and that I might have known it a day or two earlier. But, I do know that I knew it by December the 12$^{th}$.

Q All right. And you might have known it a day or two earlier but no earlier than that?

A I don't believe any earlier than that, because I was in the trial, see, until December the 10th. I had the phone call on the 12th. I know I knew it by the 12th.

Q And it would not have been the 7th, 8th, 9th or 10th because you didn't talk to Mr. Laudig? Could it have been prior to the 7th?

A It -- I don't have a recollection it was prior to the 7th. I think — my best recollection is that I knew it on December the 12th. Maybe I knew it a day or two before when we came back from Indianapolis after the trial was over, or something.

Q Would it surprise you that on August the 12th, 1982, you thought it was late November or early December when you knew that fact?

A No. It would not surprise me.

Q Why is there a discrepancy between December 12th or a day or two before and late November? Is that a trivial distinction in your mind?

A Well, it's trivial to me.

Q Yes.

A That fact is inconsequential to me. The reason I say that in the letter is I know that in late November or very early in December I became aware of that fact. I know I knew it by the 12th of December from my notation of the phone call that day. I may have known it as early as December the 7th because of another notation I made concerning this case on my time sheets. So, when I say late November or early December, it didn't make any difference to me whether Mr. Laudig was in or out of the case. But, to respond to the question, I know I knew it on the 12th when he called, because of my notation which was "withdrawn" W.D., withdrawn as counsel, which is part of that notation of phone call. I have an earlier notation of December 2nd indicating I had had some form of direct communication from Mr. Jensen and I would not have done that had he been represented by counsel. So, in responding to his letter about when these things occurred and relying on my memory without searching through boxes and boxes of files and time sheets, I responded that it was possible that I knew that late November, early December. But now I know I knew it at least by the 12th, when he called me.

Q You say you had direct communication with Mr. Jensen on December 2nd?
A I have a notation indicating that I did that, yes.
Q Do you believe it to be the truth?
A Yes.
Q All right. Would it be fair to say you would not have had a direct communication with him if you thought he were represented by counsel? Is that so?
A Exactly. I would not have knowingly communicated with a person who had been represented by counsel unless that person in communicating to me indicated he no longer had counsel. But, I was again just explaining why, in responding to his letter, without searching the files, I would have said late November or early December, in response to when I learned that fact.
Q I'll direct your attention to the eighth paragraph on this page and the language, and see if you can tell me what kind of a direct communication you might have had with Mr. Jensen on December 2nd, 1980?
A What was your question? This is what I was referring to.
Q What was your direct communication?
A Well, the communication — I said "the indication is that I wrote you a letter" --
Q Wrote Mr. Jensen a letter?
A On December the 2nd.

Q   Uh-huh. It further goes on to say that you probably would not have known that if he had been represented by counsel.
A   That's correct.
Q   I will now hand you what has been marked as Plaintiff's Exhibit "B" and ask if you can identify that?
A   Uh-hum. This is a letter dated November 25th, 1980, noted to have been mailed on December the 2nd, 1980, signed by me concerning "let's get together and discuss settlement of these actions". A letter to Mr. Laudig on the same date has the indication in my time records of the case, that I wrote a letter to Mr. Jensen.
Q   And, your statement was, you wouldn't have written to Mr. Jensen if he had been represented by counsel?
A   That's correct.
Q   This letter — well, I ask you about the parenthesis under the original date of the letter. Did your office prepare that?
A   The parenthesis underneath?
Q   Uh-huh.
A   Yes. This is nothing unusual about this. What it means is that I dictated the letter to Mr. Laudig on November the 25th, 1980. It would have been brought in to me sometime between the 25th and 2nd of December. I would have scrawled my name across it, in light of my secretary's accuracy, and it would have been mailed then — noted to have been mailed then on December the 2nd, 1980, by my secretary.
Q   And the same day that you sent a letter to Mr. Jensen?
A   Same day.
Q   Does this letter. Plaintiff's Exhibit "B", consider Mr. Laudig as Mr. Jensen's attorney?

MR, BYAL: I'll object to the question, Judge.

MR. FLETCHER: The letter of November 25th, 1980 —

BY THE COURT: Excuse me a minute, witness. Say your objection again, counselor.
MR. BYAL: I would object because the letter speaks for itself.

MR. FATOUT: Well, it's not admitted into evidence yet. It doesn't speak until it is.

MR. BYAL: In that case, we'll object to testimony concerning something not in evidence. Particularly something that has not been produced to us and contains statements in there which we find to be objectionable.

BY THE COURT: I'm going to permit counsel to develop this area. The objection is overruled. You may continue.

MR. FLETCHER: Well, I'm not sure I recall your question now.

Q I believe it was —
A Was the letter addressed to him as counsel?
Q Yes.
A The letter at the time of dictation was addressed to him as counsel.
Q Would you say it was an error or something of the sort that it was mailed when you considered Mr. Jensen not to have counsel?
A No.
Q Why?
A For the reason I said. I dictate these things, I sign them when I can, and they are then mailed out. It was mailed out on the same date when I indicated I had a notation in my records of a direct communication with Mr. Jensen. As opposed to with Mr. Laudig. It's the date of mailing as opposed to date of dictation. The letter is accurate as of the moment it is dictated. It may or may not have been accurate as of December the 2nd when the secretarial staff got around to finishing it and mailing it. I don't know when they parted company. I simply said when — I tried to answer the question when I came to have a view that he was no longer counsel.
Q This is your signature and not your secretary's?
A That's correct.
Q Is it fair to say you probably signed that some date later than November 25th?
A After date of dictation and prior to mailing, sure. But I have no idea when in that span of time.
Q Is it possible it was on December 2nd, 1980, the day it was mailed?

MR. BYAL: Objection, Your Honor, the witness has already stated he doesn't know when he signed it. Calls for speculation.

BY THE COURT: Objection is overruled. You may persist.

A   It was signed sometime between the 25th and the 2nd. My secretary is not good enough to get it out the same day I dictated it, so I would guess it was probably not on the 25th but certainly on or before the 2nd.

MR. FATOUT: All right. I would move that Plaintiff's Exhibit "B" be admitted into evidence.

MR. BYAL: We would object, Your Honor, to the introduction of Plaintiff's Exhibit "B", for two reasons. One, for the reason we addressed earlier, that the document was not produced to us and, secondly, because it contains matters which we find objectionable. Had it been produced earlier, perhaps we would have had an opportunity to address those objectionable matters. We would, however, Your Honor, agree to an excised portion of this letter.

BY THE COURT: May I see the letter?

MR. BYAL: Taking out the objectionable portions.

BY THE COURT: Have you had an opportunity to see this?

MR. FATOUT: I have not had an opportunity to see the excised portions and I find that there is no need for them to be taken out; that they are relevant to the matter, there is no reason that they should be taken out. I'd like counsel to justify why he thinks they should be out.

MR. BYAL: Well, they should be out because you didn't give us the letter when we asked for it to be produced and —

BY THE COURT: Very well. In the interest of time, counsel, I'm going to reserve ruling on the admissability of this evidence. We'll discuss it when we're not consuming the Jury's time unless you think that that approach would cause you a problem.

MR. FATOUT: I do not. Your Honor.

BY THE COURT: Very well. Let's all help each other assure that we attend to this matter in some appropriate way. Does that complete your cross examine?

MR. FATOUT: It does not. Your Honor.

BY THE COURT: Very well, you may continue.

CONTINUED CROSS EXAMINATION OF MARTIN FLETCHER

QUESTIONS BY WILLIAM R. FATOUT:

Q   Did you have any discussions with Steve Laudig in December of 1980 about the possibilities of settlement of the matters that he represented Mr. Jensen on?
A   Did I have any discussions with him in December concerning the possibilities of settlement?
Q   Yes.
A   I, of course, had a conversation with him as I indicated earlier, on December the 12th, in which that topic of settlement was mentioned.
Q   All right, fine. When Mr. Roby undertook what you understood to be the representation of Mr. Jensen for the purpose of negotiating the settlement, I believe you said that no formal offer was ever made, is that correct?
A   There was nothing made to Dan Roby that I considered to be a formal offer of settlement. Again, it was a matter of discussing the data, discussing computations, and, therefore, discussing the results of those computations. I don't believe Dan and I ever got to the point where I said — I formally said "I now offer on behalf of my client to settle".
Q   Would you be surprised if Mr. Roby testified under oath that on December 19th, 1980, you offered to settle the matters for $36,658.07?
A   Would I be surprised at that?
Q   Yes.
A   No, I would think he was using the language of lawyers.
Q   What do you mean by that?
A   Well, I mean what I said earlier. When two lawyers are sitting around trying to settle a law suit they talk. They talk back and forth and they say things like "well, do you think your client would consider thirty-six grand, if I can get my client to come up to that?" Now, is that an offer or is it not an offer. In a sense it is an offer. It's an indication of the willingness of my client to be guided

by my advice to go that far, perhaps. And, his response to that is an indication back that perhaps he will talk to his client along those lines. It's a searching out of the positions. In that sense, Dan may well view that as an offer. I would view that as an exploratory offer. Call it what you want. When I say offer of compromise is made, I mean a formal expression that my client, now through me as a duly authorized agent, offers to compromise for "X". I don't consider those kind of preliminary searchings of each other's positions to constitute formal offers, although Dan may view them, and quite logically, view them as offers. Expressions of willingness to explore that area. In that definition there were offers of compromise in this case constantly talked about. But, never a formal offer, I don't believe, until some time in March.

Q All right. Never a formal offer from you in your sense of it. Is that correct?

A That's correct.

Q But, you're saying another attorney may have a different opinion what constitutes a formal offer, and it's not inconsistent that Mr. Roby testified that you made a formal offer to him on December 19th?

A He may view that — He may view that as more binding than I would. More of a formal offer than I would.

Q And because the two of you have different ideas about what was and was not offered, would you say that one or the other of you committed perjury, for example?

A Absolutely not.

Q All right. (Pause) Attached to your formal settlement agreement, as you termed it, were a number of release agreements. Is that right?

A That's correct.

Q Did one of these involve Dan Roby?

A Yes, it did.

Q Why was that release attached to a case that he had no interest in any more?

A Why was it done?

Q Yes.

A It was attached because it is part of the general agreement of compromise that my client would take care of certain — that in addition to paying an aggregate sum of Fifty Five Thousand Dollars, my client, First Equity Security Life Insurance Company, would take care of certain of Mr. Jensen's financial obligations. We would take care of the Nyhart Company, we would take care of Dan Roby, who had money coming for representing Mr. Jensen to the extent he did. And, the agreement simply contemplates that in addition to the Fifty Five Thousand Dollars we will arrange that situation so that Mr. Jensen has those obligations taken care of and releases are executed in connection with taking care of that obligation. I think there's one in there for J. B. Tuohy and the other law firm from Indianapolis also.

Q  Did Mr. Jensen have any obligations to Mr. Tuohy and the other law firm?

A  Well, as I understood it, there was a desire to clean up a variety of things, and we simply using me, if you will, as a vehicle to achieve that. I do not know whether he had a quote obligation close quote to them or not. It was an obligation of my client under the agreement to secure these releases. We did so. We paid money when we had to, to get them.

Q  Have you seen the Motion to Correct Errors prepared by Mr. Jensen in the slander case?

A  Oh, I'm sure I did at some point in time. I have no recollection what's in it.

Q  You don't recall any of the issues raised or any of the alleged errors raised.

A  I have no -- I'm sure I would have looked at it and passed it to one of the young guys in the firm but I have no recollection of what it says. No.

Q  So you have no opinion as to whether that preserved any of these possibly reversible errors out of that case?

A  Well, I don't remember what it said so I couldn't respond to the question.

Q  Are you — do you have any knowledge as to whether an Appellant's brief was filed in that matter?

A  I do not.

MR. BYAL: I'll object to the question. Judge. I think that the testimony has already been elicited that the appeal never got beyond the preliminary stages.

MR. FATOUT: I'm trying to ascertain just what stage. He said the appeal had some value to him. I'm trying to ascertain what sort of value. I think that's a fair approach.

BY THE COURT: I'll permit the question counselor.

A   I do not believe that an Appellant's brief was filed prior to March — to the effectuation of the settlement in March.

Q   All right. Are you familiar with the Appellate Court rules?

A   Reasonably.

Q   Is there a deadline for the filing of an Appellant's brief?

A   Unless extended, there is a deadline, yes.

Q   Do you know whether that deadline was past by March 25th, 1981?

A   I do not believe that it had passed by then. I really shouldn't speak to that because I don't have a recollection of that sequence. Remember that I said we left the slander case at a certain point in time and it went on for a brief period of time, so I couldn't sit here and tell you exactly under the Apellate rules when those things occurred. I do know that I viewed the appeal as being alive in a sense that it could go forward at the time we effectuated the settlement, but I can't answer the question as to whether Mr. Jensen had sought and obtained an extension of time, or whether the time was up yet. I don't know.

Q   But, without knowing those things you still felt it had value?

A   *Oh, yes. And, therefore, I'm led to believe I must have looked at the timing, because I would have looked at that. It must have been alive or I wouldn't have thought it had any value and wouldn't have had him waive his rights.*

Q   Now, as to the contract case in Madison Superior Court. You said there was never a full trial on the merits, that bits and pieces were decided over time. Is that — are you saying that there was a trial of any kind, or there was not a trial?

A   Well, there were — there was not a trial in a sense of a judge and jury sitting in judgment of the ultimate issues. There was a trial in a sense there would be motions for summary judgment, which is a form of trying of an issue, or motion to dismiss, or motions for partial summary judgment. Those are not trials as I use the word trial. This is a trial, to me - Those are motion practice and issues would come up and be resolved in the contract cases, both of them, over time in that fashion.

Q In the fashion of motions rather than the fashion of trials?
A Sure. A decision is a decision.
Q I'm going to ask you to look at this and see if you can tell me what it is.

(DOCUMENT HANDED TO WITNESS)

A Well, it's a Court docket sheet in Cause Number S-75-828, Jensen versus First Equity Security Life Insurance Company.
Q And that was the cause of action we call the contract case?
A (Witness reviews document) I'm going through it page by page.
Q Okay. Can you answer me whether that was the contract case we're talking about?
A Yes, it is. That's what this is. That is correct.

(OFF THE RECORD REMARKS)

Q This Plaintiff's Exhibit "H" that you've identified as the docket sheet from the contract case, I'll ask you to look at the entry for August 13th, 1979, and see if you still tell me there was no trial in that matter?
A August what?
Q August 13th, 1979.
A Well the entry says "the matter was called for trial before the Court" and so forth. On the first issue as defined in the pre-trial order.
Q Was that a trial or not? Was it a trial or a motion?
A Well, the word "trial" as I say, is a term of art. A motion for certification can be a trial for purpose of determining your right to a change of venue. I said the word trial, as I said, I consider this a trial in the sense that the remaining issues, all the issues are addressed. This is a trial of one of several issues within the law suit. Is that a trial or is it not a trial? It is a piece of the law suit that came up and was resolved in some manner over these proceedings. But

it's not a trial of all of the issues because there are obviously some that remain.

Q  Is it possible to have trials at different times on different issues?
A  Sure.
Q  Is that what happened here?
A  I think basically what you have here was a bifurcation of issues and the Court taking up one now and then another one, perhaps one by summary judgment, and another one by an evidentiary proceeding. Call that a trial if you want to. Then you go on down through the issues and you ended up with some left over, which would then, in my vernacular, go to trial. Go to the ultimate decision.
Q  So as you're describing the word trial, that means only the last trial and not any of the prior trials that they are bifurcating?

MR. BYAL: Your Honor, I'm going to object to this line of questioning. I think it's getting totally out of hand. It goes to nothing to the real issues in this case. I think it's just an attempt to embarrass and harrass Mr. Fletcher. I ask that this line of questioning be ended. He answered the questions three times. He's given his opinion as to what he determines the word trial to be.

MR. FATOUT: Your Honor, this gentleman has testified in no uncertain terms about any number of subjects today. I am attempting to show the jury there is some uncertainty in the terms that he is using. He says there was no trial. The Court says there was a trial. He says there was no offer. He says that Mr. Roby may have felt there was an offer. I'm trying to show the jury that there is some imprecision in the language that he is using.

BY THE COURT: Very well. Do you think you have succeeded?

MR. FATOUT: I think I have.

BY THE COURT: Thank you.

MR. FATOUT: I would offer to admit Plaintiff's Exhibit "H" into evidence. And we have stipulated that, I believe.

BY THE COURT: Very well.

MR. BYAL: No objection. Exhibit "H" is the docket sheet, Judge.

BY THE COURT: Very well. The record will show that Plaintiff's Exhibit "H" is accepted into evidence without objection.

WHEREUPON A DOCUMENT MARKED AS PLAINTIFF'S EXHIBIT "H" WAS ADMITTED INTO EVIDENCE.

CONTINUED CROSS EXAMINATION OF MARTIN FLETCHER QUESTIONS BY WILLIAM R. FATOUT:

Q   Mr. Fletcher, you are, I presume, familiar with the work done by Mr. Laudig over the years on Mr. Jensen's cases?
A   From my viewpoint, yes.
Q   All right. From your viewpoint and in your opinion, do you think those efforts had any value whatsoever to Mr. Jensen?
A   In which case, sir?
Q   In either case. Let's take the slander case. Was there any value of Mr. Laudig's services in that case to Mr. Jensen?
A   *Regretfully, sir, I do not consider them to have advanced Mr. Jensen's cause. I considered them to be counter-productive and utterly negative in every respect. No, I consider them to be absolutely worthless.*
Q   All right. How about the contract case? Did any of the efforts of Mr. Laudig have any value to Mr. Jensen?
A   Well, in the sense that they kept the litigation alive and it did move forward, as I said earlier, I thought he did a better job in some ways in the contract action than he did in the slander action.
Q   Fine. And in the contract action you're saying that Mr. Laudig's services had some value?
A   Some value. He never won a significant point, but that's not necessarily his fault. He was able to move that case somewhat forward from where it had been with the prior counsels. So I think it had some value. But in the slander case, I'm sorry to say —
Q   (interrupting) Well, if you'll limit yourself to the contract case. I understand —

MR. BYAL: (interrupting) Your Honor, I'm going to object to counsel interrupting the witness. He's not finished.
MR. FATOUT: Your Honor, it's the same as letting him finish and then stopping and taking the time and ask that it be stricken as non-responsive.
BY THE COURT: I agree. The objection is overruled. You may continue, please.

Q   All right.  On the contract case then, Mr. Laudig's work kept the litigation alive and that had value?  Is that what you're saying?
A   Yes.
Q   Is it possible for you to say what that value was?
A   I do not truly think I could, sir.
Q   Okay.  Did you ever tell Mr. Laudig in the course of the slander litigation that the case was without merit?
A   I do not recall using those words with him.  I am sure that I oftentimes gave my view on behalf of my client that the claim was without merit.  Whether that was true or false.  That would have been my expression to him, as part of the technique of representing my client.  I'm sure I said in essence we consider this frivolous and —
Q   Are you saying that it's possible you might have said to Mr. Laudig that the slander case was without value sometime before the trial, for example?
A   Oh, I'm sure.  I'm sure that in the ordinary exchange between opposing counsel, that that kind of a position, if not those words, would have been taken.  *I would do that whether it was accurate or not in terms of my own assessment of the case.  That is a part of the technique of being a lawyer.  And, he says to me "it's worth a million dollars" and I say "it isn't worth a cent", and we try to proceed.*
Q   I understand.  Do you ever do work as a plaintiff's attorney?
A   Yes.
Q   Have you ever represented a plaintiff in a defamation action?
A   Yes.  If you'll let me use the word plaintiff to include defendants who file affirmative counterclaims.  Yes, I have represented people who affirmatively alleged actions for slander.  They happened to be defendants filing counter-claims.
Q   I understand.

MR. FATOUT:  No further questions, Your Honor.  Thank you.
BY THE COURT:  Thank you.
MR. BYAL:  I have just two questions, Judge.

REDIRECT EXAMINATION OF MARTIN FLETCHER
QUESTIONS BY RONALD C. BYAL:

Q   Mr. Fletcher, did you receive any communications from Stephen Laudig any mail, or correspondence from Stephen Laudig, after the date of December 5th, 1980?

A   After December the 5th, 1980?

Q   Yes.

A   (Witness looking through files) I believe that I would have to answer that in the affirmative. I think I did receive written communication from Mr. Laudig after December 5th, in the sense that I seem to recall his formal withdrawals from the cases came in after that. But, except for some pleading taking himself out of the case, I didn't have any letters or correspondence or stuff like that from him from Mr. Laudig.

Q   Mr. Fletcher, I'll show you what's been marked as Plaintiff's Exhibit "A" and ask if you ever received a facsimile or copy or any other document substantially the same as that one, from Mr. Laudig?

A   No, I did not.

MR. BYAL: That's all I have Your Honor.
BY THE COURT: Thank you. Any recross?
MR. FATOUT: No, Your Honor.
BY THE COURT: Thank you very much Thank you, sir, you may step down.
   (WITNESS MARTIN FLETCHER EXCUSED) *(Emphasis supplied.)*

| | | |
|---|---|---|
| STATE OF INDIANA | ) | IN THE TIPTON CIRCUIT COURT |
| | ) SS: | |
| COUNTY OF TIPTON | ) | 1983 CALENDAR TERM |
| | | |
| STEPHEN LAUDIG, | ) | |
| Plaintiff | ) | |
| -vs- | ) | CAUSE NUMBER 82-C-66 |
| REGINALD L. JENSEN, | ) | |
| Defendant | ) | |

## COURT'S CERTIFICATE

I, DANE P. NASH, Judge of the Tipton Circuit Court, hereby certify that the foregoing typewritten transcript of the evidence so taken and reported as aforesaid, contains all the testimony of Attorney Martin Fletcher given in the above stated cause on October 14, 1983, during the course of the trial by jury, as required by the Rules of the Indiana Supreme Court. The same has been examined and approved, signed and sealed, and found to be correct; and is Ordered to be made a part of the record in this cause by the Clerk of this Court; all of which is done this 17th day of March, 1984.

DANE P. NASH, Judge
Tipton Circuit Court

| | | |
|---|---|---|
| STATE OF INDIANA | ) | IN THE TIPTON CIRCUIT COURT |
| | ) SS: | |
| COUNTY OF TIPTON | ) | 1983 CALENDAR TERM |

| | | |
|---|---|---|
| STEPHEN LAUDIG, | ) | |
| Plaintiff | ) | |
| -vs- | ) | CAUSE NUMBER 82-C-66 |
| REGINALD L. JENSEN, | ) | |
| Defendant | ) | |

## REPORTER'S CERTIFICATE

I, JoAnne B. Libertore, Official Court Reporter of the Tipton Circuit Court of Tipton County, Indiana, do hereby certify that the above, within and foregoing is a true, full, complete and correct transcript of all the testimony of Attorney Martin Fletcher, a witness called on behalf of the Defendant, before the Honorable Dane P. Nash, Judge of the Tipton Circuit Court, during the course of the trial by jury held in the Tipton Circuit Court on the 14th day of October, 1983; that included herein are the objections, the rulings of the Court in respect to the admission and rejection of evidence, and exceptions taken and reserved thereto; and that the same is the original transcript of the proceedings during said testimony, as made by me from the tape recording thereof WITNESS my hand and seal this 14th day of March, 1984.

                                        Signed
                                        JoAnne B. Libertore
                                        Official Court Reporter

Tipton Circuit Court
Tipton County, Indiana

Was the slander action timely filed? The answer is on page 199, the first question and answer. The answer is "The original - we were sued within a week of the speaking of the alledged defamitory words." The suit was timely filed. As to the basic question of slander, did Eckman slander me? In the same answer on page 199, Fletcher alters his response twice. Five lines further down he says "I think the Court of Appeals would have said in light of the series of pleadings that had been made and the filing of the suit within a week of the speaking of the slanderous words that the Judge's original decision knocking out the actual dates upon which we had had communications claimed to be defamatory was erroneous." The suit was timely filed and the slander occurred. My attorneys destroyed the case.

October 17 was the third day of the trial. Laudig was on the witness stand before Fletcher's testimony and now returned to finish his testimony. Laudig used his mileage records to support the amount of time he consumed on my cases. But his auto travel expenses submitted to the court contained double and triple billings of trips he said he made on my behalf. Plus, he admitted the same bills were also submitted to his other clients. He included in his cost calculations the amount of money I had personally paid for copying and other expenses. Here's a partial transcript:

Questions to Laudig by MR. BYAL on Cross Examination
A   Mr. Jensen was responsible for the costs incurred in the pursuit of his litigation.
Q   Regardless of what the cost was, he was to pay the expenses. Is that what you're saying?
A   I wouldn't say regardless of the cost. That calls for speculation. But, whatever the cost was –
Q   If you told him the cost was fifty cents a copy would you expect him to pay fifty cents?
A   No.
Q   Okay.
A   Unless that was my actual cost, which it wasn't.
Q   And it's your testimony today that you don't know what your actual cost was?
A   Not to the — not exactly, no.

Q  Was it your testimony last week that on October 14th you attended a hearing? Take that back. October 14th, 1977, that you attended a hearing in one of these cases that lasted three hours?
A  Nineteen seventy-seven?
Q  Yes.
A  It could be. I don't recall the exact date.
Q  You testified last week from some notes. Do you still have those notes with you?
A  No, I don't.
Q  Why is it Mr. Laudig that your notes were important to you last week but they aren't important today?
A  I don't understand what you mean by the question. Do you mean why don't I have them with me?
Q  Well, you felt it necessary to testify from notes last week. Is there some reason why you don't have your notes with you today?
A  I don't have them in — I don't have them with me.
Q  I understand that. I'm asking you "why don't you have them?"
A  I wasn't asked to bring them.
Q  Did someone ask you to bring your notes when you testified last week?
A  No.
Q  Then why is it important that nobody asked you to bring them today?
A. I — the question is nonsense.

BY THE COURT: Counselor. Addressing myself to the witness.
MR. LAUDIG: I don't understand his question.
BY THE COURT: Stop. I'm talking to you. Don't comment on the questions. If you know the answer, answer it. If you don't know the answer, say so. Mr. Byal, you may proceed.
MR. BYAL: Thank you, Your Honor.

Q  Well, did you feel Mr. Laudig, that you couldn't be cross examined if you didn't have your notes here?
A  No.
Q  Are you doubting the fact that you testified on your direct examination last week that on October 14th, 1977, you attended a hearing which took approximately three hours?

A  I don't recall the exact date.
Q  Do you recall giving that testimony?
A  I don't recall the exact testimony. We went through a lot of dates.
Q  Do you recall putting it in your notes and answering to the date of October 14th, 1977, of a hearing of three hours?
A  Not that exact date, no. There are four hundred and fifty entries on there and I don't recall each and every one of them.
Q  Some of them were made up, weren't they?
A  No.
Q  Mr. Laudig, let me show you a document there and ask if that refreshes your recollection?
A  This is a copy of the document which was provided to you.
Q  Those are the notes you did not bring with you today?
A  This is a copy of the notes.
Q  And does that refresh your recollection as to whether or not you considered in those notes an entry dated October 14, 1977, of a hearing that's three hours?
A  It has notation "10/14/77, hearing this date, approximately three hours."
Q  And it's your testimony that hearing took place?
A  That's correct. My best recollection when I made this.
Q  And it was made when? Several weeks ago?
A  Within the last couple weeks.
Q  Mr. Laudig, I'll show you what has been marked as Plaintiff's Exhibit "H" and ask if you would look at that, please?
A  This is a — this is the docket sheet from the contract case.
Q  Now, do you see anywhere on that docket sheet an entry for October 14th, 1977?
A  Yes, I do.
Q  And what is that entry?
A  It says "Defendant's Motion for Summary Judgment set for hearing December 9th, 1977, 1:15 p.m."
Q  Does it say anything on that docket sheet of a hearing taking place on October 14th, 1977?
A  No.

Q I'll show you what's been marked as Defendant's Exhibit #1 and ask you to look at that, please.
A It's the same thing.
Q Can you identify that, please?
A It's the docket sheet for the contract case.
Q That's the same as your Exhibit "H". Is that correct?
A Except for the pages being rearranged.
Q I'll show you what's been marked as Defendant's Exhibit #2 and ask if you would identify that, please?
A This is the docket sheet for the defamation case.
Q Have you ever seen this exhibit before?
A Friday, I think.
Q Looking at Defendant's Exhibit #2, upon the date of October 14th, 1977, do you see an entry of a hearing on that day?
A I don't see any entry for the year 1977.
Q What are docket sheets, Mr. Laudig?
A I believe I answered it last week when I stated it was the records of documents and activities of the Court.
Q Can you explain to me, Mr. Laudig, how you can say in your own notes that you had a three hour hearing on October 14th, 1977, when there was no mention of a hearing in either of these cases on that day?
A I made a mistake.
Q You made a mistake of three hours?
A That's correct. It could have been just a meeting for three hours.
Q Or, it could not have taken place at all?
A Something happened on that date — involved with Mr. Jensen's case.
Q And you're —
A I —
Q Go ahead. I didn't mean to interrupt.
A I made a mistake and called it a hearing instead of a meeting.
Q You don't think you could have made a mistake and put something down that didn't take place at all?
A It's possible.
Q And at fifty dollars and hour that would be a hundred and fifty dollar mistake, wouldn't it?

A   I'm not claiming any compensation for 1977.

Q   Wasn't it your testimony that the records that you made in this case, in both cases, the slander case and the contract case, occurred with the same frequency in 1979 and 1980, that they did in '77 and '78?

A   What's the question? I don't understand.

Q   Well, I'll repeat it to you. You testified on your direct examination, specific dates between 1977 and November 1st, 1978. Is that correct?

A   Yes.

Q   And was it not your testimony afterwards that the frequency of the meetings and conduct in these two cases, the work you did was the same in 1979 and 1980 as it was in the period from '77 and '78?

A   No, I think my testimony was that it occurred with approximately the same frequency and that the meetings and activity increased when there was a pleading that had to be done or a hearing which occurred, at which case — during which time the level of activity increased.

Q   And did the frequency of your errors also increase?

A   I don't think so.

Q   Do you think there are any more mistaken entries in your notes for '79 and '80?

A   I don't think there are. I try not to make mistakes, but it's possible. Like I said, there were four hundred and fifty entries on there.

Q   Mr. Laudig, look at your notes again and tell me if you can find an entry that you made regarding the trip to Akron, Ohio?

A   (Looking through document) I'm sorry. What was the question?

Q   Whether or not that refreshed your recollection of the entries regarding the trip to Akron, Ohio? Have you found that in your notes?

A   Yes.

Q   How many times did you count the trip to Akron, Ohio?

A   I just meant to count it once. But it looks like I did count it twice.

Q   How many hours did you attribute to that?

A   Uh, twelve hours.

Q   So that's another twelve hour mistake in your notes. Is that correct?

A   Well, these weren't produced to be admitted as evidence.

Q  That's right. You didn't produce them at all, did you?
A  They weren't intended to. These were notes that I was referring to, and had I been asked what happened on the 20th, I would have reviewed it and seen that the entry was in here twice.
Q  Do you also have a figure of notes in there for trial 'preparation encompassing the same days as the trip to Akron, Ohio?
A  Yes.
Q  And is that a third time you've counted that same twelve hours?
A  I don't total the hours.
Q  But your notes were your basis of your estimate of your seven hundred to seven hundred and fifty hours, were they not?
A  That's exactly what it was. An estimate.

Further questions by Mr. Byal are omitted.

Questions by MR. FATOUT on redirect:

Q  If the jury were to total what the number of hours you spent and what you've testified to is what you would charge for those hours if you were charging on that basis, they would come up with a pretty large number. Exactly what is it that you're asking the jury to have Mr. Jensen pay you for your work?
A  I believe that I'm entitled to, at most, twenty-two thousand dollars, which would be forty percent of the settlement that he received on both.
Q  All right, and not seven hundred hours times fifty dollars, or a hundred dollars an hour?
A  No. *(Emphasis supplied)*

The balance of questions and answers omitted.

He withdrew his claim for payment based upon quantum meruit. His withdrawal of that claim was a tacit admission his work had no merit. He then said he was only entitled to $22,000 as 40% of the settlement I received from FESLIC. Even so, the contract between us prior to our separation called for one-third for settlement prior to trial and the contract case never went to trial. Did he think that he was entitled to payment based upon his loss of the slander action?

On October 18, the fourth day of the trial, the jury reviewed exhibits. Laudig completed his testimony. I took the stand to explain my version of events. I was asked how Laudig came to be employed, what he accomplished, and how we separated. A portion of my testimony at trial follows.

Questions by MR. BYAL:

Q   Mr. Jensen, the slander case that you had against First Equity Security Life Insurance Company and James Eckman and Retail Credit, did that case go to trial?
A   Yes, sir, it did.
Q   And when was the trial?
A   It began October 27th, 1980, and it ended on December 1, 1980.
Q   Now, Mr. Jensen, when did you first learn of the outcome of that case?
A   On November 19th — I'm sorry, November 21. It was Friday, November 21, 1980.
Q   And how did you learn of that outcome?
A   I called Mr. Laudig to find out if we were going to go back to trial the following Monday.
Q   And what was Mr. Laudig's response to you?
A   He said the trial was over, that I had lost, I had been zapped by the judge, and it was ended forever.
Q   And did you have any other discussion with him at that point on the telephone?
A   Yes, I asked him if he had a copy of the dismissal and he said "no". And I asked him what it said and he said well, I can go up to the Court and get a copy and read it myself. I asked him if he was going to appeal the case, and he said "No, he wasn't going to appeal it. There was no merit in an appeal." And I asked him if he had any objections to my appealing it myself and he said "No, he had no objections whatsoever if I go out and appeal it myself." And I told him, well, I'll get a copy of the dismissals then and then I'll come in later and pick up my papers and take it on my own. And he said "Well, that's fine but call me before you come in to pick up your papers, make sure I'm here." And I said I would.

Q At the time of that conversation, how would you describe the demeanor or the tenor between yourself and Mr. Laudig?
A Cool but courteous.
Q Was it a heated discussion?
A Not that one, no.
Q At the time that you had that discussion did you feel that Mr. Laudig was through with representing you?
A I was certain he was through. As far as I was concerned it was over.
Q And why were you certain that it was over at that time?
A For several reasons. First of all, the agreement specified that he should appeal the cause, and when he said he wouldn't appeal it, then that left it up to me. I can't appeal a law suit and pay him for it, from my standpoint. And, in order to file an appeal I'd have to use substantially all of the same documents that were used in both cases. The contract case and the slander case intermingled. It was simply impossible for me to sit in his office, using my papers, filing an appeal on a case which he had lost, while he's working on another case with an attempt to collect some money. It just didn't make any sense.
Q Mr. Jensen, prior to that date of November 21st, 1980, had you done anything to breech your agreement with Mr. Laudig?
A No, sir, I didn't.
Q And did you do anything to breech your agreement on that day?
A No, sir.
Q After that telephone conversation of November 21st, 1980, when was the next time that you had any communication with Stephen Laudig?
A It would have been the first week in December.
Q And when did that take place?
A Well, it would have been the first week in December because I called him up and told him I wanted to come down and get my papers, and wanted to make an arrangement to get it.
Q And did you then make an arrangement to meet with him?
A Yes, we did. He said to come on in on December 8th, come on in at noon and he'd talk to me then, but he had some thoughts on

whether or not he could get any money out of the cases before we finally separated.

Q  And was that a heated discussion on that occasion?
A  Not that one, no, sir.
Q  Did you then have occasion to meet with him on December 8th?
A  Yes, sir, I did. I met him at noon on December 8th.
Q  And where did that meeting take place?
A  In his office.
Q  And would you tell the Court and jury what occurred during that meeting?
A  Well, I came into the meeting — I had in my coat pocket the letter that's been introduced here asking that we settle our accounts, and, uh, I came in to get all my papers and all of my documents. And, Mr. Laudig said he thought he was entitled to some money because he had put so much time in on the law suits and he thought he ought to get some money out of it, and he said that he thought that he could get an offer of settlement from the attorneys for Retail Credit for approximately three thousand dollars to avoid filing an appeal, and he thought he could get a -- something, but he wasn't really sure if he could get anything out of First Equity but he thought maybe he could get something out of First Equity. In any event he said he was going to settle with First Equity for any amount of money that he wanted to settle for and he said he didn't care if it was twelve thousand dollars, he was going to take it. And I said "No, Steve, you're not going to take it. As far as I'm concerned we're through. I've got a letter here that I'd like you to read. I'd like you to tell me if you agree with the letter, and then see if we can separate and settle our accounts." And he read the letter, and he said he didn't think it was fair at that point in time to break off without any payment to him, other than what he had been paid up to that point of time. And I said "Well, what do you think would be fair then, Steve? What do you want?" And he said "Well, I think I can get at least three thousand dollars out of First — out of the Retail Credit Company people to avoid an appeal." He said "I think I'm entitled to forty percent of that. That's twelve hundred dollars." And, uh, we talked about the Eastern Broadcasting case. He said he was sure the attorney

for Eastern Broadcasting would offer a thousand dollars to settle that one. And, uh, I said "What about First Equity?" He said "I don't know if they'd offer anything." I said, "Well, I'll tell you what I'll do, Steve. Why don't you take one more week. Any offer you get in another week, any offer whatsoever, I'll pay you your percentages on them. When I get my checks you'll get your checks, but regardless of what happens, you find whatever offer you can get. That's my indebtedness to you. I'll make my own decisions then about whether or not I'll proceed on appeal or proceed with the cases, but that will terminate our relationship and our financial relationship." He said, "Well, in a week I ought to get some, so that's fine." He said, "I'll accept that." He said, "I know what I'll get out of the others but I don't know what I'll get out of First Equity." And I said, "Well, why don't you call Mr. Fletcher. Call him right now. Pick up the phone and telephone him and get the thing started." So he said okay. So he picked up the phone, he called Mr. Fletcher's office and Mr. Fletcher's secretary said that he was in trial in court in Indianapolis and he said well where, what court, where can I reach him down there? She said "I have no idea which court he's in. None whatsoever. I don't know what phone number to call, I'm not even sure what case he's on." She said, "I really don't know how to reach him." And he said fine and he hung up. And I said, "Well, you go ahead and check and find out whatever you want to find out, but I'm going to come back when the week is over. I'll call you and make arrangements and pick up all the rest of my documents and you tell me whatever settlement offers you have and I'll be indebted to you for that and then we're through and I'm gone." And he said, "That's fine." So, we then made arrangements to meet the following Monday at five o'clock when I could come in when his office was closing up and pick up the documents and that was the end of it.

Q   Was that a heated discussion?
A   Part of it was heated.
Q   Who was heated in this discussion?
A   Well, I think probably we both were.
Q   Had that heated part of this discussion ended at the time the two of you parted at the end of that meeting?

A  Well, I think the heated part of the discussion might have lasted for about a half an hour. We talked for about an hour or hour and a half. But I think the heated part might have lasted for about a half an hour.

Q  And did you then meet with him again the following week to pick up your papers?

A  The following Monday I came in and picked up the papers, that's correct.

Q  And what was the discussion you had with him at that time?

A  He told me that he had no formal offer or no assurance of an offer from Eastern Broadcasting but their attorney had told him that he had made a recommendation to the president of the company to settle for a thousand dollars, and I said "Well, that's fine, I owe you $333.33. I'll send that to you." I said "What happened with Retail Credit?" He said "Well, all they did was offer to settle based upon me not paying them any additional expenses for the loss of the law suit." I said "Steve, I don't know of any. I just wrote them out a check for about $500.00 for expenses and they've submitted no additional expenses. I thought I'd paid them all." He said, "Well, there are other court costs and everything they can bill you for." And I said, "Did they offer any money?" And he said, "No, they just offered to waive the expenses." And I said, "Well, I don't consider that something upon which I should pay you a commission, so there's nothing there. What happened with First Equity?" He said "Well, they never offered anything. I got no offer out of them whatsoever." I said, "Well, that's fine. I'll send you the three hundred dollars when I get it. Let me have my papers and I'll go." So I put the papers in the trunk of the car and left.

Q  Mr. Jensen, I'll show you what has been marked and admitted into evidence as Plaintiff's "Exhibit B" and ask if you would look at that please.

A  It's a copy of a letter from Martin Fletcher to Stephen Laudig dated November 25, 1980 and mailed 12/2/1980.

Q  At the time that you were in Mr. Laudig's office on December 8th, 1980, did Mr. Laudig show you that letter?

A  No, sir.

Q  Did he mention that letter in any way?

*Judicial Deception*

A   No, sir.
Q   Had you ever seen that letter prior to the trial of this case?
A   No, sir, I didn't.
Q   At the time of your meeting of December 8th, 1980, did Mr. Laudig in any way indicate to you that he could get some money from First Equity?
A   No, sir, he didn't. He told me that he thought — he said, "I'm going to take whatever settlement I can get even if it's twelve thousand." But he didn't indicate to me that he could get it. He just said that he was going to take whatever he could get.
Q   When you were first questioned by Mr. Fatout earlier in your direct examination, he kept using the word "discharge." Do you recall that?
A   Yes, sir.
Q   I believe your testimony was that you considered a discharge and a termination roughly the same term but with some differences, is that correct?
A   Yes, sir, that is.
Q   Would you explain to the Court and jury what the differences were you were referring to?
A   In my opinion if I were to come to someone and say "you are now discharged" then I have, in effect, fired them. If I were to go to someone and say "I'd like to terminate our agreement or I want to terminate our relationships" then to me that means that we're going to finalize our accounts and settle our accounts and just part company, and do it as quickly and as amicably as we can. One seems to me to have a connotation of more of a mutual arrangement, whereas as one is an absolute term on the part of one party.
Q   Did you tell Mr. Laudig he was fired?
A   No, sir, I never did.
Q   Did you ever use that word?
A   No, sir.
Q   Did you give him any written documentation saying he was fired?
A   No, sir.
Q   What terminology was used in your letter of December 8th?

A   I asked him if he would withdraw his appearances from the law suits.
Q   Did your agreement with Mr. Laudig have any provisions for the time when the agreement would be terminated?
A   No, sir, there was no time provisions.
Q   Were there any provisions in that agreement as to when it could be terminated?
A   No, sir.
Q   Any provision as to how it could be terminated?
A   No, sir.
Q   Did you believe that in the absence of any written words concerning termination that it could be terminated at will by either party?
A   That's my understanding, that the parties can terminate once each party has had adequate opportunity to perform.
Q   Did Mr. Laudig have adequate opportunity to perform under that contract?
A   I think he surely did.
Q   And did he perform everything he was obligated to perform?
A   I don't think he performed anything in the final analysis.
Q   And why do you say that, Mr. Jensen?
A   Well, the — the slander action turned out to be an absolute waste of time from beginning to end and the contract action had done nothing more than be sustained in the Court for another three or four years. I guess it was another three year period of time. The contract action had been in Court since late 1971, and as far as I could tell, all it required was a showing of — of termination and damages in order to collect the commissions. It was venued (inaudible) and by that time almost ten years. And, there were a whole series of legal documents and pleadings. Well, you can see them right here — boxes of — when you get down to them they are absolutely nothing but paper filling, that's all it is. None of it has any real significance except some of the depositions and the other basic pleadings. As far as accomplishment, nothing was accomplished at all.
Q   Mr. Jensen, the slander case, at the time that Mr. Laudig entered his appearance, was First Equity and James Eckman defendants in that case?
A   They had been dismissed as defendants, that's correct.

Q   And at the time that Mr. Laudig withdrew his appearance in that slander case had the same defendants, First Equity and James Eckman, been dismissed a second time.
A   Well, that was the third time. Not the second, but the third.
Q   During the two years that Mr. Laudig was on the case it really made no progress from when it first started. Is that correct?
A   Yes.

(OBJECTIONS AND ARGUMENTS OF COUNSEL OMITTED)

The judge sent the jury home for the night and everyone left the courthouse. It was late, past dinner time and I walked into a small restaurant across from the courthouse and saw Laudig seated in a booth reading a newspaper. When he saw me enter the restaurant, he completely covered his head and face with the newspaper he had in his hands in the hopes I wouldn't see him. He was totally embarrassed about his actions. Laudig's embarrassment about his suit caused him to announce to the judge towards the end of the trial he was not going to appeal the verdict if he lost.

During the trial, Laudig announced to the court in front of the jury I had not paid income tax on the amount of the settlement applied to the slander damages. He could have come into that information only if he had seen my income tax returns. My tax returns were private, I prepared my own and had shown them to no one. Only the IRS had a copy. It seemed to me Tuohy was the only person associated with these events who could have obtained that information. Tuohy had enough influence in Indiana so he could obtain nearly any piece of information he ever wanted to see. I informed Byal I didn't pay income taxes because slander and libel damages were exempt from taxation. Byal asked me to provide him with proof. We went into the court's law library and located the United States Treasury code, which contained the law on slander and libel damages. We reviewed the language. He agreed with me. He took the volume that contained the code section back to the courtroom and read it to Judge Nash in front of Laudig and Fatout. Judge Nash then remarked to the jury that Laudig had made an incorrect statement that had to be corrected. The judge explained to the jury I was not required to pay taxes on the slander payment.

Herrin never returned to court, so on October 19 Byal took the witness stand and read Herrin's entire deposition into the record so the jury could hear what Herrin had to say. It took him several hours to read it. Neither Fatout nor Laudig had any objections to Herrin's testimony.

On October 20, Byal completed my defense. One of the jurors became ill and had to be excused. She was replaced with the alternate juror. Judge Nash asked the parties if they would agreed to continue with only five jurors if any additional jurors had to be excused. Both sides agreed and the trial continued. Fatout presented rebuttal evidence and rested. Byal declined to make any rebuttal.

On Friday, October 21 Fatout's final argument to the Jury was that Laudig was entitled to $22,000, plus an extra $150 of uncollected expenses, presumably the telephone calls. ("Please don't forget the $150" Fatout reminded the jurors). Byal's argument to the jury was the insurance company owed me a bucket of money and I had hired Laudig to go to the company and get the bucket for me. He said Laudig then spilled the bucket on the way back. He came back with nothing. It was obvious the insurance company owed money to me because some of the debt was finally paid, but none was paid to me based upon Laudig's actions.

This was the only lawsuit in Indiana I was involved in that ever went to trial by jury. The jurors were Charles F. Zirkle, Robert N. Zell, Jack Heath, Emily J. Wilson, Leslie R. Mraz, Donald G. Burket, and Alternate, Doris McCool. Emily J. Wilson became ill during the trial and was excused. Doris McCool became the sixth juror. After several hours of consideration, the jury agreed Laudig was entitled to nothing under any conditions. The verdict was simple. It said: "We, the jury, find for the Defendant and against the Plaintiff." Byal indicated he was surprised the verdict was in my favor. He had the feeling Laudig would be awarded some amount of fees. He said he guessed it just shows a jury can be convinced to rule against an attorney. I mentioned to Byal that Fletcher had admitted FESLIC had slandered me. Byal disagreed, so I showed him Fletcher's testimony. Byal then acquiesced.

Byal prepared the form of judgment and reviewed it with me. He then finalized the judgement and Judge Nash signed it. The judgment is shown below. I paid Byal for all of his time and expenses up to that point in time.

| | | |
|---|---|---|
| STATE OF INDIANA | ) | IN THE TIPTON CIRCUIT COURT |
| | ) SS: | |
| COUNTY OF TIPTON | ) | 1983 CALENDAR TERM |

| | | |
|---|---|---|
| STEPHEN LAUDIG, | ) | |
| Plaintiff | ) | |
| | ) | CAUSE NO. 82-C-66 |
| v. | ) | |
| REGINALD L. JENSEN | ) | |
| Defendant | ) | |

## JUDGMENT

This cause having been submitted upon the merits, and evidence having been heard and concluded, the Jury now returns its verdict in favor of the Defendant.

IT IS THEREFORE, ORDERED, ADJUDGED and DECREED that Judgment be entered for the Defendant, Reginald L. Jensen, and against the Plaintiff, Stephen Laudig, and that the Plaintiff, Stephen Laudig, take nothing from the Defendant, Reginald L. Jensen, by way of Count I of his Complaint for Attorney Fees under a theory of breach of contract, and that the Plaintiff take nothing from the Defendant by way of Count II of his Complaint for Attorney Fees under a theory of quantum meruit.

IT IS FURTHER ORDERED, ADJUDGED and DECREED that costs be assessed against the Plaintiff and that Plaintiff take nothing from the Defendant.

All of which is ORDERED, ADJUDGED and DECREED this 25th day of October, 1983.

<u>Signed</u>
DANE P. NASH, Judge

What seemed strange to me was Laudig never refuted the malpractice charge by Fletcher. Fatout did cross examine Fletcher, but Laudig never took the stand to counter any of Fletcher's statements or conclusions. None of my former attorneys had the courage to appear in court and attempt to refute Fletcher's testimony about their malpractice. They knew what they had done and it would have been very embarrassing for them to be confronted in court. The Indiana Code of Professional Conduct for attorneys, Disciplinary Rule DR 2-105 said: "A lawyer shall not enter into an agreement for, charge, or collect an illegal or clearly excessive fee." The judgment in my favor in *Laudig v. Jensen* was clearly proof Laudig charged an excessive fee.

A trial judge will usually set aside a jury verdict against an attorney and award fees in any event. Awarding fees to an attorney at trial not only gives money to the attorney, it also protects the attorney from disciplinary action. Therefore, Laudig's cohorts could fully expect to force a judgment in his favor even if a jury verdict was against him.

It seemed to me Judge Nash conducted a fair trial. His rulings didn't seem to favor either party. He could have allowed the suit to be amended to bring Laudig in as the defendant in the counterclaim because Laudig had taken inconsistent positions in two equal courtrooms, but looking back on the history of the actions it was probably much better for me he didn't.

During the third day of the trial, Monday, October 17 Sam Huston, Garrison's general agent partner, went over to my apartment complex and asked the manager to let him into my apartment. He told the manager I always showed up at the office in the mornings and no one had seen me for several days. He was concerned I might be dead and he wanted to check my apartment to make sure I wasn't laying on the floor or on a bed. The manager let him in. He found nothing. On Monday, October 24 Huston explained what he had done because he believed someone might tell me he'd been in my apartment. Garrison and Huston kept a very close watch over my activities.

On December 5 I mailed a memo to Byal asking him if he had communicated with Campbell or Graham on my case against Laudig. He didn't respond, so on December 14 I called and asked if he had communicated with Campbell. He said he had not. and he received nothing from Campbell. He said he was out of town most of November.

He said he did not send a copy of the dismissal judgment because he assumed Campbell received it from someone else. He said he would mail a copy of the judgment to Campbell and tell him we are always open to talks. I had second thoughts on the timing of notifying Campbell. On December 17 I mailed a letter to Byal asking him to send the Tipton County judgment to Campbell between Christmas and New Years so 60 days had passed and it would be too late for an appeal.

On December 19, 1983, Herrin was at the Olympia Super Spa in Indianapolis at about 7 p.m. He asked how Laudig's trial turned out, he claimed he didn't know. I said Laudig lost and I would mail a copy of the judgment to him. I also said I'd send a copy of the newspaper article on Northern Indiana Public Service Company with his name on the front page. Herrin represented the power company and his name was in The Indianapolis Star in a story about the company.

On December 28 Byal wrote to Graham regarding the disposition of the Tipton case and enclosed a copy of the judgment. He asked me if we could get together in late January to begin organizing for trial in my suit against Laudig in Indianapolis. He said he wanted local counsel, maybe a good Democrat. I had no objection to local counsel, but not a Democrat.

In January, after Campbell received a copy of the judgment he traveled to Tipton to talk to Judge Nash. Byal informed me that Campbell asked the judge why he signed a judgment in my favor. Byal said Judge Nash told Campbell that Laudig came across as unbelievable and without credibility. He said the jury felt Laudig was a shyster. Byal said Campbell was quite upset with the Judge and clearly expressed it to him. Campbell spent several hours in the courthouse reviewing the records of the trial. He was probably looking for an error in procedure in search of a basis for appeal.

On January 20, 1984, Byal asked why I hadn't hired a Utah or Oregon attorney to help me against FESLIC after Tuohy withdrew. It seemed to me to be an unusual question. No attorney, even a friend, would travel several thousand miles to Indiana to live and work for months, solely on the promise of a percentage of the payment. There would need to be certainty of payment. Certainty could have existed in the contract case when Dietzen was the first attorney involved, but never after Tuohy had withdrawn. It left the impression Byal believed

I had many contacts in those states who would be happy to come to Indiana at my request. It also left the impression I had plenty of money to spend on the lawsuits. That impression of stature could have been created because of the prestige of my adversary, Tuohy. It could also have been because of name recognition since many attorneys and judges became familiar with me and my cases over such a long period of time. Byal never gave me a full explanation of the question.

On February 10, 1984, Campbell filed a Motion for Summary Judgment in the *Jensen v Laudig* Case in Indianapolis based upon the compulsory counterclaim argument. On March 16, 1984, Judge Nash signed an affidavit that was submitted to Judge Dugan saying he denied my motion for leave to amend answer and assert a counterclaim. His affidavit follows.

| | | |
|---|---|---|
| STATE OF INDIANA | ) | IN THE MARION SUPERIOR COURT |
| | ) | CIVIL DIVISION, ROOM NO. 5 |
| COUNTY OF MARION | ) | |
| | | |
| REGINALD L. JENSEN | ) | |
| | ) | CAUSE NO. S582-1389 |
| VS. | ) | |
| | ) | |
| STEVEN LAUDIG | ) | |

## AFFIDAVIT

Comes now Dane P. Nash, who being first duly sworn upon his oath, alleges and says:

1. That he is an attorney at law, duly licensed to practice in the State of Indiana.
2. That he is duly appointed Judge of the Tipton Circuit Court.
3. That the affiant presided over the trial and pre-trial proceedings in a cause of action entitled Stephen Laudig vs. Reginald L. Jensen, Tipton Circuit Court, cause no. 82-C-66.
4. That in the course of his duties as presiding judge in the cause of action outlined above in paragraph 3, the affiant held a hearing and ruled upon Reginald Jensen's motion for leave to amend answer and assert a counterclaim. That the hearing was held on March 24, 1983.
5. That the affiant denied Reginald Jensen's motion for leave to amend answer and assert a counterclaim. That in denying the motion, the affiant relied upon the representations of William DuMond, counsel for Stephen Laudig, that the amendment was not a compulsory counterclaim and that its inclusion would be prejudicial to Stephen Laudig. The proposed counterclaim was for malpractice, theft and deceit.
6. That the affiant as presiding judge in the above mentioned action repeatedly overruled subsequent motions by Reginald Jensen to assert a counterclaim in the Tipton Circuit Court during the trial of the cause. The affiant overruled said motions upon the representation and inducement of Stephen Laudig's trial Counsel William Fatout that such amendment was prejudicial to Stephen Laudig.

7. That the action entitled Stephen Laudig vs. Reginald Jensen cause no. 82-C-66, was submitted to a jury which rendered a verdict in favor of the defendant Reginald Jensen. No motion to correct errors was filed and no appeal was taken by Stephen Laudig.

FURTHER AFFIANT SAYETH NOT.
    Signed
    Dane P. Nash

Notarized by L. Shaw in Tipton, Indiana on March 16, 1984.

Laudig and his attorneys were engaged in deception before the court. Taking one position in one court and a directly opposite position in a separate court in the same jurisdiction is disingenuous. Attorneys will file several conflicting defenses hoping one will stick, but that's different from explaining the law to a judge

On April 27, 1984, the summary judgment hearing was held before Judge Dugan in his chambers. There were many courtrooms in the courthouse in Indianapolis. Judge Dugan's courtroom was number five. His office was on the west side of the courtroom. There was a very small space for his secretary and for one or two people to sit down and wait. I was standing by the judge's door to his office just before the hearing, waiting for Byal to arrive, when Herrin came through the court hallway. I mentioned to him Laudig had requested a summary judgment based on the compulsory counterclaim defense and he said "That's one good thing about being an attorney, we can have it both ways." He then went into Judge Dugan's office, closed the door, and talked to the judge for a few minutes before the hearing. After the hearing, Judge Dugan said he would grant the summary judgment in Laudig's favor. During the Tipton trial Judge Nash believed Laudig's position was honorable, Judge Dugan knew it was not.

On May 4 James Tuohy, on behalf of the Marion County Judicial Conference (Indianapolis), wrote a letter to the editor endorsing Judge Dugan for re-election. The Indianapolis Star published his letter. The letter said "The Marion County Judicial Conference comprises lawyers and others interested in our judiciary who take part in encouraging the best possible candidates to run for judge on the Democratic ticket in the primary election." The candidates endorsed were the incumbent judges, Thomas Alsip, Betty Barteau, Webster Brewer, Michael Dugan, Victor Pfau, John Tranberg and Gerald Zore, together with a new candidate Ann DeLaney, a former deputy prosecutor. There was good reason for Tuohy to make these endorsements. He received a dismissal of the malpractice suit against him by Judge Webster Brewer; he received what appeared to be a $48,000 gift from Judge Michael Dugan, via UNAC and FESLIC; and Dugan dismissed my claim against Laudig. Tuohy could have been right, those candidates might have been the best possible.

A general summary judgment order, with only a statement that the judge found no disputed facts and judgment was for the defendant, was on Judge Dugan's desk May 16 to be signed, but Judge Dugan was out of town. On May 17 Dugan signed the summary judgment, which says:

> This cause came to be heard, pursuant to Rule 56 of the Indiana Rules of Trial Procedure, on the Motion of Defendant, Stephen Laudig, for Summary Judgment, and the Court having considered all matters relevant and material to that Motion, including all pleadings filed in this cause of action, all Briefs, Memoranda of law, Affidavits and other Exhibits submitted both in support and in opposition to the Motion, and having heard argument of Counsel, now finds that there is no genuine issue of fact with respect to matters dispositive of Plaintiff's claim against Defendant, and the Court further concludes that Defendant, Stephan Laudig, is entitled to summary judgment in his favor and against Plaintiff, Reginald L. Jensen, as a matter of law, and it is hereby;
> ORDERED, ADJUDGED AND DECREED, that the Defendant, Stephen Laudig's, Motion for Summary Judgment is in all things granted, and it is further;
> ORDERED, ADJUDGED AND DECREED, that judgment shall be, and is hereby, entered against Plaintiff, Reginald L. Jensen, and in favor of Defendant, Stephen Laaudig.
> Dated: May 17. 1984.
>
> > Signed
> > Honorable Michael T. Dugan
> > Judge, Marion Superior Court
> > Room No. 5

Judge Dugan made no reference to anything that would constitute evidence to support his ruling. He made no comment whatsoever regarding compulsory counterclaim. He made a simple statement saying he considered everything (whatever everything is) and ruled in favor of Laudig. Laudig was sued for malpractice. He defends saying he didn't commit malpractice. The judge says there are no facts in dispute. Therefore, Laudig's entitled to a judgment. Figure that out. The judge should have cited the undisputed facts as to malpractice (see: Fletcher's testimoney) or the undisputed facts that demonstrated my claim was a compulsory counterclaim (see: Judge Nash's affidavit). If there were no facts in dispute the summary judgment should have been in my favor since Laudig never disputed the facts. He submitted nothing to counter Judge Nash's affidavit. Facts were never considered, only a misrepresentation of Laudig's legal position. This is the rule of law?

Campbell mailed a letter to Byal with a demand for costs amounting to several thousand dollars. Byal gave the letter to me with a comment that I might be required to pay. I mailed a letter back to Campbell saying I would pay the costs he demanded as soon as Laudig paid the costs that were awarded to me in the Tipton action. Campbell dropped his request.

Byal and I discussed appealing Dugan's decision at some length over the next few weeks. He said the other side might take the position the Marion County suit terminated when the Tipton suit went to judgment. It would have if Laudig was awarded fees in Tipton. It seemed to me a man would have to be drunk to assume the loss of a case on the merits in one court automatically gave the same loser a win in a different case in a different court without anything happening in the different case. Byal said Graham might take that position. I maintained my position that Laudig never denied malpractice and summary judgment should have been for us. Byal agreed to file the appeal. On July 13 Byal filed the motion to correct errors. Judge Dugan denied the motion on July 16. On August 3 Byal filed the praecipe for the record and a submission for pre-appeal conference with the trial court and the court of appeals. This became *Jensen v. Laudig,* Appellate Cause #4-884-A214.

The opposing attorneys and Judge Dugan didn't want the ruling appealed. Byal went to the courthouse in Indianpolis to make a copy of the file. He couldn't find it; he returned to his office in Tipton and called me. I decided to go to the Indianapolis courthouse and search for the file. It wasn't in the clerk's office so, I decided to search the courtroom. There was a file room in back of the courtroom. The file was well hidden on top of one of the file cabinets underneath a stack of other files. The Marion County Clerk made copies for me. The clerk failed to make a copy of Laudig's affidavit saying he offered to settle my cases against First Equity for $55,000. His affidavit was attached to the motion for summary judgment in the middle of other papers, which were copied. I went back to the clerk and asked her why she failed to copy Laudig's affidavit for me. She said she left it out because it wasn't file stamped. However, only the first page of every multiple-page document was file stamped. She made the copies and I took them back to Byal. Byal reviewed the court file again and found the attached exhibits to Laudig's affidavit in support of Laudig's motion for summary judgment were never attached and not in the file. This meant Judge Dugan issued the summary judgment without any supporting documents.

On October 10, 1984, Byal filed the notice of appeal. But he wasn't confident because he felt we were facing too much political pressure and influence. I gave him the opportunity to quit, but he agreed to finish the appeal and said he'd stay with me and help all he could. On October 17 Byal called and said the summary judgment was missing from the Marion County Court file. Someone removed it. The dismissal judgment *must* be included with the court record when the case is appealed. Failure to do so is fatal. I had made a practice of checking the file from time to time. It was in the file on May 17, 1984. It was in the file on Aug. 3, 1984 (certified as part of pre-appeal submission). It was not in the file Aug. 28, 1984. It was not in the file Oct. 10, 1984. After talking to Byal I went down to Indianapolis and searched all of the files again. It was in the wrong place, in the court order book in Superior 5. The court order book is a large binder with heavy covers that contains a running record of court actions. The court's copy of the summary judgment was placed between several pages in the order book. Someone didn't want to destroy it, but they didn't want it to be found either. I gave it to the clerk and had a copy certified and gave the copy to Byal. Byal completed the Petition for a Writ of Certiorari[24] and the writ. The judgment was filed with the court of appeals along with the motion to correct errors on October 19. The appeal record included Laudig's testimony at trial where he admitted to double and triple billing and Judge Nash's affidavit showing Laudig had claimed this suit was not a compulsory counterclaim.

On November 18 Byal filed the appeal brief. He and I went to dinner afterwards in a small buffet-style restaurant in Tipton. Byal said it was possible the court of appeals could charge me with filing a frivolous appeal. That didn't make any sense to me, but nothing else that was going on in Indianapolis made sense either. He also suggested I could file perjury charges against Laudig for his actions in the Tipton case. I

---

[24] A Writ of Certiorari is a command to the lower court to deliver the entire file to the higher court for review.

couldn't see any benefit to me, but I told him Judge Nash could certainly do so, if he felt he should. Was Byal preparing me for the worst or if he was just testing my bitterness over the events of the last few years? There was another possibility; he could have been talking to Campbell and just relating Campbell's conversations to me. He also said he'd calculate his hours and present me with his current billing, which I paid.

The court of appeals decision on November 25, 1985, was a memorandum decision and was in favor of Laudig. It was not for publication and was signed by Young, P., J. It said "Laudig, the attorney, was retained by Jensen to represent him in certain legal proceedings but was not paid for those services." This was a false statement by Judge Young. My affirmative defense in Tipton was Laudig had been fully compensated. The evidence in Tipton showed Laudig was paid and the jury found he was not entitled to an additional payment. The court of appeals continued to say "Trial Rule 13(A) mandates that a defendant, in answering a complaint, plead as a compulsory counterclaim all claims against the plaintiff which arise out of the transaction or occurrence that is the subject matter of the plaintiff's lawsuit." Nothing in Judge Dugan's decision referred to compulsory counterclaim. Judge Young also said when I replied to a claim for damages from Laudig that I stated I would counterclaim. No such statement is in the record, it is only part of the communication between myself and Zook. Filing a counterclaim was part of my oral communications with Braddock and Byal. Judge Young received advise from someone but not through the legal process. Judge Young was supposed to be reviewing the record in the *Jensen v. Laudig* action, which never went to trial in which only motions had been submitted. A responsible judge should give substantially more credence to an affidavit of another judge than to the defense of a litigant when the litigant's defense conflicts with his prior submissions to the court. Judge Young could easily see Laudig was making a false representations to at least one court. Yet Judge Young felt compelled to rule in favor of the party presenting falsehoods and he felt compelled to use ex parte information. Judge Young came up with many reasons as if he was ruling on the case that took place in Tipton. Even then he couldn't keep the Tipton case facts straight. As a side comment, Trial Rule 13(A) prevents a litigant from filing a lawsuit within the time prescribed by law, thus it has no validity. For example, if the statutes allow two years to file a malpractice claim the trial rules can't shorten that time. Trial rules don't take precedence over the statutes.

In common law legal systems, judges have the authority and duty to decide what the law is when there is no other authoritative statement of the law. When the facts of the case are substantially similar and an appellate court has decided what the law is, that precedent binds all future decisions of the same appellate court, and binds all lower courts in that appellate court district, until there is another authoritative statement of the law (e.g. by a legislature or higher court). The common law forms a major part of the legal systems of those countries of the world with a history as territories or colonies of the British Empire. It is notable for its inclusion of extensive non-statutory law reflecting precedent (*stare decisis*) derived from centuries of judgments by working jurists.

All courts are supposed to be open and the decision in the trial court holds only to that particular case. However, once the case goes up on appeal, the appellate court is still an open court and its decision is reviewable by all. The entire purpose is to see if the correct law has been applied to the true facts. Either the issues in the case on appeal are substantially the same as previous issues which have been resolved or something new requires a different ruling. If the ruling in the trial court doesn't follow the facts of the case, doesn't follow the law as written, or doesn't follow precedence, the lower court decision should be reversed. Otherwise, the appellate court should uphold the lower court. However, nowhere, in law or equity in any state or federal court, by any constitution or statute, have judges been granted the authority to insert imaginary facts preceding a ruling or decision the judge will issue, nor have they been granted the authority to defy existing law.

The entire purpose of the rule of law is to standardize the law so that it holds for all parties at all times in the trial and appellate courts, unless it's changed for all parties at all future times. Changes in the laws should come about because of societal changes, not changes to parties to an action. The rule of law means the law is settled on appeal and the decision applies to everyone, rich or poor, in like or similar circumstances, not to only one person. If the standardized law applies to some parties and not others at the whim of attorneys and judges, it follows that the rule of law doesn't apply to any party. The only real conclusion anyone can reach is that the rule of law in the United States is not available if a person can't seek redress in the courts and expect sane and honest people to act on the claim.

Byal took issue with Judge Young's finding of fact contrary to the jury's verdict. He filed a petition for rehearing, which specified the errors in Judge Young's not for publication memorandum ruling. Here's what Judge Young said in his ruling on the same case after the petition for rehearing had been filed. In *Jensen v. Laudig*, 480 NE 2d 405 (1986), (a published decision): "Laudig on April 22, 1981, brought suit against Jensen, his erstwhile client, alleging unpaid legal fees..." then "The trial court there refused to allow the amendment to include the counterclaim, concluding that Jensen was not required to plead malpractice as a compulsory counterclaim in Laudig's suit." What Judge Young left out was that Laudig represented to the judge in the Tipton County suit that my claim was not a compulsory counterclaim. Judge Young continues "Following a jury trial, the Tipton court on October 26, 1983, entered a judgment for Jensen on Laudig's complaint for payment of fees." So, now the court of appeals not for publication record is subtantially different than the court of appeals for publication ruling, both signed by Judge Young. The judge continues, "Thereafter, on February 9, 1984, Laudig moved for summary judgment in the Marion County suit, contending Jensen's claim was barred by Trial Rule 13(A) as a compulsory counterclaim which Jensen was required to litigate in the Tipton County action." Judge Young goes on to say: "The parties do not seriously contest whether the malpractice complaint represents a compulsory counterclaim; Jensen explicitly recognized it as such in seeking to amend his complaint in the Tipton County suit." Judge Young changed his position on my recognition of a compulosry counterclaim. Laudig argued strenuously to Judge Nash in Tipton that my suit was not a compulsory counterclaim and Judge Nash filed an affidavit to that effect in the Marion County suit and that affidavit was part of the appeal record. Laudig also argued he wanted my claim litigated in Marion County. Judge Young supports Laudig's duplicity and fails to recognize the affidavit of the trial judge. Judge Young found as a fact whatever he wanted to find as a fact to support his legal conclusion. Judge Young also said my technical arguments have no merit. Only Laudig's argument had merit in his eyes. Judge Young said I could have appealed the Tipton case results. An appeal of a judgment in my favor in Tipton would mean the court of appeals could overturn the jury verdict and award fees to Laudig. Catch 22.

I had enough of the legal system in Indiana. Ron Byal's representation was a relief after having been cheated by so many attorneys and several judges over a fifteen-year period. Still, I was supersensitive to everything that was being done and double-checked everything he did. As it turns out, Byal was honest and straightforward to the end.

It was time to complete my move to California. I advised Garrison and Huston it was time for me to leave Indiana and move to California. My first plan was to move to Southern California, but the amount of smog in the Los Angeles-area detered me. Northern California was more appealing. San Francisco was out of the question for me. San Jose is a large city at the South Bay of the San Francisco Bay and is considered the center of Silicon Valley. The weather was perfect for me, so San Jose it was. Garrison asked me to have lunch with him. At lunch, he said he had talked to Donald Roller, the general agent, for MassMutual in San Jose. Garrison said he brought Roller up to date on my history and had paved the way for me. Just before Christmas 1985, I left Indiana and traveled to Salt Lake City for the Christmas season. Mr. Rolla McAdams , chief financial officer of Rielly Chemical (now Reilly Industries), had decided to use life insurance as a supplemental benefit for several employees and it required me to take a couple of extra days to complete the work. Those two days made the trip by auto a little more interesting. As I passed through Nebraska, it began to snow quite heavily. By the time I reached Sidney, the highway pratrol had alerted motorists to stay off the highways. I continued on and drove into Kimball because I-80 was completely closed. There were no motel rooms or other accomodations in Kimball, but a truck was continuing through town and heading into the farm country away from the highway. I decidd to follow the truck even though the snow was now accumulated up to about three feet, clear up to the bottom of the windows of my auto. The truck made two grooves in the snow for my wheels to follow. The driver went up and down the farm roads for several hours at a slow speed. The snow kept falling, but the truck grooves still made my travel possible.

Eventually, the truck came back onto I-80 at Pine Bluffs and stopped at a service station. I, too, stopped to get gas. I mentioned to the truck driver that it was fortuitous for me that he knew the back roads and was able to lead me through. He said he didn't know the roads at all and that this was the first time he'd ever travelled in this area. In any event, I arrived in Salt Lake City for Christmas.

In mid-January 1986, I joined the Mass Mutual agency in San Jose. Thereafter, my communication with Byal was by phone and mail. I also subscribed to The Indianapolis Star to keep up to date on current events.

Before leaving Indiana, I had written to U.S. Senator Dan Quayle (later the United States' vice president) complaining about my treatment in the courts in Indiana. On February 3, 1986, I received a letter (dated January 24, 1986) from Senator Quayle saying he had filed a complaint with the Indiana Supreme Court Disciplinary Commission. A copy of his letter is below.

*United States Senate*

WASHINGTON, D.C. 20510

January 24, 1986

Mr. Reginald L. Jensen
PO Box 40441
Indianapolis, Indiana 46240

Dear Mr. Jensen:

Thank you for contacting me regarding your legal issue. I am pleased to have this opportunity to serve you.

I have forwarded your concern to the Indiana Supreme Court Disciplinary Commission for its review and response to me. I trust that I will receive a prompt and appropriate response to your inquiry.

Should you have additional questions during the interim, please contact Mark G. Ahearn of my Indiana staff. My Indiana Office is located at Room 447, 46 East Ohio Street, Indianapolis, Indiana 46204, (317) 269-5555.

Sincerely,

Dan Quayle
United States Senator

*Reginald L. Jensen*

I thanked Sen. Quayle by letter and also mailed the record of my disciplinary complaint against Laudig. On March 8, 1986, a letter was mailed to me signed jointly by Sen. Quayle and Sen. Richard Lugar saying they could not get involved. I had never contacted Sen. Lugar and it's unreasonable to assume Sen. Quayle discussed my situation with him without an inquiry coming from Sen. Lugar. United States senators don't have the time to compare correspondence with each other prior to communicating with all of their constituents. A copy of the letter is below:

United States Senate
WASHINGTON, D.C. 20510

February 26, 1986

Mr. Reginald L. Jensen
9000 Keystone Crossing #260
Indianapolis, Indiana 46240

Dear Mr. Jensen:

Thank you for your recent letter. We can well understand your frustration with the situation outlined, and share your concern. However, we regret to tell you that we will not be able to honor your request to intervene in this matter. We have a firm office policy against interference in legal matters, which clearly apply to this case. In any event, we see no possibility that any of our comments would affect the outcome in a favorable way.

There are various legal organizations available to assist in these types of matters. For further information you may want to contact the Indiana State Bar Association, your local Bar Association, or a Legal Services Organization.

Please feel free to contact our Indiana Office if we may provide assistance with federal matters in the future. The Address of our Indiana Office is Room 447, 46 East Ohio Street, Indianapolis, Indiana 46204, and the phone number is (317) 269-5555.

Sincerely,

Richard G. Lugar
United States Senator

Sincerely,

Dan Quayle
United States Senator

Why did these two senators take the time to prepare a joint letter to me announcing they could not and would not help? The only reasonable conclusion is that Tuohy received information from the disciplinary commission about my communication with Sen. Quayle; Tuohy then would have recommended to Sen. Lugar he remove Sen. Quayle from the equation. If the disciplinary commission complained, it would have complained directly to Sen. Quayle, not to Sen. Lugar. United States Senators shouldn't become involved in any third party litigation or attempt to influence the outcome of litigation, but they must become involved in terminating fraud and deception in the judiciary.

In mid-December 1985 the IRS asked me to bring my auto and gas receipts for the years 1981 through 1983 in for an audit. The IRS goes back three years for a normal audit and six years when searching for fraud. Since I was in the process of moving from Indiana to California, I ignored the audit letter and waited until I was settled in San Jose. In early 1986, they advised me to come into the San Jose audit division with my auto-expense receipts. When I arrived, the auditor, Steve Howells, asked me for all of my business-expense records. I brought the records the IRS requested and nothing more. Howells was visibly upset and said I should have guessed they wanted to do a complete and thorough audit of my tax returns. Why make such a guess? I did what I was told to do, no more, no less. We made a new appointment. Since I had been entering my income and expense records in my computer, I printed out the records and returned to meet with Howells again. Howells refused to review my computer records and said "garbage in, garbage out." He and I debated for quite awhile before I promised to return with more proof of expenses.

One of my expenses was my legal fees. Howells refused to accept my records of legal fees as legitimate expenses. Finally, I asked Byal to write a letter to Howells explaining my legal expenses were paid and deductible. Howells became even more verbally abusive, which caused me to complain to the IRS regional director in San Francisco about his attitude. The regional director appointed a different auditor who took over until the audit was completed. The IRS has audited my tax returns nearly every year since.

On May 20, 1986, Byal filed a petition to transfer the *Jensen v. Laudig* case to the Indiana Supreme Court. The Indiana Supreme Court denied the petition on August 18, 1986. It seemed to me that the Indiana Supreme Court didn't want me to have a fair trial before a jury because the current result was the result Tuohy ordered. (*During my legal research I came across a case where the Indiana Supreme Court ruled in favor of an appeal filed by Tuohy with the comment that Tuohy's position was totally in error. The court said that it was holding in Tuohy's favor in this instant, but for all future cases it would hold the opposite.*) As far as I was concerned my case was over, all lawsuits in Indiana were over, and there was nothing more for me to do. I made a final payment to Byal and thanked him for his services.

Dorothy was still in Salt Lake City and was quite happy to live on her own. We had now been apart for more than six years with only occasional visits in between. With a little coaxing, she finally agreed to move to California and live with me. We first lived in a condo in Santa Clara and eventually purchased a home in San Jose.

Donald Roller was the MassMutual general agent in San Jose when I first arrived. Here I was in San Jose, a new town, with a new general agent, no friends, no relatives nor contacts of any kind. Fortunately, I had learned more about split-dollar life insurance and nonqualified-deferred compensation using life insurance than anyone else in the agency. From time to time, the other agents would ask me to work with them on difficult cases. Most of the agents were highly qualified in their own fields of expertise, but it takes a lot of time and patience to read the Internal Revenue Code and regulations, as well as all of the other material in these specialized areas, and the other salesmen just didn't have the time to do both. Anyway, that gave me a start and my cold calls gave me the necessary leads to begin making a living.

Computers were just coming into fashion. I'd attended several classes on using the computer while living in Indiana, but the constant changes in hardware and softwear took a lot of time trying to keep up for the purpose of preparing presentations and documents needed in my work. I hired a man named Adisorn who was born and raised in Thailand to help me. He was very good. He took computer classes in the evenings and worked for me during the day. We were attempting to connect my computer at home with my computer at the office so we could use either computer and the same files. I purchased a book that had the technical details for establishing telecommunication for the transfer of data over phone lines. It was very complicated and cumbersome. The book described what is known today as the Internet. Addisorn didn't want to get involved with it because he felt it would never amount to anything. After about a year, he had my programs up and running so I could take over and operate without his help. I gave him three months termination notice, allowing him to work for me and to spend as much time as possible during working hours to find other employment. In less than a month, he found other work and moved to the southeastern part of the United States.

On October 18, 1986, Indianapolis Star reporter Patrick J. Traub wrote another story regarding the UNAC problem. The story explained how $500,000 was subtracted from UNAC's assets by Judge Dugan. The reduction was credited to the failure of UNAC to accept a purchase offer from another insurance company. However, the article also revealed UNAC's value was reduced when Judge Dugan and former marketing director John Flanagan invested that amount in California real estate, which included a marketing office and a home for the two men located in the South Bay area. Dugan had been in control of UNAC since 1974 and it appeared as though he was using it as his own piggy bank. It was obvious to me the Indiana Democratic leadership knew what was happening and either participated in or turned a blind eye to the fraud.

In mid-1987, I flew back to Indianapolis from San Jose and took a copy of Fletcher's trial testimony to Tuohy's office and tried to give it to Tuohy. He refused to see me and sent Herrin out to the lobby to talk to me. Herrin took the transcript from me. I then went to the state capital building in search of Chief Justice Randall T. Sheppard. I walked up to the top floor of the building and started walking around the area outside of the justices' offices. A heavy-set man about my height, but maybe a year or two older, stopped me and asked who I was looking for. I said "the chief justice". He said "That's me." I said "James Tuohy once represented me and since he's a good friend of yours; I'd like you to have a copy of an attorney's testimony at trial regarding Tuohy's representation." I handed him a copy of Fletcher's trial transcript and he promised to read it. Chief Justice Shepard had received several letters from me complaining about Tuohy and Judge Dugan prior to this meeting. By now he knew the issues very well and he should have known why I continued to complain.

One of the stock-brokerage managers in the home office of MMLISI (I believe his last name was Boodhoo) called me on the phone one day and told me to go out and start selling more stocks. I asked him which stocks to sell and he said he didn't care, just go sell stocks. I asked him which stocks he could recommend based upon his research and he said he didn't do any research, and that I needed to get out there and sell stocks. I said I had no interest in selling just any stock, I needed to have confidence the company was well managed and the stock paid regular dividends. I needed the research for support. It seemed to me I could serve the public better if I knew what I was talking about and it would be best to help people conserve their assets. It was my position very few people need someone else to help them lose money but skill is demonstrated by helping people show profits when it's difficult to show profits in investments. He became frustrated and hung up on me. Several mutual-fund firms wouldn't permit the sales of their best-performing funds unless the salesmen also sold shares in their worst-performing funds. Some salesmen, not necessarily MMLISI representatives, refused to sell funds paying low commissions and only sold the funds paying the highest commissions without regard to the funds's performances. The securities I sold were primarily mutual funds and primarily with The American Funds family.

In February 1988, the Indiana Supreme Court brought public indecency and battery charges against Judge James Young, the same court of appeals judge who couldn't keep the facts straight in *Jensen v. Laudig*. He had been arrested by the police in an adult book store. His attorney felt the charges should be dropped because the judge was sufficiently embarrassed. The worst form of punishment for a judge is embarrassment. It didn't work. Judge Young was removed from the bench in July 1988.

The disposable funds at UNAC finally came to an end. In the summer of 1988, Judge Dugan was charged with stealing more than $100,000 from UNAC with the possibility his take could be much higher. It had been twelve years since Carolyn Pickering had written the initial story for the Indianapolis Star. The Indiana Insurance Department would certainly be aware of what was happening because insurance department independent audits must be conducted at least once every three years. Recall that the insurance commissioner was a Democrat and years earlier he never objected to Judge Dugan's order sharing funds from UNAC with the various attorneys. That's a long time for a judge to be using the assets of an insurance company for his own personal gain without anyone taking action. To his credit, he shared the largess with others from time to time.

Nearly a year later, Judge Dugan was tried before a jury in Indianapolis. The action was *United States of America v. Michael T. Dugan, II*, Southern District of Indiana, Indianapolis Division, Cause No. IP88-78-CR. Other persons admitted paying bribes and taking payoffs. The jury verdict was returned May 26, 1989, finding Dugan guilty on a variety of charges of bribery and extortion, including a true bill of unlawfully obtaining money (a $1,000 bribe) from James Eckman, President of First Equity Security Life Insurance Company (which Eckman had admitted). There were 29 counts against Judge Dugan and the jury found a true bill on almost every count. Deborah J. Daniels was the prosecuting United States Attorney. Dugan was sentenced to an 18-year prison term.

Afterwards, Judge Dugan was reported to have said he wasn't concerned about his sentence because his friends would take care of his family while he was away. Apparently, he expected to return hale and hearty and financially sound with his family and friends waiting with open arms. Dugan served his time in various minimum security camps including the Federal Correctional Institution at Lompoc, California.[25] In 2006, he was working for the El Dorado Irrigation District in Placerville, California. His position at the time was human resources director. He's reported to have said he never denied being in prison when he applied for the job, he'd simply had never been asked the

---

[25] According to Zoominfo Web Summary (7/22/2006)

question. It appears as though his "friends" in Indiana weren't waiting for him to return.

On June 30, 1989, Byal filed a *Belated Petition to Transfer or in the alternative, Petition to Reopen Case Based Upon Conviction of the Trial Judge Michael Dugan for Bribery, Extortion and Racketeering* in the Supreme Court of Indiana on my behalf. Attached to the petition was the complete record of Judge Dugan's conviction as determined by the jury in his case, plus the cover pages of the Annual Statements of UNAC and FESLIC as filed with the State of Indiana, and a copy of the newspaper article identifying Judge Dugan's unsupported payments to Tuohy's law firm from UNAC's assets. The critical portions of the petition follow so a reader can see the Indiana Supreme Court had no concern with regard to providing justice in this case.

First: All requirements prior to requesting the Petition had been complied with;

Second: The petition is based upon the newly discovered evidence of corruption, fraud, bribery, and racketeering by the Trial Judge Michael Dugan. The judge has been convicted;

Third: Judge Dugan's conviction was related to UNAC. UNAC and FESLIC were associated. Both companies were located at the same address. Eckman was the president of FESLIC;

Fourth: Eckman paid a bribe to Judge Dugan in December 1982. Judge Dugan denied Jensen's motion for default judgment on January 13, 1983. Judge Dugan refused a change of venue demand by Jensen on August 9, 1983. Judge Dugan refused Jensen's motion for summary judgment on May 17, 1984;

Fifth: UNAC, controlled by Judge Dugan, entered into financial transactions with FESLIC;

Sixth: Jensen's lawsuit was against attorney Laudig whose representation of Jensen benefited FESLIC and Eckman;

Seventh: Judge Dugan's operation of the Marion Superior Court, Room 5, as a continuing criminal enterprise was unknown to the Court of Appeals at the time of its decision by Judge Young, who subsequently resigned from the bench under allegations of immoral and criminal conduct;

Eighth: Judge Dugan maintained a relationship with attorney James Tuohy whose representation of Jensen benefitted FESLIC and James Eckman.

The Indianapolis Star wrote an editorial questioning how the Indiana Supreme Court would handle the various lawsuits determined by Judge Dugan that could be subject to new trials. The Star expressed the opinion it would require considerable time on the part of the courts. I believe my request for reconsideration was the first to be filed. The Indiana Supreme Court denied my petition and, as a result, imposed fees against me. All of the justices voted to deny, including Chief Justice Sheppard. The Indiana Supreme Court quickly disposed of my petition, which prevented a flood of other requests for consideration. If the Indiana Supreme Court refused to grant relief to someone whose case was so obviously tainted and where political and personal relationships existed, there remained little chance of any case with less evidence of fraud being granted relief. That was the end of the new trial issue.

Laudig's attorney, David Campbell, contacted K. L. Mulvaney, the supreme court administrator and asked how to proceed in collecting fees from me for their costs in opposing the petition. Byal found out about the phone call and asked Mulvaney what he was doing. On November 17, 1989, Mulvaney responded to Byal that he did nothing wrong in advising Campbell to proceed in any manner he felt appropriate. Cambell claimed he made the request via a teleconference, but Mulvaney said he wasn't aware of anyone else being in on the call. Campbell's law firm dropped their request to collect fees.

FESLIC had received a lot of assistance from Richard Doermer to stay in business. Doermer controlled the investments and held most of the investments in his bank. He would exchange investments from time to time to be certain the investments were profitable. I examined FESLIC's financial statements at each year-end for a few years and found the assets on the first day of the year were usually different than the assets on the last day of the prior year. Doermer also helped FESLIC sell credit life insurance to some of Doermer's bank's corresponding banks throughout Indiana. This kept FESLIC alive for a few years, but eventually FESLIC merged with another out-of-state company and its existence came to an end. Soon afterwards, Eckman was paid to leave the surviving entity.

After Headden and Traub wrote, and the Star published, the stories about Judge Dugan, I asked Headden if the paper was going to continue to investigate Tuohy and his cohorts. She said she'd keep me posted, but she never did. I called her office and asked to have my papers returned. She didn't call back. I later went into the Indianapolis Star offices and talked to her. Her sartorial appearance had certainly improved. She looked great. I asked her to return my papers and she told me that she wouldn't. Headden only had copies of my documents, not the originals, so it made no sense to me for her to retain the copies. Reporter Pickering returned my papers after she had finished her reporting on my issues.

In 1989, Indiana Chief Justice Randall T. Shepard appointed a committee of nine judges to recommend changes to the state's Code of Judicial Conduct. What kind of a review board could he appoint to recommend changes in the Code of Judicial Conduct? The Indiana Supreme Court established the Supreme Court Committee on Character and Fitness. Who was named chairman of that committee? None other than James Tuohy! Now Tuohy was in a position to determine if any judge, from the state's chief justice on down, was ethically qualified to sit on the bench.

On August 6, 1990, four years after moving to California, I received two letters in San Jose from MassMutual about my own policies,[26] sold to me by myself, in Indiana, suggesting that I should contact the Indiana Insurance Department about any complaint I might have about the sale of the policies to me. My first response was why would I file a complaint with the Indiana Insurance Department about any misrepresentation I might have engaged in when I'm purchasing a policy on my own life? Then I found the letters were mailed to all of my policyholders in Indiana. On August 10 I wrote to Thomas Wheeler, president of MassMutual, asking him why the company mailed such a letter. His response was the Indiana Insurance Department required the company to mail the letters. The response to the mailings was a grand total of zero complaints.

---

[26] Since MassMutual is a mutual company the policyholders own the company in the same manner as stockholders own any stock company.

In mid-1991, MMLISI sent a representative from the home office to the San Jose agency and he announced they were going to get rid of all inactive registered principals in the organization. On September 5, 1991, Martha S. Richter, associate director, legal matters, MMLISI, notified me my principal's registration was terminated, which reduced my status to that of a regular salesman without the possibililty of supervising others. The stated reason was "Since you are no longer functioning in the capacity of a registered principal for MMLISI, we were required by the NASD By-Laws to terminate your registrattion as a MMLISI principal." As far as I knew, I was the only registered principal in the Bay Area and the only reason I was inactive was because the home office refused to place me in a position of supervision. I had never been functioning as a principal for MMLISI. They appointed a series of individuals to the supervisory position based on the theory each would pass the exam. None did and they were all terminated. There was never any explanation why they wanted to terminate the supervisory registration of the only person with the license, while at the same time they were trying to find others who would take the principal's exam. It made no sense to me. Seven years later they hired someone from the outside who had passed the exam.

In 1998, the IRS notified me that they had adjusted my 1997 taxable income and to send an additional $8,000 to them for unpaid taxes. The usual threats to seize my house, bank accounts, and send me to purgatory, were there. They demanded the money be sent to them immediately. The adjustment to my taxable income was minor. It didn't bother me. I had no objections to accepting the adjustment. However, the IRS tax tables created by the IRS attached to the 1040 instruction forms showed taxes due on the IRS adjusted income to be an additional $1,000. I paid the $1,000 difference and asked why the agency billed me an extra $7,000. It took the IRS five months of wrangling, threats, and posturing, before it was able to admit it made a mistake and gave up on the claim. Someone called me and said it was just human error. But there was never an apology.

Now the trials and tribulations with the courts is over and life is back to normal. Right? Dealing with irrational people in the judicial system is confined to Indiana. Right? I was about to enter a period of dealing with outrageous conduct, excess pride, mistakes, stupidity, inability to communicate, cowardice, and just plain failure of performance, by people in authority.

Suppose you're engaged in the financial services business handling money, private property, and the confidential personal information of many people. The theory is such a person needs to have integrity, be honest and trustworthy, and free of criminal conduct. MMLISI would regularly send compliance officers to the agencies to explain to the agents how important it is to keep all activities clean, honest, and follow the laws and rules precisely. They would examine our files and records and monitor our activities. Every business transaction must go through a supervisor (the principal) for approval. Eventually, MMLISI would begin to monitor our personal mail and internet communications in search of infractions or violations of the laws and rules. Our contracts required us to notify them of any lawsuit, arrests, complaints, or inappropriate conduct. Legal infractions by any representative was just cause for termination.

It was in the middle 1990s, when MMLISI sent a compliance officer to the agency to remind us again how to conduct our affairs. One officer told the story of a representative in another state who was partying one night and happened to have too many drinks. He and a friend went to a farm and found some cows in a field. The representative wanted to show off, so he went into the field and climbed under one of the cows and attempted to lift it. He finally was able to tip the cow over. The farmer was upset and reported the representative to the police. The compliance officer told us that this type of infraction caused MMLISI to terminate the license of the representative because he violated the law and embarrassed the organization. The story was designed to give a person the impression they were serious about their behavior requirements. That was the sole purpose of the lecture; conduct yourselves in a fair, honest, and nonembarrassing manner at all times or they'll get rid of you.

In early 1998, the NASD was in the process of updating their records in preparation for converting their computerized records to an Internet database format. The NASD wanted to be certain the information in its records was correct before making the information available over the Internet. The computer files and the Internet database information were recorded as Central Registration Depository records (CRD). All agency security representatives received a notice from MMLISI about the update and transfer process. The worksheet pages given to me supposedly had the same information contained in the computer files. The notice consisted of two pages that had information regarding my disciplinary record with the NASD. One page was a Tandem file and the other was a Sequent file. To my knowledge, I had no disciplinary record. If I had one, I should have known about it. I didn't understand how I, or anyone else, could be disciplined without knowing it happened. I didn't pay any attention to the forms, I just signed them and was ready to return them to the home office. As I was about to return the papers I glanced at them one more time.

There was an entry on the Sequent form given to me that said I had been held by the United States Marshall in Utah on August 12, 1983, awaiting charges for violation of the Dyer Act (interstate transportation of stolen automobiles). I couldn't believe it. Whenever someone has been arrested for any reason the brokerage firm must be notified and then it must notify the NASD.[27] The NASD was required to obtain any criminal records that existed with the FBI because a person convicted

---

[27] NASD Regulation Request for Comment 98-71 says: "Background And Discussion Current Interpretation On Disclosure. The securities industry and its regulators have established exceptionally stringent licensing and qualification requirements. Among other things, persons seeking registration to sell securities are required to file a Form U-4 with Central Registration Depository (CRD) that describes their employment and disciplinary history, including whether they have been charged with or convicted of any felony or certain misdemeanors. Form U-4 requires reporting of any charge or conviction of, or guilty and no contest pleas to: (1) any felony or misdemeanor involving investments or investment-related business, fraud, false statements or omissions, wrongful taking of property, bribery, perjury, forgery, counterfeiting, extortion, or conspiracy to commit any of these offenses (hereinafter collectively referred to as "investment-related" offenses); and (2) any other felony (hereinafter referred to as "other felony" offenses)." Included were comments about a person's capacity for fair dealing. At page 557, the committees expressed concern that the proposal could have incongruous results, *i.e.*, indefinite disclosure of insignificant misdemeanor offenses but time-limited disclosure of serious felonies. To avoid such results, some committees suggested that violent crimes against a person, certain crimes against the government (including tax evasion), and offenses involving drug trafficking should always be disclosed.

of a felony cannot work in the securities industry selling products and handling money. Any person charged with a felony was required to report to the broker/dealer all events that take place up to conviction or exoneration. It's possible for the NASD to be notified first, in which event it would notify the brokerage firm. The brokerage firm must make an investigation and report the results to the NASD so that a determination can be made as to whether or not that person can be permitted to remain in the securities business. At the very least, the person arrested is required to be notified by someone of the arrest. If the brokerage firm and the NASD have knowledge of the arrest they should certainly notify the individual he has been arrested, if for no other purpose than to make certain it isn't a case of mistaken identity. I became registered with the NASD in 1968 and had placed my license with several firms until 1983. I was registered with Transamerica Fund Sales from 1974 to 1983. I was dually registered with Transamerica Fund Sales and MMLISI from 1979 to 1983. In early 1983, MMLISI and MassMutual asked me to provide them with a set of my fingerprints and to complete a new Form U-4 (securities registration form).

On April 15, 1998, I notified Bill Bartol at MMLISI the Sequent report was wrong and whatever happened took place in 1947. I enclosed a copy of the sequent form with the word wrong written in two places with the incorrect information. I also provided Bartol with a copy of the letter from Cloninger of the United States District Court in Boise, Idaho, which said there was no record of a charge against me. Cloninger had also said any charges against me were dismissed. I had never appeared before a judge, which meant to me no charges were ever filed. I would be required to plea if they were filed.

On May 5 I talked by phone to Sophie Aksenov, assistant compliance consultant, in the MMLISI home office, and tried to explain to her I had not been under arrest on August 12, 1983, or at any other time since joining MassMutual. *She insisted the record was correct, but MMLISI didn't care what I did in my spare time, that they were only concerned about what I did during my working hours. I asked her if it was OK for me to be out robbing banks and stealing cars on my own time. She said it was OK as long as I didn't do it on company time.* I told her it was my understanding MMLISI and the law prohibited such behavior and it seemed to me her response was absurd. Then I demanded they remove the 1983 arrest information from the record. Aksenov said they would not remove it from the record unless I obtained a letter from the FBI saying I had not stolen an automobile on that date. That's another absurd position. How can the FBI certify I didn't steal a car on a certain date? I suggested she should get the letter, not me. She insisted I do it. There was no budging at the home office. There was no question in anyone's mind the report meant I had been under arrest in Utah on August 12, 1983.

I contacted attorney Christopher Taaffe in San Jose and asked him to communicate with MMLISI on my behalf. He did on several occassions. Taaffe obtained several documents from them. One was a copy of a letter from Grace Compolo of MMLISI and MassMutual to the NASD dated September 28, 1983, saying I would never be placed into a management position, but the letter was never made available for my review. There was a handwritten note on the copy of the letter retained by MassMutual and MMLISI that said to keep the letter in my files. Their letter to the NASD is below.

September 28. 1983
National Association of
Securities Dealers, Inc.
1735 K Street, N.W.
Washington, DC 20006

Re: Reginald Laurence Jensen
Social Security #xxx-xx-xxxx\
CRD # 258363

Attention: Ann Sharp
Member Firms, 5th Floor

Dear Ms. Sharp:

Mr. Reginald L. Jensen has been registered with MML Investors Services, Inc., MMLISI, as a General Securities Principal since April 21, 1983. This is to advise you that the sole purpose of this registration is to permit Mr. Jensen to solicit the products available through MMLISI. Mr. Jensen is not an officer of MMLISI

> nor will he assume any supervisory responsibilities on behalf of MMLISI.
>
> Please let us know if you need any additional information.
>
> Sincerely,
>
> MML Investors Services, Inc.
> signed Grace Campolo (dp)
>
> By:     Grace Campolo
> Assistant Administrator of
> Agency contracts/Licensing
> Massachusetts Mutual Life
> Insurance Company
>
> GC:dp

**"Please retain this in broker/dealer file"** was handwritten on the file copy of the letter.

So there it was, the reason I wasn't considered for advancement, never placed in a supervisory position and eventually demoted. This was a record created by the NASD that was used to make decisions about about my future with the organizations. All of MassMutual's and MMLISI's activities were done in secret. For fifteen years, I had been working for a company that maintained a false criminal record about me during my employment with the firm.

Unknown to me in early 1983, MassMutual conducted a new background investigation on my character on behalf of MMLISI. They mailed letters to my previous employers asking them to forward all negative information they possessed regarding me. The only negative comment given to me at Taaffe's request was a letter from WHUT's manager, Dave Butler, who complained about having to pay me the $1,000. All other letters, which eventually came into my possession, were complimentary, including a letter from Huston saying he had no negative information about me. Included was a copy of an inquiry to the state of Utah in 1986, about the 1983 arrest. The state of Utah had no information. I was never able to see any letter from FESLIC or

Eckman, if any such letter existed, nor was a copy of any investigative report given to me. All of this information was provided to Don Roller, the general agent in San Jose, without my knowledge, when I moved to California in 1986.

MMLISI could have continued my registration in 1983, without talking directly to me, only if they had talked directly to my supervisor, either Garrison or Huston. Garrison knew I wasn't under arrest in Utah because I had moved to Indianapolis in 1982 and came into his agency offices every day, including Saturdays and Sundays. I didn't have a phone in my apartment and came into the offices every day to work and use the business phone. The phone charges were billed to Garrison and I paid Garrison. There was a sign-in book with the guard at the entrance to the building where I signed in and out whenever the office was closed. That sign-in book was available to Garrison every day. Huston never acted as my supervisor, he left those duties to Garrison. Huston and I worked as co-agents on several sales, but that was the extent of his exercise of control over me. The only conclusion I could reach was Garrison deliberately let the erroneous record stand.

On May 19, 1998, Aksenov told me by letter that the NASD records reflecting my involvement in the Dyer Act back in 1947 will be displayed on the Internet via the NASD's public disclosure program unless I amend my Form U-4. She said that if I amend my Form U-4 it was necessary to provide court documents or a letter from the arresting agency giving complete details: specifically, if the charge was a midemeaner or a felony at the time of the charge or conviction. She said I should have my agency supervisor initial page 3 of the Form U-4. Fifteen years after receiving the FBI information, they said I must get a letter from the FBI saying I wasn't under arrest on August 12, 1983, and I must get copies of the court records for the 1947 arrest and that I must amend my U-4. All of this after I was demoted. I never amended the form. If I was required to amend my U-4, why didn't MMLISI or MassMutual demand I amend it back in 1983 when they found out about the arrest(s)? My guess? They didn't want me to know they had the information in their files.

Bartol had the same conversation with Taaffe on July 8 that I had with Aksenov on May 19. Bartol mailed a copy of the 1947 FBI report and said "This is the only information in Mr. Jensen's MMLISI file that references in any way the Dyer Act issue." This was a false statement. MMLISI is the organization that asked me to verify the 1983 arrest. I received a variety of documents from MMLISI with references to the Dyer Act during the next months. I told Taaffe since I had not been charged with any infraction there was no reason to amend my Form U-4 to show a charge. If there was a circumstance that required the amendment of my U-4 based upon what happened in either 1947, or 1983, or both, that circumstance existed in 1983, at the latest.

Taaffe continued corresponding with Bartol about the incorrect record. Bartol eventually agreed to cooperate to some degree. In July, Aksenov finally agreed to send an amendment to the NASD reflecting the correct arrest date to be in 1947. She was slow to get it done because the NASD didn't receive the correction until September. I believe MMLISI was still convinced the 1983 arrest record was correct, but decided to let me fight it out with the NASD since MMLISI had been relying on the NASD records from the day they received them. That seemed to be the end of it. It seemed like I had a strong case against MassMutual and MMLISI, but decided to forgo any claim and just continue my daily activities. I was now 67 years old, the damage had been done, and as long as MassMutual and MMLISI kept their word from here on out, it seemed like there wasn't much to gain from continued controversy.

On July 7, 1998, I asked my daughter, Cindy, to access the public part of the NASD Web site and locate my records. She did. The form that was printed has the following statement as part of the heading: "PUBLIC DISCLOSURE PROGRAM RESPONSE TO REQUEST FOR INFORMATION" Below was a statement outlining the disciplinary information that might appear in the report. Below that statement was a list of terms and conditions that apply to obtaining the information. Item 6. said "The Public Disclosure Program includes only information provided to the NASD." Underneath the terms and conditions was the report outlining any information which applied to me. The entire statement follows: "7/06/98 SUMMARY INFORMATION NONE" That was the totality of the report.

On September 17, 1998, Andrew Miceli, the current MassMutual general agent in San Jose, notified me by mail I wasn't allowed to solicit securities trades. He said I was allowed to make securities trades on an unsolicited basis and any such trades would have to be approved by Frank Schilero, investment specialist, or Miceli himself. This was another indication MassMutual and MMLISI still believed the 1983 arrest was correct. Miceli wasn't a registered principal, nor was Schilero. Schilero later failed the principal exam and promptly resigned from the agency. On November 20, Eileen D. Leo, assistant vice president and counsel for MMLISI, notified me that an amendment to my Registered Investment Advisor agreement allowed me to solicit securities trades. But it required me to notify my clients I was making the recommendations as an Investment Adviser and MMLISI was not responsible for these investment recommendations.

On May 20, 1999, Taaffe received a letter from the U.S. Department of Justice, Federal Bureau of Investigation, Washington, DC 20535, in response to Request No. 436668, saying every record relating to me had been destroyed in compliance with the law. The FBI no longer had any record of my arrest. (The FBI expunged the record on September 30, 1998.)

At the same time when the arrest date controversy was being discussed another issue came to the fore with MassMutual. Stephen Shearer, a stock broker in San Jose, was a current policyholder with MassMutual. His agent had left MassMutual and could no longer service his policy, so the service requirements were transferred to me. In December 1995, Shearer asked me to help him transfer a policy he owned to his two sons. I asked the legal department of MassMutual how to proceed and which forms to use. The legal department recommended the forms, Shearer signed them, and they were forwarded by me to the home office. In July 1997, a question came up about whether the transfer qualified as a tax-free gift since the total cash value of the policy exceeded the annual tax-free gift limit to one person. The problem could be easily resolved because life insurance policies can be bifarcated or severed and one half be given to each son on the demand of the owner(s). Shearer had owned policies with two other insurance companies under the same circumstances. The two other insurers agreed to bifarcate the policies and issue new policies to each son and backdated the new policies as of the date of the original transfer requests. Insurance companies do backdate policies in the regular course of business. If money is required, the companies insist the required amount of money be paid. MassMutual first agreed to correct the problem. In mid-1998 MassMutual's legal department changed its mind and refused to accommodate Shearer. Shearer was very upset and said he might sue MassMutual. He even made a trip back to the home office in Springfield, Massachusetts, to discuss the issue. The legal department wouldn't talk to him. When he returned to San Jose, Shearer told me another person in the home office told him MassMutual wanted him to sue me. I contacted my errors and ommissions insurance carrier, AIG Insurance Companies and talked to Blanch Halliman. Halliman called back and said Karen Filler at MassMutual had agreed to correct the problem. But then MassMutual reversed its position once again and refused to accommodate Shearer. Shearer said he might sue MassMutual, but he would not sue me. By August 13, 1998, MassMutual said they would sue me if Shearer sued them. I wouldn't back down and after considerable debate and threats MassMutual never sued me. That was the last I ever heard from Shearer or from MassMutual about this problem.

In December 1999 I withdrew my registration with the NASD and resigned from MMLISI, but retained my registration as an investment advisor. In early 2000 I retired as a carreer agent with MassMutual and began working for them on a brokerage basis and for several other insurance companies as well.

On November 8, 2000, the California Department of Corporations notified me annual renewals of Registered Investment Advisors will take place through the Investment Advisory Registration Depository (Web IARD) in the first half of 2001. The renewal fees must be paid directly to the NASD. The SEC and the North American Securities Administrators Association jointly developed the Web IARD to provide a single filing method. The Web IARD would make information about the Investment Advisor including the disciplinary history available to the public. California completed its transition by mid-2001. The NASD then continued my NASD assigned registration number as my personal IARD number, but required me to register as my own supervisor with a different firm number. The NASD considers its records regarding an individual to be the joint property of the NASD and the individual, but inquiries must be made through the supervisor. This gave me access to all of my own personal information on file with the NASD. I was now free to contact the NASD and make inquiries.

In 2001, the IRS decided to get into the act again. The IRS mailed a notice of an audit of my 2000 tax returns. I gathered all of my records and went down their offices in San Jose to complete the audit at the specified time. At the completion of the audit, the IRS determined I still owed an amount of money, so I wrote out a check for the amount it said was due. The audit was certified as complete and closed.

Several months later the IRS notified me taxes were due on an additional $125,000 of income in 2000. The IRS demand letter again said it would take all of my property, bank accounts, whatever they could attach, unless the amount demanded was paid immediately. It's always nice to receive such heartwarming letters. I called the IRS in the Fresno, California, office to discuss the letter with someone, anyone. The Fresno office told me to contact the San Francisco office. San Fransico sent me on to Ogden, Utah. I mentioned to the IRS office in Ogden that I'd be happy to pay taxes on the extra money if they could do one of two things; either give me the extra $125,000 so I'd have the money to pay the tax or show me any 1099, W-2, or other source of income they had in their possession that would identify the person, place, or thing, that paid the money to me. Ogden couldn't help. It gave me another phone number of an office in Tennessee and that office gave me a number to call in Atlanta, Georgia. I kept asking the person I talked to for any information the IRS possessed showing my income to be different than the income shown on the official IRS audit. No one seemed to have that information. I then asked someone to review my tax returns, the papers filed with the IRS. They said no one could find my original returns. They also said no one had copies in one place of all of the 1099s, W-2s, or any other sources of income reported on my behalf. Then I asked them to review their audit of my 2000 taxes. No one knew how to do that. Then I asked how the IRS could assess extra taxes on my income if it had no information that proved I had any income. This question seemed to baffle the people and produced no response at all. The IRS produced nothing. Finally, I asked them how they expected to force collection of extra taxes from me based upon information they didn't possess and couldn't locate. All of this work took time; hours, days and months. Seven months later, I received a notice from a woman in the Fresno office that the IRS had decided to abandon its claim for additional taxes and that the IRS really owed money to me. They accepted the original audited figures. I thanked her for their efforts. They soon mailed a check to me.

In January 2002, my son-in-law wanted to purchase a term life insurance policy. He doesn't smoke but was classified as a smoker, which meant his premiums would be considerably higher than a nonsmoker policy. MML Insurance Agency, Inc. (MMLIAI), a MassMutual company affiliated with Bisys (a joint agency), acted as an insurance broker for many other companies, which allowed me to obtain a series of quotes from different companies so my son-in-law could choose the lowest-priced policy. The Prudential Insurance Company of America (Insurance) quoted the best premium. My son-in-law made application to Insurance for a life insurance policy. The application was submitted to Insurance through MMLIAI on January 18, 2002. Prudential required me to become contracted as a life insurance broker. Prudential Financial (Financial), a holding company that owns all of the stock in Insurance as well as many other corporations, provided me with a licensing application form, which required me to authorize a background check on my character. The application form was a dual-purpose form, which included information necessary to be approved for the sale of either or both life insurance and securities. On January 22, 2002, I signed the application papers to be contracted to sell life insurance. I excluded stock brokerage authorization from the application form because I was no longer licensed to sell securities.

The Prudential Insurance Company of America had been a mutual company, which means it had no stockholders, the policyholders owned the company and were entitled to all company profits. In 2001, it converted to a stock company and formed Prudential Financial, a holding company. The holding company became the owner of all of the stock in Insurance. Financial also owned all of the stock in Prudential Securities, Incorporated (Securities). It owned a second securities company named Pruco Securities Corporation (Pruco). On July 1, 2003, Securities merged into Wachovia Securities (owned by Wachovia Bank) and Financial received 38-percent ownership in

*Judicial Deception*

Wachovia Securities. Securities came to an end. Neither Financial, nor Pruco, nor Insurance became Wachovia Securities. And Wachovia Securities did not become Financial, Securities, or Pruco. All of these companies are different. One company issues life insurance policies. Two companies are stock-brokerage firms and do not issue life insurance policies. I made application to be contracted with the life insurance company, not to be contracted by any broker-dealer or any other firm. That was very clear to everyone involved.

On March 15, 2002, I come home from work and found an overnight envelope from Prudential Insurance on Insurance and Financial stationary in my living room chair. The letter is below:

## Prudential® Financial

The Prudential Insurance Company of America
Prudential Brokerage
13001 County Road 10,
Plymouth, MN 55442
Tel 800-286-7745 Fax 800-416-5022


March 14, 2002

PERSONAL & CONFIDENTIAL
Reginald L. Jensen
5482 Walnut Blossom Dr.
San Jose, CA. 95123

Re: Request for Appointment with Prudential Brokerage

Dear Mr. Jensen:

Thank you for your interest in Prudential Brokerage. We received your request for appointment and are pleased that you are considering sales of our products.

As part of our appointment review process, we conduct background checks on all applicants. Our Compliance officer has requested additional information regarding an arrest on your record which the FBI reported 8/12/83. The exact wording is "Charge: Dyer Act, Hold for USM. (sic)

Please provide the details around this arrest including the disposition by March 28, 2002. If you have any questions about the items required, please call me at 1-800-286-7745.

Sincerely,

Signed
Kathy Schmanski
Licensing Case Manager

What's the big deal about the false arrest record going to the Prudential organizations? All false information about anyone should be immediately and completely deleted to avoid having it dispersed to others. Once the information gets into an insurance or brokerage-company records it is passed about to any other organization without a second thought. Those organizations believe they're doing a favor for anyone who inquires by passing on any and all negative information about a person. Remember how MassMutual and MMLISI requested negative information about me in early 1983?

I took the letter to attorney Taaffe and asked him how I should proceed. MMLISI had represented to me that they had removed all of this information from their files and that the NASD had corrected the information in their records. Besides, I was no longer registered with the NASD and hadn't been for more than two years. The NASD doesn't allow the public to see any information about a person who has not been registered for more than two years. A broker-dealer is considered a member of the public for all registered individuals who are not registered with its own firm. The broker-dealer can search the records of any past or current registered individual who gives them the authority to search. That authority is specific to the NASD, not a general form, and governed by federal law. That authority must be specifically granted as required by federal laws, the rules and regulations of the SEC[28] and the NASD.[29] These laws require the broker-dealer firm to have in its possession the fingerprints of an applicant for employment for securities sales along with the application for employment. If any broker-dealer accesses the information without authority from the person being considered the broker-dealer has violated federal law.

The FBI had no record of arrest in their files. It seemed as though the only other source was either MassMutual or MMLISI. It seemed someone still had a copy of the false arrest record and that record was being made available to other parties. Taaffe said it might be just an administrative mistake by some lower-level employee when entering data into the record. He showed me some of the same types of mistakes he works with on a regular basis. Taaffe said I should try to find out if it was a mistake or a deliberate act. He said he would write to Insurance and ask them to provide us with the source of their information. But, he said, they've made a claim I was under arrest on that day and, if I intend to deny the claim, I must know where I was. He said I couldn't swear I wasn't under arrest in Utah on that date if I wasn't sure of my location at the time. He said I would have to prove where I was. It was my position Insurance made the statement and it should be up to them to prove I was under arrest on that date. Taaffe insisted the proof rested with me.

I went back to my files and searched my records. I found I was with attorney Byal on that day in Tipton, Indiana, and, later in the day, we went to Indianapolis to file a document with the court in the *Jensen v. Laudig* action. I called Byal and asked him if he still had his records of our time and actions. He said his records were stored in a warehouse and he'd have to do a search. He said he was now a Chief Deputy Prosecuting Attorney and he would have to do the search on his own time. He said it would be several weeks before he could respond. When he had time available, he did the search and found his records conformed to mine. He agreed to prepare an affidavit to that effect. The affidavit follows.

---

[28] United States Securities and Exchange Commission Act of 1934, 17 f-2; Title 17, CFR 240.17 f; Title 17, CFR 240.15c 1-6; United States Securities and Exchange Commission Reg § 240.17 f2; and NASD Reg. § 17 f-2.

[29] Rules constitute laws and regulations.

Reginald L. Jensen

STATE OF INDIANA )
                 )SS:
COUNTY OF MIAMI  )

## AFFIDAVIT OF RONALD C. BYAL

Comes now the affiant, who being duly sworn upon his oath, alleges and says:

I am a licensed attorney practicing law in the State of Indiana, and have been since 1973. At the present time I am employed as the Chief Deputy Prosecuting Attorney of Miami County, Indiana. In 1983, I maintained a private law practice in Tipton, Indiana. During that time period I was retained by Reginald L. Jensen to represent him in two causes of action. One was entitled *Stephen Laudig vs. Reginald Jensen*, Tipton Circuit Court, and the other was *Reginald L. Jensen vs. Stephen Laudig*, Marion Superior Court Room 5, cause no. S582-1389.

During the month of August 1983, Mr. Reginald Jensen was employed by the Massachusetts Mutual Life Insurance Company with an office at Suite 260, 9000 Keystone Crossing, Indianapolis, Indiana 46240. He lived in Indianapolis and received personal correspondence at P.O. Box 40441, Indianapolis, Indiana.

I met frequently with Reginald Jensen in preparation for the trial in these two lawsuits. Numerous pre-trial documents had to be filed in anticipation of a trial which ultimately was held on October 6, 1983. I have reviewed my old file in this matter, including time sheets and believe that to the best of my knowledge I met with Reginald Jensen in person in my office in Tipton, Indiana, on August 9th, August 11th and August 12th, 1983. Subsequently on or about August 15, 1983, I received written correspondence from Mr. Jensen summarizing the matters we discussed. This correspondence was dated August 14, 1983, and come from his office in Indianapolis, Indiana.

I have reviewed an FBI arrest record dated January 29, 1947, which indicated that Mr. Jensen was on "hold for USM." In my experience these arrest records indicate that the arrestee was held in a local facility awaiting pick-up and transfer to a federal facility by the U.S. Marshal service. Such procedures usually take several days or more. A "hold" is not a formal disposition or conviction. Mr. Jensen was not in custody on August 12, 1983, in the State of Utah, or anywhere else.

I affirm under the penalties of perjury that the above representations are true to the best of my knowledge and belief.

Dated May 9, 2002

Ronald C. Byal

Meanwhile, on April 8, 2002, Taaffe wrote a letter to Insurance requesting the source of the arrest information. In his letter he said the arrest information was false and requested an immediate response. He was very specific. He outlined my problems with MassMutual and MMLISI, the fact that no August 12, 1983, arrest information existed with the NASD public disclosure section, and that the FBI stated on May 20, 1999, it had no arrest record. No response was received. Insurance elected to stonewall me. It would be a simple matter for them to reveal to me immediately the source of the information, especially since the authorization form provided to me by them said they would provide me with the information upon request. Neither Insurance nor Financial honored that request, which seemed to be a breach of contract.

About a month later, on May 7, Taaffe wrote a second letter and reiterated the information was not correct and to please forward the source of the information. He indicated a civil action could result if no response was forthcoming. Neither Insurance nor Financial honored this second request. However, Insurance did contract me as an insurance agent and issued the insurance policy for my son-in-law. I advised my son-in-law to pay for and keep the policy. I still wanted to clean up the record and the only way to do that was to find out who was providing false information to anyone who asked for it. Taaffe was in the process of deciding how to proceed when he died.

The only way I'd ever obtain the source of the arrest information from any Prudential organization was to file suit. Mitchell Green, an attorney in San Francisco, agreed to help me. He asked for a $15,000 retainer plus a percentage of the damages if an award was ever gained, and my guarantee to pay all expenses. He prepared a contract, which we both signed. I paid him. He filed suit in the United States District Court for the Northern District of California in *Reginald Jensen v. Massachussets Mutual Life*, San Jose, Civil No. C02 04551 JF, (Judge Jeremy Fogel) claiming libel. He demanded a jury trial. MassMutual hired attorney James J. Fleming to represent them. Fleming was about four years younger than me. Right out of the box Green reported to me Fleming told him I was "an old man who needs to sweep the ghosts out from under his bed."

Are the federal courts any different than the state courts? They should be, after all the judges have a lifetime appointment and no longer need to worry about their jobs. Federal judges are supposed to be pretty good; wise, noble, intelligent; the pillars of society. They have no need to do favors for friends or to practice deception on a party in a lawsuit to keep their jobs. But they do have obligations to keep because they weren't appointed to their jobs in a vacuum. Someone made a recommendation to a United States Senator. The senator, in turn, made a recommendation to the President of the United States. The president then made a recommendation to the entire Senate for confirmation. Judges appointed to the district courts might seek appointment to a higher court. Those in the courts of appeal might seek appointment to the United States Supreme Court. They must remain politically astute.

Green issued a subpoena to Insurance and Insurance delivered some documents to him on January 31, and February 12, 2003. On January 31 Cheryl L. Planter-Smith, a paralegal, forwarded an e-mail to Green with the following language (it was from plantersmith@prudential.com): "I briefly reviewed the documents and I believe you may already have most of them. It appears that the majority of the research conducted by Prudential was done on the NASD Website which basically is public information." I knew this was false because I searched the public records myself in 1998, and in 2001, and found nothing other than the fact I was registered in 1998; and when I checked in 2001, I found I was not currently registered but had been registered in the past. At the end of 2001, all of my information was removed from the public record section. Insurance would find no information about me from the public records of the NASD in 2002. How did they know I had ever been registered?

The documents Green received included a copy of my application to be contracted as a life insurance broker for Insurance. The top, right-hand section of the form had the name Prudential Financial. The first section looked like this:

**Licensee Name (exactly as seen on license)**: Reginald L. Jensen.
**Resident License Number:** 0365982.
**State(s) to be appointed in (attach copies of all licenses)**: CA.
**Line of business to be appointed for**: Life.
(The balance of the section was for additional personal information which was filled in as required.)

**Registered Representative NASD CRD Number (Required for Variable Product Sales):** A long line representing none.
**Broker/Dealer or Firm /Agency information. (Please check one).**
**Broker/Dealer [ ] Firm/Agency [ ]** (Neither was checked.)
**Broker/Dealer or Firm/Agency Name:** "N.A" inserted (Not Applicable).
The entire balance of the securities section was left blank.

Underneath that section was an authorization to search my history to gain information about me, just like FESLIC and MassMutual had done in the past. (Prudential Insurance claimed this section of the form authorized them to violate federal laws and NASD regulations.)

Finally: **An officer of the stock-brokerage firm must sign the application if this is an application for securities licensing.** There was no such signature since securities were not involved.

It was written in Insurance's and Financial's internal tracking document I had only applied to be contracted as a life insurance agent. I had not provided any information about my past NASD record because I was not to be contracted for securities sales. The authorization was limited to the purpose of investigating my background for the sale of life insurance only. No Prudential organization had my authority to search the NASD records. The NASD rules specify that prior to entering the NASD database in a search for information about an individual the Broker/Dealer must make a certification[30] by answering "Yes" to the following question:

> If this report is being requested by a broker/dealer, and one or more of the subjects of the report are not current or former employees, then the broker/dealer must certify (by selecting "Yes" below) that the broker/dealer is considering such subject(s) for employment and have obtained and will keep on file such subject(s) written consent to review his/her/their CRD record for that purpose. (CRD Only)
>
> Question: Is this a Pre-Hire Report Request? Yes/No (CRD Only).

---

[30] To confirm formally as true, accurate, or genuine.

I had not made an application to a broker/dealer and had not submitted my fingerprints. All of these organizations knew the rules as well as the NASD and the SEC, but as we shall see, that doesn't mean they're inclined to follow the laws.

Financial is a very large corporation. Insurance is one of the largest financial institutions in the United States. The brokerage firms Securities and Pruco were also very large. These combined firms were larger than many nations and have more facilities at hand than many nations. There's very little they cannot accomplish if they put their minds to it. Creating records is what these companies do all day long.

My experience has been that any large company will complete a thorough investigation of anyone who has threatened a lawsuit. The more information they have, the better prepared they become. They had almost a year to investigate. I'm convinced they knew everything about my Indiana experience. Yet, when subpoenaed, they delivered no records whatsoever regarding my history. They only delivered the documents they believed Green expected to receive.

One of the documents delivered was purported to be a copy of an e-mail between employees of Financial, Securities, and Insurance. Below is the language in the document from Audra Marszalek to Kathleen Schmanski, copy to Kristine Krenz:

---

**Audra Marszalek** Wednesday February 20, 2002 03:16 PM
Pre-Employment Group    212.214.1338    Fax Number: 212.214.1526

TO:      Kathleen Schmanski/PPFS/Pru@Prudential
CC:      Kristine Krenz/IIG/Prudential@Prudential
Subject: **MORE INFO - Reginald Jensen**

Hi Kathy,

The candidate has an arrest on his record which the FBI repo ted 8/12/83, the exact wording is "Charge: Dyer Act. Hold For USM."

Please have the candidate supply details of this arrest including the disposition.

Thanks

---

(See Schmanski's letter dated March 14, 2002.)

The word disposition is missing from what was represented to be the exact wording. Notice the e-mail is missing the address of the sender. The address of the sender is used for reply purposes. A fax doesn't contain the e-mail addresses of the various recipients. Also notice that PPFS/Pru@ Prudential is a different organization than Prudential@ Prudential. It leaves the impression this document was created for my benefit, but not created accurately, or it was represented to be an e-mail, but was really a fax.

Insurance delivered a thirteen-page document they represented to be a CRD report obtained from the NASD on February 20, 2002. Seven pages of the document had a copyright date of 1999-2000; while six pages had no copyright date. I had checked the NASD Website in 2002 and found the copyright appeared on the computer screen, but didn't print on the paper document. If a document is created in a particular year the copyright is applied that year when the document is created.[31] The copyright date will remain unless there are changes on the document. The copyright date is changed when changes occur in a different year. All that is required is for the new date to be inserted with the copyright notation. Any organization or person who wants to protect its documents will closely monitor the copyright process. Two pages of the document referred to the 1947 arrest, so Insurance had the 1947 arrest information in their hands. No one ever claimed they were inquiring about an arrest that happened fifty-five years ago. It became clear Insurance was only interested in the 1983 arrest date. Two pages of the document referred only to an 8/12/83 arrest report received from the FBI. One was the DOJ arrest record; the other was the Legacy Disclosure Incident Details.

One of the documents delivered under the subpoena was a copy of Insurance's contact with the National Insurance Producers Registry (NIPR) indicating they had checked on my insurance licenses. All life insurance companies belong to the NIPR thus, any information Insurance obtained in this manner was proper. Insurance would be required to enter the NIPR database to obtain the above report. The report shows NIPR information relating to me and the option of viewing the detailed report. It showed an appointment search on February 11, 2002. I contacted the NIPR and asked if they could tell me whether or not any insurance company had searched their records for information

---

[31] http://www.copyright.gov/circs/circ1.html#wccc.

about me during the last several years. The NIPR told me I must register with them to complete a search for that information. I registered, paid a fee and searched the record, but found nothing conclusive. I contacted the NIPR again and asked if my NASD licensing record would still show up when an insurance company accessed the records. They told me it would show that I had been licensed. Based upon this information, I was inclined to dismiss my lawsuit against MassMutual because this document indicated Insurance had obtained my NASD registration information from the NIPR and not MassMutual or MMLISI.

Other documents delivered included copies of worksheets and other messages discussing the arrest information.

On January 31 and February 1, 2003, I asked Green if I could sue the NASD. Green told me I couldn't because they're immune. As a self-regulatory organization it is controlled and managed by its own members, the broker-dealers, and has absolute immunity for the statutorily mandated (quasi-governmental) powers that it exercises. Those powers extend to disciplining the members and associates. But the immunity doesn't extend to acts that exceed NASD's authority or are nongovernmental.[32]

The duty rests upon the NASD to notify a person disciplinary proceedings will ensue against that person. Would immunity extend to creating a false-arrest report that extends to several documents and causes an associated person to be disciplined without ever having been made aware of the discipline, especially if the discipline restricts the person's activities and causes the person to be demoted? What happens when the NASD provides a broker-dealer with a false arrest record created by the NASD when the broker-dealer had no legal right to obtain the record? Who's liable? Which party is liable when the broker-dealer disciplines the individual without holding a hearing and without notifying the individual as required by the rules?

To quote the Exchange Act of 1934, Section 15A. h. Discipline of registered securities association members and persons associated with members; summary proceedings.

---

[32] See Sparta Surgical Corp. v. Nat'l Ass'n of Sec. Dealers, Inc., 159 F.3d 1209, 1215 (9th Cir. 1998); Barbara v. New York Stock Exch.U, 99 F.3d 49, 59 (2d Cir. 1996); Austin Mun. Sec., Inc. v. Nat'l Ass'n of Sec. Dealers, Inc., 757 f.2d 676, 692 (5th Cir. 1985).

1. In any proceeding by a registered securities association to determine whether a member or person associated with a member should be disciplined (other than a summary proceeding pursuant to paragraph (3) of this subsection) the association shall bring specific charges, notify such member or person of, and give him an opportunity to defend against, such charges, and keep a record. A determination by the association to impose disciplinary sanction shall be supported by a statement setting forth—

    A. any act or practice in which such member or person associated with a member has been found to have engaged, or which such member or person has been found to have omitted;

    B. the specific provision of this title, the rules or regulations thereunder, the rules of the Municipal Securities Rulemaking Board, or the rules of the association which any such act or practice, or omission to act, is deemed to violate; and

    C. the sanction imposed and the reason therefor.

MassMutual and MMLISI had an obligation to notify the NASD of its intent to proceed with disciplinary action against me, which included elimination of promotability, restrictions on my selling activities, and termination of my principal's license. The NASD should then notify me and a hearing would proceed. MassMutual and MMLISI were required to notify me if they proposed to discipline me because of my 1947 arrest. They would be required to notify me if they proposed to discipline me because of a 1983 arrest. Two felony arrests would require discipline if the arrests had any basis whatsoever. However, when they silently disciplined me, their conduct was outrageous, sanctimoneous, and a violation of the rules.

On February 4, 2003, at 8:19 a.m., I talked to Chris Dragos at the NASD, CRD and Records Division, about the information in my file. I asked him about the 1983 arrest information and he said there was nothing there. I asked him to check the Legacy file, which he did and again he said there was nothing there about the supposed arrest and nothing about 1983. He said the only information in the Legacy file was residential and employment. (The phone conversation was taped by the NASD.) I brought this conversation to the attention of Green.

On February 10, 2003, I talked by phone to attorney Elaine Chavez of the NASD General Counsel's office and she told me they update their copyright information whenever they make a change on any document and that the Web CRD document has been changed several times since 2000. Any CRD document obtained from the NASD in 2002 would have the 2002 copyright on the form or in the manner used at that time. The CRD document is a single product. There are a number of pages to the document, but if the page has the designation CRD printed on it, then it's part of the same document and the entire document has the same copyright. It wouldn't be possible to obtain a 1999-2000 copyright CRD document in 2002 from the NASD. It seemed to me Insurance had obtained it from someone who obtained it in 2000. MMLISI could have obtained it in 2000 to verify the accurate recording of my current status. If I could get in writing from the NASD that the document was created in 2000 and not 2002 then I'd have evidence of fraud and collusion by the Prudential and MassMutual organizations.

I phoned Richard Pullano, Associate Vice President and Chief Counsel, Registration and Disclosure, at the NASD, to verify if any Prudential organization had obtained information on my arrest from them. Pullano told me Securities had searched their records, but the NASD could not identify what, if any, information Securities had obtained. Pullano told me no Prudential organization had obtained any 1983 arrest information from the NASD. I had mentioned to Pullano and his associate, Ann Bushey, I had no intention of suing the NASD because it didn't appear to me the NASD had erred. Pullano and Bushey said they appreciated my assurances.

When I talked to Green again I mentioned that it seemed to me the Uniform Resource Locator (URL) string was placed on the 1999-2000 copyright document to make it appear as though Securities had obtained it in 2002. Green said he was convinced the document was genuine and that it was next to impossible to prove it was falsified. He said he'd try to find out from the NASD what happened.

I met with Green once more a few days later in San Francisco. He was on the phone talking to someone with the NASD trying to obtain whatever information he could provide. He wouldn't tell him anything because Green didn't have my permission to inquire. He put the call on speaker phone and I joined in the conversation over his objections. The person at the NASD said there was no database information regarding any arrest information about me. Green asked if they had any information anywhere regarding me and any arrest. The person at the NASD asked us to wait while he checked the records in another room. He came back and said the arrest information was in the files in the other room. The files were in a file cabinet. Green concluded this was proof Insurance, via Securities, obtained the information from the NASD and my case against MassMutual was in serious jeopardy. He said the false-arrest information wasn't a recoverable issue, but that MassMutual's failure to "hire" was the critical point. He said he had to determine whether or not the statute of limitations applied and if it did apply, how he could get around it.

The failure to promote me extended back to the 1980s and Green had a copy of Garrison's Christmas card to me, which should have alerted him to the probability Garrison would never agree to testify he had assured me of promotion into management. Roger Warrum would be a reliable witness, but he had moved to Ohio, then left MassMutual, and his whereabouts were unknown. Besides, after spending more than eight years in court debating the statute of limitations, there was little incentive to get involved in that type of dispute at the outset of a case. Green then said "I go where the facts take me." As far as I was concerned, the facts we had in our possession clearly showed MassMutual's and MMLISI's failure to notify me of the false-arrest record and the information passed from them to Insurance. In my mind, that failure had created an actionable case. I elected not to continue any association with Green from that time forward. I gave him instructions to dismiss the case against MassMutual and to deliver my records to me. He filed a dismissal immediately. Green kept a copy of my records and returned the originals to me.

In 2003, the IRS decided to entertain me anew. This time they mailed a demand letter for taxes on $50,000 of income in 2002 that I had never earned. The letter was like all previous letters, either pay up now or face the confiscation of your property. We went through the same routine all over again. I spent the next six or seven months trying to find anyone at the IRS in any of the cities in the United States who could produce any kind of information that would show the extra income and the source of the income. Again, it was impossible for the IRS to justify their demand. Eventually they gave up and accepted my return as filed.

On April 16, 2003, I received a letter from Bill Horn of the NIPR with a copy of my record and a copy of all firms that had made inquiry with them regarding me. It showed that in the last two years only one company, CNA, had made an inquiry, and that was on December 17, 2001. My inquiry on April 16, 2003, was also listed. No other organization whatsoever was listed on the records as having made a search in 2002. There was no producer licensing or appointments and no record in their files for 2002.

.3 14:39 FAX 816 783 8053        NAIC                                    ☒012

## Lookup Report

Entity Number: 931904
Entity Name: REGINALD L JENSEN
REGINALD LAURENCE JENSEN

| Date: | Requestor: |
|---|---|
| 12/17/2001 | CNA |
| 04/16/2003 | Prod - Self Request |

The list above represents all the PDB users that have requested a copy of the named entity's report in the past two years.

4-18-03 Bill Horn said that if anyone looked up this information on the Internet it would be recorded on this form.

*Judicial Deception*

I called Horn and asked him why the NIPR had mailed the copy of the record to me, and he said they had treated my inquiry as a Freedom of Information Act request. I asked Horn if the NIPR would still have a record of any search completed by Insurance. He assured me that it would. He said whenever anyone enters the site the NIPR makes a record of the entry. *Horn's comments convinced me the document Insurance provided to me showing they made an inquiry with the NIPR was a counterfeit document.* The credibility of the Prudential organization was in serious doubt. The authenticity of the above Lookup Report is challenged, however, the National Association of Insurance Commissioners asked me to include the following statement: "Reprinted with permission of the National Insurance Producer Registry. Further distribution of this data is strictly prohibited. Any opinions or conclusions the author may have drawn from this information are entirely the author's own. NIPR does not endorse any conclusions or opinions of the author and has not verified the accuracy of any statements attributed to NIPR personnel."

I was now about to enter into a serious dispute with the Prudential organizations and the NASD, which subsequently changed its name to the Financial Industry Regulatory Authority (FINRA). The documents now in my possession provided the basis for the dispute. The dispute carried over to a judge who should have the competency to analyze and rule on the documents. It's best to introduce the documents so you can read and recognize the reasons for the controversy. The documents make one statement and the Prudential companies, FINRA, and the judges make contradictory statements. The documents expose the arrogance and cowardice of corporations, attorneys, judges, and regulatory officials.

One page of the CRD document Insurance delivered to me is below I first became licensed as a Registered Principal in 1968. But my CRD employment history is wrong. It begins with 1971:

| | | |
|---|---|---|
| 10/1971–04/1973 | Investor's Institutional Services, Anderson, IN. | Principal |
| 01/1973–01/1979 | Eastern Broadcasting Corp., Anderson, IN | Salesman |
| 05/1974–04/1983 | Transamerica Fund Sales, Los Angeles, CA | Principal |
| 05/1974–04/1983 | Transamerica Fund Sales, Los Angeles, CA | Agent |
| 01/1979–04/1988 | Massachusetts Mutual Life Ins. Co., Springfield, MA | Salesman |
| 01/1979– | MML Investors Services, Inc., Springfield, MA | RIA |
| 04/1983– | MML Investors Services, Inc., San Jose, CA | Agent |

I was employed with MassMutual from January 1979, until January 2000, working in Indiana from January 1979, to December 1985. I then worked for MassMutual in San Jose, California, from January 1986, until January 2000. I was licensed with MassMutual as a principal from January 1979, until sometime in 1981, when MMLISI was formed, at which time my principal's license was transferred to MMLISI. I became a Registered Investment Advisor (RIA) in 1988, and did not become affiliated with MMLISI as such until 1990. I was a Principal with MMLISI until they terminated my principal's license in 1991. Insurance also delivered to me a page of the CRD document, which was titled U4 Employment History. This is supposed to represent the information on the form U4. That information is shown below:

Employment History
01/1979 – Present     MML Investors Services, Inc., Springfield, MA     RIA
04/1983 – Present     MML Investors Services, Inc., San Jose, CA     Agent

Office of Employment History Address
04/14/1983 – 12/16/1999 MML Investors Services, Inc.
        5482 xxxxxx xxxxxxx xxxxx, San Jose, CA, USA 951xx-xxxx

That information isn't correct either. Again, I became an RIA in 1988, not 1979. The address listed above is my home address. It was never the address of MMLISI and I lived at that address beginning in 1988. It appears as though there have been numerous clerical errors by the NASD in handling my records.

Pullano and I had several discussions over the phone about my NASD records, the data, and the copyright information. He attempted to memorialize our discussions in a letter to me dated June 12, 2003. The letter follows:

*Judicial Deception*

June 12, 2003

Mr. Reginald Jensen
5482 Walnut Blossom Drive
San Jose, CA 95213

Dear Mr. Jensen:

This confirms the May 20, 2003 telephone conversation that Ann Bushey and I had with you wherein we discussed a number of issues you raised in correspondence submitted to NASD relating to your Central Registration Depository (CRD) record. Our discussion focused on information received by NASD from the Federal Bureau of Investigation (FBI) in response to fingerprints submitted to it in connection with your application for securities industry registration. Pursuant to your request, this letter memorializes our discussions.

As we discussed, and as noted in your letters, your principal concern relates to a matter involving a 1947 arrest. The information surrounding this arrest, which you have acknowledged, was provided in a report NASD received on August 12, 1983 from the FBI in response to fingerprints you submitted when you applied to become a registered representative. Consistent with the practice in place at the time, NASD staff recorded the information received from the FBI in the CRD system and forwarded the report on to the MML Investors Services, Inc. (MML), the broker-dealer sponsoring your registration.

As we also discussed, NASD undertook an initiative in 1998 in preparation for the transition from the legacy CRD system to a new Web-based CRD system.[1] This initiative involved converting data from the legacy CRD system (the computerized data base in operation from 1981 to 1999) to a format that would be compatible with the new Web-based CRD system (deployed in August 1999). As part of that initiative, NASD sent to firms information/data on registered representatives employed by them (which principally included information that had been submitted on uniform securities industry registration and termination forms) that was to be transferred or migrated from the old system to the new Web-based system. Firms were asked to review these "conversion rosters" of information, and to have their registered representatives review the information, as one of several quality control measures taken before this data conversion was executed.

The conversion roster project is important because there appears to be confusion resulting from the way the information about your 1947 arrest was presented in the roster sent to MML. As we discussed, the conversion roster documents provided to MML listed the 1947 arrest as an event on your CRD record as one of the pieces of information that NASD was asking MML/you to validate. However, the roster presented a 'date' field under the event, and the date presented in that field was August 12, 1983.

---

[1] The effort also was undertaken in preparation for what was thought at the time to be an imminent implementation of on-line disclosure of disciplinary information via the NASD's Public Disclosure Program; however, on-line disclosure of disciplinary history information via the Public Disclosure Program has not yet occurred.

**Investor protection. Market integrity.**

9509 Key West Avenue
Rockville, Maryland
20850

tel 301 590 6500
www.nasd.com

*Reginald L. Jensen*

Mr. Reginald Jensen
June 12, 2003

As we discussed, the August 1983 date represents the date the NASD received the information about the arrest from the FBI, not the actual arrest date.[2] In response to the request for any corrections or clarifications to the information provided on the conversion rosters, MML requested in October 1998 that NASD check its records to make sure that the CRD system did not reflect an arrest date of August 12, 1983 for this event, but instead reflected the correct 1947 date. Our records reflect that we confirmed that the CRD system showed the correct date. We wish to emphasize again that a 1983 arrest date never appeared in the CRD system. Moreover, no information about this arrest was ever disseminated through the NASD's Public Disclosure Program (i.e., to the general public); the information appeared only in the CRD system.

I hope that this is responsive to your inquiry. If you have any questions, please contact me at 240.386.4821 or Ann Bushey at 240.386.4724.

Sincerely,

Richard E. Pullano
Associate Vice President and Chief Counsel

---

[2] The conversion roster presented information relating to events that were captured in the legacy CRD system. The roster presented a date field, but did not define what that date field represented (it simply said "Date"); however, based on the overall presentation of the event described in the roster, a reader of the information could have interpreted the date presented in that field to represent the date that the event occurred.

His letter is confusing. In paragraph one he said "in connection with your application for securities industry registration..." I had applied to be a registered principal in 1968. I was dually registered as a principal with Transamerica Fund Sales and MassMutual from 1979 to April 1981. MMLISI was formed in 1981 and my registration was transferred to them. In his second paragraph he said "was provided in a report NASD received on August 12, 1983, from the FBI in response to fingerprints you submitted when you applied to become a registered representative." In April 1983 MMLISI asked me to terminate my registration with Transamerica and to submit a fingerprint request along with a new U4 to them. I had not applied to become a registered representative, I was currently registered with them as a principal.

In the third paragraph, Pullano says the NASD was converting data from the legacy system to the Web-based system, which was deployed in 1999. Whatever was in the CRD records in 1983 remained in those files after the conversion. (No new data regarding me was added after 1999 because I withdrew my registration in December 1999, so the reason for adding the 2000 copyright date was a change in the information on the CRD pages in 2000.) He also said "As part of that initiative, NASD sent to firms information/data on registered representatives employed by them (which principally included information that had been submitted on uniform securities industry registration and termination forms) that was to be transferred or migrated from the old system to the new Web-based system." None of the 1947 or 1983 arrest information was on any registration or termination form signed by me. That information was inserted into the CRD records by the NASD.

In the fourth paragraph he said the roster presented a date field in which August 12, 1983, was inserted. In the fifth paragraph he said that was the date the NASD received the information and was not the actual arrest date. The roster page is labeled 'Sequent' and it clearly shows an arrest occurred on August 12, 1983.

In the fifth paragraph he says "We wish to emphasize again that a 1983 arrest date never appeared in the CRD system. Moreover, no information about this arrest was ever disseminated through the NASD's Public Disclosure Program, (i.e. to the general public); the information appeared only in the CRD system." First he said the 1983 arrest record never appeared in the CRD system and in the very next sentence he says it appeared only in the CRD system. I telephoned him and said the paragraph contradicted itself. He disagreed and refused to send a letter of correction or clarification. His statement "no information about this arrest" refers to the previous sentence, the 1983 arrest. The 1983 arrest showed up on several pages of the copyright 1999-2000 document. Part of Pullano's letter is factual, part is incorrect, and part consists of his opinion.

The following page is a document the NASD said it received from the FBI on August 12, 1983. This document was provided to me by MMLISI in 1998. This is identical to one of the documents given to me by the FBI in 1975.

**UNITED STATES DEPARTMENT OF JUSTICE**
**FEDERAL BUREAU OF INVESTIGATION**
**IDENTIFICATION DIVISION**
**WASHINGTON, D.C. 20537**

Use of the following FBI record, NUMBER   4 782 360   , is REGULATED BY LAW. It is furnished FOR OFFICIAL USE ONLY and should ONLY BE USED FOR PURPOSE REQUESTED. When further explanation of arrest charge or disposition is needed, communicate directly with the agency that contributed the fingerprints.

| CONTRIBUTOR OF FINGERPRINTS | NAME AND NUMBER | ARRESTED OR RECEIVED | CHARGE | DISPOSITION |
|---|---|---|---|---|
| PD Ogden UT | Reginald Lawrence Jensen 8191 | 1-29-47 | Dyer Act | hold for USM |
| | Arrest Record Meeting FBI Dissemination Criteria | | | |

The next document is the first document completed by the NASD and given to me by MMLISI in 1998, fifteen years after the 1983 arrest date. This is the Disclosure Roster – Tandem. It appears to have been created on August 12, 1983. The words "Charge: Dyer Act. Disposition: Hold for USM." added to the same line creates the impression a new charge occurred on that date. It looks like two separate charges.

## NASDR RR Disclosure Roster – Tandem

**Individual** Name: **JENSEN, REGINALD LAURENCE**
Tandem  Page 1 of 1
CRD#: **258363**              SSN: XXXXX**3832**
Firm Name: **MML INVESTORS SERVICES, INC.**
Billing Code: **098GM**

STATUS: **X**     ACTION:     FBI:     DATE: 29-Jan-1947
SOURCE: **UT**  PROVISO:

**INCIDENT; 1**

FBI REPORT RECD 8/12/83. CHARGE: DYER ACT.
**DISPOSITION: HOLD FOR USM.**

The next document is the second NASD document given to me by MMLISI in 1998. This one is the Disclosure Roster – Sequent. This is the document Pullano was referring to. This shows the error.

*Judicial Deception*

# NASDR RR Disclosure Roster - Sequent

Individual Name: JENSEN, REGINALD LAURENCE    Sequent
Page 1 of 1
CRD#: 258363    SSN: XXX-XX-XXXX
Firm Name: MML INVESTORS SERVICES, INC.
Billing Code: 098GM

**Disclosure Category: Criminal**
DRP#: 108312    Affirmative Responses 22B1B
Status: Unknown - CRD Data Conversion    Status Date:
If charge(s) were brought against an organization over which the individual exercised control:
Organization Name:
Investment-Related Business: No    Position, Title, Relationship:
Court Name    Court Location    Docket/Case Number
Last FBI Update Date:
Arresting Agency:
**Arresting Agency Location; UT**
**Charge: Other**
**Description: DYER, ACT**
**Date: 08/12/1983**    Counts:    Type: Unknown - Data Conversion
**Plea: Unknown** - CRD Data    Status: Unknown
Conversion
Product Type(s):
**Summary of Circumstances: HOLD FOR USM**
U4 Registration Form Filing Comment:
U5 Termination Form Filing Comment:

I drew a line through the "Date: 08/12/1983" and wrote the word "Wrong." Then I drew another line through "Type: Unknown – Data Conversion" information and wrote the word "Wrong" again. Before returning it to MMLISI. The two above documents, Tandem and Sequent, are NASD records.

In June 1998, Sophie Aksenov said she would send the correction form to the NASD.

(Corrected by me in May 1998 and
received by the NASD in September 1998)

# REGISTERED REPRESENTATIVES
## Roster Discrepancy Form

[NOTE: Use this form to file an amendment to a roster from the new (Sequent) format only]

Individual's CRD Number  *258363*

Individual's Name:  ***REGINALD LAURENCE JENSEN***

Type of Disclosure (circle one):

Bankruptcy   Bond   Civil Judicial   <u>Criminal</u>
Customer Complaint   internal Review   Investigation   Judgment/Lien
Regulatory Action   Termination

DRP Number.  *108312*

Sequent Roster Page Number:  1

Tandem Roster Page Number Related to Sequent Discrepancy: 1

Roster field name(s) with incorrect information:  **DATE**

Information that appears in the field(s):  **8/12/1983**

Information that SHOULD appear in the field(s):  **01/29/1947**

**FIRM CONTACT INFORMATION**

Contact Person's Name:   Sophie Aksenov
Firm Name:   MML Investors Services, Inc.
Firm CRD Number:   10409
Firm Address:   1414 Main Street Springfield MA 01144
Telephone Number:   (413) 737-8400 x423
CRD/Public Disclosure Call Center Assigned Case ID Number:  N/A

The next document is the Legacy Disclosure Summary page with the 1999-2000 copyright, created by the NASD in 1983 and retained in their records to 2004. It's part of the eleven page CRD document produced by Insurance in January 2003 and represented to have been received by Insurance from the NASD on February 20, 2002. The copyright date conflicts with their statement. There were six pages to this report with the 1999-2000 copyright information.

*Judicial Deception*

### Web CRD — Central Registration Depository

CRD Main | Forms | **Individual** | Reports

View Individual   Firm Queues

## Legacy Disclosure Summary

- View Disclosures
- Back To Previous Menu
- Current Disclosures
- Legacy Disclosures
- Reg. Arc and Z Rec.
- DOJ Arrest Records
- Disclosure Letter History
- U4 Summary Questions

Individual CRD#: 258363   Individual Name: JENSEN, REGINALD L

| Incident ID | Last Filings | |
|---|---|---|
| | Source | Action Date |
| -1 | UT | 01/29/1947 |

Back To Previous Menu | Current Disclosures | **Legacy Disclosures** | Reg. Arc and Z Rec. | DOJ Arrest Records | Disclosure Letter History | U4 Summary Questions

Back to Top

© 1999-2000, NASD Regulation, Inc. All Rights Reserved.

https://crd.nasdr.com/inm/vi/crd_inm_vii_Disc_Legacy.asp?PageName=VI_PGNM_LEGA... 02/20/2002

---

The following Legacy Incident Disclosure Details, with the 1999-2000 copyright, clearly shows only a 1983 arrest. There's nothing on this page that refers to a 1947 arrest. Prudential Insurance represented they received it from the NASD on February 20, 2002.

## Legacy Disclosure Incident Details

| Individual CRD#: 258363 | Individual Name: JENSEN, REGINALD L |

**Incident Details - #1**

| Incident Sequence | Details |
|---|---|
| 1 | FBI REPORT REC'D 8/12/83. CHARGE: DYER ACT. DISPOSITION: HOLD FOR USM. |

Back To Previous Menu | Legacy Residential Information | Legacy Employment History | **Legacy Disclosures** | Legacy Registrations | Legacy Filing History

Back to Top

© 1999-2000, NASD Regulation, Inc. All Rights Reserved.

*Judicial Deception*

The DOJ Arrest Record with the 1999-2000 copyright, has an occurrence number 400319; FBI REPORT REC'D 8/12/83. CHARGE: DYER ACT. DISPOSITION: HOLD FOR USM. The pages verify an 8/12/83 arrest. The Code of Federal Regulations (CFR) referred to in the DOJ Arrest Record was eliminated from the Code in late 1999 and reinserted after 2001

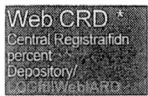

| Web CRD * Central Registraifidn percent Depository/ | | | NASD REOULAYKMt |
|---|---|---|---|
| | Individual | Reports I View | |
| | Individual | Firm Queues | |
| View Disclosures Back To Previous Menu | DOJ Arrest Record | | |
| Current Disclosures | Individual CRD#: 258363 _ Individual Name: JENSEN, REGINALD L | | |
| Legacy Disclosures | CRD System Terms And Conditions | | |
| Reg. Arc and Z Rec. DOJ Arrest Records Disclosure Letter History U4 Summary | This information is subject to the following use and disemination restrictions: Under provisions set forth in Title 28, Code of Federal Regulations (CFR), Section. 50.12, both governmental and nongovernmental entities authorized to submit fingerprints and | | |
| | Occurrence ID | Arrest/Receive Date | Arresting Agencies | Charges and Disposition |
| Questions | 400319 | | | FBI REPORT REC'D 8/12/83. CHARGE, DYER ACT. DISPOSITION: HOLD FOR USM. |

Back to Top  Back To Previous Menu j Current Disclosures | Legacy Disclosures | Reg. Arc and Z Rec. ( DOJ Arrest Records | Disclosure Letter History f U4 Summary Questions
© 1999-2000, NASD Regulation, Inc. Ail Rights Reserved.

https://crd.nasdr.com/ipm/vicrd_ipm_vii_Disc_DOJ_RAPP-asp?PageName=VI_PGNM_DO02/20/2002

The Current Disclosure Summary, with the 1999-2000 copyright date, has the language that is contained on the Composite Information page.

*Reginald L. Jensen*

| | |
|---|---|
| **Web CRD** Central Registration Depository | CRD Main \| Forms \| **Individual** \| Reports |
| LOG OFF \| Web IARD | View Individual   Firm Queues |
| View Disclosures | |
| Back To Previous Menu | **Current Disclosure Summary** |
| Current Disclosures | Individual CRD#: 258363   Individual Name: JENSEN, REGINALD L |
| Legacy Disclosures | |
| Reg. Arc and Z Rec. | ⚠ The specified individual has no disclosure that qualifies for reporting under this section. Please note that there are three types of disclosure in Web CRD: Reportable, Legacy and Archive disclosure. An individual with no reportable disclosure may or may not have Legacy or Archive disclosure. |
| DOJ Arrest Records | |
| Disclosure Letter History | |
| U4 Summary Questions | |

Back To Previous Menu | Current Disclosures | Legacy Disclosures | Reg. Arc and Z Rec. | DOJ Arrest Records | Disclosure Letter History | U4 Summary Questions

Back to Top

© 1999-2000, NASD Regulation, Inc. All Rights Reserved.

https://crd.nasdr.com/ipm/vi/crd_ipm_vii_Disc_Current.asp?PageName=VI_PGNM_LEGA 02/20/2002

The following is part of the second document was also given to me by Prudential Insurance in 2003. This is one of the pages they claimed they received from the NASD on February 20, 2002. Prudential Insurance gave me five pages like this one with no copyright information. You'll notice this document is more elaborate than the document with the 1999-2000 copyright dates. The reason is because the NASD made more

*Judicial Deception*

information available as it improved its functionality. The Composite Information page (the copyright information appeared on the computer screen, but didn't print) and the Current Disclosure Summary (copyright 1999-2000) page indicate the name was changed and the information had a different format, but the language was the same. These pages indicate the document was updated and the copyright was also updated.

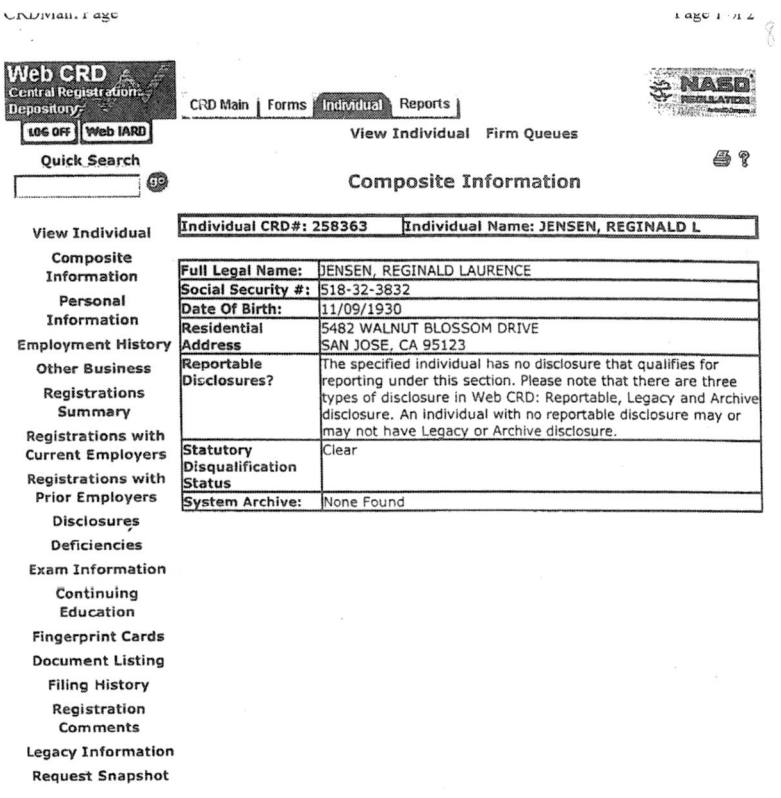

https://crd.nasdr.com/ipm/vi/crd_ipm_vii_compositeinfo.asp?INDVL_PK=258363&cbxPreh 02/20/2002

*Reginald L. Jensen*

The U4 Employment History has no copyright date, but contains data from the U4, and not from any change because of the filing of a U5, Termination of Registration. I terminated in 1999 and it should have the 1999-2000 copyright date if it wasn't changed by my termination. This is part of the 2002 document.

CRDMain Page                                                                 Page 1 of 2

**Web CRD**
**Central Registration Depository**
LOG OFF | Web IARD

CRD Main | Forms | **Individual** | Reports

NASD REGULATION

View Individual   Firm Queues

Quick Search

**U4 Employment History**

View Individual

| Individual CRD#: 258363 | | Individual Name: JENSEN, REGINALD L | | | | | |

Composite Information
Personal Information
**Employment History**
Other Business
Registrations Summary
Registrations with Current Employers
Registrations with Prior Employers
Disclosures
Deficiencies
Exam Information
Continuing Education
Fingerprint Cards
Document Listing
Filing History
Registration Comments
Legacy Information
Request Snapshot

Please note that data contained in the U-4 EMPLOYMENT HISTORY SCREEN is updated only by a U-4 and does not reflect any changes made by the filing of a U-5.

**Employment History**

| From | To | Name | Investment Related Business? | City | State | Country | Position |
|---|---|---|---|---|---|---|---|
| 04/1983 | Present | MML INVESTORS SERVICES, INC. | Y | SAN JOSE | CA | | AGENT - Agent |
| 01/1979 | Present | MML INVESTORS SERVICES, INC. | N | SPRINGFIELD | MA | | OTHER - RIA |

**Office of Employment Address History**

| From | To | Firm | Street 1 | Street 2 | City | State | Country | Postal Code |
|---|---|---|---|---|---|---|---|---|
| 04/14/1983 | 12/06/1999 | MML INVESTORS SERVICES, INC. (10409) | 5482 WALNUT BLOSSOM DRIVE | | SAN JOSE | CA | USA | 95123-2260 |

Back to Top

Composite Information | Personal Information | **Employment History** | Other Business | Registrations Summary | Registrations with Current Employers | Registrations with Prior Employers | Disclosures | Deficiencies | Exam Information | Continuing Education | Fingerprint Cards | Document Listing | Filing History | Registration Comments | Legacy Information | Request Snapshot

https://crd.nasdr.com/ipm/vi/crd_ipm_vii_EmploymentHistory.asp?PageName=VI_PGNM_  02/20/2002

*Judicial Deception*

In his June 12, 2003, letter, Pullano said *"We wish to emphasize again that a 1983 arrest date never appeared in the CRD system."* Is that a true statement? No! Anyone would conclude two arrests occurred. Pullano said the 1983 arrest date was corrected, but obviously it wasn't. All of these CRD records were available to MMLISI at any time because the request would be from an employer or former employer. These same records were available to any broker-dealer who had been authorized by me to enter the system. The authority required my signature and my fingerprints submitted on the broker-dealer form.

I repeatedly notified the NASD that the 1999-2000 document was not obtained from the NASD by any Prudential organization in 2002. Pullano continued to say he couldn't identify the document, but it appeared to him as though it could have been obtained from the NASD over the Internet in 2002 because of the URL date on the bottom of the report. I asked Pullano to check with the department at the NASD that controls the copyright protection to verify if it could have been obtained from the NASD in 2002. He said he didn't know how.

MassMutual's and MMLISI's records, which Bartol said didn't exist, look like the following, plus a variety of other documents with handwritten notes, which were delivered to me in late 1998. The next document is supposed to represent a query by MMLISI of the NASD database in a search for information about me.

Notice the separation completed by the words "KEY ANYTHING NEW WHEN READY." It separates the 1947 arrest from the 1983 arrest.

    ANOTHER CASE?
    >y

    ENTER THE RR'S CRD NUMBER, SSN, OR NAME
    >729071

    SORRY, THAT CRD NUMBER IS UNKNOWN

    ENTER THE RR'S CRD NUMBER, SSN, OR NAME

    >KK,E

```
ANOTHER CASE?
>N
ENTER COMMAND
>QUERY, 258363,SRR

CRD 258363 – JENSEN, REGINALD LAURENCE
SS#-XXX-XXXX- STATUS Y, ACTION FBI, ON 1/29/47,
SANCTIONED
BY UT, PROVISO
        INCIDENT: 1, RECORD 1.
KEY ANYTHING NEW WHEN READY

1         FBI REPORT REC'D 8/12/83, CHARGE
DYER ACT,
DISPOSITION:
2.  HOLD FOR USM

XXX-XX-XXXX -  BORN ON 11/9/30

WHAT WOULD YOU LIKE TO KNOW?
```

There's no resemblance between the MMLISI documents and the NASD documents. This document and many just like it were transferred from MassMutual's and MMLISI's offices in Massachusetts and Indianapolis to San Jose in 1986 without my knowledge at the time.

I then contacted Pullano to find out if any Prudential organization had made inquiry about me and when such inquiries were made. On June 23, 2003, Pullano wrote back saying:

> This follows up on our telephone conversation of June 19, 2003, in which you requested the names of the NASD firms that conducted a "pre-hire search" of your Central Registration Depository (CRD©) record. Pursuant to your request, below is a list of the firms that searched your CRD record between August 16, 1999, and June 17, 2003, and the dates of those searches:
>
> Prudential Securities Incorporated
> February 20, 2002

> Prudential Securities Incorporated
> April 18, 2002
> Pruco Securities Corporation
> January 21, 2003
> Pruco Securities Corporation
> January 30, 2003

All of these searches were in violation of federal laws and regulations. Prior to 2003, Prudential Insurance had already concluded the arrest information was not correct. Pullano told me by phone any search by MMLISI would not be a "pre-hire" search because I was a former employee. I asked him what the NASD would do about the violations and his response was that he didn't know.

On a July 5, 2003, I wrote in a letter to Pullano:

> On February 10, 2003, Elaine Chavez of the NASD's General Counsel's office, told me that they update their copyright information whenever they make a change on any document and that the Web CRD has been changed several times each year since 1999.

On July 28, 2003, Pullano wrote back, in reference to the 1999-2000 copyright document with the 1983 arrest information, saying:

> In your July 5 letter, you ask NASD to authenticate a document that you indicate was provided to you by Prudential Financial as information that Prudential Financial printed from the Web CRD system on February 20, 2002. While the printout appears to have been obtained from the Web CRD system, we are unable to state for certain whether and when Prudential Financial obtained this information from the CRD system.

Although Pullano couldn't say when and how Prudential Financial obtained the information from the CRD system, he could state for certain when they didn't receive it. There are two reasons for this claim. First, Prudential Financial could never obtain it from the CRD records because Financial Prudential wasn't registered with the NASD. Prudential Insurance, not Prudential Financial, claimed they received it from the NASD CRD system. Insurance wasn't registered with the NASD and it couldn't have obtained the information. Prudential Securities accessed the NASD records in 2002. Second, the copyright date would verify to him when they didn't receive it. Pullano completely ignored any reference to Chavez.

If Securities had received the NASD "arrest" information on February 20, there would be no reason to search the NASD records again after Taaffe told them the information was wrong. They would have had it in their hands and would then be able to say to me that it was my responsibillity to disprove the information. There would be no reason for Pruco, a different organization, to search the NASD records two more times almost a year later just before delivery of the documents. If they had delivered four separate identical documents with only the URL date differences, it would prove to me they received it over the Internet from the NASD. Because of Prudential Insurance's stonewalling the only conclusion left for me was that they needed the year delay to decide how to respond. Securities and Pruco produced no records whatsoever showing the request or receipt of any information from the NASD on three of those searches and they failed to reveal the searches under subpoena. The subpoena was issued to Insurance and Financial, not Securities and Pruco. The only reason they could claim they had no obligation to deliver the records would be that Securities and Pruco hadn't been subpoenaed since they were different companies.

On August 5, 2003, I submitted all of this information to Judge Fogel and asked him to reopen my action against MassMutual. He refused. I then hired John Teter, an attorney in San Jose with twenty years of experience in federal court, and paid him a substantial fee to help me prepare the pleadings for a lawsuit against the Prudential organizations. The preparation took about a month. I filed the suit against four firms, Prudential Financial, Prudential Insurance Company, Prudential Securities, and Pruco Securities, in federal court in San Jose in 2003. The case was assigned Number C-03-4608-JF. The case went before Judge Fogel. I hired a professional process serving firm to complete service. Every organization doing business in California must appoint a person in California to act as agent for service of process. And every organization using a fictitious name must file that name in the county where their principal office is located. Financial had failed to do both. Since there was no agent for service of process in California for Financial, the servers mailed the complaint back to New Jersey to be delivered by an associate in that state. I also mailed a duplicate copy through the United States Post Office. The process service firm notified the court service had been properly completed. I also notified the court but I had made a spelling error in one word of my notification and forwarded a corrected copy to the court. I fully expected the defendants to move to dismiss my case because I would be appearing Pro Se.

In federal court, the plaintiff need only file a notice pleading. Neither party argues or proves their case in the complaint and answer. This means the plaintiff must put the defendant(s) on notice as to the purpose of the complaint. Federal Rule 9(e)(1) says each averment of a pleading shall be simple, concise, and direct. No technical forms of pleading or motions are required. The rule in federal court[33] is explained as follows:[34]

> As discussed in Kolupa v. Roselle Park District, federal complaints are to plead claims rather than facts. In fact, the federal rules provide models to illustrate how to plead a short and simple claim for relief under Rule 8(a). Accordingly, plenty of cases have held that a narrative explanation of a claim for relief is unnecessary. E.G. Swierkiewicz v. Sorema N.A., 534 U.S. 506 (2002); McDonald v. Household Int'l, Inc., 425 F.3d 424 (7th Cir. 2005).
>
> On the other hand, the McDonnell Douglas standard is not meant to test the sufficiency of the complaint. Rather, McDonnell Douglas is a screening mechanism to weed out inferential cases that are insufficient for trial. In other words, "the prima facie case under McDonnell Douglas ... is an evidentiary standard, not a pleading requirement." See Swierkiewicz, 534 U.S. at 510. To

---

[33] Federal Rules of Civil Procedure, Rule 9(b).
[34] http://www.wislawjournal.com/archive/2006/0215/finerty-021506.html

invoke the evidentiary standards in McDonnell Douglas, a defendant has a number of other options, including a motion for judgment on the pleadings or a motion for summary judgment under Rule 56.

The court in Kolupa admonished judges and litigants about dismissing pleadings: "Any district judge (for that matter, any defendant) tempted to write 'this complaint is deficient because it does not contain...' should stop and think: What rule of law requires a complaint to contain that allegation?"

The Defendants knew why they were being sued.

Robert Spagat in San Francisco and Linda S. Husar in Los Angeles, of the large, highly respected national law firm Thelen Reid & Priest LLP, appeared for Insurance. No appearance was filed for the other three firms. They claimed Insurance was the only organization that had been served. (Here they claimed there were four different companies who had been sued, but later they and the courts will claim "Prudential" is the only defendant.) Because they failed to appear they were in default. I filed a default motion including the exhibits showing a professional service firm had completed service on the other companies. Judge Fogel ignored my Motion for Default.

After graduating from law school, Spagat served for one year as a law clerk to Judge Patrick D. Sullivan of the Indiana Court of Appeals in Indianapolis in 1991-92, right after the conviction of Judge Dugan and the expulsion of Judge Young from the Indiana Court of Appeals. Judge Sullivan was elected to the Indiana Court of Appeals in 1968 and was retained on the court by election in 1972, 1982, 1992 and 2002. Judge Sullivan and James Tuohy were compatriots in Indianapolis. It's no stretch of the imagination to assume one judge will talk to another. Judge Sullivan could be a perfect conduit between Spagat and Judge Fogel even if Spagat never directly communicated with Judge Fogel in this regard. The Prudential organizations picked the right person to represent them. The Complaint was adequate, yet Judge Fogel dismissed my complaint without prejudice, which left me the right to amend and refile. The parties and the judge knew exactly what was transpiring.

Spagat and I talked for a few minutes outside the courtroom in San Jose after the first hearing. He told me large corporations like Financial and Insurance never engage in deception, libel, or the like, because it isn't necessary for them to do so for the purpose of continuing in business. I said there are many instances of large corporations like Financial and Insurance who do engage in those activities and that Insurance had a history of engaging in illegal activities from time to time.

It seemed as though Spagat needed a reality check. I contacted the Florida Financial Department, which had a record of Insurance engaging in substantial fraud in the 1990s by misrepresenting life insurance policies as retirement plans to thousands of retired people. A substantial amount of the retiree's cash was consumed in commission payments to the agents and managers. Insurance was fined millions of dollars and ordered to make restitution. I mailed a copy of the record to Spagat. Spagat believed I had filed the document with the court and he filed a Motion to Supress. I notified the judge that I had simply mailed the document to Spagat and not to the court. Judge Fogel then ruled that a motion to supress was moot. (As an aside, in August 2006, Securities agreed to pay $600 million to settle civil and criminal charges for improper securities transactions.)

I did refile the dismissed complaint and reduced the number of paragraphs so that the judge could more easily understand it. Spagat asked for a second dismissal through another motion (demurrer) challenging the facts outlined in the second complaint without answering. The paragraphs of the amended complaint included defamation (with the attached document), oppression, and invasion of privacy.

Judge Fogel had not yet ruled on my default motion. Spagat and Elizabeth McCrohan, senior vice president of Insurance, objected to my motion for default against the three defendants. Each filed affidavits saying they had not personally been served on the date of service, therefore, default did not happen. The affidavits swore to something that didn't happen, not to something that did happen. If they knew something didn't happen on a certain date, they would know which date it did happen. They made no sworn statement as to date of service. Spagat wasn't agent for service of process, he was outside counsel and an employee of his law firm. He wouldn't be aware of the complaint until notified by his client. McCrohan was an employee of Insurance, not employed by any of the other three firms, and not an agent for service of process for any of the Defendants. Judge Fogel accepted their affidavits as adequate. The judge denied my default motion. The judge also dismissed my Amended Complaint with prejudice (can't amend and refile). Judge Fogel had the words not for publication stamped on the dismissal.

I contacted Pullano again and asked him to remove the arrest information from the NASD record. He said I needed a court order to have the record removed. I suggested obtaining a court order to that effect could be time consuming and perhaps impossible. What proof would a judge require to determine I had not been arrested on August 12, 1983? Pullano held his ground and wouldn't complete the removal, so I contacted the FBI and asked them how to proceed. On April 14, 2004, the FBI notified me that it had requested the removal of the arrest information from the NASD files. The NASD complied. I didn't need a court order. As it turns out, the NASD's initative to correct the records of the registered representatives, which took place in 1998, and the notification to them about changing their incorrect information regarding me all came to naught. They simply refused to remove the false information without instructions from the FBI. Those instructions came five and one-half years after the NASD received the corrections.

In June 2005, MassMutual's Board of Directors fired Chairman, President, & CEO Robert O'Connell for cause. It was reported O'Connell had arranged to receive Nonqualified Deferred Compensation funds based upon a shadow investment account. A shadow account is usually set up with an employee of a company, which allows the company to assign a certain number of its shares to an account. This is simply a ledger book accounting arrangement with no shares trading back and forth. If the performance of the company is good, the increased value of the shadow stock will be calculated and the dollar amount of the increase will be paid to the employee at a predetermined future date, otherwise the employee receives nothing. Since MassMutual had never issued stock there could be no legitimate shadow investment account.

O'Connell decided to use stock in some other unrelated companies. It was reported in the national press and The Insurance Forum,[35] that he didn't use the stock of a NYSE well established firm (which would be inappropriate in its own right), but used the stock in Initial Public Offerings (IPOs) where the stocks were considered hot. Hot means the shares had been oversubscribed and were guaranteed to increase in value as soon as the IPO was completed. He couldn't purchased any stock in the initial offering, but he credited his account with a purchase anyway. This benefited his account by $18.9 million. Another transaction involving late trading benefited his account by another $4.7 million. These were no risk transactions that had absolutely nothing to do with the performance of MassMutual or any of its subsidiaries. The entire arrangement was absurd. MassMutual attempted to deny O'Connell's claim to the money.

An arbitration panel determined that O'Connell was not entitled to $23.6 million. But the arbitration panel gave him other funds. It determined O'Connell was entitled to about $50 million as severance payment. This was an outstanding reward for O'Connell. It amounted to more than ten times the compensation of any previous Chief Executive Officer at MassMutual. O'Connell was paid approximately $11,400,000 in 2005 as total direct compensation. How much did he really earn? His performance was mediocre at best. The primary growth and development of MassMutual occurred under the management of Thomas Wheeler, the former President and CEO.

I appealed the dismissal of my action against the various Prudential organizations to the United States Ninth Circuit, *Jensen v. Prudential Financial, et. al.* No. 04-16608. Byal had appealed my case in Indiana and he gave me a little insight in how to proceed. But I had no experience whatsoever with filing an appeal in federal court and I had no experience in preparing and filing an appeal without assistance. There are time restraints. There was a lot to learn. So, I obtained the federal rules on filing an appeal and did my share of studying. It was a challenge.

The first issue to be established is jurisdiction, a person must establish the court of appeals has jurisdiction over the case. It took some research

---

[35] Published by former Professor Joseph Belth (Indiana University), October 2006 issue of The Insurance Forum. See also, Vol. 24, Nos. 1 & 2, January/February 2007.

to find the section of the statutes that applied. Then it was necessary to compose the appeal document. The rules of the court of appeals was my guide.

As the appellant, I had to outline what I considered to be the errors in the court below and then present those arguments in the appeal document. *Since Judge Fogel had found as a fact that "Prudential" obtained the NASD legacy documents from the NASD I was required to argue from that position in the appeal.* I finally completed the appeal and made a timely filing with the Ninth Circuit. After an appeal has been perfected, a panel of three judges is supposed to absorb the information and prepare to hear oral arguments. The rules prescribe the appellant is allowed to argue his position in person before the appellate judges and the appellee is permitted to rebut. Would the Court of Appeals grant this pro se litigant the same rights the rules prescribe? The Ninth Circuit ruled against me without allowing me to make oral arguments.

Our federal constitution doesn't provide for the dismissal of a lawsuit by a judge. Any common law provision is overridden by our right to a jury trial. Dismissal of any federal lawsuit prior to jury consideration is a serious infringement on our Constitutional protections. Consider the statistical margin of error again, which was stated in the Foreward. The normal statistical margin of error is 3 percent. When published appeals are less than 3 percent, it simply means, statistically, no case is ever appealed. Yet, our United States Constitution guarantees an appeal of every criminal action and every civil action in excess of a stated amount, which changes from time to time. Less than 2 percent of all cases, criminal and civil, are tried by a jury, and 2 percent or less of all cases tried are appealed. If anyone goes to court, the odds are one in fifty the person will receive a jury trial and substantially lower that any case will be appealed. Some cases not tried but dismissed by a judge can go to appeal, such as my case, but since it's not for publication it really doesn't count. How does that stack up with the rule of law and the United States Constitution?

The complete language of Judge Fogel's two decisions and the ruling of the Ninth Circuit Court of Appeals will follow shortly. You'll be able to compare the ruling of the Ninth Circuit with Judge Young's ruling in Indiana. Both Judge Young and the Ninth Circuit established their own facts to support their decision, which is the purpose of a not for publication or not for citation decision.

In August 2005, I appealed the dismissal of my action by the ninth circuit with the filing of a Petition for a Writ of Certiorari to the United States Supreme Court, *Jensen v. Prudential, et. al.,* Docket No. 05-193. If the Supreme Court believes it might disagree with the decision below it grants the writ and reviews the case. If the Supreme Court decides it doesn't want to review the decision below it denies the writ. This allows the Supreme Court to take up the same issue at a later time, which means the current case can be allowed to stand while a different case can reverse the decision. This allows the courts to rule for and against any party below and to rule the opposite for a different party with the same or identical issues.

What does the United States Constitution say about the function of the Supreme Court? Article III, Section 2. (second paragraph) says:

> The Supreme Court shall have appellate jurisdiction, both as to law and fact, with such exceptions, and under such regulations as the Congress shall make.

The rules of the Supreme Court make it very difficult to have a petition for a writ granted. Here is one of the rules:

> Part III. Jurisdiction on Writ of Certiorari. Rule 10. Considerations governing review on certiorari: A petition for a Writ of Certiorari is rarely granted when the asserted error consists of erroneous factual findings or the misapplication of a properly stated rule of law.

Rule 10 seems to contradict the Constitution. Congress makes the regulations, not the Supreme Court. Any rule that restricts or expands the Court's duties are regulations controlled by Congress. Correcting erroneous factual findings and the misapplication of law seems to be mandated by the Constitution to the Supreme Court. But the Supreme Court decides for itself what it will or will not consider. The interpretation of the Constitution can only be in the hands of the entity that drafted and authorized the document. Interpreting a document as it applies to two other unrelated parties is one thing, but interpreting a document, not created by the interpreter, governing how the document applies to the interpreter is completely unrealistic. In speaking to the United States government, Thomas Jefferson had this to say: "[T]hat the government created by this compact was not made the exclusive or final judge of the extent of the powers delegated to itself; since that would have made its discretion, and not the Constitution, the measure of its powers."[36] Madison said: "When the people have formed a Constitution, they retain those rights which they have not expressly delegated...If we advert to the nature of republican government, we shall find that the censorial power is in the people over the government, and not in the government over the people."[37] Who decides the authority and powers of the judiciary? The judiciary, the Congress, the president, or the people? In the United States it's the people. Every interpretation of our Constitution as it applies to the federal courts must go back to the people (either directly by Congress or through Congress), no matter how inconvenient that process might be. The failure of the judiciary to hold itself accountable to the Constitution and the laws simply means the United States is in a downward spiral to the loss of our democratic process. It has been said previously by others that the Constitution, the creation of the people, becomes the people's tyrant. In this case the tyrant is the judiciary, which believes it controls the Constitution. Jefferson also had this to say about the Supreme Court in a letter to Senator Giles "If a member of the executive or legislature does wrong, the day is never far distant when the people will remove him. They will see then and amend the error in our Constitution which makes any branch independent of the nation."[38] Jefferson believed the appointment of judges should be for four or six years and renewed by the president and the senate. Today, such a plan would work with the exception that the judges would go before the people in the renewal process. Every four years, one third of the justices should be submitted to the citizens of the United States for renewal of their term or removal from the court based upon their actions on every case submitted to it. The public could then decide if the justices were applying the laws to the facts or were satisfying their own personalities and prejudices.

---

[36] Draft of the Kentucky Resolution," October 1798
[37] Speech in Congress on "Self-Created Societies." November 27, 1794.
[38] Jefferson to W. B. Giles. April 20, 1807; Works, v.65.

No judge should ever be allowed to determine the facts in a lawsuit. No lawsuit should proceed until the facts are stipulated by the parties or a jury has determined which facts were true and the law should be applied to those facts. Every lawsuit presented to the higher courts should first contain a certification that the parties had agreed to the facts in dispute, or the facts that were found by a jury, and so state those facts. The appellate courts would review the actions to certify the facts and then to affirm or change the law(s) as required. If the lower courts' rulings on fact and law are correct, there's no reason for the Supreme Court to take jurisdiction, it should simply state the facts and cite the law, then certify the law applied to the facts below was correct. If the lower courts' rulings on law and fact are incorrect, then the Supreme Court must take jurisdiction to correct the errors below. That's what an appeal is all about. Every action submitted to the Supreme Court should be verified or reversed and be published. No case should ever be turned away without analysis.

R. M. MacIver has this to say:[39]

> But men have struggled toward democracy not for the sake of the form but for the way of life that it sustains. Any monopoly of power is a threat to this way of life, for any ruling group that is not subject to control is tyrannous. Any group endowed with irresponsible power, no matter whether it be of the rich or of the poor, of the right or of the left, is suppressive of democratic liberties. Any such group drives a wedge through the community, denies the equal participation of all groups in the affairs of the community…Whereas in a democracy the government that rules by law is itself ruled by law.

The Supreme Court does not exist without a superior body over its entity, the people, but it operates as though it does.

---

[39] *The Web of Government,* The MacMillan Company, New York, 1948 (pp. 204-5)

The Petition for a Writ of Certiorari is below. It incorporates what I consider to be the appealable items. It contains the rulings by the Court of Appeals and both trial court decisions. The trial judge's incorrect determination that there is no law in California governing oppression isn't appealable according to the rules of the Supreme Court. Other errors committed by the trial judge are not appealable.

My stated reasons for granting the petition begins on page 3 of the writ. You'll notice at the end of the petition there is a waiver signed by Thomas E. Hill, lead partner in the Los Angeles office of the firm Thelen Reid & Priest LLP. He waived filing a response to my petition. The opposing side should file a response if the petition contains inaccuracies. The record showing the denial of the writ by the Supreme Court comes after the waiver. When I filed with the Supreme Court my paperwork was returned to me because of technical errors. I corrected the errors and refiled. It was then accepted for review.

The Petition for a Writ of Certiorari places the last events first. The ruling by the court of appeals is first, after the petition.

Docket No. <u>05-193</u>
In The
# SUPREME COURT OF THE UNITED STATES
REGINALD L. JENSEN,

v.

PRUDENTIAL FINANCIAL, INC.,
A New Jersey Corporation
THE PRUDENTIAL INSURANCE COMPANY OF AMERICA,
A New Jersey Corporation
PRUCO SECURITIES CORPORATION
A New Jersey Corporation
PRUDENTIAL SECURITIES INCORPORATED
A Delaware Corporation
Respondents.

# PETITION FOR WRIT OF CERTIORARI
To The United States Court of Appeals for the Ninth Circuit

Reginald L. Jensen
*Pro Se*
5482 Walnut Blossom Drive
San Jose, CA 95123-2260
(408) 225-4227

# QUESTIONS FOR REVIEW

A. **INVASION OF PRIVACY.** Do the United States Constitution, Amendment 14; the California Constitution, Article 1, Section 1; the Freedom of Information Act; federal securities laws; state laws; and National Association of Securities Dealers rules and regulations; control access to information regarding an individual or does an individual's signature on a restricted and limited, standard, vague authorization form overcome the application of these legal provisions? *Department of Justice v. Reporters Committee*, 489 U.S. 749, 762-763, 764 n.16 (1989).

B. **VALIDITY OF AN AUTHORIZATION.** Is an authorization valid in California if the maker is a New Jersey corporation using a fictitious name not in compliance with California code § 7918?

C. **LIBEL.** Can a court consolidate various corporations into one entity for the purpose of applying privilege in the transfer of false information? The Ninth Circuit Court of Appeals ruled that California Civil Code § 47(c) controls. However, this code applies only to communications between previous and potential employers. The Ninth Circuit has granted privilege to noninterested parties, to parties where no intention of employment existed.

D. **DEFAULT,** Can the Court of Appeals ignore this Court's ruling on willful default? See; *United States v. Bryan* 339 U.S. 323,327, (1950)

**PARTIES TO THE PROCEEDINGS AND STATEMENT PURSUANT TO RULE 29.6** The parties to the proceedings below were Reginald L. Jensen, (as Appellee) and respondents Prudential Financial, Inc. ("Financial"), a New Jersey Corporation; Prudential Securities Incorporated "Securities") a New Jersey Corporation; The Prudential Insurance Company of America ("Insurance") a New Jersey Corporation; and Pruco Securities Corporation ("Pruco") a New Jersey Corporation, (as appellants).

Pursuant to Rule 29.6, petitioner Reginald L. Jensen states that he is an individual.

# TABLE OF CONTENTS

Question Presented .................................................................. i

Parties to the Proceeding and Statement Pursuant to Rule 29.6 ....... ii

Table of Cited Authorities ........................................................ iv

Opinions Below ........................................................................ 1

Statement of Jurisdiction ......................................................... 1

Statutory Provision Involved .................................................... 1

Counsel of Record .................................................................... 1

Statement of the Case .............................................................. 1

Reasons for Granting the Petition ............................................. 3
    A.  Invasion of Privacy                                          3
    B.  Validity of an Authorization                            9
    C.  Libel                                                                       10
    D.  Default                                                          13

Conclusion .............................................................................. 21

## TABLE OF AUTHORITIES

| | |
|---|---|
| UNITED STATES CONSTITUTION<br>AMENDMENT XIV, Section 1 | 8 |
| CALIFORNIA CONSTITUTION,<br>ARTICLE 1, SECTION 1 | 7 |
| 5 U.S.C. § 552, as amended<br>by Public Law No. 104-231, 110 Stat 3048 | 8 |
| U.S.C. TITLE 15, 15q(f)(2) | 11 |
| U.S. Securities & Exchange<br>Commission Act of 1934, 17f-2 | 5 |
| 15USCA78a | |
| Fed. R. Civ. P. 417, 23<br>TITLE 17, CFR. 240.17f. | 5, 11 |
| TITLE 17, CFR.240.15c 1-6 | 7 |
| U.S. Securities & Exchange<br>Commission Reg. §240.17f-2 | 5, 11 |
| Cal. Bus. & Prof Code § 17918 | 9 |
| Cal. Civ. Code § 45 | 325 |
| Cal. Civ. Code § 47(c) | 11, 13, 326 |
| Cal. Code, Title 10. Investment. | 6 |

| | |
|---|---:|
| Cal. Corp. Code § 1215-1215.16 | 16 |
| Cal. Corp. Code § 1700-1701 | 16 |
| Cal. Ins. Code § 1600, 1602 | 16 |
| NASD Reg. § 240.17f-2 | 11 |
| Coastal Abstract Service. Inc. v.<br>First American Title Ins. Co. 173 F.3d 725 (9th Or. 1999) | 11, 13 |
| Cramer v. Consol Freightways, Inc.,<br>(9 Cir. 2000) 209 F.3d 1122 | 13 |
| Department of Justice v.<br>Reporters Committee 489 U.S. 749 (1989) | 9 |
| Eitel v. McCool, 782 F.2d 1470 (9th Cir. 1986) | 13 |
| Hill v. Nat'l Collegiate Athletic Ass'n.,<br>865 P.2d 633 (1994) | 3, 13 |
| Kahn v. Bower, 284 Cal. Rptr. 244(1991) | 11, 13 |
| Masson v. New Yorker Magazine, Inc. 501 U.S. 496 (1991) | 13 |
| United States v. Bryan 339 U.S. 323 (1950) | 9 |

## OPINIONS BELOW

The District Court's order (per Fogel, J.) denying Plaintiffs motion for default judgment and granting Defendants' motion to dismiss with leave to amend on February 25, 2004, is not for citation. The District Court's order (per Fogel, J) granting Defendants's motion to dismiss without leave to amend; and deeming moot Defendants' motion to strike on July 21, 2004, is not published and not for citation. The Ninth Circuit Court of Appeals is a memorandum opinion and is not published (per Pregerson, Canby, and Thomas).

## STATEMENT OF JURISDICTION

JURISDICTION of the District Court is under 28 U.S.C.A. §1332.

JURISDICTION The Court of Appeals entered judgment on May 9, 2005, which was filed on May 13, 2005. This Court has jurisdiction pursuant to 28 U.S.C. § 1291.

## STATUTORY PROVISION INVOLVED

28 U.S.C.A.§ 1332 based upon diversity of citizenship because the Defendants are incorporated in and have their principal places of business in states other than California and the amounts in controversy exceeds $75,000.

## COUNSEL OF RECORD

Counsel of record and all parties are listed on Pet. App. #3A-5A.

## STATEMENT OF THE CASE

Reginald L. Jensen, Petitioner, Pro Se, Plaintiff and Appellant below, is a life insurance agent.

There are four Defendants in this cause of action:

1. Prudential Financial, Inc. ("Financial") is a holding company;
2. The Prudential Insurance Company of America ("Insurance") is a life insurance company;
3. Prudential Securities, Incorporated ("Securities") is a stock brokerage firm;
4. Pruco Securities Corporation ("Pruco") is a stock brokerage firm.

This action filed on October 14, 2003, claims **Invasion of Privacy** against Securities and Pruco, **Libel** against Financial and Insurance and **Oppression** against Insurance.

On November 12, 2003, only Defendant Insurance responded by filing a Motion to Dismiss. The Motion to Dismiss said the other three Defendants had not been served. Footnote 1, on page 2 of said Motion says:

> Defendant The Prudential Insurance Company of America (hereafter "Prudential" or "Defendant") is the only defendant who has been served, and accordingly, only Prudential (as herein defined) appears by this motion. Nonetheless, the arguments set forth herein are equally applicable to each of the named defendants.

On December 9, 2003, Jensen moved for a Default Judgment against Financial, Securities, and Pruco.

On December 10, 2003, Financial, Securities, and Pruco filed an appearance. (Pet. App. D, 19A) Subsequently, the Motion for Default Judgment was denied by the District Court. Thereafter, the Defendants' Motion to Dismiss was granted and Jensen was given the opportunity to amend, which he did. Jensen attempted to file an appeal of a ruling by the District Judge, but the Ninth Circuit Court of Appeals denied jurisdiction. A new Motion to Dismiss was filed by all Defendants and that Motion was granted. Jensen filed an appeal and the Ninth Circuit Court of Appeals upheld the dismissal. Jensen now files this Petition for a Writ of Certiorari to the United States Supreme Court.

## REASONS FOR GRANTING THE PETITION

In the District Court's Order (1) Denying Plaintiff's Motion for Default Judgment and (2) Granting Defendants' Motion to Dismiss with Leave to Amend, filed Feb. 25, 2004, the Court said *"The fact that Prudential allegedly violated applicable rules is neither here nor there."* (Emphasis supplied) (Pet. App. #D, 23A). The District Court also said in Order Granting Defendants' Motion to Dismiss Without Leave to Amend; and Deeming Moot Defendants' Motion to Strike, filed July 23, 2004, *"the fact that Defendants may have violated applicable SEC rules (which Defendants deny) is immaterial with respect to Jensen's claim for invasion of privacy."* (Emphasis supplied) (Pet. App. #C, 14A) The fact that all four defendants violated "applicable" rules, which are laws, is the very issue before the court. For what other purpose do the courts exist? The laws (rules) prohibit libel, oppression, and invasion of privacy. The *Rule of Law* prohibits Defendants's and others from engaging in these and other herein cited violations of laws. It's weird and incomprehensible for a federal court to announce that violations of "applicable" rules are "neither here nor there" and "immaterial." The United States Ninth Circuit Court of Appeals upheld these violations of the "rules." Hence, this Petition for a Writ of Certiorari.

**A. PRIVACY.** On the issue of Privacy the Court of Appeals ruled:

> Prudential Insurance Company of America, Prudential Securities, Inc., Prudential Financial, Inc. and Pruco Securities Company ("Prudential") did not commit an unauthorized intrusion into Jensen's privacy by completing a background check prior to hiring him as a life insurance agent because Jensen authorized the background check and released Prudential from any and all liabilities, claims, or lawsuits with regard to the information obtained. *See Cramer v. Consol. Freightways, Inc.*, 209 F.3d 1122, 1130 (9th Cir. 2000) *(citing Hill v. Nat'l Collegiate Athletic Ass'n.*, 865 P.2d 633 (1994)" (Pet. App. A, 2A)

The Court of Appeals relied upon a standard authorization form prepared by Prudential Financial which was restricted and limited by Jensen and signed by Jensen as the basis for its ruling. Jensen completed and signed a standard dual **application** form prepared by Prudential Financial that was used by applicants to be appointed either as life insurance agents, stock brokers, or both. (Cmpt. #12, P.3) The **authorization** is included as part of the application form. A portion of the authorization is cited by the District Court and is reproduced as follows:

> I hereby: Authorize Prudential and its authorized agents to investigate my background, references, characters, past employment, education, criminal or police reports, including those mandated by both public and private organizations and all public records for the purpose of confirming the information contained on this application and/or obtaining other information which may be material to my qualifications for my appointment.
>
> Release Prudential, its authorized agents and any person or entity which provides information pursuant to this authorization, from any and all liabilities, claims or lawsuits in regards to the information obtained from any and all of the above referenced sources.

(Pet App. #C, 10A)

Below Jensen's signature the sentence reads: **"An Officer of the Firm/Agency or Broker/Dealer must sign if this is a Firm/Agency or Broker/Dealer Appointment Request."** Above Jensen's signature in the middle of the form are the words "Broker/Dealer or Firm Agency Name:" Followed by "NA" inserted by Jensen. (Cmpt Ex. #12, P. 3) Jensen applied only to Insurance to be a life insurance agent. (Pet. App. #A, 2A and #C, 9A) (See also Motion to Dismiss filed 11/12/2003, Footnote #1, page 3) Jensen excluded the authorization from being used by a stock brokerage firm. Securities (a stock brokerage firm) obtained incorrect arrest information from the NASD and provided that information to Insurance and Financial. (Pet. App. #C, 12A)

There is no information in the record showing Insurance or Financial authorized any agent to investigate Jensen's background. Securities and Pruco are not investigative agencies.

Securities and Pruco only hire life insurance salesmen if the applicants and employers comply with 15q (f)(2) of Title 15, United States Code, which provides:

> Every member of a national securities exchange, broker, dealer, registered transfer agent, and registered clearing agency shall require that each of its partners, directors, officers, and employees be fingerprinted and shall submit such fingerprints, or cause the same to be submitted, to the Attorney General of the United States for identification and appropriate processing. The Commission, by rule, may exempt from the provisions of this paragraph upon specified terms, conditions, and periods, any class of partners, directors, officers, or employees of such member;, broker, dealer, transfer agent, or clearing agency, if the Commission finds that such action is not inconsistent with the public interest or the protection of investors. Notwithstanding any other provisions of law, in providing identification and processing functions, the Attorney General shall provide the Commission and self-regulatory organizations designated by the Commission with access to all criminal history record information.
>
> This section is implemented by Section 240.17f of Title 17, Code of Federal Regulations.

Prior to and during the process of employing a person to become a representative for a securities firm all parties must comply with SEC Reg §240.17f-2, the NASD fingerprint Regulation §240.17f-2, and the NASD application certification requirements. The NASD regulation is a statement that it has adopted 17f-2 of the Securities Exchange Act of 1934. (Cmpt Ex. #26) Jensen was never asked to provide and never did provide fingerprints. None of the Defendants complied with any of the above laws.

As of May 20, 1999, the Federal Bureau of Investigation (FBI) had no record of arrest or criminal conduct by Jensen. (Cmpt Ex. #18) *(See* Pet. App. #C, 13 A)

Insurance did investigate Jensen's background. On or about February 18, 2002, Insurance conducted a criminal investigation of Jensen's background through CARCO Group, Inc. and found that Jensen had no federal criminal record. (Cmpt Ex. #18, Pp. 2-3) *(See* Pet. App. #C, 12A)

Securities and Pruco also investigated Jensen's background. On February 20, 2002, Securities obtained a WebCRD NASD report stating Jensen has an arrest on his record. (Pet. App. #C, 10A) Only a broker/dealer could access the NASD files in reference to Jensen. (Cmpt Ex. #25, Pp. 1-3) *(See also:* Plaintiffs Supplemental Objection to Motion to Dismiss First Amended Complaint. Pages 1-3.) The NASD certification requirement is as follows for stock brokerage firms in accessing information in reference to those not currently or formerly employed by the firm:

> If this report is being requested by a broker/dealer, and one or more of the subjects of the report are not current or former employees, then the broker/dealer must certify (by selecting "Yes" below) that the broker/dealer is considering such subject(s) for employment and have obtained and will keep on file such subject(s)'s written consent to review his/her/their CRD record for that purpose. (CRD Only)

The California law on dual employment of securities personnel California Code. Title 10. Investment. Chapter 3, Subch 2. Article 9. §260.216.16 *Dual Employment of Affiliation,* says:

> It shall constitute a "fraudulent, deceptive or manipulative act or practice," as used in Section 25216 of the Code, for any agent, officer, director, partner, managing employee or controlling person of a broker-dealer to become concurrently associated with another broker-dealer or with an issuer as an agent, officer, director, partner, managing employee or controlling person unless prior to establishing such concurrent affiliation (I) such person gives written notice to both affiliates regarding such dual relationship, (i) both affiliates consent to such concurrent affiliation, (ii)

both affiliates establish appropriate procedures designed to correct any conflict of interest arising out of such relationship and to guard against violation of Sections 260.216, 260.216.3, 260.216.4, 260.216.7 or 260.218.4, etc. (including 17 FR240.15cl-6 and 15USCA78a).

The Court of Appeals cited *Cramer v. Consol. Freightways, Inc.* 209 F. 3d 1122, 1130 (9th Cir. 2000). In *Cramer* the Court held that consent is normally a defense in a privacy action. And note 9 of the consent issue said that they must proceed under a general **tort** claim under the California Constitution. Article 1, Section 1. That section says:

> All people are by nature free and independent and have inalienable rights. Among these are enjoying and defending life and liberty, acquiring, possessing, and protecting property, and pursuing and obtaining safety, happiness, and privacy.

The District Court said "California does not recognize such a **tort**." (Pet. App. C, 13A)

Jensen did proceed under the California Constitution, Article 1, Section 1, and the common law (Am. Cmpt. P.8. L.25 - P.9. L.2) but the Court of Appeals ignored these requirements.

The Court of Appeals cited *Hill* v. *Nat'l Collegiate Athletic Ass'n*, 865 P.2d 633 (Cal. 1994). (Pet. App. #A, 2A) In *Hill,* at 643, speaking to the California Constitution Article 1, Section 1, the California Supreme Court said:

> Emphasizing that the concerns underlying the Privacy Initiative extended to the conduct of both governmental and nongovernmental entities, the court observed: "Common experience with the ever-increasing use of computers in contemporary society confirms that the [Privacy Initiative] was needed and intended to safeguard individual privacy from intrusion by both private and governmental action. That common experience makes it only too evident that personal privacy is threatened by the information-gathering capabilities and activities not

just of government, but of private business as well. If the right of privacy is to exist as more than a memory or a dream, the power of both public and private institutions to collect and preserve data about individual citizens must be subject to constitutional control. Any expectations of privacy would indeed be illusory if only the government's collection and retention of data were restricted." (Id., at p. 1043, 264 Cal Rptr. 194).

The United States Constitution, Amendment XIV, Section 1, also applies. Section 1 says:

> All persons born or naturalized in the United States and subject to the jurisdiction thereof, are citizens of the United States and of the State wherein they reside. No State shall make or enforce any law which shall abridge the privileges or immunities of citizens of the United States; nor shall any State deprive any person of life, liberty, or property, without due process of law; nor deny to any person within its jurisdiction the equal protection of the laws.

The <u>Freedom of Information Act</u>., 5 U.S.C. § 552, as amended by Public Law No. 104-231, 110 stat 3048. prohibits obtaining unauthorized information from the NASD. If the NASD is covered by the Freedom of Information Act (a new question) then it also applies:

> § 552. Public information; agency rules, opinions, orders, records, and proceedings (a) Each agency shall make available to the public information as follows:--
>
> (b) This section does not apply to matters that are— (6) personnel and medical files and similar files the disclosure of which would constitute a clearly unwarranted invasion of personal privacy.

The U. S. Supreme Court said: "(B)oth the common law and the literal understanding of privacy encompass the individual's control of information concerning his or her person." *Department of Justice v. Reporters Committee* 489 U.S. 749 762-63, 764 n. 16 (1989). Therefore, if an individual says to one organization: "Yes, you can investigate my background." And says to another: "No! You cannot investigate my background." that prohibition stands.

## B. VALIDITY OF AN AUTHORIZATION.

<u>Prudential Financial</u> is a fictitious trade name. Prudential Financial, Inc. is a holding company. The words Prudential Financial are used on various forms and letterheads by and for different companies under the control of Prudential Financial, Inc. <u>Prudential</u> is a fictitious trade name used without specificity by Financial. Defendants use the term **"Prudential"** to identify Insurance. (See: Motion to Dismiss filed 11/12/2003, Footnote #1. supra: page 3) During 2002 the name *Prudential Financial* had not been filed with a county in the State of California as an assumed (fictitious) business name as required by California Code § 17918. (See; Motion for Judgment by Default Against Defendants Pruco Securities Corporation, Prudential Financial and Prudential Securities Corporation, filed December 9, 2003) The authorization was provided by Prudential Financial to Jensen. (Cmpt.Ex. #12,P2&P3)

California Business and Professional Code § 17918 says;

> No person transacting business under a fictitious business name contrary to the provisions of this chapter, or his assignee, may maintain any action upon or on account of any contract made, or transaction had, in the fictitious business name in any court of this state until the fictitious business name statement has been executed, filed, and published as required by this chapter. For the purposes of this section, the failure to comply with subdivision (b) of Section 17917 does not constitute transacting business contrary to the provisions of this chapter.

> (Subdivision (b) of 17917 is not pertinent to this case.)

The authorization is not valid. Neither the District Court nor the Ninth Circuit Court of Appeals ruled on this law. The authorization form is a contract. A strict interpretation of the code demonstrates the authorization is not valid.

Assuming the authorization form is declared to be legally valid, the issue remains as to whether a standard form authorizing a background investigation by one entity can be used by other entities which have been excluded by the authorization form. The Ninth Circuit Court of Appeals ruling means the authorization applies, but the specific exclusion contained in the authorization does not apply (Pet. App. #A, 2A).

**C. LIBEL** The District Court said (Pet. Add. #C, 11A-12A) "Jensen's defamation claim is based upon an email dated February 20, 2002 that apparently was sent between Prudential employees regarding the background check on Jensen. The email, which is attached to Jensen's amended complaint, was sent by **Audra Marszalek** to **Kathleen** Schmanski, with courtesy copy to **Kristine Krenz**. The subject of the email was "MORE INFO-REGINALD JENSEN," and reads in full as follows:

> Hi Kathy,
>
> The candidate has an arrest on his record which the FBI reported 8/12/83, the exact wording is "Charge: Dyer Act. Hold for USM"
>
> **Please have the candidate supply details of this arrest including the disposition.**
>
> Thanks."

(Emphasis supplied)

On the issue of libel the Ninth Circuit Court of Appeals ruled:

> The district court also properly dismissed Jensen's claim because the e-mail communication between

two Prudential employees who were responsible for processing Jensen's application was privileged. *See* Cal. Civil Code § 47(c). In any case, the e-mail did not convey a false factual implication that Jensen was guilty of a Dyer Act violation, only that he had an arrest on his record requiring further inquiry. *See Coastal Abstract Service. Inc. v. First American Title Ins, Co.* 173 F.3d 725, 732 (9th Cir. 1999) (citing Kahn v. Bower, 284 Cal. Rptr. 244, 248 (1991) (Emphasis supplied)

First, the Complaint speaks to *arrest*, not *guilt*. The District Court reached the conclusion "Accordingly, it appears on the face of the pleadings the statement in the email was true — that is, that there was an FBI report regarding the Dyer Act charge." (Pet. App. #C, 13A) The pleadings and documents in evidence contradict this conclusion. The FBI said there was no arrest record regarding Jensen on May 20, 1999. If the courts accepted the E-mail as evidence, they would also be required to accept the letter from the FBI which said no FBI record existed. (Cmpt Ex. #3) On 8/12/83 Jensen was in the office of an attorney in Tipton, Indiana, and was not under arrest. (Cmpt Exh.. #18)

Second, the District Court said: "As part of its background check of Jensen, Prudential accessed the website of the National Association of Securities Dealers ("NASD")-The NASD website apparently contained information that Jensen had been arrested in1983 for violation of the Dyer Act (the National Vehicle Theft Act), 18 U.S.C § 2311. Prudential asked Jensen for additional information about this arrest." (Pet. App. D, 18A, and # C, 10A) Securities obtained the information from the NASD (Cmpt Exh #27) and then passed it on to Insurance through Financial.

This action was in violation of U.S.C. Title 15, 15q, (f)(2); C.F.R. Title 17, 240.17f, Securities and Exchange Commission Regulation § 240.17f2; the NASD fingerprint regulation § 240.17f-2; 5 U.S.C § 552, as amended by Public Law No. 104-231, 110 Stat. 3048; Cal. Civ. Code § 45a (Pet. Add. #C, 12A), and Cal. Civ. Code § 47(c) (since is was the transfer of information from the NASD to Securities then to Insurance). (Pet. Add. #C, 10A, 12Aand 13 A)

The District Court said the arrest information was obtained from the NASD and that there were at least **three** parties involved in the E-mail. The NASD was an additional (fourth) party. (Pet. App. #C, 12A): (Emphasis supplied)

California Civil Code § 47(c) specifically applies ONLY to communications between a potential employer and a previous employer. California Civil Code §47(c) states in its entirety:

> "In a communication, without malice, to a person interested therein, (1) by one who is also interested, or (2) by one who stands in such a relation to the person interested as to afford a reasonable ground for supposing the motive for the communication to be innocent, or (3) who is requested by the person interested to give the information. *This subdivision applies to and includes a communication concerning the job performance or qualifications of an applicant for employment, based upon credible evidence, made without malice, by a current or former employer of the applicant to, and upon request of, one whom the employer reasonably believes is a prospective employer of the applicant.* This subdivision authorizes a current or former employer, or the employer's agent, to answer whether or not the employer would rehire a current or former employee. This subdivision shall not apply to a communication concerning the speech or activities of an applicant for employment if the speech or activities are constitutionally protected, or otherwise protected by Section 527.3 of the Code of Civil Procedure or any other provision of law." (Emphasis supplied)

Jensen has never been employed by and was not applying for employment with the NASD. Nor was Jensen applying for employment with either Financial or Securities or Pruco. Jensen's previous employer was MML Investors Services, Inc. (Cmpt Exh.

#23, P.4) The Circuit Court of Appeals reached the conclusion that Cal. Civ. Code § 47(c) applied. (Pet. App. #A, 2A) This is a validation of the District's Court's reasoning that Prudentials's violations of "applicable rules is neither here nor there." or is "immaterial" (Pet. App. #D, 22A; and #C, 14A)

The Circuit Court of Appeals cited *Coastal Abstract Serv., Inc. v. First Am. Title Ins. Co.,* 173 F 3d 725, 732 (9th Cir. 1999) (citing *Kahn. V. Bower,* 284 Cal. Rptr. 244, 248 (1991). (Pet. App. #A, 2A) *Coastal Abstract* refers to opinions expressed by the defendant. At 732, *Coastal Abstract* says: "[5, 6] An opinion that does not convey a false factual implication is not defamatory under California law." None of the Defendants ever claimed to be expressing an opinion about Jensen being arrested and nothing in evidence demonstrates such a conclusion. (Cmpt Ex. #s 3, 18, & 20) *Coastal Abstract* simply doesn't apply here. *Kahn,* at 248, III says: "The stated basis for the trial court's entry of judgment was its conclusion that the challenged statements "are statements of opinion and not statements of fact and therefore do not constitute actionable libel."" *Kahn* doesn't apply either.

Malice applies because Insurance knew from the Carco investigation on or about February 18, 2002, Jensen had no criminal record. (Pet. App. #C, 11 A) (*See also* Cmpt Ex. #18, Pp.2-3) This is also a jury Issue. In *Masson v. New Yorker Magazine, Inc.,* 501 U.S, 496 (1991), an appeal from the Ninth Circuit, the U.S. Supreme Court held "the evidence presents a jury question whether Malcolm acted with requisite knowledge of falsity or reckless disregard as to the truth or falsity of five of the passages." The Court of Appeals should have sent the case back for jury trial on the issue of libel.

**D. DEFAULT** On the issue of Default under Fed. R. of Civ. P. 4. The Court of Appeals said:

> The district court did not abuse its discretion by denying Jensen's motion for default judgment as the record reflects that Prudential Securities, Inc., Prudential Financial, Inc., and Pruco Securities Company were not properly served with summons and complaint. *See* Fed. R. Civ. P. 4; *see Eitel v. McCool,* 782 F.2d 1470, 1471 (9th Cir. 1986).

The *Eitel* citation refers to a situation whereby the Plaintiff interfered with the service. Defendants have never claimed Jensen has interfered and Jensen made no contact with Defendants other than to effect service through a professional service firm and the United States Post Office. The professional process servers completed their work in compliance with the rules of the Court. *Eitel* doesn't apply here. Any error on Jensen's part was inconsequential and failed to interfere with Defendants's ability to timely respond. The Court Docket shows the facts of service are as follows:

A. **10/14/2003.** Civil Docket Case #: 5:03-cv-04608 filed.

B. Summons Issued as to Prudential Securities Incorporated (gm, COURT STAFF)(Entered:10/14/2003)[40]

C. **10/14/2003** ADR SCHEDULING ORDER: Case Management Statement due by 2/17/2004, Case Management Conference set for 2/23/2004 at 10:30 AM. (gm, COURT STAFF)(Entered: 10/14/2003)

D. **11/12/2004** Certificate of Interested Entities by Prudential (sec) Insurance Company of America, (gm, COURT STAFF)(Entered: 11/14/2003)

E. **11/12/2003.** Motion to Dismiss *for failure to state a claim* filed by The Prudential Insurance Company of America. Motion Hearing set for 1/26/2004 09:00 AM. (gm, COURT STAFF) (Entered: 11/14/2003)[41]

F. **11/12/2003** Received Order re [4] *Motion to dismiss* by The Prudential Insurance Company of America, (gm, COURT STAFF)(Entered: 11/14/2003)

---

[40] SUMMONS IN A CIVIL CASE issued. Defendants given 20 days to respond or "judgment by default will be taken against you." (Court record)

[41] This Motion sets the defendants apart as four separate entities, not as a single unit.

G  CERTIFICATE/PROOF OF SERVICE by The Prudential Insurance Company of America re[], [4] (gm, COURT STAFF)(Entered; 11/14/2003)

H.  **12/02/2003.** "SUMMONS Returned Executed byReginald L. Jensen, Pruco Securities Corporation. Pruco Securities Corporation served on 10/22/2003; answer due 11/12/2003; **Prudential Financial served on 10/21/2003, answer due 11/10/2003;** Prudential Securities Incorporated served on 10/22/2003, answer due 11/12/2003; The Prudential Insurance Company of America served on 10/22/2003, answer due 11/12/2003. (gm, COURT STAFF) (Filed on12/2/2003) (Entered: 12/05/2003)" (Emphasis supplied)

I.  **12/02/2003.** CERTIFICATE OF SERVICE by Reginald L. Jensen re [6] Summons Returned Executed, CORRECTED NOTIFICATION OF SERVICE OF SUMMONS ON ALL DEFENDANTS (gm, COURT STAFF) (Filed on 12/2/2003) (Entered: 12/05/2003)

J.  **12/03/2003.** REQUEST for the Court Clerk to certify service of summons on **all** defendants as completed by Reginald L. Jensen, (gm, COURT STAFF) (Filed on 12/3/2003) (Entered: 12/05/2003)

K.  **12/09/2003.** Declination to Proceed Before a U.S. Magistrate Judge by Reginald L. Jensen, (gm, COURT STAFF) (Filed on 12/9/2003) (Entered; 12/10/2003)

L.  L. **12/09/2003.** MOTION for Default Judgment as to Defendants Pruco Securities Corp., Prudential Financial and Prudential Securities Corp. filed by Reginald L. Jensen, (gin, COURT STAFF) (Filed on 12/9/2003) (Entered 12/10/2003)

M.  **12/9/2003.** Received Order re Motion for Default Judgment [10] by Reginald L. Jensen, (gm, COURT STAFF) (Filed on 12/9/2003) (Entered 12/10/2003)

N.  **12/10/2003.** Joinder in Motion to Dismiss [4] by Pruco Securities Corporation, Prudential Financial, Prudential

Securities Incorporated, The Prudential Insurance Company of America, (gm, COURT STAFF) (Filed on 12/10/2003) (Entered: 12/12/2003)

Insurance holding companies are governed by the California Insurance Code Section 1215-1215.16

Agent for service of process is governed by the California Insurance Code. The code reads as follows:

> 1600. The commissioner shall require every foreign insurer, as a condition precedent to receiving and holding a certificate of authority, to file and maintain in the commissioner's office a writing designating an agent for service of process. The agent designated may be any person residing in this state, including, but not limited to, any corporate officer of the insurer. The writing shall state the name of the agent and his or her place of business in this state with sufficient particularity so that he or she can readily be found by peace officers or process servers. Appointment of an agent reasonably available for service of papers, notice, proof of loss, summons or other process during business hours shall be continuously maintained by every admitted insurer subject to this article while it holds a valid and unrevoked certificate of authority.
>
> 1602. Any notice provided by law or by a policy, and any proof of loss, summons or other process may be served on such agent in any action or other legal proceeding against the insurer, and such service gives jurisdiction over the person of such insurer.

The California Corporations Code Provides:

> 1700. In addition to the provisions of Chapter 4 (commencing with Section 413.10) of Title 5 of Part

2 of the Code of Civil Procedure, process may be served upon domestic corporations as provided in this chapter.

1701. Delivery by hand of a copy of any process against the corporation (a) to any natural person designated by it as agent or (b), if a corporate agent has been designated, to any person named in the latest certificate of the corporate agent filed pursuant to Section 1505 at *the* office of such corporate agent shall constitute valid service on the corporation.

Service was made on the authorized agent for service of process for Insurance, Securities, and Pruco, and on Financial directly. (Court Docket: 12/02/2003 through 12/10/2003).

On February 2, 2004, Elizabeth McCrohan, Vice President and Corporate Counsel of **Insurance,** and Robert Spagat, attorney for the Defendants, filed Declarations saying that to their knowledge service of process and complaint had not been made on Financial, Securities, and Pruco., as of November 12, 2003. ***Elizabeth McCrohan*** said:

> 2. On information and belief, Defendant Prudential Insurance Company of America ("PICA") was served on October 22, 2003. To my knowledge, and on information and belief, PSI and Pruco had not been served with summons and complaint as of November 12, 2003, when Defendant PICA filed its motion to dismiss pursuant to "Rule 12 of the Federal Rules of Civil Procedure (the "Motion to Dismiss"). Also, to my knowledge as of November 12, 2003, PFI had not been served with summons and complaint. (Defendants's Declaration of Elizabeth McCrohan filed 02/02/2004))

***Robert Spagat*** said:
2. On November 12, 2003, Defendant PICA filed a motion to dismiss pursuant to Rule 12(b)(6) of

the Federal Rules of Civil Procedure. That motion currently is set for hearing on February 23, 2004. To my knowledge, and on information and belief, PSI and Pruco had not been served with summons and complaint as of November 12, 2003, when Defendant PICA filed its motion to dismiss pursuant to Rule 12 of the Federal Rules of Civil Procedure (the "Motion to Dismiss").

Also, to my knowledge as of November 12, 2003, PFI had not been served with summons and complaint. PSI, PFI and Pruco did not appear and join ir. PICA'S motion to dismiss on November 12, 2003, based on my understanding that they had not been served at that time. (Defendants's Declaration of Robert Spagat filed 02/02/2004)).

Elizabeth McCrohan was not employed by Financial, Securities, or Pruco, Robert Spagat, Defendants's counsel, was not the listed Agent for Service of Process with the State of California for any of the Defendants.

Neither McCrohan nor Spagat offered any statement as to the date service was completed. *If they knew that service was not completed as if November 12, 2003, they would have known and should have stated the date service was completed* **A person cannot swear something did not happen on or by a certain date if they did not know which date it did happen.** Their affidavits are worthless.

The Defendants's attempts at self-serving and unsupported denials of having been served cannot override the requirements of the Federal Rules of Civil Procedure 4. Nothing was ever filed by Financial, Pruco, or Securities to demonstrate they had not been timely and properly served, or to affirm the date(s) of service. (All Defendants were named individually on the face page of the complaint.) The Court of Appeals was simply wrong.

The Court of Appeals has failed to properly apply the position of the United States Supreme Court in which it found a party in default when the defaulting party announced it will not respond to the complaint.

In *United States v. Bryan* 339 U.S. 323, 327, (1950) the Supreme Court said:

> "Default" is, of course, a failure to comply with the summons." "A proclaimed refusal to respond, as in this case, makes that intent plain. But it would hardly be less plain if the witness embarked on a voyage to Europe on the day before his scheduled appearance before the committee.
>
> "Of course a witness may always change his mind. A default does not mature until the return date of the subpoena, whatever the previous manifestations of intent to default. But when the Government introduced evidence in this case that respondent had been validly served with a lawful subpoena directing her to produce records within her custody and control, and that on the day set out in the subpoena she intentionally failed to comply, it made out a prima facie case of wilful default."

A Defendant can change its mind about responding before the date to answer, but not after, once the party has determined it will not answer. Defendants have filed motions, but have not filed an answer to this date.

In *Bryan* (supra) at 335. the Supreme Court went on to say

> "The question is no less than whether courts must put up with shifts and subterfuges in the place of truth and are powerless to put an end to trifling. They would prove themselves incapable of dealing with actualities if it were so, for there is no surer sign of a feeble and rumbling law than timidity in penetrating the form to the substance. "Loubriel v. United States, 9 F.2d 807, 808(1926).""

*******************

The Ninth Circuit Court of Appeals decision is inconsistent with the United States Constitution, the California Constitution, federal and state laws, and relevant decisions of this Court.

The law should apply to the facts; the facts should not be adjusted to satisfy a preferred law. There has been a rush to judgment in this case by the lower courts.

## CONCLUSION

This Court should accept this Petition to correct a manifest injustice and enforce the rule of law. The integrity of the judicial system should be upheld.

For the foregoing reasons, this Court should grant the petition for a writ of certiorari.

Respectfully submitted,

Signed
Reginald L. Jensen

Petitioner, *Pro Se*
5482 Walnut Blossom Drive
San Jose, CA 95123-2260
(408) 225-4227
E-mail: regj@pacbell.net

1A

APPENDIX A[42]
NOT FOR PUBLICATION
UNITED STATES COURT OF APPEALS FOR THE
NINTH CIRCUIT
No. 04-16608 MEMORANDUM*
D.C. No. CV-13-.04608-JF
Filed May 13 2005 CATHY A. CATTERSON,
CLERK U.S. COURT OF APPEALS

Reginald L. Jensen

*Plaintiff-Appellant* v.

Prudential Financial, Inc., a New Jersey Corporation;
Prudential Securities, Inc., a New Jersey Corporation;
Pruco Securities Corp., a New Jersey Corporation;
The Prudential Ins. A New Jersey Corporation,

Defendants-Appellees.

Appeal from the United States District Court for the Northern District of California, Jeremy Fogel, District Judge, Presiding

Submitted May 9, 2005**—Decided May 13, 2005 Before: PREGERSON, CANBY, and THOMAS, Circuit Judges.

*This disposition is not appropriate for publication and my not be cited to or by the courts of this circuit except as provided by Ninth Circuit Rule 36-3.

**This panel unanimously finds this case suitable for decision without oral argument. *See* Fed R. App. P, 34(a)(2)

---

[42] Face page and Index page omitted.

## 2A

Reginald L. Jensen appeals pro se the district court's dismissal of this diversity action alleging defamation, "oppression," and invasion of privacy under California law. We have jurisdiction pursuant to 28 U.S.C. § 1291. We review de novo a dismissal for failure to state a claim, see *Brunette* v. *Humane Soc'y of Ventura County,* 294 F.3d 1205, 1209 (9th Cir. 2002), and we affirm.

The district court properly held that Prudential Insurance Company of America, Prudential Securities, Inc., Prudential Financial, Inc., and Pruco Securities Company ("Prudential") did not communicate an unauthorized intrusion into Jensen's privacy by completing a background check prior to hiring him as a life insurance salesman, because Jensen authorized the background check and released Prudential from any and all liabilities, claims, or lawsuits with regard to the information obtained. *See Cramer* v. *Consol. Freightways, Inc.,* 209 F.3d 1122, 1130 (9th Cir. 2000) (citing *Hill* v. *Nat'l Collegiate Athletic Ass'n.,* 865 P.2d 633 (1994).

The district court also properly dismissed Jensen's libel claim because the e-mail communication between two Prudential employees who were responsible for processing Jensen's application was privileged. *See* Cal. Civil Code § 47(c). In any case, the e-mail did not convey a false factual implication that Jensen was guilty of a Dyer Act violation, only that he had an arrest on his record requiring further inquiry. *See Coastal Abstract Serv., Inc.* v. *First Am. Title Ins. Co.,* 173 F.3d 725, 732 (9th Circ. (1999)(citing *Kahn* v. *Bower,* 284 Cal. Rptr. 244, 248 (1991)).

3A

## APPENDIX A

The district court did not abuse its discretion by denying Jensen's motion for default judgment as the record reflects that Prudential Securities, Inc. Prudential Financial, Inc., and Pruco Securities Company were not properly served with the summons and complaint. See Fed_ R. Civ. P. 4; *see Eitel* v. *McCool,* 782 F2d 1470, 1471 (9th Cir. 1986).

Jensen's remaining contentions lack merit.

**AFFIRMED.**

A TRUE COPY
CATHY A. CATTERSON
Clerk of Court
ATTEST
June 06 2005
By: <u>Ruben Talavera</u>
Deputy Clerk

INTERNAL USE ONLY: Proceedings include all events. 04-16608 Jensen v. Prudential Financial, et al

| REGINALD L. JENSEN | Reginald L. Jensen |
|---|---|
| Plaintiff- Appellant | 408/255-4227 |
| | [NTC prs] |
| | 5482 Walnut Blossom Drive |
| | San Jose, CA 95123 |
| v. | |
| PRUDENTIAL FINANCIAL, a New Jersey Corporation Defendant-Appellee | Robert Spagat, Esq. FAX 421-1068 415 415/392-6320 Suite 2200 [COR LD NTC ret] |

4A

## APPENDIX A

THELEN REID & PRIEST, LLP

           101 Second St.
           San Francisco, CA 94105-3601
           Linda S. Husar
           FAX 213/576-8082
           213/576-8000
           29th Floor
           [CORLDNTCret]
           Thelen Reid & Priest
           333 South Hope Street
           Los Angeles, CA 90071-3048

PRUDENTIAL SECURITIES, INC.,
a New Jersey Corporation
    Defandant-Appellee

           Robert Spagat, Esq.
           [CORLDNTCret]
           (See above)

           Linda S. Husar
           (See above)
           [CORLDNTCret)

Pruco Securities Corp. a   Robert Spagat, Esq.
New Jersey Corporation      (See above)
  Defendant-Appellee         [COR LD NTC ret]

           Linda S. Husar
           (See above)
           COR LD NTC ret]

THE PRUDENTIAL INS.     Robert Spagat
a New Jersey Corporation   (See above)
           [COR LD NTC ret]

5A

APPENDIX A

Linda S. Husar
(See above)
[COR LD NTC ret]

Docket as of February 8, 2005 11:12 pm   Page 2 NON-PUBLIC

6A

APPENDIX B
UNITED STATES COURT OF APPEALS
FOR THE NINTH CIRCUIT
No. 04-16608
D.C. No. CV-03-04608

**JUDGMENT**

FILED
JUN 09 2005
Richard A. Wieking
Clerk, U.S. District Court
Northern District of California
San Jose

Reginald L. Jensen

*Plaintiff-Appellant*

v.

Prudential Financial, Inc., a New Jersey Corporation; ET AL.,

Defendants-Appellees.

Appeal from the United States District Court for the Northern District of California (San Jose).

This cause came to heard on the Transcript of the Record from the United States District Court for the Northern District of California (San Jose) and was duly submitted.

7A

## APPENDIX B

On consideration whereof, it is now here ordered and adjudged by this Court, that the judgment of the said District Court in this cause be, and hereby is **AFFIRMED.**

Filed and entered Friday, May 13, 2005

A TRUE COPY
CATHY A. CATTERSON
Clerk of Court
ATTEST
June 06 2005

By:    Ruben Talavera
         Deputy Clerk

8A

EXHIBIT C
NOT FOR CITATION
IN THE UNITED STATES DISTRICT COURT
FOR THE NORTHERN DISTRICT OF CALIFORNIA
SAN JOSE DIVISION

Filed
July 23 2004
RICHARD W. WIEKING
Clerk U.S. District Court
Northern District of California
San Jose

REGINALD L. JENSEN
Plaintiff

v.

PRUDENTIAL FINANCIAL, et al.
Defendants

Case Number C-03-4608-JF

ORDER GRANTING DEFENDANTS' MOTION TO
DISMISS WITHOUT LEAVE TO AMEND; AND
DEEMING MOOT DEFENDANTS' MOTION TO STRIKE
[Docket Nos. 32, 40]

Defendants' motion to dismiss the above-entitled action was argued on May 24, 2004. Plaintiff did not file a substantive opposition prior to the hearing because he had filed an appeal with respect to the Court's Order of February 25, 2004, dismissing his original complaint with leave to amend. At the hearing, the Court explained that Plaintiff's appeal did not stay the action,[43] and requested that Plaintiff file opposition on or before June 7, 2004

---

[43] The Court of Appeals subsequently dismissed the appeal for lack of jurisdiction.

9A

EXHIBIT C

and that Defendants file their reply on or before June 14, 2004. The Court stated that once briefing was completed, the matter would be taken under submission without further oral argument. The matter has been fully briefed. Having carefully reviewed Plaintiffs amended complaint filed March 10, 2004 and having considered the arguments of the parties, the Court concludes that Plaintiff has failed to state a claim upon which relief may be granted and that further amendment would be futile. The Court therefore will grant Defendants' motion to dismiss without leave to amend.

On June 14, 2004, Defendants filed a motion requesting that a Settlement Stipulation and Consent Order entered in another case be stricken from the record. Defendants' motion asserts that this document was attached to Plaintiff's brief in opposition to the motion to dismiss. Plaintiff filed a response on June 16, 2004, stating that the document was provided to counsel but was not filed with the Court. The document is not attached to the opposition filed with the Court. Accordingly, Defendants' motion to strike appears to be moot.

## I. BACKGROUND

Plaintiff Reginald L. Jensen ("Jensen"), proceeding *pro se*, filed this action on October 14, 2003 against Prudential Financial, Prudential Securities Inc., Pruco Securities Corporation and The Prudential Insurance Company of America (collectively "Prudential"). The action arises out of Jensen's application to be licensed as a life insurance agent for Prudential and Prudential's background check of Jensen as part of that application process. Jensen submitted two separate written applications, both dated January 22, 2002 and both of which were attached to his original complaint. The applications are on identical forms, which provide in relevant part as follows:

10A

EXHIBIT C

I hereby:

Authorize Prudential and its authorized agents to investigate my background, references, characters, past employment, education, criminal or police reports, including those mandated by both public and private organizations and all public records for the purpose of confirming the information contained on this application and/or obtaining other information which may be material to my qualifications for my appointment.

Release Prudential, its authorized agents and any person or entity which provides information pursuant to this authorization, from any and all liabilities, claims or lawsuits in regards to the information obtained from any and all of the above referenced sources.

As part of its background check of Jensen, Prudential accessed the website of the National Association of Securities Dealers ("NASD")- The NASD website apparently contained information that Jensen had been arrested in 1983 for violation of the Dyer Act (the National Vehicle Theft Act), 18 U.S.C. § 2311. Prudential asked Jensen for additional information about this arrest. Jensen explained that the information was erroneous. Jensen was not arrested for a

11A

EXHIBIT C

Dyer Act violation in 1983, although he was arrested for a Dyer Act violation in 1947. Prudential ultimately accepted Jensen's application and registered him to sell Prudential life insurance policies.

Jensen's original complaint asserted eleven claims against Prudential, three for fraud and eight for invasion of privacy. His amended complaint contains three claims: (1) defamation, (2) oppression (3) invasion of privacy.

## II. LEGAL STANDARD

"A court may dismiss a complaint only if it is clear that no relief could be granted under any set of facts that could be proved consistent with the allegations." *Hishort v. King & Spaulding*, 461 U.S. 69, 73 (1984V *see also Argabright v. United States*, 35 F.3d 472, 474 (9th Cir. 1994). For purposes of a motion to dismiss, the plaintiff's allegations are taken as true, and the Court must construe the complaint in the light most favorable to the plaintiff. *Jenkins v. McKeithen*, 395 U.S. 411, 421 (1969); *Argabvrighi*, 35 F.3d at 474. The pleadings of *pro se* litigant is held to a less stringent standard than a pleading drafted by an attorney, and is to be afforded the benefit of any doubt. *Holmes v. Kerner*, 404 U.S. 519, 520 (1972); *Karim-Panahi v. Los Angeles Police Department*, 839 F.2d 621, 623 (9th Cir. 1988). Further, *a, pro se* litigant must be given leave to amend unless it is absolutely clear that the deficiencies of the complaint could not be cured by amendment. *Lucas v. Department of Corrections*, 66 F.3d 245, 248 (9th Cir. 1995).

## III. DISCUSSION

### A. Defamation.

Jensen's defamation claim is based upon an email dated February 20, 2002 that apparently was sent between Prudential

12A

EXHIBIT C

employees regarding the background check on Jensen. The email, which is attached to Jensen's amended complaint, was sent by Audra Marszalek to Kathleen Schmanski, with courtesy copy to Kristine

Krenz. The subject of the email was "MORE INFO-REGINALD JENSEN," and reads in full as follows;

> Hi Kathy,
>
> The candidate has an arrest on his record which the FBI reported 8/12/83, the exact wording is "Charge: Dyer Act. Hold for USM."
>
> Please have the candidate supply details of this arrest including the disposition.
>
> Thanks.

Jensen asserts that Audra Marszalek "had in her possession or available to her" documents indicating that Plaintiff did not have such an arrest on his record. He further asserts that the statement in the email was false and defamatory and that the circulation of the statements has caused him emotional distress and damaged his personal and business reputation.

To state a claim for libel, Jensen must allege that Defendants published a statement that is false, defamatory and unprivileged. Cal. Civ. Code § 45. Moreover, unless the statement is

13A

EXHIBIT C

defamatory on its face, Jensen must demonstrate that he suffered special damages. Cal. Civ. Code § 45a. Attached to the amended complaint as Exh. 6 is a printout from the NASD stating as follows: "FBI REPORT REC'D 8/12/83. CHARGE: DYER ACT. DISPOSITION: HOLD FOR USM." Accordingly, it appears on the face of the pleading the statement in the email was true - that is, that there was an FBI report regarding the Dyer Act charge. The email does not state that Jensen was guilty of the charge, but merely reported - accurately - that the FBI had reported such a charge. A statement that such charge had been reported and an inquiry for further information is not defamatory. Moreover, the statement appears to be privileged under Cal. Civ. Code § 47(c), providing that a statement is privileged if it is made without malice to a person interested therein by one who also is interested. Section 47(c) applies to statements made in the context of an application for employment. Finally, Jensen fails to allege any facts showing that he suffered special damages. After Prudential clarified that the statement was erroneous, it granted Jensen's application and licensed him to sell its products.

It does not appear that Jensen would be able to amend his complaint to state a viable claim for defamation in light of the facts already alleged. Accordingly, the defamation claim will be dismissed without leave to amend.

### B. Oppression.

California does not recognize such a tort. To the extent the allegations of oppression are intended to support a claim for punitive damages, such claim fails because Jensen has failed to allege adequately an underlying tort.

14A

EXHIBIT C

Accordingly, this claim also will be dismissed without leave to amend.

### C. Invasion of Privacy.

Jensen asserts that Defendants invaded his privacy by accessing NASD records in violation of applicable rules of the Securities and Exchange Commission. As was discussed at length in the Court's Order of February 25, 2004, the fact that Defendants may have violated applicable SEC rules (which Defendants deny) is immaterial with respect to Jensen's claim for invasion of privacy. In essence, Jensen's claim is for intrusion. Such a claim has two elements: (1) intentional intrusion into a private place, conversation or matter, (2) in a manner highly offensive to a reasonable person. *Marich v. MGM/UA Telecommunications, Inc.*, 113 Cal.App.4$^{th}$ 415, 421 (2003). Here,

Jensen explicitly granted Prudential and its agents permission to do a background check. Under these circumstances, no reasonable person could be "highly offended" that Prudential accessed Jensen's NASD records, even assuming that such records otherwise could be considered "private matter." Moreover, even if Prudential's conduct could support a viable claim for invasion of privacy, Jensen explicitly released Prudential and its agents from "from any and all liabilities, claims or lawsuits in regards to the information" obtained during the background check. Accordingly, the invasion of privacy claim will be dismissed without leave to amend.

## IV. ORDER

Defendants' motion to dismiss is granted without leave to amend as to all claims. The matter is dismissed with prejudice.

DATED: 7-21-04

15A

EXHIBIT C

<u>SIGNED</u>
Jeremy Fogel
United States District Judge

16A

EXHIBIT D

NOT FOR CITATION
IN THE UNITED STATES DISTRICT COURT
FOR THE NORTHERN DISTRICT OF CALIFORNIA
SAN JOSE DIVISION

Filed
JUL 23 2004
RICHARD W. WIEKING
Clerk U.S. District Court
Northern District of California
San Jose

REGINALD L. JENSEN
Plaintiff
v.
PRUDENTIAL FINANCIAL, et al.
Defendants

Case Number C-03-4608-JF

JUDGMENT

The Court having issued an order dismissing the amended complaint without leave to amend and dismissing the action with prejudice,
IT IS HEREBY ORDERED that judgment be entered for Defendants.

DATED: 7-21-04

Signed

JEREMY FOGEL
United States District Judge

17A

EXHIBIT E
NOT FOR CITATION
IN THE UNITED STATES DISTRICT COURT
FOR THE NORTHERN DISTRICT OF CALIFORNIA
SAN JOSE DIVISION

Filed
Feb 25 2004
RICHARD W. WIEKING
Clerk U.S. District Court
Northern District of California
San Jose

REGINALD L. JENSEN
Plaintiff
v.
PRUDENTIAL FINANCIAL, et al.
Defendants

Case Number C-03-4608-JF
ORDER (1) DENYING PLAINTIFF'S MOTION FOR DEFAULT JUDGMENT AND (2) GRANTING DEFENDANTS' MOTION TO DISMISS WITH LEAVE TO AMEND

[Docket Nos. 4, 10]

On February 23, 2004, the Court heard (1) Plaintiff's motion for default judgment against Defendants Pruco Securities Corporation, Prudential Financial and Prudential Securities Corporation and (2) the motion of all defendants to dismiss the action. The Court has considered the moving and responding papers as well as the oral arguments presented at the hearing. For reasons discussed below, the motion for default judgment will be denied and the motion to dismiss will be granted with leave to amend.

18A

EXHIBIT E

## I. BACKGROUND

Plaintiff Reginald L. Jensen ("Jensen"), proceeding *pro se,* filed this action on October 14, 2003 against Prudential Financial, Prudential Securities Inc., Pruco Securities Corp. and The Prudential Insurance Company of America (collectively "Prudential"). The action arises out of Jensen's application to be licensed as a life insurance agent for Prudential and Prudential's background check of Jensen as part of that application process. Jensen submitted two separate written applications, both dated January 22, 2002 and both attached to his complaint. The applications are on identical forms, which provide the relevant part as follows:

> I hereby:
>
> Authorize Prudential and its authorized agents to investigate my background, references, characters, past employment, education, criminal or police reports, including those mandated by both public and private organizations and all public records for the purpose of confirming the information contained on this application and/or obtaining other information which may be material to my qualifications for my appointment.
>
> Release Prudential, its authorized agents and any person or entity which provides information pursuant to this authorization, from any and all liabilities, claims or lawsuits in regards to the information obtained from any and all of the above referenced sources.

19A

EXHIBIT E

As part of its background check of Jensen, Prudential accessed the website of the National Association of Security Dealers ("NASD"). The NASD website apparently contained information that Jensen had been arrested in 1983 for violation of the Dyer Act (the National Vehicle Theft Act, 18 U.S.C. § 2311. Prudential asked Jensen for additional information about this arrest. Jensen explained that the information was erroneous. Jensen was not arrested for a Dyer Act violation in 1983, although he was arrested for a Dyer Act violation in 1947. Prudential ultimately accepted Jensen's application and registered him to sell Prudential life insurance policies.

Jensen asserts eleven claims against Prudential: claims 1 through 3 are for misrepresentation and fraud, while claims 4 through 11 are for invasion of privacy. Prudential moves to dismiss all claims. The motion to dismiss was filed on behalf of The Prudential Insurance Company of America. Footnote 1 on page 2 of the motion states that the arguments set forth in the motion are applicable to all defendants, but that the motion was made on behalf of one defendant because the others had not been served. On December 9, 2003, Jensen filed a motion for default judgment against Pruco Securities Corporation, Prudential Financial and Prudential Securities Corporation. The next day, on December 10, 2003, these defendants filed a notice of appearance and joinder in the motion to dismiss. These defendants filed an opposition to Jensen's motion for default judgment on February 2, 2004.

## II. MOTION FOR DEFAULT JUDGMENT

20A

EXHIBIT E

The motion for default judgment as to Pruco Securities Corporation, Prudential Financial and Prudential Securities Corporation will be denied. Jensen failed to obtain a clerk's entry of default with respect to these defendants. They filed an appearance on December 10, 2003. Accordingly, default judgment is not appropriate. Moreover, even had a clerk's entry of default been obtained, it is clear that these defendants always intended to defend the action and that any delay in appearing was caused by confusion as to when service of process was effected. Under these circumstances, and absent any showing of prejudice by Jensen, the Court would be inclined to set aside any default.

## III. MOTION TO DISMISS

"A court may dismiss a complaint only if it is clear that no relief could be granted under any set of facts that could be proved consistent with the allegations." *Hishon* v. *King & Spaulding,* 467 U.S. 69, 73 (1984); *see also Argabright* v. *United Slates,* 35 F.3d 472, 474 (9th Cir. 1994). For purposes of a motion to dismiss, the plaintiffs allegations are taken as true, and the Court must construe the complaint in the light most favorable to the plaintiff. *Jenkins v. McKeithen,* 395 U.S. 411, 421 (1969); *Argabvright,* 35 F.3d at 474. The pleadings of pro *se* litigant is held to a less stringent standard than a pleading drafted by an attorney, and is to be afforded the benefit of any doubt. *Holmes* v. *Kerner,* 404 U.S. 519, 520 (1972); *Karim-Panahi* v. *Los Angeles Police Department,* 839 F.2d 621, 623 (9th Cir. 1988). Further, *a pro se* litigant must be given leave to amend unless it is absolutely clear that the deficiencies of the complaint could not be cured by amendment. *Lucas v. Department of Corrections,* 66 F.3d 245, 248 (9th Cir. 1995).

**Fraud:**

21A

EXHIBIT E

The elements of a claim for intentional fraud under California law are: (1) a misrepresentation or omission, (2) knowledge of falsity (scienter). (3) intent to defraud, (4) justifiable reliance and (5) resulting damages. *Lazar* v. *Superior Court,* 12 Ca 4th 631, 638 (1996).

The bases for Jensen's fraud claims are unclear. With respect to claim 1, it appears that Prudential received a subpoena for records referencing Jensen in connection with another lawsuit in this Court, *Jensen v. Massachusetts Mutual Life Insurance Company,* Case No. C-02-4551-JF. Prudential produced the records. On January 31. 2003, a Prudential paralegal, Cheryl L. Plantersmith, sent an email (attached to the complaint in this action) to Jensen's attorney in the *Massachusetts Mutual case,* stating that the records had been sent by Airborne Express. Ms. Planter-Smith also stated as follows: "I briefly reviewed the documents and I believe you may already have most of them. It appears that the majority of the research conducted by Prudential was done on the NASD Website which basically is public information." Jensen appears to be construing this statement to be a representation by Prudential that it obtained the erroneous information regarding Jensen's arrest from *the public* portion of the NASD website. Jensen alleges that this representation was fraudulent because the information actually came from the "members only" portion of the NASD website that is not open to the general public.

Jensen's reading of Ms. Planer-Smith's email is contradicted by the plain text of the email itself, which did not make any representations as to where the arrest information came from. The email stated that "the majority of the research" on Jensen was done on the NASD website and gives Ms. Planter-Smith's opinion that this website contains public information.

22A

EXHIBIT E

Moreover, Jensen does not allege facts demonstrating that Ms. Planter-Smith had authority to speak for Prudential. Finally, Jensen does not allege facts demonstrating the elements of a claim for fraud. For example, he does not allege how he relied upon Ms. Planter-Smith's email statements or how he was injured by her statements.

Claim 2 appears to be based upon the Planter-Smith email and fails for the reasons discussed above.

Claim 3 appears to be based upon one of the documents produced by Prudential in response to the subpoena. The document in question, entitled "Available Information," lists three categories: demographics, producer licensing and appointments. The document provides the date each category was "Last Updated." Jensen contends that this document is "false and fraudulent," but does not explain how it is false, or how the other elements of a fraud claim were met by Prudential's production of the document in response to a subpoena.

**Invasion Of Privacy:**

Jensen does not specify whether his claims for invasion of privacy are based upon intrusion or public disclosure of private facts. A claim of intrusion has two elements: (1) intentional intrusion into a private place, conversation or matter, (2) in a manner highly offensive to a reasonable person. *Marich* v. *MGM/UA Telecommunications, Inc.,* 113 Cal. App.3d 118, 126(1983).

As an initial matter, it appears that any claim for invasion of privacy are barred by the language of Jensen's applications to Prudential explicitly granting Prudential and its agents permission to do a background check and releasing Prudential and its agents from liability arising from information obtained during such

23A

EXHIBIT E

background check. Jensen argues that this language did not give Prudential the authority to search the "members only" portion of the NASD website. Jensen further argues that Prudential violated applicable rules for searching the "members only" portion of the NASD website. The language granting Prudential permission to do a background check is quite broad and clearly would encompass website searches. The fact that Prudential allegedly violated applicable rules is neither here nor there. Moreover, Jensen clearly released Prudential from any claims arising out of information obtained during his background check.

To the extent Jensen assets claims for intrusion, he does not allege how a website search constitutes intrusion into a "private place, conversation or matter," nor does he allege that a website search would be highly offensive to a reasonable person. To the extent Jensen asserts claims for public disclosure of private information, it is unclear how information contained on the NASD website - even that portion open to members - could be considered "private."

**Leave To Amend**

Given the exhibits attached to the complaint, containing among other things the email from Ms. Planter-Smith and Jensen's application to be licensed as a life insurance agent for Prudential, the Court has grave reservations as to whether Jensen will be able to amend his pleading to cure the defects noted above. However, because Jensen is proceeding *pro se* and because Defendants' motions are addressed to the original complaint, the Court will afford Jensen an opportunity to amend.

## IV. ORDER

24A

EXHIBIT E

Defendants' motion to dismiss is granted with leave to amend as to all claims. Any amended pleading shall be filed and served within twenty (20) days after service of this order.

Dated 2-23-04

<u>Signed</u>

JEREMY FOGEL
United States District Judge

*Reginald L. Jensen*

# WAIVER

## SUPREME COURT OF THE UNITED STATES

Supreme Court Case No. _____05-193_____

Reginald L. Jensen        Prudential Financial, Inc., et al.
(Petitioner)                   (Respondent)

I DO NOT INTEND TO FILE A RESPONSE to the petition for a writ of certiorari unless one is requested by the Court.

Please check one of the following boxes:

[X] Please enter my appearance as Counsel of Record for all respondents.

[ ] There are multiple respondents, and I do not represent all respondents. Please enter my appearance as Counsel of Record for the following respondent(s):

_____

I certify that I am a member of the Bar of the Supreme Court of the United States (Please explain if your name has changed since your admission):

Signature ___Signed by Thomas E. Hill_____

Date: ___9/02/05_____

(Type or print) Name _____Thomas E. Hill, Esq._____

[X] Mr.     [ ] Ms.     [ ] Mrs.     [ ] Miss

Firm    Thelen Reid & Priest LLP

Address 333 South Hope Street, Suite 2900

City & State _____Los Angeles, CA_____ Zip 90071

Phone (213)576-8000

A COPY OF THIS FORM MUST BE SENT TO PETITIONER'S COUNSEL OR TO PETITIONER IF *PRO SE*. PLEASE INDICATE BELOW THE NAME(S) OF THE RECIPIENT(S) OF A COPY OF THIS FORM. NO ADDITIONAL CERTIFICATE OF SERVICE IS REQUIRED. SEE REVERSE FOR INFORMATION CONCERNING THE STATUS OF A CASE ON THE DOCKET.

CC: Reginald L. Jensen

## Supreme Court of the United States
## Office of the Clerk Washington, DC 20543-0001

William K. Suter
Clerk of the Court
(202) 479-3011

October 11, 2005

Mr. Reginald L. Jensen 5482 Walnut Blossom Drive
San Jose, CA 95123-2260

Re:     Reginald L. Jensen
v. Prudential Financial, Inc., et al.
No. 05-193

Dear Mr. Jensen:

The Court today entered the following order in the above-entitled case:

The petition for a writ of certiorari is denied.

Sincerely,

Signed

**William K. Suter,** Clerk

On page 11A, (These page numbers refer to the pages in the Petition for the Writ.) Judge Fogel said "His amended complaint contains three claims: (1) defamation, (2) oppression (3) invasion of privacy." He then established the reasons behind each claim. The complaint was coherent enough to allow the judge to find facts and rule against the facts he found. It means the complaint was adequate to withstand a motion to dismiss. My complaint contained claims that require no proof for the case to proceed to discovery.

There are several serious errors committed by the courts in this suit. Several of the errors are so obvious it doesn't take an attorney to recognize them. The first is that the defendants and Judge Fogel understood the basis of the complaint.

None of the defendants ever answered, but Insurance filed a motion to dismiss under the theory I failed to state a claim. Some jurisdictions refer to this as a demurrer. It means that, even if everything stated in the complaint is true, there is no basis for a lawsuit. A party can't make a denial through a demurrer. They must answer the complaint if they intend to make a denial. Judge Fogel acknowledged Insurance's Motion to Dismiss contained a denial. See; Appeal P. 14A, Exhibit C. Invasion of Privacy, lines 5-6).

Judge Fogel found I was not defamed; there was no invasion of privacy (the applicable rules are neither here nor there and are immaterial); and no California law existed regarding oppression. He had to find facts to reach those conclusion. Finding facts is a jury requirement. Then he had to apply the law to the facts so found, which effectively eliminated each of my claims.

Some words spoken or printed are defamation per se, which means there is no need to prove malice. A statement that someone has been arrested for a felony, when no such arrest took place, is defamation per se.[44] The republication of a false accusation of the commission of a felony is also defamation. This means the person who repeats the words,

---

[44] Private persons must prove only that a false defamatory statement was published with negligence -- carelessness, or lack of reasonable care under the circumstances. Carelessness can be nothing more than copying information incorrectly or misidentifying a person who has been arrested. http://journalism.nyu.edu/ethics/handbook/legal/

even if that person has no direct knowledge of whether or not the words are true, had defamed the other person with malice.

Judge Fogel decided to dispose of defamation at pages 11A-12A. Audra Marszalek obtained the arrest information from someone. On February 18, 2002, Marszalek obtained an FBI investigative report through CARTCO, the agent of Insurance. CARTCO found no FBI record existed. At that moment, Marszalek knew no current FBI record existed. Nevertheless, Insurance provided a document to me that they said was an E-mail from Marszalek instructing Kathleen Schmanski, an employee of Insurance, to send a letter to me requesting my response to the arrest record of 1983. A copy of this instruction was given to Kristine Krenz. The Defendants demonstrated the arrest information passed through two or three different corporations. If they received the information from the NASD, only Securities could have obtained it. If it came from MMLISI, it constituted libel. Then it was passed to Financial and Insurance, because both were involved in investigating my background.

The judge reached the conclusion the communication between the three employees of "Prudential" was a communication between three employees of the same company and all four companies were one, Prudential. Thus he found the statement was privileged under California Civil Code § 47(c). (Exhibit C, Page 12A.) California Civil Code § 47(c) says:

> In a communication, without malice, to a person interested therein, (1) by one who is also interested, or (2) by one who stands in such a relation to the person interested as to afford a reasonable ground for supposing the motive for the communication to be innocent, or (3) who is requested by the person interested to give the information. This subdivision applies to and includes a communication concerning the job performance or qualifications of an applicant for employment, based upon credible evidence, made without malice, by a current or former employer of the applicant to, and upon request of, the prospective employer. This subdivision shall not apply to a communication concerning the speech or activities of an applicant for employment if

*Judicial Deception*

the speech or activities are constitutionally protected, or otherwise protected by Section 527.3 of the Code of Civil Procedure or any other provision of law.

The NASD wasn't a current, prospective or former employer. Securities and Pruco weren't current, prospective or former employers, nor did they have any interest whatsoever in me. There is nothing in the record that indicated the communication was from MassMutual or MMLISI to Insurance. The judge had to change the facts that apply to defamation and privilege to dismiss this section of the complaint, so that's what he did.

The NASD isn't the FBI. The NASD never arrested me. The judge had in his possession the 1999 letter from the FBI that said no arrest record existed. Yet, he found the NASD records showed I had been arrested in 1983. (Exhibit C, Page 10A). He said:

> As part of its background check of Jensen, Prudential accessed the website of the National Association of Securities Dealers ("NASD"). The NASD website apparently contained information that Jensen had been arrested in 1983 for violation of the Dyer Act (the National Vehicle Theft Act), 18 U.S.C. § 2311.

"Apparently" doesn't constitute proof. And if the NASD information was wrong it was libel. Judge Fogel also said: "Prudential clarified that the statement was erroneous,..." (Exhibit C, Page 12A). Insurance said the NASD records were false, which the Judge affirmed.

Legacy Incident Details is one document before the court. (Exhibit C, Page 12A) The judge said:

> Attached to the amended complaint as Exh. 6 is a printout from the NASD stating as follows: "FBI REPORT REC'D 8/12/83. CHARGE: DYER ACT. DISPOSITON: HOLD FOR USM." Accordingly, it appears on the face of the pleading the statement in the email was true – that is, there was an FBI report regarding the Dyer Act charge. The email does not state that Jensen was guilty of the charge, but reported – accurately – that the FBI had reported such as charge.

This printout showed the NASD possessed a document that said it had received an arrest report from the FBI in 1983, it doesn't prove the FBI had an arrest report in 2002. The FBI never reported that I had been arrested in 1983. Judge Fogel had to find a way around this circumstance. The judge determined a statement (which is not known to be true or false) that a person was arrested for a felony is not libelous unless the statement claims a person is guilty of such a charge.

Next, Judge Fogel had to dispose of oppression. He ruled "California does not recognize such a tort." (Exhibit C, page 13A) That took care of the oppression claim. California law expressly provides that oppression is actionable as a tort.[45] California Civil Code Section 3294(a) states:

> In an action for the breach of an obligation not arising from contract, where it is proven by clear and convincing evidence that the defendant has been guilty of oppression, fraud, or malice, the plaintiff, in addition to the actual damages, may recover damages for the sake of example by way of punishing the defendant.

Finally, Judge Fogel had to get rid of the invasion of privacy claim. Invasion of privacy is protected by Article I, Section 1, of the California Constitution. Invasion of privacy is the intrusion into the personal life of another, without just cause, which can give the person whose privacy has been invaded a right to bring a lawsuit for damages against the person or entity that intruded. It encompasses workplace monitoring, Internet privacy, data collection, and other means of disseminating private information. The judge had to change my complaint from invasion of privacy to "intrusion."

Judge Fogel ruled (Page 14A):

> In essence, Jensen's claim is for intrusion. Such a claim has two elements: (1) intentional intrusion into a private place, conversation or matter, (2) in a manner highly offensive to a reasonable person.

---

[45] A tort is defined as a wrongful act for which a civil action will lie except one involving a breach of contract.

Judge Fogel had to change my privacy claim to intrusion so as to avoid any complications that might arise under his dismissal based upon California's Constitutional protection.

Judge Fogel's ruling meant I could authorize (the authorization form provided to me by Insurance) any Prudential organization (and others) to violate the law. So, Judge Fogel had to remove the applicable laws and regulations. At page 13A, he ruled:

> The fact that Defendants may have violated applicable SEC rules (which Defendants deny) is immaterial with respect to Jensen's claim for invasion of privacy.[46]

In his February 25, 2004, order, on page 23A, Judge Fogel said "The fact that Prudential allegedly violated applicable rules are neither here nor there." What rational judge would sign such a decision?

That took care of the laws!

Judge Fogel explains his authority to dismiss a complaint. He said, under II. LEGAL STANDARD at page 11A. "A court may dismiss a complaint only if it is clear that no relief could be granted under any set of facts that could be proved consistent with the allegations." He continues on with "For the purposes of a motion to dismiss, the plaintiff's allegations are taken as true,…"

Not for citation was placed on the decision. Not for Citation on a trial court order has no meaning or value to any lawsuit other than a message to the higher court reflecting the opinion of the trial court that the case should be dismissed forthwith. A trial court decision can't be cited for any purpose. Only a decision by the court of appeals can be cited in another court.

*Not for publication* was stamped on the decision by the court of appeals. Not for publication allows the judges and the courts to do anything they want to do, to rule in any manner with impunity.[47] Not for citation and not for publication have the same primary meaning. If the case is published, it can be cited in other cases. If the case can't be cited after appeal, the law need not apply to the facts; and the facts as stated by the judges need not be the true facts. (The entire purpose of

---

[46] My signature on an authorization form can't give a party the right to violate federal laws.

[47] http://www.nonpublication.com/KenCommentWerdegar.htm

appeal is to be certain the proper law has been applied to the established facts in the trial court.) Kenneth J. Schmier[48] said:

Re: Comments on Werdegar Committee Report

> The committee has, by majority vote, deliberately chosen not to make mandatory the publication of decisions that meet the standards set out in Rule 976.
>
> The committee thus leaves appellate courts free to decide any case, even those establishing a new rule of law, in a manner that is completely free of the constraints of stare decisis. If an appellate court can decide a case according to rationale that by virtue of being unpublished, cannot be cited in the future, then any constraints imposed upon the judicial branch by the making of precedent are rendered ineffective.
>
> Before persisting in this folly the committee should answer these simple questions: By what mechanism is the rule of law enforced upon the judiciary if judges are free to make a new rule of law that is not for everyone but only effective at one time and place? And, if new rules of law are not published to the general community, how are citizens to know the law, and how may they criticize it? Given that – by your own survey – 50 percent of appellate judges are relying upon unpublished decisions for the rationales of decision, how are errors to be caught before being replicated?

Kenneth J. and Michael K. Schmier added these comments to the report:[49]

---

[48] Chairman, Committee for the Rule of Law, 1475 Powell Street, Suite 201, Emeryville, California 94608. January 11, 2006.

[49] Kenneth J. Schmier is the chairman and Michael K. Schmier the director of the Committee for the Rule of Law. They are the authors of "Has Anybody Noticed the Judiciary Has Abandoned Stare Decisis?" in the Journal of Law and Social Challenges and maintained www.nonpublication.com.

Justices Carve Exception to No-Cite Rule
The Recorder
November 4, 2005

Fifty California appellate justices, half the bench, were caught violating the same court rule they insist on enforcing against litigants — the rule prohibiting reliance on unpublished appeal decisions. The Judicial Performance Commission must now decide whether to sanction them.

The embarrassing violations of Rule 977(a) came to light when the Supreme Court Advisory Committee on Rules for Publication ("Werdegar Committee") released its preliminary report two weeks ago. A survey taken by the committee revealed 58 percent of 86 justices responding rely upon "unpublished" appellate opinions. California's "no-citation" Rule 977 says unpublished opinions "must not be cited or relied on by a court or party."

California appellate courts have repeatedly rejected challenges to Rule 977. Rule 977 and other no-citation rules have spawned a great deal of controversy over the past decade. Many high ranking judicial officers have argued no-citation rules must be rescinded.

"A lawyer ought to be able to tell a court what it has done," said new Chief Justice John Roberts Jr. Supreme Court nominee Samuel Alito Jr. has said that the three decade old experiment with no-citation rules has proved to "conflict with basic principles underlying the rule of law."

Alito and Roberts are among those backing the adoption of Federal Rule of Appellate Procedure Rule 32.1, which Alito wrote for the Federal Appellate Rules Committee and "abolishes such rules and requires courts to permit unpublished opinions to be cited."

Rule 32.1 is expected to be approved by the U.S. Supreme Court by May. In considering Rule 32.1 the federal rules committee called upon the Federal Judicial Center to investigate defenses of no-citation rules offered by Ninth Circuit U.S. Court of Appeals Judge Alex Kozinski and California Chief Justice Ronald George. It found their assertions to be without substance.

Nonetheless the California judiciary, its chief justice, its judicial council, the attorney general, and, most importantly, the appellate courts, have resolutely defended the validity of Rule 977. To paraphrase the late Johnnie Cochran, if the rule is fit, the appellate bench too must submit.

But half are not submitting. A comment included in the Werdegar Committee's report said, "Most justices who rely on unpublished opinions indicated that they do so in order to consider the rationale or analysis used in a similar decision or to ensure consistency with their own rulings or with those in their district/ division." Justices are deciding cases by relying upon unpublished decisions in the same way they would use decisions marked 'Certified for Publication' — except without citation. Apparently the admission escaped the attention of the committee's chair, Justice Kathryn Mickle Werdegar, and the members of her committee specially chosen by Chief Justice George.

We concur with Justices Roberts and Alito, the American Bar Association, the American College of Trial Lawyers, 21 states, including New York, Texas, Illinois, Michigan and New Jersey: rules like 977 must go. Yet, we are the ones who complained to the Commission on Judicial Performance that justices are violating Rule 977. Given the poor regard in which we hold Rule 977, why did we do so? We invoke the rule of law to attack it. The rule of law requires that law—bad or good—be applicable to all, including the appellate bench. If the appellate bench finds abiding by Rule 977 awkward, the rule of law forces the bench to change it. It is not acceptable that judges, who made and enforce the rule that forbids us to rely on unpublished decisions, secretly violate the same prohibition. "Violating rules relating to court administration" constitutes judicial misconduct, according to the CJP. But is the CJP sufficiently independent of the judicial establishment to issue charges?

We are giving the CJP an opportunity to prove its rectitude.

The complaint is not frivolous; there is great harm in what the justices are doing.

Clandestine reliance upon unpublished decisions deprives litigants and attorneys of any opportunity to argue against their validity. Worse, these decisions have never been vetted before the tens of thousands of court watchers, incentivized by citability and *stare decisis*, who monitor published appellate decisions. Among these court watchers is vast expertise regarding all manner of issues that come before appellate courts. Vetting decisions before them serves as a realistic and vocal quality control mechanism for the enormous volume of appellate dispositions.

But court watchers, and justices too, have been misled by Rule 977 into believing unpublished decisions do not influence the determination of future cases, and rarely criticize them. Unpublished opinions lack the crucial dignity of standing for something. They are not supposed to count, except for the parties, who are often shocked, and many devastated, by their "result orientation." The warranty of rightness is stripped when unpublished opinions circumvent court watcher inspection. Yet the Werdegar Committee report reveals that these opinions are calcifying into decision-determining lines of secret precedent anyway.

Our strategy depends upon the CJP to enforce Rule 977. Will it? It's already waffling. Its executive secretary, Bernadette Torivino, responded to our complaint the day it was received. She wrote that the investigation will not go forward until we name the justices and "specify exactly, what action or behavior of each judge is the basis for your complaint." When 50 of 101 justices have admitted a serious violation in writings held by a Supreme Court advisory committee, it is hard to believe the CJP does not have enough information to move forward. Sounds like evasive bureau-speak to us.

We cannot identify the specific justices because, despite open government Proposition 59, the committee met in secret and will not release to us the survey responses or other records of their meetings. We have sued the Judicial Council to gain access, but the Judicial Council, represented by Morrison & Foerster, aggressively defends its questionable right to hold all of its policy-making subcommittee meetings in secret and to keep their papers from the public.

So we shall name all of the appellate justices and rely upon the CJP to use its investigative powers to defend the rule of law, and hope for the best. (Reprinted with permission.)

The federal Ninth Circuit Rule Number 36-3 provides for circumstances under which the case can be cited. Those conditions are related to the same case only, but have nothing to do with establishing or following precedence. The decision can't be tested. A bad decision contrary to law and common sense can't be challenged. If the decision can't be applied to any other case, which has similar or identical facts, it has no meaning. There is no provision to verify the facts below and to certify the applicable law. The judges do whatever they want to do and reach any conclusions they want to reach without being subject to oversight by any entity whatsoever. This is the definition of anarchy. There is no superior power in anarchy. The superior power in a judicial system is supposed to be the law and the citizens, not the judges. The law is supposed to control the judges, not the reverse.

What surprises me is that the not for publication process has taken hold without the general public noticing the usurpation of the laws by the judiciary itself. What started out as what appears to be an unsupported method of reducing the caseload and record keeping requirements has now become part of the permanent record of the errors of learned men who are supposed to be responsible for administering justice in a serious and thoughtful manner. The citizens of the United States rely on these people to conduct their affairs with honesty, integrity, and without bias or prejudice. But that isn't happening.

Reporter Fredric N. Tulsky[50] wrote a story published in the San Jose Mercury News about how the California Supreme Court has amended the rules in an attempt to make the judicial system more open on appeal.[51] In that article, Tulsky deals with the not-for-publication issue. The court itself admitted it has not been dealing honestly with the public. The California Supreme Court said more decisions must be published and issued using legally correct protocol without regard to potential embarrassment to judges and other members of the judiciary. So, higher courts refuse to issue rulings using correct protocol because someone might be embarrassed? If that's so, they're protecting themselves. This is really a bazaar state of affairs. Here we have the courts admitting incompetence, secrecy and malpractice. The rule of law, again!

The failure to publish permits all kinds of miscarriages of justice as the California Supreme Court has demonstrated. The applicable section of the California Constitution follows.

ARTICLE 6 JUDICIAL

> SEC. 14. The Legislature shall provide for the prompt publication of such opinions of the Supreme Court and courts of appeal as the Supreme Court deems appropriate, and those opinions shall be available for publication by any person. Decisions of the Supreme

---

[50] Fredric N. Tulsky earned a law degree, passed the Pennsylvania bar, and earned a Pulitzer prize in 1987. He was also a Pulitzer finalist in 2001.
[51] San Jose Mercury News, *Tainted trials, stolen justice*, December 13, 2006. Morning Final, Local Editions, 1B.

Court and courts of appeal that determine causes shall be in writing with reasons stated.

California is following its Constitution. California has given the state Supreme Court the right to decide the cases it will publish. California also permits a judge to dismiss a case if the judge believes the result will be a miscarriage of justice:

ARTICLE 6 JUDICIAL

SEC. 13. No judgment shall be set aside, or new trial granted, in any cause, on the ground of misdirection of the jury, or of the improper admission or rejection of evidence, or for any error as to any matter of pleading, or for any error as to any matter of procedure, unless, after an examination of the entire cause, including the evidence, the court shall be of the opinion that the error complained of has resulted in a miscarriage of justice.

The judges have been given an extraordinary amount of power in California. The California Constitution allows the judges to make a whole host of errors, and the person harmed has no recourse. The judges decide if there's been a miscarriage of justice. We should give a lot of credit to the California Supreme Court for self-correcting some of its abuse of discretion.

There is no provision in the U.S. Constitution for unpublished decisions. There's no guidance for the judiciary. This is a glaring failure by the judiciary. Since no guidance has been provided, it's a violation of the United States Constitution[52] for the judiciary to follow the practice of not publishing some appeals they believe are not worth publication. It appears as though Congress and the United States Supreme Court have now changed the requirements for citation of unpublished decisions.[53]

---

[52] See: <u>Anastasoff v. United States of America</u>, U.S. Court of Appeals, 8th Circuit, No. 99-3917EM (2000).

[53] U.S. SUPREME COURT ALLOWS CITATION OF UNPUBLISHED OPINIONS IN ALL FEDERAL COURTS. December 1, 2006: Federal Rule of Appellate Procedure 32.1, which ends former prohibitions forbidding us to cite unpublished appeal court opinions, is now effective as of this date as <u>the Congress made no changes in the language adopted by the U.S. Supreme Court on April 12,</u>

Did Congress approve the rule or did the Supreme Court conclude that since Congress took no action on the proposed rule the failure to act was an approval of the new language? In any event, the next step is to eliminate not for publication in its entirety, publish all decisions, and to publish all decisions which were previously designated not for publication. And Congress should consider it an impeachable offense if any judge fails to read, research, and affix his or her name to any decision of the court.

Even though an unpublished decision may now be cited, it's nearly impossible for anyone to locate any or all decisions that are not published. Published decisions are indexed, unpublished decisions are not. Consider the following comments by attorneys Lynn Paul Mattson and Peter Van Dyke:[54]

> To lawyers, the controversy ought to be much more significant than whether printed and signed authority can be used for arguments in briefs, why? Because the not-for-publication stamp on the decision has repeatedly resulted in decisions and awards so contradictory, unclear, and in some cases just plain arbitrary, the task of advising clients who operate in several jurisdictions about legal-risk management has become close to a guessing game. The uncertainty caused by inconsistent application of precedent essentially mandates inconsistent business practices to account for legal variations between jurisdictions. Worse,

---

2006. *The new rule reads as follows: Rule 32.1. Citing Judicial Dispositions. (a) Citation Permitted. A court may not prohibit or restrict the citation of federal judicial opinions, orders, judgments, or other written dispositions that have been: (i) designated as "unpublished," "not for publication," "non-precedential," "not precedent," or the like; and (ii) issued on or after January 1, 2007. (b) Copies Required. If a party cites a federal judicial opinion, order, judgment, or other written disposition that is not available in a publicly accessible electronic database, the party must file and serve a copy of that opinion, order, judgment, or disposition with the brief or other paper in which it is cited.* Committee for the Rule of Law. (Emphasis supplied.)

[54] Not For Publication Rules Versus Stare Decisus…If It's Not Picked for Publication It Doesn't Exist But Who Does The Picking? https://papers.ssrn.com/sol3/papers.cfm?abstract_id=945414. See also: Barnett, Stephen R., No-Citation Rules Under Siege: A Battlefield Report and Analysis. UC Berkeley Public Law and Legal Theory Research Paper Series. US Berkeley School of Law, Boalt Hall, Berkeley, CA 94720. http://ssrn.com/abstract=485823. See also: www.NonPublication.com

many courts routinely ignore their own nonpublication rules and actually rely on unpublished decisions from their own or other jurisdictions, ignoring the published decisions. This makes many critical business decisions legal gambles. Our system of precedent, once seemingly settled and consistent, is in jeopardy because of a growing body of private, unpublished rulings out of the same or other jurisdictions. This problem forecasts a judiciary and lawyers uncertain of precedent on critical issues.

The fact is that over eighty percent of all federal appellate decisions are not precedential law. They are soley the law of the case, or collateral estoppel because they are stamped "not for publication." So how do cases make it into the selective twenty percent of decisions that should become full-blown precedent available for citation? There are variant guidelines in each jurisdiction. There was a pending federal rule to deal with nonpublished decisions, but the reality is that judges appear to pick and choose, largely as they please, which cases become "law" and which do not. As of this writing, only about twenty percent of the decisions in the twelve federal circuits become precedent and nobody knows exactly how they are picked.

THE APPEAL. The record above at 1A, states "Submitted May 9, 2005**—Decided May 13, 2005, Before: PREGERSON, CANBY, and THOMAS, Circuit Judges." The judges were Harry Pregerson, in Los Angeles, California; William C. Canby, Jr., in Phoenix, Arizona; and Sidney R. Thomas, in Billings, Montana. The Memorandum, not-for-publication decision is a de novo review (p. 2A). De novo means anew or starting over. They said they examined all of the evidence from the beginning just as though it had not been tried below.

The appellate judges obviously didn't read the file. The normal time period for the court of appeals to consider and rule on any appeal is nine months. The judges received the appeal on May 9 and decided on May 13. At most, they had five days to review the file. But they probably had the appeal request for three or four days because of the press of other business and the normal procedure in any office. Copies of the entire file, not just the decisions by Judge Fogel, would have to go to Los Angeles, Phoenix, and Billings. Each judge must read the district court file to determine the facts, then research the law. It would take several days for each judge to read the entire record. It would take more time for them to confer and a bit more time for them to reach a conclusion after testing the facts and the law. Having done that they would let one judge reach a decision and the others would compare that decision with their own notes. Four or five days of consideration were really an absurdly short time period for a de novo review. I believe a clerk read Judge Fogel's decision and issued the order upholding the court below. It's my opinion that no appellate judge ever saw the appeal.[55]

Stephen R. Barnett makes the same point in his UC Berkeley Public Law and Legal Theory Research Paper No. 143 (2004).[56] The clerk was careful to exclude any reference to Fogel's contradictory language. Only unrelated cases were cited. The primary difference between a judge and a clerk is intellectual awareness, but the disposition of each is the same

---

[55] Committee for the Rule of Law – Mission Statement. "The committee brings to light that the courts of appeal across America have become judicial assembly lines dispensing inconsistent product rather than wisdom, often without significant involvement of any authorized justice, let alone *three* independent, qualified and prepared jurists. As a result the law is so inconsistently applied that the Chief Justice of California has publicly said, "You'd have a hard time telling the wheat from the chaff" when reviewing Court of Appeal decisions." http://www.nonpublication.com/CRLMission.html. See also: Joshua Hold v. California Supreme Court, CV 07-05107 THE, United States District Court of Northern California, San Francisco.

[56] University of California at Berkeley School of Law "No-citation Rules Under Siege: A Battlefield Report and Analysis." http://ssrn.com/abstract=485823. (See footnote 44). California's addiction to unpublished opinions may reflect habits of undue leisure on the part of the state's Court of Appeal justices. One judge who sat for twenty-one years on that court reported that "too many appellate court justices viewed the court as a kind of retirement." Craig Anderson, *Front-Row Seat at the Rerun*, S.F. Daily J. 1 (Dec. 19, 2002) (profile of former justice Marcel Poché). The *average* number of published opinions produced annually by justices of the California Court of Appeal, in the latest year reported, was nine. See *2003 Court Statistics, supra* n. 106, at 20, tbl. 1 (total written opinions of courts of appeal 12,056, and full-time judge equivalents 92.7); *id.* at 31, tbl. 9 (seven percent of opinions published, producing 844 published opinions). It may be asked whether the public is getting its money's worth from appellate judges who produce, on average, well under one citable opinion per month. (The average number of *un*published opinions per judge was 121. See *id.* **But unpublished opinions are more likely to be delegated entirely to staff and not to trouble the judge.)** (Emphasis supplied)

when the goal is to get rid of the litigant. If the clerk in the appellate court handled my case and no judge was involved, my case has not been heard by the court of appeals. The cases are still on appeal and the appellate and Supreme Court must consider them in a proper and authorized fashion.

The Court of Appeals said (P. 2A):

> The district court properly held that Prudential Insurance Company of America, Prudential Securities, Inc., Prudential Financial, Inc., and Pruco Securities Company ("Prudential") did not communicate an unauthorized intrusion into Jensen's privacy by completing a background check prior to hiring him as a life insurance salesman, because Jensen authorized the background check and released Prudential from any and all liabilities, claims, or lawsuits with regard to the information obtained. *See Cramer v. Consol. Freightways, Inc.*, 209 F.3d 1122, 1130 (9th Cir. 2000) (citing *Hill v. Nat'l Collegiate Athletic Ass'n.*, 865 P.2d 633 (1994)."

Only one company had the ability to hire me as a life insurance agent, that was Insurance. Libel was filed against Financial and Insurance. Oppression was filed against Insurance. Invasion of privacy was filed against Securities and Pruco. The court of appeals ruled I had filed invasion of privacy claims against all four and that all four companies were authorized to investigate my background. (And they called their review a de novo review?) Only Insurance responded to the suppoena while Securities and Pruco never revealed, as required by law, they had searched the NASD files.

The court of appeals failed to read the release. The release is a contract, which is why the court held I was bound by the release. A contract consists of the entire document. The entire document excluded the involvement of any securities firm. The court of appeals ruling also validated the lower Court's finding that the applicable laws are immaterial and neither here nor there when it said it completed a de novo review.

The court of appeals then ruled the e-mail communication between two Prudential employees was privileged. The court of appeals, at page 2A, continued with:

> [T]he e-mail did not convey a false factual implication that Jensen was guilty of a Dyer Act violation,…

The word guilty was never in the complaint; it was not an issue of fact or law. The court of appeals continued:

> [O]nly that he had an arrest on his record requiring further inquiry.

I had no arrest record in 2002, thus it was not "…on his record."

The Court of Appeals at page 3A, added:

> The district court did not abuse its discretion by denying Jensen's motion for default judgment as the record reflects that Prudential Securities, Inc., Prudential Financial, Inc., and Pruco Securities Company were not properly served with summons and complaint.

Oops! The *record* reflected that those companies were properly served with summons and complaint. If a de novo review had taken place, it would have revealed the Defendants had been properly served.

Notice the difference between the process in this federal lawsuit and the process in the first lawsuit filed by Walter Dietzen in Indiana. Dietzen filed the claim, it was answered, evidence and proposed testimony were prepared, and the case went to trial. Dietzen placed me on the stand, marked the contract and termination documents, had me identify the contract and termination documents, placed the actuary on the stand to state the amount of damages due to me, then he closed the case. (Martin Fletcher moved for dismissal because the contract and termination had not been placed into evidence.) The process is the same for all state and federal courts.

In this above case no answer was ever filed, no witnesses ever testified, no evidence was ever submitted, no proof established, and no damages shown (which is what the judge and defendants needed to avoid). Yet the courts treated the entire proceeding as though all of these events took place. The judge(s) rephrased assertions of fact as opinions, created facts for the purpose of applying laws, ruled on the facts, ruled the applicable laws aren't applicable, redesignated parts of my complaint, then used existing judicial rulings inappropriately. The courts and judges created a massive structure out of thin air. Nothing substantive had been properly submitted to the court other than the complaint. Based upon nothing definitive before them they established something and then ruled. The courts have universally held that nothing vitiates fraud, except, of course, in instances where the judges and attorneys conclude it's beneficial to them.

The Supreme Court believes it has the discretion to hear a case. It only reviews one-tenth of one percent of the cases submitted to it. Attorney and judge Richard A. Posner is a celebrated author and advocate of economics as applied to the law. Posner and William M. Landes completed a paper for The Law School, The University of Chicago, in April 2008. The title is *Rational Judicial Behavior: A Stastitical Study*.[57] This is an extensive study regarding the reasons United States Supreme and appelate court judges rule as they do. Their research extends back over the last seventy years. The authors concluded it is the tendency in the appelate courts for liberal judges to cast conservative votes in criminal cases and that the liberal side of a civil case is usually the plaintiff's side. (Page 25.) (A conservative vote is against the defendant and a liberal vote is for the defendant. (Page 27.)) Republican presidents appoint conservative judges and Democratic presidents appoint liberal judges. (Judge Posner granted authority to use portions of the article up to 20%.)

But the law specifies an outcome that is the same whether the judge leans toward the conservative or liberal side. The law is specific, the judges are not specific. The judges must do the same thing a jury does, decide the facts first, or accept the facts decided by a jury, then decide the law as it applies to the facts. The legal theory is every judge will decide a case the same way whether the judge is conservative or liberal, because the facts determine the outcome. The Landes-Posner study illustrates otherwise. The judges don't vote according to the law, because the law is fixed. The outcome is decided by the mindset or emotional condition of the judges.

---

[57] The Chicago Working Paper Series Index: http://www.law.uchicago.edu/lawecon/index.html and the Social Science Research Network Electronic Paper Collection: http://ssrn.com/abstract=1126403.

From January through February 2006, the San Jose Mercury News' reporter Tulsky wrote a series of articles titled "Tainted trials, stolen justice" describing the failures in the judicial system. The articles were comprehensive and a service to the public. Tulsky investigated the function and accuracy of the judicial system in charging, trying, and sentencing criminals in the South Bay area of California. The investigation included Santa Clara (San Jose) and Santa Cruz counties (part of California's Sixth Judicial District). Tulsky found a small number of individuals were charged with and convicted of crimes they never committed. He set out to find the failures in the judicial system. He found serious flaws on the part of everyone who participated. He found incompetent prosecution, incompetent defense, and incompetent judges. His articles began with how the Santa Clara County criminal justice system failed one man.[58] Then he wrote how the justice system failed others, enough to warrant the series of articles. He wrote about how prosecutors were over the line.[59] Three veteran litigators were identified as participating in wrongful convictions punctuated by acts of questionable conduct tolerated by their supervisors. He moved on to explain how judges favor the prosecution.[60] He concluded some judges help to undermine the defendants and how the 6th District Court of Appeal attempts to preserve guilty verdicts."[61]

His articles weren't an indictment of the entire system, but an indication enough professionals failed to live up to their duties, which brought an indictment on the system. It clearly demonstrated some members of the legal profession really didn't care about following the letter and spirit of the law. Even though the judiciary in California has been given extraordinary power by the California Constitution, the judges in particular failed to adhere to their power. Errors by judges cause a loss of confidence in the judicial system.

Judge Fogel wrote the following response to the articles that the Mercury News published entitled "Justice denied is a national problem"[62]

---

[58] San Jose Mercury News, January 22, 2006, AA.
[59] San Jose Mercury News, January 23, 2006, 1A+.
[60] San Jose Mercury News, January 25, 2006, A+.
[61] San Jose Mercury News, January 26, 2006, 1A+.
[62] (http://www.mercurynews.com /mld/mercurynews/news/editorial/13854269.htm?template=c)] February 12, 2006, (Page 1P, 3P).

"Tainted Trials, Stolen Justice," the Mercury News' recent series about Santa Clara County's criminal justice system, focused needed attention on the ways in which the daily reality of that system falls short of our expectations. The research for the articles was carefully done; even those who disagree with the writer's conclusions have been hard-put to identify any glaring factual inaccuracies. There is a risk, however, in viewing a single community in isolation.

Looking at something under a microscope necessarily makes what one is looking at appear larger in relation to everything else than it really is. Without context, our local problems too easily may be seen only as the mistakes of individuals rather than as evidence of much broader social dynamics and imperfections in our legal culture. While the articles tell the truth, there are important ways in which they don't tell the whole truth.

I've been a judge for more than 24 years. I spent the first 16 1/2 of those years in Santa Clara County's trial courts; I've worked in the more rarefied air of the federal court system for the past eight. I've taught legal and judicial ethics for more than 20 years and served for seven years as a peer counselor for California judges facing discipline for misconduct.

Some of the people who were criticized in the series are my former colleagues. A number of the problems discussed in the articles have become issues in this year's race for the district attorney's office. I want to be very clear that in expressing my personal views, it is not my intention to take sides or to defend or criticize anyone. As a federal judge with lifetime tenure and an ethical obligation to maintain political neutrality, I don't have a dog in the fight. The facts in the articles speak for themselves; my purpose is simply to provide perspective.

There are three points, each of which received only brief mention in the Mercury News' series, that bear particular emphasis. The first is the extent to which the potential for injustice is inherent in our country's adversarial legal system. The second is the pervasive impact of economic inequality on the quality of justice people receive. The third is the way in which electoral politics affect the balance between the rights of criminal defendants and the interests of the state.

From the first day of law school, would-be lawyers learn not how to seek the truth, but how to advocate effectively for a client's version of the truth, expressed as a legal position. While codes of professional conduct prohibit outright dishonesty, lawyers nonetheless are taught that they have a duty of zealous advocacy, which often includes putting the most favorable spin on unfavorable facts, avoiding unnecessary disclosure of damaging evidence to their opponents, and making aggressive use of legal procedures to limit the effectiveness of an adversary's case.

It shouldn't surprise us that some lawyers instinctively view even unambiguous obligations to cooperate with the other side as narrowly as possible. It's not that the truth doesn't matter; rather, it is assumed that the truth will emerge through the process of each side trying to win.

This system works reasonably well when the lawyers on both sides of a case follow the law, act professionally and have relatively equal skill, but things can go terribly wrong when a lawyer cares too much about winning or too little about being prepared and professionally competent.

The Mercury News' series identified embarrassing local examples of such behavior, such as a prosecutor who apparently withheld evidence helpful to a defendant -- a practice prohibited many years ago by the Supreme Court in Brady vs. Maryland -- and a defense lawyer who abandoned her client. But problems like these exist virtually everywhere. Most legal ethics courses still teach lawyers what they absolutely can't do rather than how to think about what they *should* do.

If we want things to be different, either locally or at the state or national level, we have to start both by recognizing the roots of the problem and by being clear about what we want done differently.

It's not necessarily apparent from the articles, but I seriously doubt that any of the defendants whose stories were highlighted had financial resources like O. J. Simpson's.

Although there have been instances in which well-funded defense lawyers have taken advantage of poorly prepared or overworked prosecutors, inappropriate professional behavior usually occurs when the defendant cannot afford a proper defense. When an inexperienced or ineffective defense lawyer fails to conduct an adequate investigation or make a crucial motion or objection, the system's ordinary checks and balances fail, not because the prosecutor is trying too hard to win but because the defense lawyer isn't trying hard enough or, even worse, doesn't know how to try.

One of the great ironies of our system in actual practice is that the poorest defendants -- those who qualify for the typically excellent services of career public defenders -- often get much better representation than the working poor whose families go deeply into debt to hire private attorneys of dubious ability and reputation. While I don't have statistical studies to prove this, I doubt that many experienced trial judges would disagree with me.

Economic inequality undercuts one of the core premises of the adversarial paradigm: that both sides will have the same ability to present their case, and that the real truth will emerge from their competing versions of the truth. There are things we can do in response to this situation, such as implementing minimum levels of training and experience for lawyers handling serious criminal cases.

We also can increase the rates of compensation for lawyers who are appointed by the court because the public defender's office has a conflict. While there are some notable exceptions, criminal defense lawyers generally don't make a lot of money, and without adequate compensation from their court-appointed cases, they are forced to charge higher fees to their private clients, who are often the working poor. If we want to make good legal services more widely available, we as taxpayers have to be willing to pay for them.

District attorneys and trial-level judges in California are elected officials. And California's appellate judges -- who are appointed by the governor -- are subject to periodic public referendums as to whether they should be retained. I can't think of too many instances in which people have campaigned successfully for these offices on a platform of being fairer to criminal defendants; for many years the focus has been almost exclusively on being tougher on crime.

In 1986, California voters overwhelmingly ousted three members of the state Supreme Court whom they considered too defendant-oriented. Until very recently, a majority of the lawyers appointed or elected to Santa Clara County's trial courts were former prosecutors.

The composition of the 6th District Court of Appeal, which was the subject of pointed criticism in the series, reflects the concerted effort of two conservative governors -- George Deukmejian and Pete Wilson -- to appoint justices who, in addition to their excellent professional qualifications, had a well-documented conservative approach in criminal matters. Even our two most recent governors, both of whom are viewed as more moderate than their predecessors, have been wary of judicial candidates with criminal defense backgrounds.

It paints with much too broad a brush to suggest that judges simply follow their own political philosophy in deciding cases. While there are people with personal agendas in every profession, including mine, I believe that the great majority of judges try to decide cases based upon the law and the facts presented. But philosophy and life experience do sometimes matter with the close calls, the decisions that could go either way.

There are literally dozens of decisions judges make in a criminal case that aren't cut and dried and that involve the exercise of discretion: which witnesses to believe in pretrial hearings, what questions to ask in jury selection, what evidence to admit or exclude during trial, what jury instructions to give or refuse to give. Appellate courts can reverse these decisions only if the way the trial judge exercised his or her discretion was clearly unreasonable and there is a reasonable possibility that the error affected the outcome of the trial.

The concept of ``harmless error'' -- that is, error that in the judgment of the appellate court did not affect the outcome of the trial -- has existed since our country was founded. It no doubt is applied somewhat more broadly today in California than it was 20 years ago, with the result that a greater percentage of criminal convictions are affirmed on appeal. This is not because judges are less intellectually honest than they used to be; it's because California voters by and large have expressed a preference for judges (and for governors) who have a less expansive view of the rights of criminal defendants. If one sees that as a problem, the solution in large part must be a political one.

Vigorous enforcement of ethical standards for prosecutors, defense attorneys and judges is essential if the public is to have confidence in our criminal justice system. All of the declared candidates for district attorney recognized this in their published responses to the series, as did the presiding judge of the Superior Court.

Beyond the efforts of our local leaders, California's State Bar and the Commission on Judicial Performance should receive enough legislative and fiscal support that they are not limited, as they often have been, to dealing with only the worst cases of misconduct.

Particularly in the case of the State Bar, there needs to be a commitment to adequate staffing, prompt and thorough investigation of potentially meritorious complaints, and meaningful progressive discipline for ethical lapses and incompetent representation.

Integrity and professional competence are minimum requirements for all of us who do the public's work. From law school on, we need to train lawyers (some of whom will become judges) that winning for its own sake is not an appropriate goal and that *our system of justice is only as trustworthy as the conduct of the people who work in it*. At the same time, going forward, I hope that we remember that the problems the Mercury News' series brought to light are not local aberrations but rather are symptomatic of much larger and deeply embedded realities in our legal system -- and in our society.

*JEREMY FOGEL is a judge of the U.S. District Court in San Jose. He wrote this article for Perspective.* (Emphasis supplied.) (Reprinted with permission.)

If a person gives serious thought to what Judge Fogel had to say it should cause grave concern to the average person. Judge Fogel is an intelligent man. He graduated from Stanford University and earned his law degree at Harvard University. These are two schools that cater to the intellectually gifted. He recognizes that gift in his comments about his accomplishments and the rarefied air of the federal judiciary. (That sounds elitist to me.) There's nothing rarefied about the air of being a federal judge. Compentency and integrity are the required primary ingredients of a sitting federal judge. He recognizes that dishonest judges and attorneys exist. Perhaps the judges are not less intellectually honest than they used to be, but that doesn't reassure us that their intellectual honesty in the past is anything to be proud of. It appears as though he's saying they're just as bad as they were in the past and it's the public's fault. In my opinion the employees of the federal judiciary must be trustworthy beyond question.

He said in reference to the potential for injustice "From the first day of law school, would-be lawyers learn not how to seek the truth, but how to advocate effectively for a client's version of the truth, expressed as a legal position." A client's version of the truth might be the truth as he/she sees it, a perception. That doesn't preclude seeking the truth. Since the judge has this awareness shouldn't he direct the attorneys to advance the truth? Facts are truths, spinning the facts are versions of the truth. The judge advanced the belief the legal process is reduced to the knowledge and skills of the advocates. He said both sides should have relatively equal skill. When he notices a lawyer is inexperienced or ineffective he should point the lawyer in the right direction and make certain that same lawyer isn't blindsided. He also said "Economic inequality undercuts one of the core premises of the adversarial paradigm." In Judge Fogel's court, the uneducated representing themselves will automatically lose when facing wealthy defendants and skilled attorneys. Why? Because Judge Fogel knows what's happening; he knows what's going on in his court. He just explained it. The person he believes to be more knowledgeable of the law than him will win as the judge in Indiana explained. Yet, he indicates he has no interest in cutting through the fog, dealing with substance instead of form. Judges have an obligation to insist the facts and truth prevail and the laws and rules are followed by the competent and incompetent. As a matter of practice every lawsuit should be reduced to the essence of truth and simplicity. Socrates said in The Apology "A judge's duty is not to make a present of justice, but to give judgment; and he has sworn that he will judge according to the laws, and not according to his own good pleasure." Judge Fogel leaves the impression he believes a person without funds is always represented by an attorney without the proper skills and knowledge. But an attorney's competency isn't determined by the size of his paycheck.

Judge Fogel referred to the ouster of the California Supreme Court judges in 1986. He attributed the reason for their ouster was because the judges were defendant-oriented. This is his reference to injustice resulting from political interference. In my opinion, the judges were ousted because they failed to adhere to the California Constitution.

It's my understanding Judge Fogel believes the failures outlined in the Mercury News' articles are nationwide. Remember what the judge in Indianapolis said to me, that he rules in favor of the attorneys from the large firms in the large offices, because they have more knowledge than him? (Compare his approach to the Chicago judge who insisted the attorneys stick to the facts and leave their show in the hall outside of the courtroom.) Judge Fogel used different words to say the same thing, he rules in favor of wealth.

I wrote a letter to the editor of the Mercury News in response to Judge Fogel's article. It was my position he might pay attention to some cases, but he certainly didn't pay any attention to the decisions he signed in my case. I quoted his reasoning in his decisions that "applicable rules are neither here nor there," and "immaterial." Carol Scholl of the Mercury News letters section said my letter was too long for publication and it would "run today in the on-line letter section without any edits." I looked for it and didn't see it anywhere, so I wrote back and asked what happened. *She said my letter was too personal to publish.* Most letters to the editor and most items in newspapers are personal. Judge Fogel said his writing was personal. The title of his article was "Another view." I wrote the following letter to Ms. Susan Goldberg, the Executive Editor of the Mercury News:

> Enclosed you'll find copies of e-mails written by me to the Letters to the Editor department. The e-mails concern an article written by federal judge Jeremy Fogel and my experience with the judge in his courtroom.
>
> You'll notice Carol Scholl first said the letter would run in the on-line letters section on 2/13/06, without any edits, but it would not run in the paper because of its length. I checked the on-line section and found no reference to my letter. I edited the letter for length and resubmitted it to the Mercury News. Scholl then said it would not run because it really doesn't express an opinion but speaks about my personal experience with the judge.
>
> Judge Fogel's article expressed the facts as he sees them regarding the integrity and professionalism of the federal courts and about his integrity and professionalism in particular. My comments are a direct response to his position. It would be unfair on my part to express an opinion without first laying the groundwork by stating the facts at hand. If I intend to dispute a person's position

on an issue it is only appropriate for me to first establish the factual reasons why I'm so disputing. If I have no facts to support my position I should remain silent.

I don't believe the Mercury News intends to silence me or anyone, especially when comments are made relating to articles printed in the paper. It seems to me the format of my Letter to the Editor might be wrong, but it also seems to me that it would be more appropriate for my response to be printed in the same place the Judge's comments were printed. For that reason, I'm attaching my response which should satisfy your paper as Another View article.

Sincerely,

Reginald L. Jensen
5482 Walnut Blossom Drive
San Jose, CA 95123-2260
(408) 225-4227 E-mail: regj@pacbell.net

Attached:

ANOTHER VIEW
for the Mercury News

Judge Jeremy Fogel expressed his views in the Mercury News on February 12, 2006, based upon his perspective as a federal judge. He believes the judicial system should and does represent the interests of the public in the application of the laws and legal procedure. He cites his extensive legal background, his lifetime tenure, his ethical teachings to other attorneys, and other evidence, in support of his position.

There is no question Judge Fogel was regarded as a well-informed and fair practitioner prior to his appointment to the federal bench, otherwise he would never have received confirmation. Judge Fogel is still held in high regard by the legal profession based upon his fairness and professional performance based upon information available to me.

However, if someone is looking at the landscape only from his own perspective it's easy to fail to notice the perspective of others. Judges and attorneys could benefit from receiving feedback from litigants in both civil and criminal actions from time to time. I know a judge makes the final decision and will usually find the loser in an action biased against the judge's decision. But that isn't always the situation and sometimes the responses from the litigants will help avoid future hardship. I recently was a pro se litigant in Judge Fogel's courtroom. I believe the judge ruled as he felt he should rule, however, I think the results should have been different. My action was *Jensen v. Prudential, et. al* Case Number C-03-4608-JF. The defendant's attorneys took the position my pleadings were not properly prepared. (I never mentioned in court that I had retained an attorney with more than twenty years experience in both state and federal court to assist me in preparing the pleadings.) Judge Fogel dismissed with the provision that I could file an amended complaint. The dismissal was dated February 25, 2004, and contained the language "The fact that Prudential allegedly violated applicable rules is neither here nor there."

I filed an Amended Complaint, prepared only by me, which Judge Fogel also dismissed on July 23, 2004. He ruled: "B. Oppression. California does not recognize such a tort." California Civil Code Section 3294 (a) states "In an action for the breach of an obligation not arising from contract, where it is proven by clear and convincing evidence that the defendant has been guilty of oppression, fraud, or malice, the plaintiff, in addition to the actual damages, may recover damages for the sake of example by way of punishing the defendant."

His decision continued: "As we discussed at length in the Court's Order of February 25, 2004, the fact that Defendants may have violated applicable SEC rules (which Defendants deny) is immaterial with respect to Jensen's claim for invasion of privacy."

I appealed to the United States Ninth Circuit and it upheld the dismissal citing, what appears to me to be unrelated case law. I then filed a Petition for a Writ of Certiorari (Supreme Court docket number 05-193) which was denied.

It seems to me as a layman that the legal reasoning in my case was flawed. If the rules, which are federal law, are applicable they certainly are not "neither here nor there," nor are they "immaterial." Perhaps Judge Fogel was correct in dismissing my action and perhaps there exists relevant case law which is right on point in support of his decision which the Ninth Circuit could cite. But, from my perspective it appears as though the judges could have paid more attention to detail when considering my case.

Steve Wright wrote back to me saying he was in charge of the editorial page. He said Judge Fogel's decision might have been flawed from my point of view, but it was about a single case and he didn't believe it had much relevance for the community at large. However, he did say he would retain my comments in his files. Is that really how the press works?[63] Tulsky focused on criminal defendants who were cheated in court. Each flawed decision affected one person. My focus has been on civil trials.

One year later, Tulsky wrote another article discussing the improvements by the appellate court, which required publication of more

---

[63] Wright's son entered the military and was sent to Iraq. Wright himself was opposed to the war, but he fully supported his son's decision to fight for his country. Wright wrote several poignant, touching and human editorials (March 21, and December 30, 2007) about how his family was affected by this event.

decisions.[64] The comment here was that the appellate court reversed more cases and tolerated fewer errors. Why would they tolerate any errors? If they know an error exists, they have an obligation to correct it. The entire purpose of the higher courts is to correct all errors, not some errors. Should they tolerate those they believe are inconsequential, those they believe will not be challenged or should they correct all errors? Grammatical errors might be harmless, but errors of fact and law can't be harmless. Errors the judges believe are not important can come back to raise havoc in the community.

Tulsky reported that, after twenty years, the court of appeals ruled a man had not received a fair trial, because of prosecutorial error. The man had died in prison. One prosecutor was now a judge and the other was now a district attorney. A public defender said she would train her attorneys to testify truthfully in court. (Attorneys need to be trained in their duty to testify truthfully? Come on, now.)

Nowhere in the United States Constitution does it say judges may dismiss cases upon their own pleasure. Nowhere does it say a litigant may have a jury trial only if the judge agrees to allow it. Nor does it say a litigant may not have a jury trial if the courts are crowded, if there isn't enough time for the court to handle it, if it isn't convenient; or that the judge may dismiss and throw the plaintiff out of court if he believes a litigant isn't entitled to a trial. You can go down the list of reasons why the courts fail to allow jury trials to litigants and you'll find the reasons are to satisfy their own personal needs.

According to the Library of Congress, from March 4, 1789, to June 5, 2007, 44,806 federal laws have been passed by Congress and placed on the books.[65] Add to that the laws passed in the several states, plus the laws and ordinances of the counties, cities, and municipalities. That's just a start because each and every published decision entered by any court of appeals, federal and state, also becomes case law, in the parlance of the legal profession. There are a few million of them. In case law there are cases, either published or unpublished, that have been decided

---

[64] San Jose Mercury News. "Tainted trials: one year later". January 28, 2007. 1A+

[65] Public Services Division, Law Library of Congress, 101 Independence Ave., SE. Washington, D.C. 20540-3120. URL: < http://www.loc.gov/rr/law/ >. E-Mail: < http://www.loc.gov/rr/askalib/ask-law.html >

for, against, and neutral on nearly every subject. A good research project is to locate the various case decisions affecting the payment of interest. Interest can be set at nearly any rate beginning and ending at nearly at time. If you go to court, whatever your claim happens to be can be compromised because there are cases on the books, which can be referred to by the attorneys and judges, which say you win, you lose, or you neither win nor lose. Any attorney worth his salt can find myriad case law that supports his position. A competent opposing attorney can find the opposing case laws by simply searching. The attorneys can decide the case by agreement and demonstrate to their clients the case was either decided properly or improperly.

What's the purpose of most laws? When a law is written the purpose is for one person or faction to cause another person or faction to do what the first person or faction wants done. Rather than use a gun, the first person or faction causes a law to be enacted. The second person or faction then finds a method of retaliation by causing a different law to be enacted, which favors the second person or faction. If you wonder about that just read the tax code. The ten million words in the code and regulations[66] are designed to cause one faction to pay less in taxes than a separate faction. Otherwise, there would be a fixed rate or a set schedule, which applied to everyone without preference. It would take less than 100 words. Factions can control specific areas of life. Factions can control specific judges. Factions, rather than a national institution, vie for supremacy. You see it happening now. Here's a very simple example of what could happen if the rich and powerful failed to adhere to the rules. We drive our automobiles down the road to a corner with a semaphore, which controls the flow of traffic. The light turns red and all drivers going in our direction stop to allow the cars travelling in a different direction to proceed. If the rich and powerful decide the rules don't apply to them, they will continue through the intersection. Accidents, chaos, deaths, and injuries occur. In such instances, the people on the scene would ignore the regulatory agencies and take control themselves. As the people become more aware of what transpires in any domain, they'll take more control.

---

[66] Congressman George Radanovich (Rep), CA, 19th District, Website August 9, 2007.

In 2005 the IRS increased my 2004 income, this time by $17,000. As usual, they threatened to take all of my property to satisfy any tax liens. At issue were unpaid, self-employment taxes and taxes on the additional income assessed by the IRS. They said I had not paid self-employment taxes in the amount of $1,700. It was less than that amount, closer to $1,000, because one insurance company had deducted and paid employment taxes on my behalf for some of the commissions paid to me. But I mailed a $1,700 check to the IRS. In checking my return I found the increased income to be unsupported. I disputed their accounting discrepancy several times. Each time they adjusted my income to conform to the errors I disclosed, but then added the income back at a different location on the 1040. Finally, I decided to file a notice of appeal of their actions. My case was assigned to the San Francisco tax court. I met with the hearing officer on April 25, 2007. The hearing was to be informal and if all issues weren't resolved then the case would be set for trial.

The hearing officer reviewed the records created by the IRS and reviewed my records. I mentioned to her the previous audits and how the IRS made me jump through hoops for about nine months each time they increased my income, forcing me to make calls all over the United States to different IRS offices. I said that I didn't mind a little horseplay from time to time, in fact I might even play myself, but enough is enough. She said that an auditor should be able to bring up all of my records in any location just by pushing a couple of buttons on the computer. I told her about the *Laudig v. Jensen* trial where Laudig told Judge Nash that I hadn't paid taxes on the slander damages paid to me by FESLIC and that my attorney explained to the judge that slander damages were not taxable at that time. Since I prepared my own returns, I and the IRS are the only ones who had copies. Someone had to have obtained copies of my returns either from the IRS files or from my home and given the information to Laudig. She said the greatest majority of IRS employees are completely honest, but there are always a few who will skirt the laws. She concluded that, based upon payment of self-employment taxes, my returns were correct and the IRS had erred on the additional income. She said she would recalculate my taxes and send me a new notice. It appeared as though no additional taxes would be due.

On May 18, 2007, the hearing officer mailed a proposed stipulation and decision showing the removal of the additional income. My wife and I signed the decision and returned it to the IRS. The stipulation and settlement was signed by the judge and returned to me on June 27, 2007. On September 4, 2007, we received a refund check in the amount of $265.54.

On August 19, 2007, I checked the attorney listings in Rockville, Maryland, Pullano's FINRA office location, and found his listing as a practicing attorney at 716 Anderson Ave. 20850-2103. I asked FINRA about its position on allowing staff attorneys to engage in private practice. A response was never received. Several weeks later, the listing was removed. Then it seemed to me to be best to ask FINRA one more time to clarify its position on the conflicting accounts of the copyright dates on the CRD documents and the conflict between the copyright of 1999-2000 with the URL 02/20/2002 date. I wrote to Mary Schapiro, CEO of FINRA, and asked her if the document could have been obtained in 2002. Schapiro gave my letter to James Cummings, executive vice president, who gave it to Pullano. The dispute regarding Pullano's knowledge or integrity in response to my inquiry was returned to Pullano for a decision. In a letter dated September 28, 2007, Pullano wrote back:

> As we informed you in 2003, we cannot affirmatively authenticate the document as a CRD printout because we have no direct knowledge of when it was printed or by whom. It seems that whoever produced the document would be in the best position to provide more definitive information on that point. We can confirm that the URL (uniform resource locator) referenced at the bottom of the document was a URL used by the Web CRD system. Based on the date referenced in the footer, we would presume that it was printed from Web CRD on February 20, 2002.
>
> While we cannot conclusively state that this document was printed from Web CRD, we can confirm (or reconfirm) that the information contained in the document was available to MML through the CRD

system (either the Legacy CRD system or Web CRD) to MML from the time it was received (August 1983) until it was removed from the CRD system in late 2003 or early 2004...Because the information was available through the CRD system until that time, it is possible that it could have been printed in 2002.

Pullano's conclusion "it is possible that it could have been printed in 2002." is a misrepresentation. It could have been printed by one of the Prudential companies in 2002, but not obtained from FINRA/NASD. Any Prudential organization could reproduce the complete document if it so desired. Pullano ignored my request for information regarding the copyright dates. Copyright rules specify that a collection of items published over a number of years shall record the date of the first published item and the date of last published item connected by a hyphen.[67] Even though Pullano knew Chavez said the document would have a 2002 copyright date if it was retrieved in 2002, he never said he had conferred with Chavez and she was mistaken. He infers the arrest information went to MassMutual and MMLISI. His response includes only the information he's willing to provide.

He said in his June 12, 2003, letter (next to last paragraph, page 197):

> MML requested in October 1998 that NASD check its records to make sure that the CRD system did not reflect an arrest date of August 12, 1983, for this event, but instead reflected the correct 1947 date. Our records reflect that we confirmed that the CRD system showed the correct date.

In his September 28, 2007, letter Pullano said the record was never corrected. Yet he maintained several years earlier that the record had been corrected.

---

[67] The information contained in the section of the Cataloger's Reference Shelf is based on Graphic Materials - Rules for Describing Original Items and Historical Collections, compiled by Elisabeth W. Betz; Cataloging Distribution Service, Library of Congress, Washington, D.C.; 1982. It includes 1996 Updates based on the Cataloger's Desktop CD, Issue 4, 1997. http://www.itsmarc.com/crs/graph0163.htm

On November 19, 2007, after receiving a repetitive letter from Pullano, I decided to send enough material in my possession to Schapiro and Pullano for them to understand Pullano was incorrect in his assumptions about FINRA's record of my arrest and the 1999-2000 copyright document. My letter said, in part:

> FINRA (a/k/a NASD) created a false 8/12/83 arrest record about me. Mr. Richard Pullano and I have been discussing this arrest for some time. He has now forwarded a new letter to me dated November 12, 2007, defending his position on issues which I claim him to be incorrect. He is incorrect in both fact and law. I need to cover the issues one-by-one so that the conflict can be identified and hopefully resolved.
>
> **Issue # 1. Was the 8/12/83 arrest date always accurately reflected in the CRD system?** On page 2 of his November 12, 2007, letter, first paragraph, beginning with the fifth line from the end, he says *"In any event, I note two things: (1) the information was always accurately reflected in the CRD system (i.e. both dates appeared and were identified correctly.)"* (My emphasis; all quotes in the letter are in Italics.) He is factually incorrect.
>
> Enclosed are the Pre-Web based CRD system documents (all separate) provided to me by MML in 1998, with the arrest report identified as 1-A, and the CRD documents identified as 1-B and 1-C. A letter to FINRA from MassMutual (MM) and MML Investors Services, Inc. (MML) stating I was being disciplined for the arrest, is identified as 1-D.
>
> 1-A. The FBI arrest record of 1-29-47.
>
> 1-B. NASDR RR Disclosure Roster – Tandem.
> Status: X Action: FBI Date: 29-Jan-1947 Source: UT
> Proviso Incident: 1
> FBI Report Rec'd 8/12/83. Charge: Dyer Act.

Disposition: Hold for USM.
(This is where the error began.)

1-C.   NASDR RR Disclosure Roster – Sequent.
Disclosure Category:  Criminal
Status: Unknown – CRD Data Conversion
Arresting Agency Location;  UT
Charge:  Other
Description:  Dyer Act
Date:  08/12/1983
Counts: Type: Unknown – Data Conversion
Plea:  Unknown – CRD Data
Status: Unknown Conversion
Product Type(s):
Summary of Circumstances:  HOLD FOR USM
**(This document created an arrest date of 8/12/83.)**

1-D  MM's and MML's letter to the NASD indicating they were in the process of disciplining me.

On page one of his latest letter; Mr. Pullano refers again to his June 12, 2003, letter in which he says *"a 1983 arrest date never appeared in the CRD system."* In this November 12, 2007, letter he says *"I explained to you in detail in a May 20, 2003 telephone conversation the purpose of the roster report, and confirmed that the information in the CRD system accurately reflected your arrest date. I confirmed that conversation in a June 12, 2003 letter,..."* The above (1-C) is a 1983 arrest date, which appeared in the CRD system unless the document provided by MML is counterfeit. This is the document which Ms. Sophie Aksenov referred to when she said MML didn't care what I did on my own time, whether robbing banks or stealing cars (attached). MM and MML firmly believed I was under arrest for violation of the Dyer Act in 1983.

The letter from MM and MML to the NASD indicates that I was disciplined for this arrest. I had previously been in insurance company management and I was the only person who possessed a Principal's license in MM's Indiana and San Jose, California agencies. When I became employed by MM it was with the understanding that I would be promoted into management if my performance was satisfactory. The discipline consisted of a decision that I would not be promoted, in fact, I was later demoted to representative status. This discipline took place without my knowledge and in violation of FINRA's disciplinary rules (attached).

Mr. Bill Bartol at MML said FINRA created the false arrest document. FINRA enjoys absolute immunity from suit for any and all regulatory conduct, but it does not have immunity for nonregulatory conduct.[68] I've indicated to you and stand by it, I have no intention of filing a legal challenge; which seems to be a decent trade-off for a candid exchange of information, especially since all CRD information relating to me is deemed by FINRA to be our joint property.

**Issue #2. Verifying the authenticity of a document.**

In the third paragraph of page two, Mr. Pullano said *"Note that it states "FBI REPORT REC'D 8/12/83." This presentation is consistent with what was available in Web CRD regarding the arrest event before it was deleted."* On page three, paragraph one, he said *"Let me be as clear as I can on this point. The arrest record in question was available in the CRD system from August 12, 1983 until it was deleted (we believe the deletion took place in late 2003 or early 2004); however, the CRD system never reflected the arrest as having occurred in 1983."* The word "never" is inappropriate. This might be correct as an opinion as to what was reflected in

---

[68] See: Sparta Surgical Corp. v. Nat'l Ass'n of Sec. Dealers, Inc., 159 F.3d 559 (D.C. Cir. 1996); D'Alessio v. New York Stock Exch., Inc., 258 F.3d 93, 105 (2d Cir. 2001).

the CRD system after 1998, but it is not factually or legally correct. If other individuals, organizations, and the courts interpret the Legacy Disclosure Incident Details to mean an arrest took place on 8/12/83, then his opinion is not correct. He also said on page two (last paragraph) of his November 12, 2007, letter (as well as previously) that the above document with the copyright date of 1999-2000 "appears to have been printed from the Web CRD on February 20, 2002."

At the end of January 2003, The Prudential Insurance Company of America (Insurance) delivered a so-called NASD CRD document to me which was represented to be the Web-based CRD document (identified as 2-A through 2-M, a single document).

On February 4, 2003, I talked to Mr. Chris Dragos at the NASD by phone at 8:19 a.m. PST. He said *"There isn't anything in the Legacy system about any arrest in 1983."* On February 10, 2003, I talked to Elaine Chavez of the NASD's General Counsel office and she told me that they update their copyright information whenever they make a change on any document and that the Web CRD document has been changed many times since 1999.

Document 2-A through 2-M was presented to me in the form as attached. The pages with the copyright date at the bottom were collated with the pages without the copyright. Notice the language under Reportable Disclosures on page 2-B and page 2-C. Page 2-B is an updated page 2-C. Notice the listings of available information on the left-hand sides of the pages and at the bottom of the pages. At 2-K, the language under CRD System Terms And Conditions was removed from the CFR in 1999 and replaced after 2001. It's clear to the naked eye that these are two different documents when the pages are separated and aligned according to the copyright and noncopyright pages.

Page 2-I is the page which I submitted to the court in Jensen v. Prudential, et.al. This page makes no reference whatsoever to 1947. Prudential told the court that it received this document from the NASD on February 20, 2002, and that it was the NASD who created the document, thus Prudential's inter-company transfer of the arrest report didn't make them liable for libel. Prudential also said the report was received as part of its investigation of my previous employment, from one previous employer to a potential employer. (As an aside on this point, Mr. Pullano mentioned in his November 12, 2007, letter, footnote #1, *"As you are aware, the federal securities laws require that anyone applying for securities industry registration be fingerprinted."*) I never made application for employment to Prudential Securities nor to Pruco Securities and never provided either firm or any Prudential organization with fingerprints, but both firms certified to FINRA that I had made such employment application and had provided them with my fingerprints in 2002, all in violation of federal laws and FINRA regulations. I believe it constitutes perjury.

The District Court agreed with Prudential and ruled *"The NASD website apparently contained information that Jensen had been arrested in 1983 for violation of the Dyer Act (the National Vehicle Theft Act), 18 U.S.C. § 2311."* (Enclosed, page 2) The Court recognized that I explained the report was in error (page 3). On page 4, the court ruled *"Attached to the amended complaint as Exh. 6 is a printout from the NASD stating as follows: "FBI REPORT REC'D 8/12/83. CHARGE: DYER ACT. DISPOSITION: HOLD FOR USM." Accordingly, it appears on the face of the pleading the statement in the email was true – that is, that there was an FBI report regarding the Dyer Act charge. The email does not state that Jensen was guilty of the charge, but merely reported – accurately – that the FBI had reported such a charge."* On this subject, the Ninth Circuit Court of Appeals said at

## Judicial Deception

the bottom of page 2, *"In any case, the e-mail did not convey a false factual implication that Jensen was guilty of a Dyer Act violation, only that he had an arrest on his record requiring further inquiry."* (Attached) A Petition for a Writ of Certiorari was filed with the U.S. Supreme Court, Docket No. 05-193, which was denied.

Incidentally, the dismissal by the judge in the District Court included the language that California doesn't recognize oppression as a tort. Yet, California law expressly provides that oppression is actionable as a tort.[69] Additionally, the judge said *"As was discussed at length in the Court's Order of February 25, 2004, the fact that Defendants may have violated applicable SEC rules (which Defendants deny) is immaterial with respect to Jensen's claim for invasion of privacy."* In his February 25, 2004 ruling the judge said *"The fact that Prudential allegedly violated applicable rules is neither here nor there."* If the judge had said the cited laws and regulations were not pertinent to my claim he would have made sense, but he chose not to say that. However ill conceived, the decision is still the law of the case.

Mr. Pullano has never properly addressed my questions about the copyright dates. I know that in 2000 the NASD placed the copyright notice on the document, but in 2002 the NASD placed the copyright notice on the computer screen and it did not print on the paper document. Document 2-A through 2-M is clearly two separate documents; one document created in the year 2000 and the other document created presumably on 2/20/2002. I've asked Mr. Pullano to explain the discrepancy to me on many occassions, by phone and

---

[69] *California Civil Code Section 3294(a)* states: In an action for the breach of an obligation not arising from contract, where it is proven by clear and convincing evidence that the defendant has been guilty of oppression, fraud, or malice, the plaintiff, in addition to the actual damages, may recover damages for the sake of example by way of punishing the defendant.

letter, yet he's failed to address the issue adequately. Mr. Pullano could have easily printed out a copy of the CRD report and reviewed it to accertain whatever he could perceive to be a discrepancy, but he's never done that.

Mr. Pullano now says he's contributed considerable time to answering my questions. He's failed to recognize that I've suffered substantially as a result of FINRA's creation of the 1983 arrest document (1-C) and MM's and MML's failure to follow procedure in disciplining me for the arrest and for their failure to notify me they had such an arrest report.

**Issue #3. Did one of the Prudential organizations obtain the documents with the 1999-2000 copyright date from the NASD or MM or MML?** My question remains, how did the Prudential organizations come into possession of the document with the copyright 1999-2000? Prudential said they obtained it from the NASD on 2/20/2002. The evidence demonstrates the document was created in 2000, not 2002.

FINRA took the coward's way out when it refused to respond to my letter. A regulatory agency demands complete, exact, detailed answers to any inquiry they present to others. For them to refuse to respond is unthinkable. If my responses to inquiries from FINRA were in the same nature as its responses to me, FINRA would have me hanging by my thumbs thirty feet above the sand in the middle of the Gobi desert.

Congresswoman Zoe Lofgren (CA 16th District) invested considerable effort in attempting to compel FINRA to respond to my specific questions. FINRA still refused to respond. On November 27, 2007, she said, in reference to her research as to whether or not Congress can require FINRA to respond to my questions:

> At the conclusion of this research, it is clear that because FINRA is a non-governmental agency it is not obligated to respond to Congressional inquiries in the same manner as governmental agencies must. In addition, based upon what FINRA, CRS [Congressional Research Service]

and the SEC explained to my office, there is nothing under their regulatory authority or current law that can be done to compel further action from FINRA.

The NASD was created in 1939, in response to the 1938 Maloney Act amendments to the Securities Exchange Act of 1934.[70] The SEC authorizes the creation and termination of any self-regulatory agency or organization. Through the SEC rule-making authority and oversight FINRA must comply with United States laws. If FINRA fails to comply with the laws, its authority can be terminated and its registration revoked by the SEC (see § 78s(G)). The President appoints the SEC commissioner. Congress approves the appointment. The commissioner must respond to Congressional inquiries. It appears to me that, since the SEC exists under federal law and FINRA also exists under the same federal law, FINRA must respond to Congressional inquiries.

Did FINRA act punitively towards me in 1983? Not in my opinion. They made numerous clerical errors. They had incorrectly recorded my license information, my residence information, my employer's information, my dates of employment, and a date of arrest. Did FINRA act punitively towards me in 2002 and later? My answer is absolutely yes!

So, what happens when people in positions of authority lose their compass, their integrity? The public must endure unnecessary suffering and pain. The problems aren't confined to the judiciary. Too many regulators have taken the same approach. Regulators sit in positions of authority similar to a judge or jury. And their decisions are compromised in a manner similar to members of the judiciary. Here are several examples. We go from minor failures that somehow increase until the nation is harmed.

Most Health Savings Accounts (HSA) are forms of mutual funds offered for sale along with medical insurance plans in the United States. All mutual funds are securities registered with the SEC. These securities are sold through broker-dealers, many of which are owned by banks or insurance companies. I posed the question to the SEC as to whether medical insurance brokers should be registered to sell securities when they sell HSAs. I mailed a brochure to the SEC, which contained

---

[70] United States Code Title 15, Chapter 2B, § 78s. Registration, responsibilities, and oversight of self-regulatory organizations.

Reginald L. Jensen

complete identification of the HSA as mutual funds being marketed by a registered broker-dealer. However, the HSA was and is being marketed by medical brokers who are not registered to sell securities. The e-mail response from the SEC follows along with my reply.

| | |
|---|---|
| Date: | Wed, 27 Aug 2008 14:38:08 -0400 (EDT) |
| From: | "U.S. Securities and Exchange Commission" <oiea@sec.gov> |
| To: | "Jensen, Reginald" <regj@pacbell.net> |
| Subject: | SEC Response – File HO1287882 |

Dear Mr. Jensen,

Thank you sending the materials to me about Health Savings Accounts. In your letter, you seem to question whether HSAs are securities that are being sold by unlicensed brokers.

I have reviewed the documents you provided. There is nothing I could find in the materials about the offer or sale of securities. In contrast to a variable annuity, which is a security, HSAs do not appear to me to offer a component of investing in securities. As such, I do not see how HSAs are securities that we would oversee.

Thanks again for submitting the information.

Sincerely,

ROBERT T GREENE
Office of Investor Education and Advocacy
U.S. Securities and Exchange Commission
100 F St, NE
Washington, DC 20549-0213
(202) 551-6331

| | |
|---|---|
| Date: | Fri, 29 Aug 2008 21:08:18 -0700 (PDT) |
| From: | "Reginald Jensen" <regj@pacbell.net> |
| Subject: | Re: SEC Response - File HO1287882 |
| To: | "U.S. Securities and Exchange Commission" <oiea@sec.gov> |

Mr. Greene,

I direct your attention to an exhibit I thought I forwarded to you. The exhibit is Wells Fargo Kaiser Permanente Thrive: Take Charge of Your Health, Your Savings and Your Future.

*Judicial Deception*

1. Back Page: "Investment in any mutual fund is not insured or guaranteed by the U.S. Government, the FDIC, the Federal Reserve System or any other federal agency. Shares of a mutual fund are not obligations, deposits or guaranteed by Wells Fargo or its affiliates and are subject to investment risk, including possible loss of principal."

2. Page 5. not including the cover page. "Health Savings Account (HSA) Options. Your Wells Fargo HSA can be a powerful tool for helping save and invest for future health care expenses. You will be able to choose from the following mutual fund investment options - from conservative to aggressive - to match your personal financial goals and investment style. Risk & Return Characteristics: Most Conservative - Most Agressive.

Fund:
Wells Fargo Advantage Government Money Market Fund A. Ticker WFGXX
Wells Fargo Advantage Total Return Bond Fund A. Ticker MBFAX
Wells Fargo Advantage Moderate Balanced A. Ticker WFMAX
Wells Fargo Advantage Growth Balanced A. Ticker WFGBX
Wells Fargo Advantage Asset Allocation A. Ticker SFAAX
Wells Fargo Advantage Diversified Equity A. Ticker NVDAX"

A partial quotation of the words underneath "Not FDIC Insured - No Bank Guarantee - May Lose Value" (at the bottom of the page). "Representatives can assist with general information about Wells Fargo Advantage Funds, but are not able to provide advice about which funds you should invest in for your HSA. If you have questions about your HSA, please call the toll-free number listed on page six. Wells Fargo Funds Management, LLC. a wholly owned subsidiary of Wells Fargo & Company, provides investment advisory and administrative services for Wells Fargo Advantage Funds. Other affiliates of Wells Fargo & Company provide sub-advisory and other services for the Funds. The Funds are distributed by Wells Fargo Funds Distributors, LLC, member FINRA/SPIC, an affilliate of Wells Fargo & Company."

Mr. Greene, I've afraid HSAs are securities. I can provide additional information, or you might want to check with other divisions of the SEC.

Thanks,

Reginald Jensen


SEC Response - File HO1287882

Wednesday, September 10, 2008 5:38 AM
From:
"U.S. Securities and Exchange Commission" <oiea@sec.gov>
Add sender to Contacts
To:
"Jensen, Reginald" <regj@pacbell.net>

Dear Mr. Jensen,

Thank you for your follow-up email. I will take a look at the information you have provided.

Sincerely,

ROBERT T GREENE
Office of Investor Education and Advocacy
U.S. Securities and Exchange Commission
100 F St, NE
Washington, DC  20549-0213
(202) 551-6331

Neither Greene nor the SEC has contacted me in a follow-up. If a regulatory agency is going to regulate something it should know what it is the agency regulates. Why would the SEC ignore its responsibilities in this area? Broker-dealers have little interest in selling medical insurance plans. The contributions to HSAs might average $100.00 per month. A commission of $1.00 or $2.00 per month to a broker who would spend many hours explaining how HSAs work, then assist in the implementation of the plan, has little interest to people who might otherwise earn commissions of several hundred thousand or even millions of dollars a year sitting on the phone. So, why regulate them? Those HSAs can accumulate to large sums of money over a twenty or thirty year period just like an IRA. As the size of the accounts increase so does the temptation for others to acquire the money. It's better to take control at the very beginning.

Remember in the beginning of this book I explained how the SEC was present at the decision reading of the case of ICOA Life Insurance Company v. Oregon Insurance Commissioner where the Commissioner claimed life insurance policies were not authorized for sale in Oregon. The court upheld ICOA. The SEC attempted to claim the insurance policies were securities. Here, where securities are admitted to be such by the selling organizations, the SEC determines the mutual funds are not securities. Is an invisible hand involved?

## Judicial Deception

On page 46 of this book, I referred to Lincoln Hanks representing Oregon National Life Insurance Company in his offer to take over ICOA. He wanted to arrange for several different insurance companies to reinsure their business so each company could take credit for the insurance sold by one company, which would allow each company to present terrific results to their shareholders. Later, in the 1990s a man by the name of Martin Frankel did something similar. He took control of Franklin American Life Insurance Company of Tennessee. Then he took control of several other insurance companies and transferred the reserve assets back and forth between the companies when they were audited by the insurance departments. The transfer of funds between the companies made each company appear to be solvent. The purpose was to finance his outrageous lifestyle. Those reserves should have been secured in bank vaults and available only to Frankel with the permission of the insurance department. Both parties should have held one of two keys required to open the boxes holding the securities. The losses to investors amounted to somewhere in the neighborhood of $200 million.[71] The several states involved were required to tap the assets of solvent insurance companies to make up the losses. This was a small-scale Ponzi scheme compared to the one going on in New York.

The SEC demonstrated it protects its friends and companions just like FINRA. A CNN cable news report aired December 25, 2008, examining the Bernard Madoff $50 billion[72] (that's a lot of money) Ponzi scheme indicated the primary purpose of the executives of the SEC is to protect the executives of the regulated organizations for the purpose of preserving future jobs in private industry for members of the SEC. The breakdown in the rule of law and the consequent damage to the citizens can be demonstrated by the following excerpts of a news report.

---

[71] You can read about these transactions at the Tru tv-Crime Library, http://www.trutv.com/library/notorious_murders/clasics/frankel/5html.

[72] MassMutual is reported to have lost $3.5 billion in funds delivered to Madoff.

*Provided By* **Associated Press**

# Ex-Nasdaq chairman arrested on fraud charge in NYC

## Ex-Nasdaq chairman arrested on securities fraud charge in NYC; accused of $50B `Ponzi scheme'

- Larry Neumeister, Associated Press Writer
- Friday December 12, 2008, 8:11 am EST

NEW YORK (AP) -- A Wall Street powerbroker for nearly 50 years who built an influential firm has confessed to a massive fraud scheme that will cost investors at least $50 billion, federal authorities say.

Bernard L. Madoff, 70, facing a single count of securities fraud, declined to speak with reporters after a federal magistrate judge in U.S. District Court in Manhattan ordered him released Thursday night on $10 million bail.

Andrew M. Calamari, associate director of enforcement in the Securities and Exchange Commission's New York office, said the SEC had filed a civil securities fraud charge as well and was alleging "a stunning fraud that appears to be of epic proportions."

The SEC said it was seeking emergency relief for investors, including an asset freeze and the appointment of a receiver for the firm. A hearing was scheduled for Friday.

If the allegations contained in a criminal complaint are true, it may be the largest fraud ever blamed on a single individual. Nearly all of the allegations stem from an FBI agent's recounting of what Madoff told two FBI agents and three senior employees of his firm, Bernard L. Madoff Investment Securities LLC.

It would be a steep fall for Madoff, a former Nasdaq stock market chairman who founded his business in 1960 with $5,000 he earned in part working as a lifeguard on Long Island beaches.

His firm was a market maker, handling trades in some of the largest securities on various stock exchanges, matching buyers and sellers. Investigators say Madoff's crime originated in a separate and secretive investment-advising business that served between 11 and 25 clients and had a total of about $17.1 billion in assets under management.

The criminal complaint signed by FBI Agent Theodore Cacioppi said Madoff told at least three senior employees at his Manhattan apartment Wednesday that the investment adviser business was a fraud and had been insolvent for years, losing at least $50 billion.

Madoff told the employees he was "finished," that he had "absolutely nothing," that "it's all just one big lie" and it was "basically, a giant Ponzi scheme," according to the complaint filed in court.

The employees understood Madoff's admission to mean that "he had for years been paying returns to certain investors out of the principal received from other, different, investors," said the complaint, which did not identify the investors impacted by the scheme....

Cacioppi said two senior Madoff employees told him that Madoff said during the Wednesday meeting that he planned to surrender to authorities in a week but first wanted to distribute $200 million to $300 million he had left to certain selected employees, family and friends...

Shortly after leaving law school, Madoff founded his firm in 1960. It was one of five broker-dealers most closely involved in developing the Nasdaq Stock Market, where he served as a member of the board of governors in the 1980s and as chairman of the board of directors.

*Reproduced with permission of The Associated Press Copyright© 2008. All rights reserved.*

Here's the SEC's 2008 response to the claims of fraud by Madoff:

## Cox says SEC staff failed to probe Madoff

Tue Dec 16, 9:17 pm ET Associated Press

WASHINGTON – Staff at the Securities and Exchange Commission repeatedly failed over the past decade to fully investigate credible allegations of wrongdoing by money manager Bernard Madoff, the head of the SEC said Tuesday, calling it a serious agency breakdown.

SEC Chairman Christopher Cox said he is "gravely concerned by the apparent multiple failures" by staff to look into claims about Madoff's business and to seek formal authority to investigate....

The SEC has come under criticism for having looked into Madoff's business in 2007 and not referring the matter to the agency's commissioners for enforcement action. Questions arose of whether the agency was lax in failing to scrutinize the operations of Madoff — an influential Wall Street figure who had been chairman of the Nasdaq Stock Market — and to respond to alarms raised about them.

Cox said in the statement that he and fellow commissioners have met multiple times since late last week "to seek answers to the question of how Mr. Madoff's vast scheme remained undetected by regulators and law enforcement for so long."

"Our initial findings have been deeply troubling," Cox said. They learned that "credible and specific allegations" regarding Madoff's misconduct, dating to at least 1999, were repeatedly brought to the SEC staff's attention but not formally acted on.

*Used with permission of The Associated Press Copyright© 2008. All rights reserved.*

## Judicial Deception

President Barack Obama replaced SEC Commissioner Cox with Schapiro. Harry Markopolis, who worked as an industry executive and fraud investigator in Boston, New York, and Washington, D.C., told the United States House Financial Services Sub-Committee on February 4, 2009, he had notified the SEC on many occasions that the Madoff scheme was a scam. He said he believes FINRA is corrupt and was corrupt under Schapiro. Several management staff members of the SEC followed Markopolis in their appearance before the same subcommittee on the same day. Schapiro instructed them to refuse to answer any questions posed to them by members of Congress. They complied.

It's clear to me that trading favors by attorneys, judges, and people in positions of authority, contributes to the breakdown of the legal system. One favor deserves a repayment, which creates an endless chain. After the favor has been granted the person who received the favor has only one method of protection, to expose the person who granted the favor as untrustworthy without creating self-incrimination. The better method of preserving a nation of laws, and not of men, is to respond to the favor request with a statement "If it's within the law and I can accommodate you, yes, I'll do it. Otherwise, the answer is no."

I began this book with an explanation of the extent of prostitution in the court system in Oregon. I'm going to end the book with the published extent of prostitution in the highest office in the State of New York. Eliott Spitzer was a crime-busting, corruption-busting attorney general in New York. His successes helped elect him to the office of Governor of New York. He left office pretty rapidly. Here's the story.

Spitzer took on the largest United States insurance company because of false dealings with its customers. Spitzer found American International Insurance (AIG) companies were engaged in various methods of freezing its customers out of obtaining competitive quotes for insurance business. It was reported in the news media that AIG companies were also arranging kickbacks to insurance brokers and clients. These arrangements are illegal in all states, but the New York Insurance Commission has the toughest enforcement system in the United States. At least it had the reputation of the toughest enforcer. Spitzer uncovered the scam and forced AIG to make restitution to some policyholders and to the state of New York. Hundreds of millions of dollars of restitution was involved.

Spitzer's reward was his election as Governor of New York. After serving about a year as governor, Spitzer was caught up in a prostitution sting. Spitzer had been prosecuting prostitution in New York while he was prosecuting AIG. But he also participated in the benefits prostitutes can offer. It was his downfall.[73] Was this payback for Spitzer's prosecution of the AIG misdeeds?

But AIG still had more work to do. AIG is an insurance holding company, not an insurance company. AIG didn't issue insurance policies. However, it did issue interest-rate swaps that were supposed to insure derivatives of mortgages that were sold by brokers to many investors. The sales mushroomed into the trillions of dollars because the swaps were suppose to be insurance against losses based upon the change in mortgage-interest rates, which could cause mortgages to default. The buyers of the derivatives lose if the mortgages default. The swaps were created to protect the buyers. Many of the mortgages defaulted, the investors wanted their losses covered by the swaps and the brokers wanted the insurance policies to pay off. There weren't any insurance policies and AIG couldn't pay, AIG didn't have enough billions of dollars. If someone enters into a contract and collects money from the other party under a promise to pay, without any knowledge of the risk and obligations involved; while the party paying the premium has been led to believe the first party is knowledgeable and competent, the first person is committing fraud in my opinion.

What happened? U.S. Treasury Secretary Henry Paulson and Federal Reserve Chairman Ben Bernanke asked Congress to come up with $750 billion to bail out AIG, the brokers, and the banks. They created the Troubled Asset Relief Program (TARP) for the purpose of protecting the banks. Well, the brokerage firms are also known as banks and it became hard to tell who was being bailed out. The TARP funds, $350 billion of them, were distributed, but no one seemed to be able to properly account for the money. In fact, it's been reported no one may ever be able to complete a proper accounting. It's my

---

[73] You can read about his downfall in The New York Times March 10, 2008, issue with the headline "Spitzer Is Linked to Prostitution Ring " by <u>Danny Hakim</u> and <u>William K. Rashbaum</u>

opinion the United States government is bailing out those who engage in fraud. The argument advanced by Paulson and Bernanke, which convinced Congress and the President, is that those who committed the acts, whether or not legitimate, are too big to fail. That's where our tax dollars went. It's better to have no financial system at all than to have one governed by greed and fraud.

An interesting discussion took place between Martin Feldstein, the renowned economist teaching at Harvard University and James Galbraith, the renowned economist teaching at the University of Texas at Austin.[74] Feldstein claimed the banks and brokers needed to pay millions of dollars in bonuses to the officers of the firms that created the financial disaster because those same officers might leave their current firms and begin working for a competitor. Galbraith claimed those same officers who caused the financial disaster should be turned out to pasture and told to look for work elsewhere. Who's right? Feldstein represents the Wall Street view. Galbraith represents the views of the rational public.

If those in authority, including attorneys and judges, would follow the law it would make it much easier for others to do the same. It would also make the following statement true: We are a nation of laws.

This is a good place to insert the words of Thomas Paine: "Where knowledge is a duty ignorance is a crime; and if any man whose duty it is to know better has encouraged such an expectation, he has either deceived himself or them."[75] People who have been placed in positions of authority in the United States have received that election or appointment for the purpose of serving their fellow citizens with integrity and respect. The wealthy should receive exactly the same attention, consideration, and rulings that would apply to those without wealth. It's my understanding that money and power act as a narcotic on some people in the same manner as cocaine, heroin, and alcohol. When we see people behaving as if they've had a snort or two, their authority should be removed until they return to sobriety.

---

[74] PBS broadcast on the Lehrer News Hour on January 29, 2009.
[75] <u>Public Good</u>, December 30, 1780.

Despite all of the evidence placed before people that the United States is not governed by the rule of law, people still believe it is so governed. It's like believing in Heaven. If a person believes in Heaven, that person should have an open mind regarding the possibility that he or she might be wrong. But you have a better chance of going to heaven than the United States has of being a nation of laws unless the citizens reclaim control. Perhaps you've heard the words caveat emptor; you should learn the words caveat publicum, let the public beware. When fraud and deception is nipped in the bud it prevents much heartache and financial devastation. But when the authorities become participants in the fraud and deception it mushrooms until the damage is no longer controllable. At that point the organizations involved should be allowed to die quickly and we all begin anew.

END

# Index

## Entities

### A

American Guarantee Life Insurance Company 21
American Management Association (AMA) 25, 26, 27, 35
Anderson 7, 70, 74, 75, 76, 78, 80, 81, 82, 83, 87, 89, 90, 91, 95, 96, 97, 99, 100, 101, 105, 107, 108, 109, 110, 112, 113, 129, 131, 132, 133, 134, 135, 136, 144, 145, 146, 147, 149, 150, 152, 159, 164, 166, 174, 176, 285, 381, 400
Anderson Agency, Inc 74, 82
Atlanta 62, 80, 269

### B

Baker 18
BanLife 32, 42
Barnes & Hickam 81, 143, 165
Benson Hotel 17, 18
Boise 10, 18, 75, 262
Bowles & Tillinghast 62

### C

California Corporations Commissioner 17
California Insurance Department 67
Chicago 20, 73, 109, 143, 174, 384, 393

Coeur d'Alene 13
Coos Bay 28, 51
Credit Lyonnais 67

### D

Davies, Biggs, Strayer, Stoel and Boley 60
Dillon, McCarty, Hardeman and Cohen 109
Diogenes 53

### E

Eastern Broadcasting Company 93, 132
Equitable Life and Casualty Insurance Company 13
Eugene 23, 38, 47, 51, 59
Executive Life Insurance Company of California (ELIC) 64, 65, 66, 67, 68
Executive Life Insurance Company of New York 64

### F

Fair Credit Reporting Act 80
Farmers Home Administration 55
FBI 75, 82, 109, 115, 261, 263, 265, 267, 272, 273, 275, 279, 289, 290, 292, 293, 297, 302, 308, 5, 10, 11, 353, 368, 369, 370, 402, 404, 406

First Equity Security Life Insurance Company (FESLIC) 70, 71, 72, 73, 74, 75, 76, 77, 78, 79, 80, 81, 82, 84, 85, 86, 88, 90, 91, 92, 96, 97, 98, 99, 100, 102, 105, 106, 107, 108, 110, 115, 116, 117, 122, 124, 129, 130, 131, 133, 135, 140, 143, 144, 146, 148, 149, 151, 152, 154, 156, 159, 161, 162, 166, 167, 168, 169, 170, 175, 177, 179, 182, 186, 187, 189, 193, 203, 211, 213, 225, 226, 234, 237, 241, 255, 256, 257, 264, 277, 399
First Executive Corporation (FEC) 64, 65, 66, 67, 68
Franklin National Life Insurance Company 80
Frisch's Big Boy 95
Ft. Wayne 27, 79, 84, 145, 146, 148, 151, 162, 175

# G

George S. May Company 20

# H

Henry County prosecutor 101
Howard Nyhart Company 83, 106, 187
Hult Lumber Company 51

# I

ICOA 25, 28, 30, 31, 32, 33, 34, 35, 36, 37, 38, 39, 42, 43, 44, 45, 46, 47, 48, 49, 50, 51, 52, 53, 59, 60, 61, 62, 63, 64, 67, 412, 413
*ICOA v. Insurance Commissioner* 37
Idaho Falls 9, 10
Indiana Disciplinary CommissionIndiana Disciplinary Commission 105
Indianapolis Judicial Nominating Commission 89
Indianapolis Star 55, 109, 110, 113, 168, 171, 237, 241, 249, 253, 255, 257, 258
Indiana Supreme Court 113, 134, 150, 156, 218, 249, 252, 254, 256, 257, 258
Individual Retirement Accounts (IRAs) 98, 99, 109
Insurance Company of America 17, 21, 23, 25, 27, 32, 37, 270, 271, ii, 2, 3, 14, 15, 16, 17, 343, 350, 358, 359, 382, 405
Insurance Company of North America (INA) 25, 99
Insurance Company of Oregon 23
Internal Revenue Service (IRS) 55, 58, 106, 233, 251, 259, 269, 270, 283, 284, 399, 400
*Investment Service Company (Oregon) v. Columbia Softwood Lumber Company, Buehner Lumber Company, Vulcan Mountain Lumber Company, Thelin Lumber Sales, and Henry A. Buehner* 40
Iowa Attorney General 55, 56
*Iowa District Court for Polk County* 56
*Jensen v. First Equity Security Life Insurance Company Cause #71-1083* 90, 100
*Jensen v. First Equity Security Life Insurance Company Cause #71-1084* 90, 100

## J

Jensen v. First Equity Security Life Insurance Company Cause #73-C-185 92, 102
Jensen v. First Equity Security Life Insurance Company, Madison County Cause No. S-75-828 107, 129, 176, 177, 190, 213
Jensen v. James Eckman and First Equity Security Life Insurance Company Cause #S72-697 81
Jensen v. Tuohy, Marion County (Indianapolis) cause number S276-735 111

## K

Kansas City Life Insurance Company 16

## L

La Grande 18
Laugh In 8
Laymen Life Insurance Company 70
Life Insurance Company of North America (LICNA) 99, 100, 109
Lincoln National Life Insurance Company 27
Lodi 55
Los Angeles 16, 22, 68, 248, 285, 306, 314, 345, 352, 360, 364, 380, 381

## M

Madison County Democratic Party 78
Marion County Democratic Central Committee 110
Marion Hotel 19, 39, 45, 60
Merrill Lynch Pierce Fenner and Smith 68
Metropolitan Life Insurance Company 37
Milliman and Robertson 19, 21
Monterey 31

## N

National Association of Insurance Commissioners (NAIC) 90, 285
National Association of Securities Dealers (NASD) 68, 171, 259, 260, 261, 262, 263, 264, 265, 266, 268, 269, 272, 273, 275, 276, 277, 278, 279, 280, 281, 282, 283, 285, 286, 289, 290, 292, 293, 294, 295, 298, 301, 302, 303, 304, 308, 310, 4, 5, 6, 8, 11, 12, 351, 353, 354, 355, 359, 361, 362, 363, 368, 369, 370, 382, 401, 402, 403, 405, 406, 407, 408, 409
National Underwriter 34, 35, 36
New Jersey Insurance Department 32
New York City 5, 15, 25, 26, 28, 32, 35, 51, 69, 99, 108
Normandy Securities 68, 69
Northwestern Mutual Life Insurance Company (NML) 46
Nyhart Company v. Reginald L. Jensen, Cause # S74-506 95

## O

Occidental Life Insurance Company of California 27

Occidental Life of California 93
Odgen 10
Onterio 18
Oregon Auto Insurance Company 23, 24
Oregon Corporations Commissioner 17
Oregon Evangelical Trust 55, 56, 57
Oregonian 56
Oregon Insurance Commissioner 19, 30, 69, 412
Oregon Life Underwriters Association (OLUA) 34, 37
Oregon National Life Insurance CompanyOregon National Life Insurance Company 46, 413
Oregon State Bar 53, 54, 58, 59
*Oregon State Bar v. Wright* 54
Oregon State Legislature 21, 23

## P

Pacific Power and Light Company 60
Panama 10
Pasadena 27
Peat Marwick Mitchell & Co (PMM) 51
Pendleton 18
Portland 17, 18, 20, 21, 23, 24, 40, 41, 46, 49, 50, 51, 60, 67
President's Association 25
Prudential Insurance Company of America 32, 37, 270, 271, ii, 2, 3, 14, 15, 16, 17, 343, 350, 358, 359, 382, 405

## R

Rapid City 70

Reliance National Life Insurance Company 12
Republic National Life 31
Retail Credit Company 80, 81, 90, 96, 97, 111, 125, 126, 128, 133, 143, 228
*Robert J. Wright v. Reginald L. Jensen & ICOA Life Insurance Company* 47
Rockwood, Davis, Biggs, Strayer, & Stoel 40
Roseburg 20, 48, 52
Rothberg, Gallmeyer, Fruechtenicht, and Logan 79

## S

Salem 17, 18, 19, 20, 22, 28, 29, 31, 35, 37, 39, 40, 46, 47, 51, 52, 60, 61, 69, 71, 77, 78
Salt Lake City 9, 10, 12, 13, 16, 17, 18, 23, 136, 140, 145, 170, 248, 249, 252
San Francisco 17, 68, 69, 73, 248, 251, 269, 275, 283, 306, 345, 381, 399
Schortemeier, Eby & Wood 89
Sears Roebuck 10
Seattle 19, 75
Security National Life Insurance Company (SNLIC) 30, 31
Silicon Valley 16, 248
Southeast Furniture Company 13
Spirit of St. Louis 72
Standard Insurance Company 23
Standard & Poor's 500 Index 69
St. Anthony 9, 10
*State of Oregon ex rel. Oregon State Bar, Respondent v. Robert J. Wright,*

*Appellant* 54
St. George 14

## T

Teamsters Union 82
The Church of Scientology 93
The Dalles 18
The Economist 67
The Employees Retirement Income
    Securities Act (ERISA) 98
Transamerica Insurance Company of
    California 93
Trans-Pacific Enterprises 55
Tuohy, Gleason and Mercer 110, 187

## U

Underwriters National Assurance
    Company (UNAC) 105, 109,
    110, 157, 168, 171, 241, 253,
    255, 256
Union Bank 65
United States Constitution 3, 4, 5,
    310, 311, i, 8, 20, 378, 397
United States Court of Claims 58
United States National Bank 17, 40,
    49, 50, 60, 61, 62, 63
United States Securities & Exchange
    Commission (SEC) 37, 38, 42,
    44, 189, 268, 273, 278, 3, 5,
    354, 371, 377, 378, 396, 407,
    409, 410, 412, 413, 416, 417
University of Oregon 77
University of Utah 10, 13
Utah Corporation Commissioner 14

## W

Wall Street Journal 67
Weyerhaeuser Lumber Company 38
WHUT 93, 94, 111, 133, 167, 175,
    264
Willamette Valley 18, 19, 39, 41
WLHN 94, 133
Wood Tuohy Gleason & Mercer 89
*Wright v. ICOA Life Insurance Company*
    *38, 39*

## Y

YMCA 91

# People

## A

Aksenov, Sophie  262, 263, 265, 266, 293, 294, 403
Alexander, Dean  40, 49
Appley, Lawrence A.  25

## B

Balika, Mary  171
Barnett, Stephen R.  379, 381
Bartol, Bill  262, 265, 266, 301, 404
Beck, Jack  77
Belth, Joseph  309
Bernanke, Ben  418, 419
Biggs, Hugh  60, 61, 63
Bothum, David  43
Bowles, Tom  62
Braddock, Charles  146, 156, 157, 158, 159, 160, 163, 164, 165, 245
Brewer, Webster  111, 241
Brown, Clarke  52
Buehner, Henry  20, 32, 39, 49, 59
Burket, Donald G.  234
Butler, David  93
Byal, Ronald C.  165, 166, 167, 168, 170, 171, 172, 173, 174, 175, 176, 191, 200, 221, 225, 233, 234, 236, 237, 238, 241, 243, 244, 245, 247, 248, 249, 251, 252, 256, 257, 273, 309

## C

Campbell, David  160, 257
Canby, William C. Jr.  380
Carr, Fred  65, 66
Carroll, Dennis  110
Chavez, Elaine  282, 303, 405
Churchill, Marian  18
Churchill, Thomas  17
Clase, Steve  146
Cloninger, Coite E.  75, 76
Compolo, Grace  263
Cox, Alva  83, 102
Cox, Christopher  416
Crosby, Bing  31
Crosby, Larry  31, 42
Cross, Travis  59
Cummings, James  400

## D

Davis, George B.  98, 116
Dean, Daryl J.  83, 86
Deborah, Daniels J.  255
Dietzen, Walter  78, 112, 179, 383
Doermer, Richard  72, 96, 257
Drager, Peg  37
Dragos, Chris  282
Drudge, Forrest  82
Dugan, Michael  105, 157, 241, 256
Duncan, Marshall  34
Duncan, Robert  20
Dunn, Charles  93

## E

Earle, Hugh  20, 21, 49
Eckman, James  70, 74, 80, 81, 97,

119, 122, 123, 124, 127, 129, 152, 186, 226, 232, 233, 255, 257

## F

Fatout, William R. 170, 175, 176, 180, 183, 187, 188, 191, 194, 196, 198, 199, 200, 207, 208, 209, 212, 214, 215, 216, 217, 225, 231, 233, 234, 236, 239
Faulstich, James R. 69
Feldstein, Martin 419
Filler, Karen 268
Fleming, James 275
Fletcher, Martin 79, 81, 84, 134, 158, 159, 176, 218, 219, 230, 383
Fogel, Jeremy 275
Forst, Otto 64, 65, 68
Fox, Howard 63
Francis, C. Edwin 17
Friedland, Daniel 106, 107, 122

## G

Galbraith, James 419
Gallmeyer, Thomas A. 72
Garamendi, John 67
Garrison, Thomas 132, 133, 136, 137, 138, 139, 154, 155, 156, 162, 163, 164, 172, 236, 248, 265, 283
George, Al 164, 165
Giannini, Albert 27
Giuliani, Rudy 5
Goldberg, Susan 393
Goode, Melvin 44, 49
Grassley, Charles 55

Greene, Robert T. 412
Green, Mitchell 275
Griffis, Brandon 114, 134

## H

Hahn, Gregory 110
Hanks, Lincoln 17, 20, 46, 413
Hanley, Marshal 81
Harvey, Harmon T. 20
Hatfield, James 20
Hatfield, Mark 20, 23, 43, 48
Hay, Douglas 47
Headden, Susan 171, 258
Healy, Frank 19, 53
Heath, Jack 234
Herman, Peter 44
Herrin, John 89, 96, 167
Herzinger, Bruce 20
Hicks, Loren 43
Higgins, George 61
Hill, Thomas E. 314
Hinkle, Ernest 20
Howells, Steve 251
Husar, Linda 306
Huston, Sam 163

## I

Ingham, Clifford 17
Irwin, Stewart 111

## J

Jefferson, Thomas 312
Jensen, Cindy 17, 77, 136, 266
Jensen, Dorothy vii, 10, 12, 17, 18, 72, 77, 78, 93, 136, 137, 140,

145, 170, 252
Jensen, Harold A. vii, 20, 35
Jensen, Leslie vii, 17, 77, 145, 234
Jensen, Wendy vii, 12, 17, 77
Johnson, Paul 118
Johnstone, Robert 128, 143, 165

## K

Kelly, Clarence 109
Kelsay, Betty 52
Kelsay, "Bun" 20
Ketner, Joseph 74
Key, Claude 61
Korlann, Walter G. 23

## L

Lake, Hayden 13
Landes, William M. 384
Laudig, Stephen 114, 118, 122, 147, 156, 177, 178, 181, 182, 190, 217, 227, 230, 235, 239, 240, 242
Leo, Eileen D. 267
Libertore, JoAnne B. 219
Lofgren, Zoe 408
Lugar, Richard 250

## M

MacIver, R. H. 313
MacIver, R. M. 7, 313
Madison, James 312
Madoff, Bernard 413, 416, 417
Mahoney, Mike 24
Markopolis, Harry 417
Marszalek, Audra 278

Martindale, William (Bill) 22
McCool, Doris 234
McCrohan, Elizabeth 307
McCullough, Billie R. 111
Miceli, Andrew 266
Milkin, Michael 65
Miller, Tom 56
Montgomery, Monte 23
Mraz, Leslie R. 234
Mulvaney, K. L. 257
Murphy, Stephen 81
Musser, Dean 19

## N

Nash, Dane P. 166, 167, 174, 218, 219, 233, 234, 235, 236, 237, 238, 239, 240, 241, 243, 244, 245, 247, 399
Newman, Thomas Jr. 110
Nunn, Warne H. 59

## O

Obama, Barack 417
O'Connell, Robert 308
Ormiston, Tom B. 58
Osborn, Harry 63
Ouelette, Gerry 162

## P

Paulson, Henry 418
Pickering, Carolyn 109, 168, 255
Posner, Richard 384
Potts, Ray 17
Pregerson, Harry 380
Pullano, Richard 282, 286, 289, 290,

292, 301, 302, 303, 304, 308, 400, 401, 402, 403, 404, 406, 407, 408

## Q

Quayle, Dan 249, 250, 251

## R

Ratliff, Wesley 100
Redding, Charles W. 40
Rich, Lewis 13
Riebenack, Walter 79, 84, 177
Robb, Dave 37
Robertson, Stuart A. 19
Roby, Dan 146
Roby, Richard 145
Roller, Donald 248, 252, 265
Rosen, Ben 28
Ross, David 13
Ross, "Doc" 13
Ross, Galen 13
Ross, Ray 13, 17

## S

Sammons, E.C. 63
Schapiro, Mary 400, 402, 417
Schmanski, Kathy 272
Schmier, Kenneth J. 372
Schmier, Michael K. 372
Scholl, Carol 393
Schriber, Ronald 63
Shapiro, Lou 93
Shearer, Stephen 267
Sheppard, Randall T. 253, 257
Shrenker, Paul 79, 116

Silna, Dan 72
Silna, Ozzie 72
Sivin, Eric 108
Spagat, Robert 306, 307, 17, 18, 344, 345
Spitzer, Elliot 417
Sulmonetti, Alfred T. 63

## T

Taaffe, Christopher 263, 264, 265, 266, 267, 272, 273, 275, 304
Teter, John 304
Thomas, Sidney R. 380
Tookey, Clarence 27, 35, 36, 43
Tookey, Robert 27
Traub, Patrick 171, 253, 258
Trichet, Jean-Claude 67
Tulsky, Frederic N. 377, 385, 396, 397
Tuohy, James 89, 116, 241, 253, 257, 258, 306

## W

Warrum, Roger 131, 132, 133, 136, 146, 155, 283
Wayne, Fort 72, 176, 184
Wheeler, Thomas 258
Wilcox, Ann 158
Wilson, Emily J. 234
Wright, Robert J. 38, 47, 54, 55, 58, 59
Wright, Steve 396

## Y

York, Robert 95, 164

Young, James  245, 247, 248, 254, 256, 306, 310

## Z

Zell, Robert N.  234
Zirkle, Charles F.  234
Zook, Linda  153, 158, 169, 245

LaVergne, TN USA
14 February 2010
172996LV00002B/9/P